Penguin Education

Group Processes

Edited by Peter B. Smith

✔ KU-548-418

Penguin Modern Psychology Readings

General Editor

B. M. Foss

Advisory Board

P. C. Dodwell
Marie Jahoda
S. G. M. Lee
W. M. O'Neil
R. L. Reid
Roger Russell
P. E. Vernon
George Westby

WITHDRAWN

N 0017577 3

Group Processes

Selected Readings
Edited by Peter B. Smith

Penguin Books

Penguin Books Ltd, Harmondsworth,
Middlesex, England
Penguin Books Inc., 7110 Ambassador Road,
Baltimore, Md 21207, U.S.A.
Penguin Books Australia Ltd,
Ringwood, Victoria, Australia

First published 1970
This selection copyright © Peter B. Smith, 1970
Introduction and notes copyright © Peter B. Smith, 1970

Made and printed in Great Britain by
Cox & Wyman Ltd, London, Reading and Fakenham
Set in Monotype Times and Univers

Contents

Introduction

This volume attempts to introduce the reader to the rapidly developing study of behaviour in small groups. A recent bibliography listed 3200 publications in this field since the last war and it was by no means exhaustive. In introducing the topic one might ask what it is that has attracted researchers into this field in such numbers, and whether on balance the findings to date have repaid such a concentration of effort.

Traditionally psychologists have tended to develop explanatory models of human behaviour which focus on the individual as the key concept, while sociologists for their part have attended more to the properties of institutions and classes. Empirical findings in both disciplines have indicated the need for an analytic concept in between these two levels. To take a few examples, it is found that individuals respond to mass communications such as advertising not only in relation to their own values, but equally in relation to the values of those with whom they associate; it is found that theoretically constructed models of bureaucracy only partially describe individual behaviour in large organizations – some behaviour is explicable only in terms of loyalties of people to one another, rather than responses to the abstract rules of organization; it is found that psychological experimenters can influence the way their subjects behave, even if their subjects happen to be rats. In a word, behaviour is social. One can only define an individual in relation to his context.

Some social relationships are transient, while others last a lifetime, but most people would probably agree that the social structure that is found in more durable groups constitutes the central subject matter of the study of groups. However, the severe methodological problems of obtaining experimentally based findings have led many workers to focus on the more controllable transient relationships. Ultimately hypotheses about group behaviour will need to stand up both to experimental testing and to more naturalistic study, and this volume accordingly includes some naturalistic studies and some experimental ones. The divergence between the methods of adjacent chapters will no doubt be only too apparent. Many published discussions on group processes lean rather heavily on a number of 'classic' studies which were conducted in the thirties and forties, whose significance with the passage of time is becoming increasingly a historical one. Such studies have been omitted from this volume, although several of them are referred to in the Part introductions. The goal has been to provide examples of more recent research conducted in the fifties and sixties, much of which derives from the early leads given by the classic studies.

It may help the reader to find his way through what is to follow if a simple and idealized model is presented of what might happen when a number of people come together for the first time. Suppose that a number of students meet, with or without explicit purpose. While they meet, each one behaves according to his personality predispositions subject to the limitations of the environment within which they meet, say, the student cafeteria. Some of the behaviours each person can do may be irrelevant and others downright impossible within this particular setting. But some at least are possible. These behaviours elicit consequences for each person. For some, they satisfy a goal they value, whether that goal be swapping lecture-notes, exchanging friendship and so on. For others, the behaviours satisfy a goal, but not to the same extent as they can achieve in other settings. For yet others, the behaviours may not achieve much goal satisfaction, but it is still more than they can achieve elsewhere.

The second of these types will not seek to continue or repeat the meeting; they will not become part of the incipient group. The first and third types will form a group. Since they are deriving different amounts of rewards from the group meetings, they will tend to behave in different ways, that is to say there will develop in the group an implicit differentiation of roles. Those who are highly rewarded will tend to talk and initiate, while those who are not rewarded will remain silent or express dissatisfaction.

Since large numbers of people cannot all communicate with one another at once, durable groups will tend to be quite small. Larger groups will be more frustrated and more likely to splinter into a number of semi-autonomous smaller groups. If the student group continues to achieve goals for its members, they will begin to want to conserve it. If Alan's behaviour leads to group goal achievement, members will not only anticipate that that is how Alan *usually* behaves, they will begin to feel that that is how he *ought* to behave for the good of the group. Alan's role is now normatively defined. If he fails to behave as he should he risks the group's displeasure. As for Alan so for all the other members, there will be certain standards of behaviour, or norms, whose maintenance will ensure continued goal achievement. For the student group this would most likely include times at which one should come to meet the others and what sort of topics are to be discussed. If the goals achieved are very much more valuable than those that the members can achieve elsewhere, the group will be highly cohesive and the norms will not be much violated. If goal achievement is only marginally better than could be attained elsewhere, violation of norms will be widespread. In such groups the norms may be made more explicit, for example by putting them in writing. Such speci-fications arise precisely because of the danger that the norms and role definitions will be violated. In such a way the group may pass from being a small group to being a small organization, with hand-books of procedural norms and organizational role definitions. This would happen if our student group transformed itself into a society with officers and constitution.

Here then is a picture of how a group might develop over time. Whether it does or not depends on the nature of the specific goals achieved, the sort of environment in which it is placed and the stance of other groups with which there may be contact. The selections in this volume should clarify this idealized model at many points. They will also make it very clear that any general theory of group behaviour is still a long way off. George Homans has recently argued that the problems of the social sciences derive from the 'historicity' of its subject matter. In other words in attempting to predict the behaviour of A in a group today, it matters a great deal what sort of groups he has previously belonged to, such as his family, peer groups in school and so forth. Compare this with the problem of predicting the behaviour of a gas molecule which has previously formed numerous chemical compounds, but is unchanged by these reversible experiences. If we are to cope with the problems posed by historicity, we shall need much better measures of the important variables in group behaviour. Particu-larly we shall need better measures of personality as manifested in groups and we shall need better measures of the different tasks with which groups are faced. Although interaction between personality and task underlies much of what follows, they are but crudely measured. Even when we have these better measures we shall still need to find ways of studying groups which take account of the interrelatedness of the different aspects of a group. Most research has necessarily concentrated on whether A affects B, such as whether leadership style affects performance. But leadership style no doubt affects many other things, such as the other roles in the group, the emergent norms, the group's cohesiveness, relationships with other groups and so on, and each of these may well also affect performance. Analysis will need to be multivariate, and not concerned with over simply derived causes and effects.

If this picture seems an unduly pessimistic one, it may be as well to close this introduction with an assessment of what has so far been achieved in the analysis of group processes. A number of valuable new research methods has been developed which enables us to examine social behaviour in ways hitherto restricted to individual behaviour. These methods have enabled us to develop useful descriptive models of group processes. Using comparable concepts we can describe groups of students, managers, shop-floor workers, soldiers or nurses. We can show the ways in which membership in such groups influences behaviour. Such descriptive findings have cast considerable doubt on earlier theories of, for example, the behaviour of organizations, and of responses to the mass-media. At a number of points it is possible to go further than this and to make predictions about how group members will respond to particular inputs. Examples of such predictive models can be found in the work on communication nets (discussed by Shaw in Reading 5), on interpersonal attraction (Newcomb, Reading 7), and on leadership (Fiedler, Reading 13). It should be possible in the next few years to refine such models and slowly to extend their generality.

The editor gratefully acknowledges the assistance of Herbert Pollack, Troy Langley, Rustom Gandy and Angela Pead in the preparation of this volume.

Part One Defining the Small Group

We begin on a somewhat gloomy note. Golembiewski follows through some of the twists and turns in the development of the concept group, or small group. He leaves us in no doubt there is still a good deal of conceptual confusion. Rather often the temptations of fully controlled research in the laboratory have kept researchers away from natural-state groups which more fully satisfy the theoretical definitions of what a group is. For the present we must accept the findings of both laboratory and field studies while keeping a weather eye open for differences in findings which may be due to variations in research setting rather than to the variable under consideration. We can adopt only the minimal definition that a group is a number of people interacting with one another.

Cartwright and Zander examine the relationship of these difficulties of method to the development of adequate theories of group behaviour. In the following two Readings we shall look in more detail at two of the principal traditions in the theoretical explanation of small group behaviour, namely those emphasizing environment and personality respectively.

1 R. T. Golembiewski

The Development of the Genus 'Group'

Excerpt from R. T. Golembiewski, *The Small Group*, University of Chicago Press, 1962, pp. 34–45.

The early history of the study of 'groups' can be written in terms of a series of leaps (society, primary group, reference group, membership group and small group) from one vaguely defined or inconvenient research level to another. In the process, as Newcomb (1951, pp. 37–8) noted: 'The term "group" ... has achieved no standard meaning. ...' Thus when it comes to indicating the precise limits of a macroscopic 'group' of any kind, recourse is often taken in obvious, if sometimes elegant, tautologies. As Parsons, Shils and Olds (1951, p. 192) phrased their particular contribution of this sort:

The concept of a boundary is of crucial significance in the definition of a collectivity. The boundary of a collectivity is that criterion whereby some persons are included as members and others are excluded as non-members. The inclusion or exclusion of a person depends on whether or not he has a membership role in the collectivity. Thus all persons who have such roles are members; they are within the boundary. Thus the boundary is defined in terms of membership roles.

The point is simply that the empirical determination of such 'boundaries' and 'membership roles' for different types of collectivities has been almost untouched (see, for example, De Gré, 1949).

Small-group analysis has not yet sharply broken this long tradition. The range of existing working designations of the term 'small group' is wide. Begin with a 'base line' designation of the small group derived from the early studies. A small group:

1. Consists of a small number of individuals in more or less interdependent status and role relations.

2. Has an indigenous set of values or norms which regulates the behavior of members at least in matters of concern to the group.

This may be called Designation I.

Heavy concentrations of studies, however, cluster around two other designations of what small-group analysis is about. The first of these designations, more common in laboratory studies, specifies that a 'group' is 'any number of persons engaged in a single face-to-face meeting or a series of meetings in which each member receives some impression of the others as a distinct person *even though it was only to recall that the other was present* ' (Bales, 1950, p. 33; Golembiewski's italics). This may be called Designation II.

Designation III, common in studies of natural collectivities, uses the term 'group' in a simple aggregative sense. Thus one study dealt with a 'relatively stable group of college students'. 'Stable' was defined as lack of newcomers or dropouts. The group was a formal one of forty-two girls taking the same course of study (Venable, 1954).

In sum, Designation I is both relatively size specific and content-filled; Designation II is relatively size specific but almost content-less; and Designation III is neither size specific nor content-filled. Studies in the small-group area are scattered over the full range of the three designations. Any summary treatment, then, must to some extent deal with the proverbial horses and apples.

This is regrettable, but explainable. The lack of designational convergence is a function of four general factors:

1. The widely held opinion that a 'structural homology' exists between groups conceived of as human aggregates.
2. The fact that small-group analysis has developed 'between' existing disciplines.
3. Procedural convenience.
4. The different degrees of reality accorded to the 'group' concept.

The term 'group', first, may be used generically. But it has been used indiscriminately to imply that a 'group' is a 'group'. Thus George Homans, for example, not only used the term 'group' to refer to a primitive tribe, a street corner gang, a roomful of factory workers, and a New England village, but he also used the results of studies of these social units (if that is what they were) *in combina-*

tion in *The Human Group* (1950). The underlying and convenient assumptions are, of course, that all human aggregates are groups and that although groups may differ in accidents such as size and research utility, they are not essentially different.

At the very best, this 'structural homology' is a very broad hypothesis indeed. But its influence has been wide, as Designation III and the considerable amount of work done in connection with it document. Much work in small-group analysis also has assumed that the collectivities with which it is concerned are homologous enough to be considered in the aggregate. The evidence, however, does not permit such a liberty. As will be shown, there are different classes and subclasses within the genus 'group' which have different properties. The subclass 'small group' also contains a number of types.

Thus the generic term 'group' is a useful one, just as the term 'animal' is. But it is useful only within limits. These limits are particularly important when it comes to setting up laboratory groups, the real test of knowledge. Sanderson (1938) suggests these limits when he notes of the term 'animal' that 'it does not help us much to deal with protozoa and elephants without distinguishing that they are radically different sorts of animals'.

Second, small-group analysis has developed on the margins of several disciplines. Thus Hare, Borgatta and Bales (1955, pp. v–vi) note that small-group analysis involves the study of subcultures, of small social systems and of personality development. These students concluded that:

[The study of small groups'] strategic significance ... is that it related all three of these types of structure to a common base – the social processes out of which they arise and ... change. This field of research does not 'belong' to any one of the recognized social sciences alone. It is the common property of all.

In the longer run, perhaps, this multisource interest in the small group may result in the comprehensive analysis of the study area. For the present, however, results have been less encouraging. An approximate explanation may be provided. Sociologists, social psychologists and anthropologists have in general discovered the small group in working down from their traditional concern with macroscopic social units. These students also tend to approach the study of the small group in terms of the traditional macro-analytic problems and general concepts. In the main, on the other hand, psychologists and psychotherapists have discovered the small social unit in working up from their traditional concern with personality. These students have tended to approach the small group as a convenient medium in which to observe and/or guide individual behavior rather than to study the small group *per se*.[1] Designations II and III both reflect this concern with the study of the individual in some context. They also reflect the neglect of the 'content' of these various contexts.

Third, procedural convenience has played an important role in the lack of convergence of working designations in small-group analysis. The homology hypothesis, for example, is a convenient working myth in the short run when the data available for any specific class or subclass of group are in short supply. Designation II is also convenient in the short run because it legitimates, *ipso facto*, the 'creation' of laboratory groups in the course of limited interaction. Designation III also has an apparent convenience. In the long run, of course, such approaches are self-defeating. The research usefulness of a study area is based upon cumulative results achieved. A vague study area must encourage much research which is neither comparable nor cumulative.

The fourth and final general factor explaining the designational divergence of small-group analysis concerns the differential degrees of 'reality' accorded to the group. It is convenient to discuss the point under four separate heads.

The group as a reification

Much of the literature of social organization is based upon a 'group mind' or 'collective consciousness' variation of the simple and sovereign principles. The essential point of such explanations is that 'groups' or 'crowds' have mental characteristics like those of individuals. Floyd H. Allport has most comprehensively attacked

1. M. W. Horowitz, Joseph Lyons and H. V. Perlmutter (1951, p. 61) are novel only in their openness on this issue: '... although this experiment has been described as "group research", actually is it is a misnomer. We are really dealing with a group only as it affects the responses of individuals in a group situation. All data obtained are individual data.'

the 'group-mind' approach. His formulation and its many variations have also been extended more or less indiscriminately to groups as a genus. The large volume of work using Designations II and III attests to this influence.

In part, Allport's argument was a vitally needed one against the non-empirical speculations *re* the 'group mind', Allport, however, went to the other extreme and developed a theory of social behavior based on the simple but additive physical transmission of stimuli from individual to individual. Thus, as Allport (in Newcomb, 1954, p. 625) put it, '[t]he individual in the crowd behaves just as he would behave alone, *only more so*'. This is the skeleton of the theory of 'social facilitation'. In a more developed way, Allport (1924, p. 4) thus contrasted his position with the 'group-mind' approach:

Impressed by the closely knit and reciprocal nature of social behavior, some writers have been led to postulate a kind of 'collective mind' or 'group consciousness' as separate from the minds of the individuals of whom the group is composed. No fallacy is more subtle or misleading than this.... (1) There is no psychology of groups which is not essentially and entirely a psychology of individuals.... (2) Psychology in all its branches is a science of the individual. (3) To extend its principles to larger units is to destroy their meaning.

Allport's argument is not conclusive. Consider the two propositions at the heart of Allport's argument: that psychological processes occur only within individuals; and that 'the actions of all are nothing more than the sum of the actions of each taken separately' (Allport, 1933, esp. pp. 13–15). The first proposition is incontrovertible. The second rests on a fundamental assumption which, if consistently applied, would prohibit all natural science. This fundamental assumption presupposes a sharp cleavage between two types of data, 'things' and the 'relations between things'. 'Things' are concrete, real. 'Relations between things' are abstractions, 'phases of our experience with which we can deal only by thinking or talking about them. They cannot be heard, seen, or pointed to with any part of our bodies....' In speaking of individuals, Allport argues, one is dealing with real, concrete 'things'. To speak of groups in any sense but as the actions of numerous reciprocally facilitating individuals is to commit the 'group fallacy', to reify a construction of the imagination.

Allport's distinction is an important one. But his position that such relational constructs imply a reification is untenable. There could be no physical science without such concepts as magnetic and electrical fields – all 'relations between things'. Allport's implied 'hard' conception of reality, moreover, is not consistent with the scientific criteria for reality and existence. For scientific existence is tentative. Any concept 'exists' if it explains, if it is related to other concepts, and if it is operationally defined in a way which permits consistent testing.[2]

A concomitant difficulty is Allport's apparent acceptance of 'The fallacy of misplaced concreteness'. The fallacy assumes that anything 'real' must have 'simple location' in physical space-time.

Allport's concept of 'social facilitation' is apparently an effort to provide such a 'simple location' for behavior in the individual. But Allport had to use terms such as 'mind', 'consciousness' and 'individual'. To these he had to attribute logically a 'thing-like' definiteness with a 'simple location'. In the case of the 'individual', however, the sense in which one can be referred to as a 'thing' with 'simple location' is quite limited. Thus all people are complex 'relations of things'. They are many 'selves', even though they are not often Jekylls and Hydes.

Weak or not, however, the position has been a popular one. Its effect, often reflected in small-group analysis, has been the neglect of the group as an object of study. Hence the 'individual' is considered the relevant research unit, even when a group situation is being studied. Designations II and III reflect this bias.

This makes group study (and attacks on the usefulness of such study!) too easy. If, however, a group is conceived as a form of organization, a cheap victory is no longer possible. For, as Mac-

2. The development of such relational, or 'field', concepts was central to modern physical science. Pre-nineteenth-century work premised a conception of natural phenomena as the result of forces existing *between one body and another*. The 'field' approach postulated quite a different analytical frame. As Albert Einstein and L. Infeld (1938, p. 259; Golembiewski's italics) noted of the relational construct of the electro-magnetic field: 'It needed great imagination to realize that *it was not the charges nor the particles but the field in the space between the charges and particles* which is essential for the description of physical phenomena.'

Leod notes, the research question then becomes this more formidable one:

Are there characteristics of groups, of a psychological order, which can be studied without any necessary reference to the characteristics of any particular member of the group? This I submit, is a reasonable question for research, and I do not think that the answer is obviously in the negative.[3]

The 'group' as a nominal entity

The conception of the group as a nominal entity underlies much of the present work in small-group analysis. This is especially so of work based upon Designation II. 'Group' in this approach, as Malinowski (1939, p. 938) put it, is a term used to refer to 'an assemblage of individuals'. The individual, as in the first approach, is the only reality. Thus only the behavior of individuals, singly or collectively, requires investigation. Group, or the total extra-individual, phenomena are found in the briefest interactions. Groups are recognized, then, but only barely.

This position is a difficult one. Even Allport, who held the extreme parent position most consistently, at times acknowledged that persons act *as if* groups were real. Moreover, the results of numerous studies have established that a 'structure of relations' emerges *in time* out of interaction in small groupings. The existence of this 'structure of relations' is a force influencing the behavior of individuals in the grouping. It may be preserved even in the face of a rapid turnover of members under certain conditions.

The failure of traditional theoretical statements to account for such 'structures of relations' was instrumental in the swift popularization of small-group analysis. But the breaking of old patterns of thought underlying those traditional explanations and the establishment of the 'group' as more than a nominal entity have been less complete and rapid. Thus many studies assume a nominally conceived 'group'. These studies, Warriner (1956, p. 549) concluded, have some bearing upon interpersonal relations. But, he concluded, 'by no stretch of the imagination can they be called studies of groups'.

3. MacLeod (1951), pp. 216–17. See Boodin (1913) for just such a statement of the 'group-mind' position.

The group as a 'less basic' entity

The conception of the 'group' as a 'less basic' entity is a further slide down the ladder from Allport's original position. It combines his emphasis upon the study of the individual, and his admission that individuals do act as if groups were real. The approach seems the most influential present orientation toward the study of the small group. It significantly influences work employing Designations II and III. The general approach is conveniently presented in Krech and Crutchfield's *Theory and Problems of Social Psychology*. It may be summarized in this way:[4]

1. The term 'group' refers to a 'perceptual reality' which exists in the minds of its members or observers.
2. '[W]hen a person perceives several people acting together ... the resulting perception will be organized and certain properties of these groups of people will be perceived *that are different* from the properties of the individuals comprising the group.'
3. But this 'perceptual reality' must not be confused with 'objective reality', which is conceived of as being somehow 'more real'.
4. Although the group has some practical research utility *for studying individual behavior*, the individual is the 'more basic' unit of investigation as well as 'objectively real'.

Again, the basis for the approach is a distinction between 'things' and 'relations between things'. The difference is that the relational construction 'group' is accorded a somehow lesser 'subjective reality'. In the previous approaches, the 'reality' of the 'group' was (almost always) denied.

This last approach, however, does not improve much on the others. First, what a person perceives or feels about a certain experience is quite as 'real' as that which the experience 'really' is. The two types of judgements ('social facts' or 'social reality' *v.* 'objective fact') are distinct. They must be treated as such. But to maintain that one type is not 'real', or not 'as real' as the other, is

4. See Krech and Crutchfield (1948), pp. 19 and 391. They conclude on a much more restrictive note, however. They note that the 'fact that a person's behavior in the group *is not determined entirely* by the structure and nature of the group ... testifies to the dangers that may inhere in *completely* disregarding individual considerations when dealing with groups' (p. 373). Golembiewski's italics.

to extend the point too far. Moreover, it is trite but true that all science rests upon observation. And all observation must deal (if in a particular way) with 'subjective reality' rather than with 'objective reality'. That is, it must deal with 'reported fact' as conceptualized and operationalized, rather than with 'apprehended fact'.

Second, the approach perverts the 'levels' approach to a study area. Thus Krech and Crutchfield (1948, pp. 13 and 14) distinguish three levels of analysis of social phenomena:

1. The level of the social behavior of the individual.
2. The level of the behavior of 'social groups', conceived of as relatively small and informal and of relatively short duration.
3. The level of the operation of social organizations or institutions, conceived of as macroscopic units such as 'army', 'society' and 'class'.

These seem a reasonable enough place to start. However, the authors go on to use the analogy of the study of the behavior of a volume of gas to demonstrate the more 'basic' nature of level 1. On the aggregate level, they note, a description of a gas is possible in terms of volume, pressure, and temperature. They also note, however, that if the physicist wishes 'to understand *more basically*' why such relations exist, 'he is required to examine the situation ... from the point of view of the single molecule'.

This analogical moral to emphasize the individual, however, limps. For even brief consideration of the concept of 'integrative levels' establishes the fallacy of rank-ordering more or less 'basic' levels. Novikoff's (1945, p. 209) brief description of the concept in biology will serve this purpose:

Each level of organization possesses unique properties of structure and behavior, which though dependent on the properties of the constituent elements, appear only when these elements are combined in the new system. Knowledge of the laws of the lower level is necessary for a *full* understanding of the higher level; yet the unique properties of phenomena at the higher level cannot be predicted, *a priori*, from the laws of the lower level. The laws describing the unique properties of each level are qualitatively distinct, and their discovery requires methods of research and analysis appropriate to the particular level. These laws express the new organizing relationships, i.e. the reciprocal relationships of elementary units to each other and to the system as a whole.

The 'group' as a conceptual reality

The general argument underlying the conceptual reality of the 'group' may be summarized in terms of three propositions. First, the 'group' is as real as the 'person'. Second, both the 'group' and the 'person' are analytical concepts, not concrete entities. The content of both concepts can be established scientifically. Third, the 'group' may be described in terms of social processes on its own level, without any *necessary* reference to personality characteristics of members.

The position has become more respectable of late, because of the recent wide study of small social groupings. This study has moved the argument about the reality of groups from the level of philosophy to an often more substantial empirical level.

Two facts, however, limit the influence of this fourth approach to the 'group'. First, substantial disagreement about the 'small group' concept exists even among those who accept the group as a conceptual reality. Second, there has been a too enthusiastic application of the work on small social units to broader groups. The friends of small-group analysis, in short, often are its worst enemies. For such overenthusiasm can only hurt small-group analysis over the long haul.

References

ALLPORT, F. H. (1924), *Social Psychology*, Houghton Mifflin.
ALLPORT, F. H. (1933), *Institutional Behavior: Essays Toward a Reorienting of Contemporary Social Organization*, University of North Carolina Press.
BALES, R. F. (1950), *Interaction Process Analysis: A Method for the Study of Small Groups*, Addison-Wesley.
BOODIN, J. E. (1913), 'The existence of social minds', *Amer. J. Sociol.*, vol. 19, pp. 1–47.
DE GRÉ, G. (1949), 'Outlines for a systematic classification of social groups', *Amer. soc. Rev.*, vol. 14, pp. 145–8.
EINSTEIN, A., and INFELD, L. (1938), *The Evolution of Physics*, Simon & Schuster.
HARE, A. P., BORGATTA, E. P., and BALES, R. F. (eds.) (1955), *Small Groups: Studies in Social Interaction*, Knopf.
HOMANS, G. (1950), *The Human Group*, Harcourt, Brace & World.
HOROWITZ, M. W., LYONS, J., and PERLMUTTER, H. V. (1951), 'Induction of forces in discussion groups', *Hum. Rel.*, vol. 4, pp. 57–76.
KRECH, D., and CRUTCHFIELD, R. S. (1948), *Theory and Problems of Social Psychology*, McGraw-Hill.

MacLeod, R. B. (1951), 'The place of phenomenological analysis in social psychological theory', in J.H.Rohrer and M.Sherif (eds.), *Social Psychology at the Crossroads*, Harper & Row, pp. 215–41.

Malinowski, B. (1939), 'The group and individual in functional analysis', *Amer. J. Sociol.*, vol. 44, pp. 938–64.

Newcomb, T. M. (1951), 'Social psychological theory: integrating individual and social approaches', in J.H.Rohrer and M.Sherif (eds.), *Social Psychology at the Crossroads*, Harper & Row, pp. 31–49.

Newcomb, T. M. (1954), *Social Psychology*, Dryden Press.

Novikoff, A. B. (1945),' The concept of integrative levels in biology', *Science*, vol. 101, pp. 209–15.

Parsons, T., Shils, E. A., and Olds, J. (1951), 'Values, motives and systems of action', in T. Parsons and E. A. Shils (eds.), *Towards a General Theory of Action*, Harvard University Press, pp. 47–275.

Sanderson, D. (1938), 'Group descriptions', *Social Forces*, vol. 16, pp. 309–19.

Venable, T. C. (1954), 'The relationship of selected factors to the social structure of a stable group', *Sociometry*, vol. 17, pp. 355–7.

Warriner, C. K. (1956), 'Groups are real: a reaffirmation', *Amer. soc. Rev.*, vol. 21, pp. 549–54.

2 D. Cartwright and A. Zander

Theoretical Orientations

Excerpt from D. Cartwright and A. Zander, *Group Dynamics*, Tavistock, 1953, 3rd edn 1969, pp. 26–31.

Theoretical orientations

The student of group dynamics must be prepared to encounter and make constructive use of a wide variety of theoretical approaches. It is not possible to summarize here all of the many theoretical orientations to be found in the field. The different approaches derive from all the social sciences and reflect the many schools of thought within each. As an aid to identifying points of view and 'placing' particular studies, we will list a few of the major orientations that have most influenced work in group dynamics. Then we will discuss some of the reasons for the great diversity of orientations and concepts and, finally, attempt to identify the more important theoretical issues that underlie all the different orientations. In reading the following list it should be understood that these are not schools of thought to which individuals belong; an investigator may be influenced, even in a single research project, by several of these orientations.

A list of orientations

1. Field theory. This is the name given to the theoretical approach originated by Lewin (1951). It derives this name from its basic thesis that behavior is the product of a field of interdependent determinants (known as life space or social space). The structural properties of this field are represented by concepts from topology and set theory, and the dynamic properties by means of concepts of psychological and social forces. For an overview of this approach reference may be made to articles by Cartwright (1959a and b) and Deutsch (1954).

2. *Interaction theory*. As developed especially by Bales (see 1950, ch. 30), Homans (1950) and Whyte (1951), this conceives of a group as a system of interacting individuals. The basic concepts of this approach are activity, interaction and sentiment, and the attempt is made to construct all higher order concepts from these terms.

3. *Systems theory*. The view that a group is a system, adopted by the interaction theorists is also found in a wide variety of forms in other writings. These may be referred to as *systems theories*. Thus, 'systems of orientation' and 'systems of interlocking positions and roles' are central conceptions in the work stimulated by Newcomb (1950); the notion of 'communication system' has been widely employed in research following the leads of communications engineering; and the conception of a group as an 'open system', derived from biology, may be found in the writings of Miller (1955) and Stogdill (1959). Systems theories place major emphasis on various kinds of 'input' and 'output' of the system, and they share with field theory a fundamental interest in equilibrating processes.

4. *Sociometric orientation*. Originated by Moreno (1934) and elaborated by Jennings (1943), this is concerned primarily with the interpersonal choices that bind groups of people together. The remarkably large quantity of research conducted within this orientation has been effectively reviewed by Lindzey and Borgatta (1954), who point out that little systematic theory has yet resulted.

5. *Psychoanalytic theory*. Psychoanalytic theory focuses upon certain motivational and defensive processes within the individual and was first extended to group life by Freud (1922). In more recent years, especially as a result of the growing interest in group psychotherapy, it has been elaborated in various ways by such writers as Bach (1954), Bion (1948–50, 1952), Ezriel (1950), Scheidlinger (1952) and Stock and Thelen (1958). Of especial relevance to group dynamics are its concepts of identification, regression, defense mechanisms and the unconscious. Although comparatively little experimental or quantitative research on groups has been conducted within this orientation, concepts and hypotheses from psychoanalytic theory have permeated much of the work in group dynamics.

6. *General psychology orientation.* Since groups consist of individuals, it is to be expected that conceptions of human behavior developed in general psychology will be found in work on group dynamics. And, in fact, the influence of each of the major theories of motivation, learning and perception can be seen. Perhaps the most influential of these to date has been a broad approach referred to as *cognitive theory.* This is not, strictly speaking, a theory but a point of view that insists on the importance of understanding how individuals receive and integrate information about the social world and how this information affects their behavior. Important contributions to the study of groups have been made within this orientation by Asch (1952), Festinger (1957, ch. 10), Heider (1958) and Krech and Crutchfield (1948).

7. *Empiricistic statistical orientation.* This maintains that the concepts of group dynamics should be discovered from statistical procedures, such as factor analysis, rather than constructed on *a priori* grounds by a theorist. Those working in this orientation make considerable use of the procedures developed in the field of personality testing. Good illustrations of this approach may be found in the writings of Borgatta, Cottrell and Meyer (1956), Cattell (1948) and Hemphill (1956), who have concentrated to date on ascertaining the orthogonal dimensions in terms of which groups can be characterized.

8. *Formal models orientation.* In sharp contrast to this last orientation is the work of a group of writers who have attempted to construct *formal models* with the aid of mathematics in order to deal rigorously with some rather limited aspects of groups. Although these models ordinarily contain some assumptions drawn from one or another of the social sciences, the emphasis is more on formal rigor than on comprehensive substantive theory. Examples of this approach may be found in publications of French (1956), Harary (1959), Hays and Bush (1954), Rapaport (1963) and Simon (1957).

Some sources of diversity

These, then, are some of the major approaches to the study of groups, and there are many others that could be enumerated.

Although many of these appear to be in competition with one another, a careful study of them will reveal that the different theories and explanations do not actually contradict but instead augment and amplify one another. In order better to understand these various approaches and their interrelations, the reasons for the existence of so many theoretical orientations should be known.

Variety of groups and social settings investigated. It cannot be said of group dynamicists that they have confined their research to a narrow range of groups or to a limited segment of society. While it is true that they have conducted many studies on college students, they have also worked in a variety of other social settings. Thus, studies have been conducted on children in classrooms and summer camps, on military units, on committees and boards at all levels of business and government, on neighborhood groups, on voluntary groups as different from one another as labor unions and the League of Women Voters, on athletic teams, on therapy groups, on research teams, on international conferences and on work groups in industry. In view of this great diversity it is only to be expected that different investigators will emphasize in their theorizing different phenomena and explanatory principles.

Differences in social problems motivating research. A project that is stimulated by interest in some social problem tends to concentrate on particular phenomena and social situations. An investigator who seeks to find ways of improving group efficiency may limit his attention to work groups and be especially concerned with the division of responsibilities among members, their acceptance of group goals and the adequacy of their communication. A person who wishes to reduce intergroup conflicts may focus on sources of frustration, autistic hostility and the transmission of stereotypes among group members. And the researcher who seeks to learn how to make groups more effective media for changing attitudes, behavior or personal adjustment may pay special attention to group cohesiveness, social pressures generating conformity and the emotional atmosphere created by trainers or therapists.

Number of disciplines contributing to the field. People coming to the study of groups from different disciplines bring with them the special vocabularies of these disciplines and certain assumptions about the relative importance of various aspects of group life. Thus, a political scientist may be especially interested in social power and want to account for as much as possible in terms of this variable. An economist may believe that the dominant determinants are economic resources and technological skills. A sociologist may emphasize the place of the group in an organized society. An anthropologist may stress the importance of culture. A psychoanalyst may maintain that unconscious processes and ego defenses within group members are of the greatest significance. A psychologist may insist that events occurring in groups depend basically upon the way members view the group and the relationships among members.

The various circumstances surrounding the conduct of research generate a diversity of terminology and a variety of conceptions as to what the important determinants of group life are. Many of the more obvious disparities of terminology that derive from the special languages brought to the study of groups will undoubtedly be eliminated as research techniques become more standardized and as people from different disciplines become accustomed to communicating with one another about the same research material. And much of the disagreement as to which variables are the most important will disappear when it is realized that different writers are referring to different kinds of groups and social settings.

The understandable tendency of an investigator to generalize his findings from a particular setting to 'groups in general' is another source of confusion. It is a legitimate objective of group dynamicists to construct a general theory applicable to all types of groups, but this does not mean that any particular finding will be applicable to all groups in all conceivable settings. The task of deriving general principles from diverse findings is a most difficult one. It is the essential nature of a general law that it specifies what effects may be anticipated under specified conditions. The achievement of such a law demands, therefore, that great care be exercised in specifying the conditions which generate any particular findings. Only confusion will result unless one is careful to determine what limits should be imposed upon findings from a particular type of investigation or a particular type of group. Such different findings, when properly conceived, can be made to supplement one another in a comprehensive theory.

Some basic theoretical issues

All the conflicting points of view in group dynamics cannot, however, be eliminated by doing away with terminological misunderstandings or excessive zeal in generalizing from particular studies. Certain fundamental questions remain unanswered concerning the best ways to proceed in research and theorizing. Many genuine differences among the various approaches lie in the different answers people give to these questions. Four questions are of greatest importance: (a) What is the proper relation between data collection and theory building? (b) What are the proper objects of study and techniques of observation? (c) What are the basic variables that determine what happens in groups? (d) How can the many factors affecting group life be combined into a comprehensive conceptual system?

The development of any science seems to work progressively toward a satisfactory answer to the question of how data collection and theory building should be related. It appears that all the sciences have stemmed initially from armchair speculation; most can be traced back to a definite tradition in philosophy. For each developed science it can be said that at some point in history some people became dissatisfied with speculation and undertook to observe carefully and objectively the phenomena in question. Often the rebellion against speculation created an extreme position that ignored theory and let the data 'speak for themselves'. Finally, as a branch of science became more mature, theory building and data collection assumed a more interdependent relation to each other. In its advanced stage the scientific enterprise consists of developing hypotheses and theories from observations, checking these theoretical formulations by new observations and experiments, revising the hypotheses, checking these new hypotheses in new investigations and so on, over and over again. In the process, more and more comprehensive theoretical systems emerge, each part of which has a firm empirical basis.

Research and theorizing in group dynamics illustrate this trend quite well. Until the beginning of the present century the study of groups was in the speculative era. Then the empiricist rebellion held sway, with most energy being devoted to 'fact finding' and improving techniques of research. Finally, during the past three decades or so, group dynamics has entered progressively into the third stage of development, with more and more of its research being motivated by an interest in testing hypotheses that are 'derived' from a larger body of theory. There do remain, however, genuine disagreements among those working in this third stage about the exact way in which testable hypotheses should be constructed.

Some investigators believe that such methodological problems as those of developing measuring instruments and of demonstrating their reliability should come before much theorizing. They hold that the empiricist era should not be left too rapidly for fear that premature theorizing will get the research into blind alleys. Those working in the empiricistic-statistical orientation, for example, maintain that the basic dimensions of groups should be revealed through such procedures as factor analysis in which a large sample of reliable measurements of group phenomena are analysed to determine homogeneous factors. The sociometrists, too, have tended to concentrate upon the development of sociometric tests before building an elaborate theory of group structure. And the interactionists have devoted energy to creating standardized systems for recording and categorizing various kinds of interaction on the assumption that theorizing will develop more rapidly as a body of standardized 'facts' is developed.

In sharp contrast are those who feel that in the past the collection of data has been inefficient because so few findings can be added up to a comprehensive formulation. They prefer to let theory exert a more guiding influence in the design of research. According to this second view one should not select devices for recording and measuring before one knows what it is that needs to be studied. Until the variables necessary for developing a given theory or testing a hypothesis have been defined, these investigators hold, one has no real basis for deciding whether to use an interaction chronograph, a sociometric test, a personality test, a certain questionnaire or some other device.

If we take the view that group dynamics is ready for the third stage of scientific development in which theorizing and data collection mutually contribute to our understanding by a process of approximation, the conflicts between these two views do not seem irreconcilable. The collection of standardized data can help formulate theory, provided the data are not collected just because the standardized instrument is available. Similarly, each new formulation of a hypothesis may call for a refinement or revision of the data-gathering instruments. And it is certainly to be hoped that investigators will not invent new procedures when existing ones are satisfactory, because such innovation only serves to make it difficult to compare findings from one study to the next.

It is apparent, then, that the way a person attempts to solve the problem of data collection and theory building will greatly influence his selection of specific phenomena for investigation and his methods of research. Thus, for example, the investigator who believes that rigorous theorizing is dangerous at the present stage of development may prefer broad exploratory field studies in order to gain a more intuitive grasp of the variables with which subsequent theorizing should deal. On the other hand, an investigator who wants to test some restricted hypothesis derived from a theory or conceptual model may desire to conduct a rigidly controlled experiment in which some limited number of variables are varied systematically. The same investigator may choose one method in one study and quite a different one in another, depending upon his judgement of how well developed a given theoretical area is.

Because of the heterogeneous background of group dynamics and its recent history of being in the empiricist era, the phenomena selected for observation and measurement are quite diverse. As a result different researchers may observe the same group discussion, let us say, and yet come out with widely different descriptions of what happened. One, who adheres to the interactionist orientation, will present a frequency distribution of the interactions for each of a set of categories of interaction. Another, who is primarily interested in sociometry and group structure, will relate his observations to the sociometric structure of the group. Another, who holds to the psychoanalytic orientation, will attempt in various ways to detect the prevailing emotional and unconscious determinants. And yet another, who adopts the view of cognitive theorists that perceptions and cognitions determine the events in groups, will describe the content of communication and the beliefs held by various members. If it were evident, as is often the case when different kinds of groups are being studied, that all these different descriptions actually point to different phenomena, there would be no insurmountable difficulty. The basic task would then be to determine how each of these aspects relates to the others both conceptually and empirically. But unfortunately it is not always clear to what degree these different descriptions may be different ways of talking about exactly the same things. A great deal of work remains to be done before this problem can be solved and much will be gained by broadening the range of data collected from the same groups. Many needless confusions would never arise if interaction records, sociometric tests, interviews and projective tests, let us say, were all employed in the same research project. It would then become evident that all of these make important contributions to understanding a particular group, but it would also become possible to discover how these various kinds of data relate to one another empirically.

The most important task for group dynamics as it works in the third stage of scientific development is to establish a generally accepted set of basic variables and concepts having clear empirical and conceptual meanings. The essential problem may be posed in this way. The basic laws of group dynamics toward which all investigators are working are to be stated in terms of functional relations of the type: $x = f(y)$; x is a certain function of y. How are we to select and name the xs and the ys in our research? In working toward a resolution of this issue it is well to keep separate two of its aspects that are rather different. One part of the problem is to isolate the actual unitary variables or dimensions that make discernible differences. The other part consists of giving these variables appropriate names and conceptual properties.

The determination of unitary variables can be accomplished only by empirical work which discovers what regularities are invariably found among measurements and observations. Factor analysis and other methods of detecting invariant empirical associations can help here. The achievement of a common language of concepts that will permit the ordering of variables into a coherent conceptual system is more difficult. If the variables are to be employed in a conceptual system in such a way that derivations can be made to new empirical data and relations, then their conceptual properties must be clearly specified. These properties indicate the place of each variable in the conceptual system and the kinds of logical or mathematical operations that may be performed upon it.

Despite the importance of conceptual systems and models, at the present time there is no single language that all theorists will agree upon. Furthermore, there is little prospect that such a language will soon emerge. Fortunately, however, the conceptual systems that are currently in use are not completely incompatible with one another. In a general sense those who employ one set of terms can 'understand' those who employ another, even though a dictionary of translations has not been worked out. This possibility of sensing when two differently oriented theorists are talking about essentially the same thing provides the way in which a generally agreed upon set of terms can be achieved. When two theorists can agree that they are talking sufficiently about the same thing that the same operational definition can be given to the differing terms, then a rigorous translation can be made between the two languages and eventually the two will become amalgamated as one.

At the present time most of the theoretically oriented research in group dynamics consists of specific investigations of how two or three variables are related to one another. Thus, one study may investigate how variations in the cohesiveness of a group affect the strength of pressures on group members toward homogeneity of opinions. Another may seek to determine how variations in cohesiveness affect members' readiness to express hostility. And yet another may examine how the degree of similarity of opinions affects the cohesiveness of the group. There have as yet been few efforts to put these variables together into one coherent theoretical system. A promising lead, however, has been provided by March and Simon (1958), who have developed several 'maps' which show how the relations among variables reported by different investigators may be combined. These maps make it clear that a fully adequate understanding of the determinants of group life will involve a specification of a network of causal relationships. One of their maps indicates, for example, that the extent to which goals are perceived as shared and the number of individual needs satisfied in the group jointly determine the frequency of interaction in the group, which influences the strength of identification with the group, which in turn affects the extent to which goals are perceived as shared and the number of individual needs satisfied in the group. In other words, there is a circular chain of causal interactions.

The field of group dynamics appears to be ready for rapid progress in the construction of such maps. As attention shifts from isolated causal relations between variables taken two at a time to configurations of relations, a more penetrating understanding of the nature of group life will quickly emerge. And, as a result, the practical value of group dynamics theory will be greatly enhanced, since practitioners must be concerned, not with single relationships, but with the total ramifications that stem from the modification of any particular variable.

References

Asch, S. E. (1952), *Social Psychology*, Prentice-Hall.

Bach, G. R. (1954), *Intensive Group Therapy*, Ronald Press.

Bales, R. F. (1950), *Interaction Process Analysis*, Addison-Wesley.

Bion, W. R. (1948–50), 'Experiences in groups', *Hum. Rel.*, vol. 1, pp. 314–20, 487–96; vol. 2, pp. 13–22, 295–303; vol. 3, pp. 3–14, 395–402.

Bion, W. R. (1952), 'Group dynamics: a re-view', *Inter. J. Psychoanal.*, vol. 33, pp. 235–47.

Borgatta, E. F., Cottrell, L. S., and Meyer, H. J. (1956), 'On the dimensions of group behavior', *Sociometry*, vol. 19, pp. 223–40.

Cartwright, D. (1959a), 'A field theoretical conception of power', in D. Cartwright (ed.), *Studies in Social Power*, Institute for Social Research, Ann Arbor, Michigan, pp. 183–220.

Cartwright, D. (1959b), 'Lewinian theory as a contemporary systematic framework', in S. Koch (ed.), *A Study of a Science*, vol. 2, McGraw-Hill, pp. 7–91.

Cattell, R. B. (1948), 'Concepts and methods in the measurement of group syntality', *Psychol. Rev.*, vol. 55, pp. 48–63.

Deutsch, M. (1954), 'Field theory in social psychology', in G. Lindzey (ed.), *Handbook of Social Psychology*, Addison-Wesley, pp. 181–222.

Ezriel, H. (1950), 'A psychoanalytic approach to group treatment', *Brit. J. med. Psychol.*, vol. 23, pp. 59–74.

Festinger, L. (1957), *A Theory of Cognitive Dissonance*, Row, Peterson.

French, J. R. P., Jr (1956), 'A formal theory of social power', *Psychol. Rev.*, vol. 63, pp. 181–94.

Freud, S. (1922), *Group Psychology and the Analysis of the Ego*, Hogarth Press.

Harary, F. (1959), 'A criterion for unanimity in French's theory of social power', in D. Cartwright (ed.), *Studies in Social Power*, Institute for Social Research, Ann Arbor, Michigan, pp. 168–82.

HAYS, D. G., and BUSH, R. R. (1954), 'A study of group action', *Amer. soc. Rev.*, vol. 19, pp. 693–701.

HEIDER, F. (1958), *The Psychology of Interpersonal Relations*, Wiley.

HEMPHILL, J. K. (1956), *Group Dimensions: A Manual for their Measurement*, Bureau of Business Research, Ohio State University.

HOMANS, G. (1950), *The Human Group*, Harcourt, Brace & World.

JENNINGS, H. H. (1943), *Leadership and Isolation*, Longman.

KRECH, D., and CRUTCHFIELD, R. S. (1948), *Theory and Problems of Social Psychology*, McGraw-Hill.

LEWIN, K. (1951), *Field Theory in Social Science*, Harper & Row.

LINDZEY, G., and BORGATTA, E. F. (1954), 'Sociometric measurement', in G. Lindzey (ed.), *Handbook of Social Psychology*, Addison-Wesley, pp. 405–48.

MARCH, J. G., and SIMON, H. A. (1958), *Organizations*, Wiley.

MILLER, J. G. (1955), 'Toward a general theory for the behavioral sciences', *Amer. Psychol.*, vol. 10, pp. 513–31.

MORENO, J. L. (1934), *Who Shall Survive?*, Nervous and Mental Diseases Publishing Co., Washington.

NEWCOMB, T. N. (1950), *Social Psychology*, Dryden Press.

RAPAPORT, A. (1963), 'Mathematical models of social interaction', in R. D. Luce, R. R. Bush and E. Galanter (eds.), *Handbook of Mathematical Psychology*, vol. 2, Wiley, pp. 493–579.

SCHEIDLINGER, S. (1952), *Psychoanalysis and Group Behavior*, Norton.

SIMON, H. A. (1957), *Models of Man: Social and Rational*, Wiley.

STOCK, D., and THELEN, H. A. (1958), *Emotional Dynamics and Group Culture*, New York University Press.

STOGDILL, R. M. (1959), *Individual Behavior and Group Achievement*, Oxford University Press Inc.

WHYTE, W. F., JR (1951), 'Small groups and large organizations', in J. H. Rohrer and M. Sherif (eds.), *Social Psychology at the Crossroads*, Harper & Row.

Part Two Structural Models

One strong tradition in the study of groups has conceptualized the group as a unit and examined its relationships with the environment. Lewin's (see Cartwright, 1959; Lewin, 1935) early writing has had continuing influence, although his system of 'topology' whereby he sought to depict the interrelations of persons or groups and their environments has not won acceptance. The model of Trist, Higgin, Pollock and Murray (Reading 3) illustrates a Lewinian approach as modified to permit the study of natural-state groups within functioning organizations. Collins and Guetzkow (Reading 4) provide an integrated summary of work attempting to compare the productivity of groups with that of an equivalent number of individuals working separately. Their findings illustrate the utility of a model of group behaviour which takes account of the type of task with which the group is faced.

The most rigorous attempt to provide experimental verification of the impact of environmental structure on group process has been the communication-net studies discussed by Shaw (Reading 5). These experiments are conducted within a highly artificial setting in which subjects who are strangers to one another may only communicate by written note. The studies have none the less generated findings which are increasingly in line with those from more naturalistic studies. For example the impact of task on communication-net performance can be compared with Collins and Guetzkow's conclusions, and those on role development in the nets with the Fiedler model (Reading 13).

The three Readings in this Part are somewhat diverse, but they each attempt to account for group behaviour not in terms of personality variables, but by the environmental or structural constraints within which a group operates. This contrasts with Part Three which focuses instead on the behaviour which arises in the group as an outcome of personality needs of the members.

References

CARTWRIGHT, D. (1959), 'Lewinian theory as a contemporary systematic framework', in S. Koch (ed.), *Psychology: A Study of a Science*, McGraw-Hill, pp. 7–91.
LEWIN, K. (1935), *A Dynamic Theory of Personality*, McGraw-Hill.

3 E. L. Trist, G. W. Higgin, A. E. Pollock and H. A. Murray

Sociotechnical Systems

Excerpts from E. L. Trist, G. W. Higgin, A. E. Pollock and H. A. Murray, *Organizational Choice*, Tavistock, 1963, pp. 5–10, 20–28.

The sociotechnical approach
The development of the concept

This presentation of research studies by the Tavistock Institute of Human Relations in a number of pits in north-west Durham is concerned with the interaction of technological and social factors in industrial production systems – here represented by a variety of mining methods at differing levels of mechanization. The approach adopted, that of considering each production unit as a *sociotechnical system*, originated in the first mining study carried out by the Institute (Trist and Bamforth, 1951). The usefulness of the concept having been demonstrated by subsequent work (Trist, 1953; Wilson and Trist, 1951), it has been further developed in two parallel Tavistock projects, one in the Indian textile industry (Rice, 1958), the other the present research. Wilson (1955) has noted that work on similar lines has developed independently in various countries and that similar findings have emerged (Touraine, 1955; Walker and Guest, 1952; Westerlund, 1952).

The propositions underlying the present studies may, following Trist and Bamforth (1951), be stated as follows:

The longwall method will be regarded as a technological system expressive of the prevailing outlook of mass-production engineering and as a social structure consisting of the occupational roles that have been institutionalized in its use. These interactive technological and sociological patterns will be assumed to exist as forces having psychological effects in the life-space of the faceworker, who must either take a role and perform a task in the system they compose or abandon his attempt to work at the coal face. His own contribution to the field of determinants arises from the nature and quality of the attitudes and relationships he develops in performing one of these tasks and in taking one of these roles. Together, the forces and their effects constitute the psychosocial whole which is the object of study.

Rice (1958) continues more generally:

The concept of a production system as a sociotechnical system designates a general field of study concerned with the interrelations of the technical and sociopsychological organization of industrial production systems....The concept of a sociotechnical system arose from the consideration that any production system requires both a technological organization – equipment and process layout – and a work organization relating to each other those who carry out the necessary tasks. The technological demands place limits on the type of work organization possible, but a work organization has social and psychological properties of its own that are independent of technology. . . . A sociotechnical system must also satisfy the financial conditions of the industry of which it is a part. It must have economic validity. It has in fact social, technological and economic dimensions, all of which are interdependent but all of which have independent values of their own.

It is, of course, the sociopsychological (the people) and the technological (the things) which are the substantive dimensions. The economic dimension measures the effectiveness with which human and technological resources are used to carry out the primary task (cf. Williams, 1950). The importance of the distinctiveness of territory has been discussed by Miller (1959). Emery and Trist (1960, p. 94) have further shown that the sociotechnical concept requires to be developed in terms of open rather than closed system theory, especially as regards the enterprise–environment relation and the elucidation of the conditions under which a steady state may be attained:

Considering enterprises as 'open sociotechnical systems' helps to provide a more realistic picture of how they are both influenced by and able to act back on their environment. It points in particular to the various ways in which enterprises are enabled by their structural and functional characteristics ('system constants') to cope with the 'lacks' and 'gluts' in their available environment. Unlike mechanical and other inanimate systems they possess the property of 'equi-finality'; they may achieve a steady state from differing initial conditions and in differing ways. Thus in coping by internal changes they are not limited to simple quantitative change and increased uniformity but may, and usually do, elaborate new structures and take on new functions. The cumulative effect of coping mainly by *internal* elaboration and differentiation is generally to make the system independent of an increasing range of the predictable fluctuations in its supplies and outlets. At the same time, however, this process ties down in specific ways more and more of its capital, skill and energies and renders it less able to cope with newly emergent and unpredicted changes that challenge the primary ends of the enterprise.

Inherent in the sociotechnical approach is the notion that the attainment of optimum conditions in any one dimension does not necessarily result in a set of conditions optimum for the system as a whole. If the structures of the various dimensions are not consistent, *interference* will occur, leading to a state of disequilibrium, so that achievement of the over-all goal will to some degree be endangered and in the limit made impossible.[1] The *optimization* of the whole tends to require a less than optimum state for each separate dimension.

Focusing on the sociopsychological system

This approach does not imply that in all circumstances a detailed study of all three dimensions must be carried out. It does, however, underline the importance, when any aspect of a production system is examined, of taking into account the manner and extent of its interdependence with the other dimensions. In the present mining studies the research focus is the *sociopsychological* system. It is through the people who comprise this system that technological and economic changes are successfully or unsuccessfully implemented. For such changes to be effectively introduced, understanding of the latent as well as the manifest functioning of the sociopsychological system is necessary (Blau, 1955; Jaques, 1951; Merton, 1949).

The sociopsychological system may be studied at different organizational levels in the coal as in other industries: at the level of the individual worker, the work group, the seam, the pit, the Area, the Division or at the level of the National Coal Board itself, that is, the enterprise as a whole, when a very wide economic, political and sociocultural environment must be taken into account. The unit

1. Such dissonances between system characteristics may be similar to those described by Festinger (1957) in the field of cognition, though it is beyond the scope of this book to press such a comparison.

of study on which the present research is centred, however, is the *primary work group*. This is the smallest group whose membership carries out the whole set of activities constituting the unitary cycle of coal face operations. The boundaries of this social unit are defined in terms of the technological unit – the work cycle which it has to perform.[2] Just as the technical system of a coal face forms part of a larger system – the seam – in which it must be integrated for effective working, so does the primary work group – the cycle group – form part of a larger social system. The research is therefore concerned not only with the component work groups at the coal face which make up the cycle group but also with other individuals and groups in the seam population with whom they have immediate relations and who constitute the surrounding 'seam society'.[3]

At the level of the cycle group, the technological, economic and sociopsychological dimensions differ in the degree to which they constrain modification of the system by the group. There is least freedom in the technological system for other than very minor modifications, decisions on the mining side rarely being taken below pit level and frequently involving higher management. In the economic dimension there is somewhat more, though still limited, opportunity for change, as in initiating local negotiations regarding the basis or amounts of payment. Strict account, however, must be taken of the framework of existing agreements, which may be seam 'prices' or local colliery settlements; and at an early stage any proposal has to be considered in terms of county and national agreements. It is the sociopsychological system which affords the greatest opportunity for either formal or informal change at the level of the cycle group – in such matters as altering the pattern of work group organization.

It was not within our terms of reference to consider aspects of the economic system such as the capital, operating, maintenance and wages costs, or the level of wages or piece-rate prices, as such. None the less, the form of the wages system has considerable bearing on the structure and functioning of the sociopsychological

2. Cf. von Bertalanffy (1950) for the need to represent the mediating boundary conditions (here the technology) among the system constants in order to show how an open system achieves a steady state.

3. Cf. Lewin (1951) for the importance of adjacent systems both above and below the focal level.

system and in this context is taken into account. Our principal concern is to examine that aspect of the sociotechnical whole – the sociopsychological – within which the primary work group has relatively greater opportunity to develop various forms of work organization within imposed technological and economic limits. A set of concepts for describing the sociopsychological dimension is called for, which can be co-ordinated to concepts used in describing the technological.

The research opportunity

Over a number of years pilot studies of a variety of mining methods had been made by the Institute in a number of coalfields. Because these studies could be made only as opportunity arose, and because the seam conditions, customs, practices and attitudes differed in each locality, systematic and detailed comparison of the mining methods was scarcely feasible. Further progress required that these should be simultaneously available for study and that pits using them should be in one Area of a coalfield so as to minimize differences in background and tradition. The opportunity to undertake such studies in an older Area of the Durham coalfield was particularly welcome. In the collieries offered for study there existed – often in the same pit and all actively functioning in the present – a wide variety of mining systems ranging from traditional unmechanized working, through partially mechanized conventional methods, to more highly mechanized emergent systems. Since the faces concerned were in the same low seam, the geological structure of which was noted for its constancy, a comparative study of systems at different levels of mechanization was made possible under conditions more closely similar than any hitherto available.

In the most widespread of the conventional technologies in Durham there also existed two radically different forms of work organization, one of which had its roots in the earlier traditions of the coalfield, the other reflecting a form of organization more widespread in manufacturing industries. Comparison of alternative forms of work organization within the same technology therefore became feasible. The hypotheses emerging from the earlier Institute studies made the carrying out of such an 'experiment of opportunity' a matter of central scientific interest.

The co-existence in the present of a historically related range of mining methods, the growing importance of low seams as the higher were exhausted and the increasing use of more highly mechanized methods in low seams also presented an unusual opportunity to observe, as they occurred, the sociopsychological aspects of technological change. [...]

The appraisal of sociotechnical systems in mining

Primary task

The concept which integrates the technological, economic and sociopsychological aspects of a production system is the *primary task* – the work it has to perform (Bion, 1950; Rice, 1958). Work in this sense is the key transaction which relates an operating group to its environment and allows it to maintain the steady state (Emery and Trist, 1960). The production system with which we are concerned is the coal *face system*, although this must be studied in the context of the larger *seam system* of which it is a part. The primary task of a face system engaged in three-shift longwall working is the daily completion of a production cycle under all the given conditions that prevail.

The underground situation

The underground situation can vary greatly from one face to another and from one type of system to another, but common to all is the absence of fixed and consistent conditions in the physical environment. The complex of factors affecting work at the coal face is of the kind that would confront a factory if productive machinery had to be moved and re-set every day; if every operator had to contend with constant minor changes in the material he was working on; and, at the same time, look to keeping the walls and roof of his work area supported because they were imminently liable to collapse; if all supplies had to be brought in and products removed through two narrow passages; and if, despite the absence of uniform working conditions, supervisors could visit the operators only occasionally throughout one shift. Unlike the factory situation, where a high degree of control can be exercised over the production process since working conditions can be maintained in a passive and constant state, in the underground situation the threat of instability from the environment makes the production task much more liable to disorganization. Under the dangers, stresses and difficulties of the underground situation, certain qualities, evolved from the experience of successive generations and characteristic of traditional mining systems, are especially appropriate for the organization of work groups (cf. Gouldner, 1955):

1. Acceptance of responsibility for the entire cycle of operations.
2. Recognition of the interdependence of one man or group on another for effective progress of the cycle.
3. Self-regulation by the whole team and its constituent groups.

How far a work group is capable of such *responsible autonomy* and is able to adapt itself in correspondence with changing conditions indicates the extent to which its social structure is appropriate to the demands of the underground situation. The concept of responsible autonomy introduced by Trist and Bamforth in their original study of longwall in relation to traditional systems is intended to summarize these requisite[4] characteristics.

Activity structure

Analysis of the activity structure in these terms is basic to an understanding of work group organization – the way in which those who carry out the necessary tasks are related to each other. Although the technology places limits on the kind of work organization possible, it does not uniquely determine its form, which may be analysed in terms of the five following aspects, each of which is more fully considered in subsequent paragraphs:

1. The quality of the *work roles* to which each system gives rise through the division of labour.
2. The kinds of *task group* – the groups who together carry out given operations at the coal face and share a common paynote.
3. The *work culture* – customs, traditions and attitudes – which governs how these groups are built up and conduct themselves.
4. The nature of *intergroup relations* between task groups making up the face team.
5. The *managing system* through which the work of all faces in the seam is supervised, supported and co-ordinated.

4. For the term 'requisite organization' *vide* Brown (1960).

Work roles

In analysing any mining system, or in comparing one with another, the first consideration is to make a systematic examination of work roles. By work roles are meant the jobs which people do every day and with which they become identified – cutters, fillers, pullers, stonemen, etc. In thinking of themselves as such they gradually take on certain common characteristics and may be said to acquire the *character* of their role. In an industry such as mining, the role with which a man is identified becomes a way of life. Work roles vary both within and between mining systems, in their nature, their quality, the demands they make upon their occupants, the satisfactions they afford, and the degree and type of stress to which they expose those who carry them out.

A work role – what a man does, where, when and with whom – is primarily determined by the formal division or allocation of the tasks constituting the cycle of operations among the men who form the cycle group. A distinction must, however, be made between the formal or specified work role (the 'model') and the actual role which develops under a particular set of operating conditions. This distinction between formal and informal functioning applies also to other aspects of the social system. Recognition of such differences may not only indicate the efficiency of system functioning but also point the direction in which explicit technological or social change may profitably develop to achieve a better fitting together of the different aspects of the system as a whole.

A formal work role usually constitutes a main task together with such sub- and ancillary tasks as are associated with it. Since in certain systems the shifts on which main tasks are carried out are fixed, it is meaningful to talk of *task-shift roles*. According to the system of organization, tasks may or may not be specific to particular roles. The range of tasks and shifts comprising a work role may be narrow or wide depending on whether there is formal *rotation of shifts and tasks*. The *task range* of a role may also be increased by disorganization, as when the work a man normally does becomes unavailable because of cycle breakdown and he is required to undertake activities properly belonging to another role. The delineation of work roles is, therefore, to some extent a function of the period of time over which the role content is observed.

The task content of work roles must also be examined in relation to the level of skill involved, a consideration of importance where questions of degree of specialization or interchange-ability arise. How far the activities of a role comprise a self-completing whole task which occupies a full shift or how far the man has to fill out part of his shift by undertaking other activities has bearing on the extent to which he can experience satisfaction and identify himself with his role. In work systems where there is a large number of different work roles, some, because of the position they occupy in the cycle, may gain in status, power and reward at the expense of others, to a degree which is disproportionate to any real difference in skill and effort.

All roles at the coal face are stressful, but the pattern varies with the different roles. The physical effort required, the liability to interference from factors beyond the control of the facework group, the cruciality of the tasks for cycle progress, the monotony or variety of tasks, the permanency of the roles and the shifts on which they are carried out, are all factors which contribute to the *stress pattern*. When conditions become bad, certain roles are more exposed than others so that undue stress falls on those concerned. Casualties arise if there can be no relief. The pattern of absence, accidents and sickness is, therefore, relevant in an examination of work-role stress.

Task groups

The whole team of men responsible for the operations of a particular unit is the *cycle group*. This is sometimes referred to as the 'face' or 'panel' team. In any seam, the cycle groups, together with the other piece and day workers in the seam, constitute the *seam population*, which includes the younger men who are aspiring to facework, as well as older men who have retired to jobs away from the coal face. Depending on the system of working and the form of organization, the cycle group may contain a number of distinct subgroups. Where the cycle of operations is spread over more than one shift, there will be different *shift groups*. If a production unit has two faces – a double unit – there may be two *face groups*.

A group of men carrying out a particular operation in a particular location on the coal face is referred to as an *activity group*.

These groups may vary in size – according to the particular activity or activities carried out – and in the kinds of relationships between the men constituting the group. According to the system of work organization, the membership may be permanent or may vary, systematically or otherwise. Those activity groups which share a common paynote and in which membership is permanent are referred to as *task groups*.

Task groups, which are the basic units in a study of facework organization, vary in size and differ according to the kind of relationships the men have with each other in the work situation. In *identical-role* groups all concerned are supposed to do the same amount of the same task and work more or less independently of each other. In *reciprocal-role* groups the interdependent component activities of a main task are shared out among two or more persons who work together in order to complete it. There are also task groups of one, *isolate roles*, in which a man carries out a main task alone. The first step in the analysis of the characteristics of each task group is to determine the extent to which the structure of the task places limits on the kinds of relationship that are possible between the men in the group – whether work may be carried out independently or in subgroups of two or three; whether the level of skill or effort required is the same for all members of the group; whether or not stress arising from the task is likely to affect all members equally, etc.

Work culture

For a fuller understanding of the behaviour of facework groups – whether cycle, shift, face, activity or task – it is necessary to examine the pit and seam *culture* – the customs, traditions and attitudes which regulate how men achieve membership of the various groups and conduct themselves as group members. In the underground situation of high risk, self-dependence and the good use of discretion are necessary. It follows, as was pointed out at the beginning of this chapter, that to a considerable degree face groups must be autonomous and self-regulating. This can only come about if groups develop customs and traditions for regulating their behaviour and relationships which are internal to themselves and binding by force of the authority of the group itself. The psychological climate of a group and the kinds of relationship it has with other groups involved in completing the same primary task is to a considerable degree determined by the way in which the groups are built up. It is important to determine the route through which men achieve membership of particular groups, the permanency of membership and the route by which men leave. To do this an examination must be made not only of the various facework groups, but of the wider seam population. The earlier history of the seam has to be examined in order to gain an understanding of the way in which some of the on-going pit customs and practices have evolved.

Intergroup relations

In longwall working especially, the various task groups need some system of intergroup relations to enable them to co-operate successfully in the over-all task of cycle completion. An appraisal must, therefore, be made of the way in which task groups are related to each other and the extent to which their activities and attitudes facilitate or hinder completion of the over-all goal. The *degree of segregation* of the various task groups comprising the cycle group, their number and work relatedness to each other determines the basic pattern of intergroup relations. Within task groups there may be a number of activity groups whose membership may or may not be permanent. Role allocation may be to varying degrees flexible. At one extreme are fixed roles, at the other systematic patterns of rotation; in between are *ad hoc* exchanges of jobs. The extent to which all members of a cycle group share a common experience must be examined in relation to the way each constituent group carries out its work, since this can affect the conditions with which later groups have to cope.

The technological interdependence of activities is such that task groups are to varying degrees dependent on preceding groups. A situation of this kind tends to give rise to differences in status and power – according to the relative independence of a group's work and its cruciality for cycle completion. Where differences in status and power arise they may be reflected in differences in the level of earnings. It is in this connexion that account must be taken of the way in which the payment system operates. The earnings of a group may be dependent to varying degrees on completion of the over-all cycle task, on completion of its own main task, on the efficiency with which preceding groups carry out their tasks, and on the amount of unpredictable interference with their work arising from causes beyond the control of the cycle group. When the earnings of one group are too greatly dependent on the skill and attitude to its work of another, conflicts may arise and a state of tension develop between successive groups. As a protective measure against loss of earnings caused by the inability to complete main tasks regularly, groups may also, wittingly or unwittingly, go into collusion to carry out work in ways which, though economically mutually advantageous to the task groups concerned, may militate against the efficient completion of the production cycle.

The managing system

Because main task groups share work places and equipment on successive shifts, over-all co-ordination and continuity are required for smooth running of the *face system*. This is provided by the managing or governing system – which includes the total means adopted to maintain the boundary conditions of given 'operating systems' (Rice, 1958; Rice and Trist, 1952). These must be examined not only at face level but at the level of the seam. The *seam system* includes the face systems together with their common *service system* which covers everything supporting the productive operations of faces – transport facilities for coal and supplies, communications, manpower reserves, repair work, development work, etc. The formal managing system of the seam embraces the deputy, overman and undermanager – officials who are external to the face team; but some co-ordinating and regulating functions may reside within the face team and its constituent groups. These may sometimes be carried more or less explicitly by 'team captains'.

Important for a differentiation of systems of work organization is the extent to which co-ordination of task groups is *internal* or *external* – is carried out by the cycle group itself or effected by management external to the face team. Specific activity and task groups may be internally self-regulating without accepting responsibility for co-ordinating themselves as a shift group. Shift co-ordination may be provided entirely by the deputy who, when his shift overlaps others, also provides continuity between them. It is, therefore, necessary to identify the level at which responsibility is taken for co-ordinating the cycle group as a whole and the means by which this is done.

Since at any time the progress of operations on a face may be affected by what is happening in other parts of the seam system, each face 'shift supervisor' – the deputy – must be related to the seam 'shift supervisor' – the overman – whose responsibilities vary according to which shift he is on and the character of the seam system. It is at the level of the undermanager that the two facets of seam management – co-ordination of the cycle of operations on each face and co-ordination of the seam system on all shifts – become the responsibility of one person. An examination of the managing system at each level in the seam must explore the way in which information is generated, received and transmitted, the kinds of decisions that have to be taken, the means by which they are implemented and the nature of the stresses and strains to which officials are exposed. At the deputy and overman levels in particular, which are usually filled by promotion of qualified men from the face, conflicts may be experienced between the pressures of tradition and custom on the one hand and the technological and economic demands of higher management on the other. The nature of these conflicts and the habitual methods of coping with them must be ascertained. Finally an attempt must be made to assess in terms indicated in the earlier paragraphs of this chapter [see original source], the extent to which the managing system functions so as to enable the production units to carry out their primary task under the ever-present difficulties of the underground situation.

References

BION, W. R. (1950), 'Experiences in groups: V', *Hum. Rel.*, vol. 3, pp. 3–14.

BLAU, P. (1955), *The Dynamics of Bureaucratic Structure: A Study of Interpersonal Relations in Two Government Agencies*, University of Chicago Press.

BROWN, W. B. D. (1960), *Exploration in Management*, Heinemann and Wiley.

EMERY, F. E., and TRIST, E. L. (1960), 'Socio-technical systems', in C. W. Churchman and M. Vershulst (eds.), *Management Sciences Models and Techniques*, vol. 2, Pergamon, pp. 83–97.

FESTINGER, L. (1957), *A Theory of Cognitive Dissonance*, Row, Peterson.

GOULDNER, A.W. (1955), *Patterns of Industrial Bureaucracy*, Routledge & Kegan Paul.

JAQUES, E. (1951), *The Changing Culture of a Factory*, Tavistock.

LEWIN, K. (1951), *Field Theory in Social Science*, Harper & Row.

MERTON, R. D. (1949), *Social Theory and Social Structure*, Free Press (rev. edn 1957).

MILLER, E. J. (1959), 'Technology, territory and time: the internal differentiation of complex production systems', *Hum. Rel.*, vol. 12, pp. 243–72.

RICE, A. K. (1958), *Productivity and Social Organization: The Ahmedabad Experiment*, Tavistock.

RICE, A. K., and TRIST, E. L. (1952), 'Institutional and sub-institutional determinants of change in labour turnover (the Glacier Project – VIII)', *Hum. Rel.*, vol. 5, p. 347.

TOURAINE, A. (1955), *L'évolution du travail ouvrier aux usines renault*, Centre National de la Recherche Scientifique, Paris.

TRIST, E. L. (1953), *Some Observations on the Machine Face as a Socio-Technical System*, a report to the General Manager, no. 1 area, East Midlands Division, T.I.H.R., no. 341.

TRIST, E. L., and BAMFORTH, K. W. (1951), 'Some social and psychological consequences of the Longwall method of coal-getting', *Hum. Rel.*, vol. 4, pp. 3–38.

VON BERTALANFFY, L. (1950), 'The theory of open systems in physics and biology', *Science*, vol. 3, pp. 23–9.

WALKER, C. R., and GUEST, R. H. (1952), *The Man on the Assembly Line*, Harvard University Press.

WESTERLUND, G. (1952), *Group Leadership*, Nordisk Rotogravyr, Stockholm.

WILLIAMS, R. H. (1950), *The Theory of Action in Operations Research and in Social Sciences*, Johns Hopkins Press.

WILSON, A. T. M. (1955), 'Some contrasting socio-technical production systems', *The Manager*, December.

WILSON, A. T. M., and TRIST, E. L. (1951), *The Bolsover System of Continuous Mining*, a report to the Chairman, East Midlands Division, N.C.B., no. 290.

4 B. E. Collins and H. Guetzkow

Group and Individual Performance

Excerpts from B. E. Collins and H. Guetzkow, *A Social Psychology of Group Processes for Decision-Making*, Wiley, 1964, pp. 14–32.

Comparisons of the group and its individual members are a good place to begin this book on the group processes in decision making. In the first place, the relatively large amount of experimental works allows us to illustrate the way in which the *findings* from experimental social psychology form the foundation for a model about group process. Second, the contrast between the individual working alone and individuals working together introduces us to many of the central problems of social psychology which will be discussed further in later chapters. Third, these experiments emphasize the close relationship between individual psychology and group psychology. Both individual and group psychologies are important in the decision-making group. Finally, the studies to be reported have immediate practical implications. The administrator must frequently decide whether a matter for decision should be assigned to a conference, to an individual, or to some combination of both. The results of these studies may help him with these decisions.

An emphasis on the conditions under which groups are superior to individuals

Lorge and his colleagues made an extensive and critical review of the literature of individual and group comparisons up to 1958:

In general, in the evaluation of the relative quality of the products produced by groups in contrast to the products produced by individuals, the group is superior. The superiority of the group, however, all too frequently, is not as great as would be expected from an interactional theory. In many studies, the product of the 'best' individual is superior to that of the 'best' group (Lorge, Fox, Davitz and Brenner, 1958, p. 369).

It is not possible to state simply that group productivity is or is not superior to the productivity of individuals working in isolation. 'It depends ... !' Thus, our major task here is to specify the conditions under which groups will and will not be superior to individuals. For purposes of both theory and application, it is necessary to understand *why* the group is not always superior, which usually means that we must specify the conditions under which groups are superior and the conditions under which individuals are superior.

Observers of group interaction are impressed with the great differences among groups and among the individuals in each group. One group may be successful while another is not. For the moment, however, let us set aside these important differences among groups and individuals. Rather, let us contrast the performance of individuals working in a group with the performance of these *same* individuals working in isolation. Because this chapter is devoted to over-all differences between groups and individuals, considerations of different personalities and different patterns of interpersonal relations will be postponed for later chapters.

The nature of the task

The world is complex. We cannot discuss comparisons between individuals and groups without also discussing the task on which they are working. For this reason, we must find ways to characterize different group tasks before we turn to the data from group versus individual comparisons. Hopefully, we work toward a method of identifying those tasks on which groups will excel and those tasks on which the individuals will excel face-to-face groups.

Roby and Lanzetta (1958, p. 95) suggest that we analyse a task in terms of its *critical demands*:

We may expect that the most useful method of classifying group tasks will be with reference to those aspects of group behavior or procedures which these tasks bring to the foreground. In other words, we would expect that the distinctive features of particular tasks will be the degree to which they require certain group behaviors for adequate performance. Such behavioral requirements will be referred to as 'critical demands'.

For example, groups are likely to perform particularly well when they are able to divide the labor of the task among the group members. For this reason we would expect that 'division of labor' will be an important critical demand for tasks which are used to compare individuals and groups. There is little reason, for example, to assume that a group of individuals would do a better job than would a single individual of plotting the geographical locations of branch units with pins on a map. It is true that a group of kibitzers might catch an occasional oversight, but there is little that the extra 'members of the group' can contribute to a single member's map work. All twenty-five members of a group might see that a pin representing a branch should be placed in Cleveland; but since there is only one pin and one map, the twenty-five individual efforts can appear but once in the group product. Since the task is simple and routine, twenty-five members would redundantly replicate each other's efforts with little gained by the multiple checks.

Even in group interactions on complex tasks where the group is most likely to excel, only one person can speak at a time; and while one member is speaking, the others must listen. One listener may be stimulated to make a valuable criticism or modification later; but, for the time being, the other members are partially 'idle' in the sense that they are not *overtly* producing information, alternatives or conclusions for the benefit of the other group members.

Much the same argument will apply to less extreme examples. If a problem is so simple that the major difficulty is the time it takes to fill in the correct responses to an agency questionnaire, a group hardly could be expected to improve on the effort of one of its members. If the major portion of the task is 'writing words', and only one person will write at a time, there is little that the extra members can do to help. On the other hand, if the problem required a wide range of backgrounds in order to discover all the answers, a group of individuals might do a better job than its most capable member.

Although some divisions of labor may allow a group to utilize its full resources, other divisions might limit the group to the ability of its poorest member. If the decision requires unanimous agreement, as is the case in some boards of directors or government commissions, the inability of one member to understand a technical solution could seriously delay the group decision. We must recognize that the task or problem on which the group is working influences the extent to which a group is – or is not – superior to its individual members working in isolation.

B. E. Collins and H. Guetzkow 57

Propositions about individual and group productivity: division of labor and consolidation of information

We shall focus on three general ways in which the output of a group of individuals differs from the output of single individuals working separately. In this first section propositions concerning the 'group's' utilization of its potentially greater resources are presented. [. . .]

In many senses the topics of this chapter comprise a varied and heterogeneous list; but – in at least three senses – these topics are appropriate for an early chapter in a book on the social psychology of group processes. First, these topics introduce the reader to most of the broader issues which are developed more fully in later chapters. Second, each proposition gives us insight into the way in which the 'group' differs from the 'individual'. Finally a list which contrasts individuals and groups provides insight into group processes. If we remain alert to the processes which distinguish individuals from a group, we are likely to discover those variables which will help us distinguish one group from another.

It should be understood throughout this book that the phrase 'other things being equal' is implicit in each proposition.

Proposition 2.1. When several individuals work collectively on a single task their activities will overlap and/or make a division of labor possible.

The experimental and field data to be used in building our propositions in this part encompass a wide variety of problems – from the almost trivial (estimating the number of beans in a bottle) to the more serious (finding satisfactory ways to increase significantly the output of an assembly line). Whether overlap and division of labor increase the adequacy of the group will depend on the critical demands of these tasks and on the effectiveness of the group's pattern of internal relations.

Proposition 2.1–A. For tasks involving random error, combining several individual estimates or solutions into a single group product will increase accuracy.

Many tasks (working arithmetic problems, guessing weights and room temperature, estimating branch office sales, forecasting clientele reactions, etc.) involve many sources of error. It is a statistical axiom that, for problems which involve random errors, the average of several judgements will be more accurate than a single judgement. The greater the number of separate judgements included in the final answer, the more accurate will be the final average. The errors tend to cancel out each other.

In her unpublished master's thesis, Hazel Knight (1921) had college students estimate room temperature. According to Lorge *et al.* (1958, p. 344): 'The judgements of the individuals ranged from 60° to 85°; the "statisticized" group judgement was 72·4°, approximating the actual room temperature of 72°. The "statisticized" group judgement was better than that of 80 per cent of the individual judgements....'

This increase in the accuracy results from the arithmetical combination of individual hypotheses and does not depend on the criticism and evaluation of group members. It has been demonstrated that such individual judgements do not need to be made in the presence of the other individuals (Farnsworth and Williams, 1936). All that is required is that a number of separate hypotheses which contain a random error be combined in some manner. Stroop (1932) reports that accuracy was increased by combining five separate judgements of the same individual. The responses of single individuals are, of course, more likely to contain a constant bias which will not be cancelled out by combination.

On the other hand, a series of hypotheses taken from different individuals often contains a constant bias that may be accentuated by the grouping of answers. Error cancellation requires that the errors be random. The individuals whose judgements are pooled must have been subjected to varying and heterogeneous background experiences. Farnsworth and Williams (1936) used a task which required the subjects (Ss) to estimate the weight of three objects. One object was lighter than the others, but also larger in size. In this case the individual errors were not random; since all individuals had experienced larger objects as heavier, they made mistakes in the same direction. The average of the pooled judgements was not superior to individual performance on this task.

Gordon (1924) had students rank objects by weight and then correlated these rankings with the rankings obtained by physical measurement. The average correlation of individual rankings with the true ranking was only 0·41. But, then she averaged several individual estimates together and correlated this 'group' estimate with the true scores. These 'group' correlations were considerably higher; the average rank order correlation between 'groups' of fifty averaged individual judgements and the true order was 0·93.

Stroop (1932) was the first to indicate that the increased size of the correlations was a 'mathematical' rather than a 'social' phenomenon. He replicated Gordon's findings, and also executed several additional variations in the design. He demonstrated that the increased accuracy was almost exactly that which would be predicted from a statistical formula (the Spearman–Brown Prophecy Formula), and then showed that grouping increased the correlation size even with data generated randomly from card sorting. Similar results have been reported by other experimenters.[1]

In summary, the combined estimate of several group members is likely to be more accurate than the estimate of any single member. This is true only when each individual estimate contains random sources of error so that the errors tend to cancel out. Combination does not eliminate a constant bias.

Proposition 2.1–B. For tasks which involve creating ideas or remembering information, there is a greater probability that one of several persons will produce the information than that a single individual will produce it by himself.

In 1955 Lorge and Solomon published a detailed mathematical model which predicts the degree to which a group will surpass its individual members on a problem where the answer is 'obvious' to everyone as soon as it occurs to anyone in the group. It seems reasonable that when one person has a certain probability of discovering the answer by himself, then there is an even greater

1. Smith (1931) applied the Knight technique (see above) to groups of five, ten, twenty and fifty undergraduates who worked individually judging personality and behavior traits of children from written reports of their behavior. The correlations with the criterion increased with the size of the group.

Bruce (1935) had subjects judge the weight and number of buckshot in a sample. The correlation for the statisticized group was higher than the average individual correlation.

Klugman (1945) obtained similar results when high school students judged the number of unfamiliar objects in a bottle, although there was no significant difference for familiar objects. Schonbar (1945) found that interacting pairs were more accurate than individuals in estimating the length of lines.

probability that at least one of several group members will discover it. By the same reasoning, the group is likely to stumble on the answer faster than a single person working alone. After having individuals solve a relatively complicated problem individually and then resolve it in groups, Tuckman and Lorge (1962, p. 51) conclude: 'The evidence in this study suggests that groups are superior to individuals, not so much on account of the greater effectiveness of groups in solving problems, but rather on account of the greater probability of getting a good solution from a group of five than from any one individual.' Hoppe (1962) finds that the Lorge and Solomon model accurately predicts the degree to which groups will exceed individuals in recalling nonsense syllables. Although they suggest qualifications to be discussed in Proposition 2.3, Davis and Restle (1963) report that a greater proportion of groups reached a correct solution within the time limit than did individual members working alone. Yuker (1955) reports an experiment in which individuals tried to reproduce three times a story which had been read to them. First they worked separately, then groups were formed to prepare a common story and finally the same Ss again attempted to reproduce the story individually. 'The group recall was superior to the average initial individual recall, the initial individual recall of the persons with the best memories, and to the average final individual recall' (Yuker, 1955, p. 22). In summary, the data confirm our proposition. Several individuals are more likely than a single person to hit on an improbable but obviously correct idea.

The argument to this point can be extended to situations where the group seeks more than one alternative. For instance, several individuals would be more likely to stumble on five separate alternatives than a single individual would be. Gibb (1951)[2] found that the number of different solutions suggested by a group increased with the size of the group in a negatively accelerated function. In other words, the number of extra solutions increases rapidly as the

2. '1152 college students [were] drawn at random from a group of students in elementary psychology classes.... Groups of varying sizes were given a set [of instructions] to produce as many solutions as possible to a series of problems permitting multiple solutions. The groups varied in size, containing one, two, three, six, twelve, twenty-four, forty-eight or ninety-six members. Each group session lasted exactly thirty minutes after the instructions containing the set were read' (Gibb, 1951, p. 324).

first few members are added, and then the gain per individual begins to drop off.

Proposition 2.1–C. Groups will be efficient when the critical demands of the task emphasize the gain from a duplication of effort and/or from the division of labor.

So far in Proposition 2, we have seen how the group can eliminate random errors and has access to a greater pool of alternatives. Now we see that these facts can be either strengths or weaknesses – depending on the task environment. A larger number of available solutions, for instance, would increase the productivity of larger groups only when a larger number of solution alternatives are necessary for optimal output. For many problems the surplus of alternatives may lead merely to conflict and would not increase the quality of the final product. Of course, multiple estimates of the same judgement can increase the accuracy of the group product, but this effect may be more than canceled by the time spent sorting out twenty alternatives when four would have been enough for a particular task. Furthermore, both the number of alternatives added per person and the increased accuracy per person drop off as the group becomes larger.

In 1938 Thorndike conducted an experiment to test the hypothesis that the superiority of the group over the individual will be highest for tasks which afford a wide range of possible solutions.[3] In general, the hypothesis was confirmed. It appeared, however, that composing a crossword puzzle was so complex a problem that Thorndike's newly formed groups were unable to organize themselves adequately for the task. Husband (1940) found that pairs

3. Thorndike (1938) had college subjects meet for four sessions, each of which was one week apart. Each subject worked as an individual twice and in a group twice. All tasks were completed within a session. All tasks were designed in two forms, one form with a wide range of alternatives and another with a narrow range.

Groups were superior when working on 'fill in blank' vocabulary tests (versus multiple choice) and when filling in three lines of a limerick (versus one line). The fact that the individuals had a greater superiority over groups when composing a puzzle (versus completing a crossword puzzle) suggests that extremely complex tasks may require so much interpersonal organization within the group that group superiority is thereby lessened, at least for newly formed groups.

were superior to individuals when working on problems requiring some originality or insight, but not on the more routine arithmetic problems. Perhaps the arithmetic problems were so easy that no random errors were involved.

Implications of propositions 2.1. These propositions have important implications for the utilization of groups for decision making in government and industry. When quantitative judgements must be made, it is well to increase the size of the group and to include persons with widely varying experiences relevant to the matter at hand. It would seem wise, for example, for the Internal Revenue Service to assemble personnel with a large variety of experiences in assessment of tax write-offs when the impact of new regulations is being estimated. When a large variety of information must be brought to bear and unusual solution alternatives must be produced, it again would seem that increasing the size of the group would improve the quality of productivity. These considerations might well prompt an industrial firm to bring its foremen together and have them suggest alternative proposals for a new plant which the architects then would work over before completing their final drawings. But remember – the improvement with increasing size yields diminishing returns. Finally, the superiority of the group may be washed out in organizational confusion if the task requires a high degree of patterning of the internal relations.

Proposition 2.2. When several individuals are limited to a single product, it will be selected from available ideas and information.

In other words, the final *group* product will not contain all of the information which each group member might have used in his *individual* product. Up to this point, we have stressed the fact that the group has access to more information than a single individual. But, more often than not, the group must select from the information which it has available. Few solutions are so obvious that the group does not have to choose among several alternatives in order to make its final decision.

Proposition 2.2–A. The final group product will exclude some of the ideas and information potentially available to each member.

In the first place, each individual is aware of only a few of the events in his environment and can 'bring to mind' only a small fraction of his total knowledge. Second, each individual will report only a small fraction of the events in his awareness to the group. The total information available in the group is still further pruned when the other group members fail to assimilate everything reported by their fellow members. Furthermore, the other group members will reject as 'false' or 'not up to par' many of the individual contributions which are assimilated. For that matter, the group interaction may lead an individual to reconsider an idea which he himself proposed.

It has been possible to isolate a portion of this selective process in a series of experiments which compare an interacting group with a nominal or synthetic group. Lorge *et al.* (1958) use the term 'concocted', but we shall use 'synthetic' because it connotes both the artificial nature of the 'groups' and the fact that they are constructed from separate and independent parts. In experiments on synthetic groups, the researcher has individuals work out a common decision in face-to-face group interaction; then he has an equivalent set of individuals work on the problem independently. The *experimenter* then combines the results of the individual efforts into a single group product; he eliminates ideas which overlap and credits the entire 'group' with all solutions achieved by any single individual. Note that the synthetic group *does not complete the process of problem solving*. Members of synthetic groups only can generate a wide number of alternative solutions; it remains for someone else to select one or edit out the overlapping alternatives.

Proposition 2.2–A argues that the solutions of the face-to-face group usually contain fewer alternatives than those of the synthetic group because the contributions of the interacting group have undergone the entire selective process of face-to-face group interaction. Furthermore, the superiority of the synthetic groups should be most evident on tasks (such as those described in Proposition 2.1–B) where little is to be gained from the criticism and selectivity uniquely present in face-to-face group deliberation.

An experiment by Faust (1959) serves to illustrate the reliable superiority of synthesized groups over interacting groups for problems which require little sophistication and otherwise do not allow for division of labor or criticism. Faust had his subjects work for an hour on two tasks: one set of tasks in which the problem was presented in a diagram and a verbal description, Ss were to 'draw' the answer; the second set of tasks was three anagrams. The anagrams were placed in envelopes within envelopes in such a way that Ss were forced to work jointly on each step of a multiple step problem. Note how this latter limitation makes the problem relatively routine and prevents the members from dividing the work.

Groups of four working together performed better than a single individual working alone, but a group synthesized from the products of four individuals (who had actually worked separately) was superior to the product of four interacting group members (who had actually worked together). Similar results have been found by Watson (1928)[4] and in a study by Taylor, Berry and Block (1958).

Taylor, Berry and Block (1958) formed twelve groups of four men each and compared the productivity of these groups with the results of forty-eight individuals working separately. The researchers gave both groups and individuals a set of instructions designed to increase creativity (i.e. no criticism, wild ideas en-

4. Watson (1928) divided 108 graduate students in education into twenty newly created experimental groups of three to ten members. Subjects were given a set of envelopes containing jumbled letters and were asked to form a word from the letters. 'The first ten-minute period was spent by each person making as many words as he could by himself. . . . After a brief intermission, the group came together for a group-thinking process. The group secretary kept the list of words, and each person called his contribution aloud. Ideas, just in the process of becoming suitable words, were expressed in the group and others helped to supply the desired term or modification. This continued for exactly ten minutes' (Watson, 1928, pp. 329–31).

In other words there were four sessions separated by a brief intermission: (a) ten minutes alone, (b) ten minutes in group, (c) ten minutes in group and finally (d) ten minutes working alone. Scores were compiled for the sessions each individual worked separately, the time spent in the cooperative face-to-face group, and for a synthetic group based on the sum of individual member scores during the individual sessions.

Taking the average individual production as 100 per cent, 'the poorest person had an efficiency of 55 per cent, the best of 150 per cent, the cooperative group of 231 per cent, and the compiled [synthetic] group ... would average 268 per cent. In every group the group thinking [face-to-face interaction] produced more words than the best individual of the group. In [only] five of the twenty groups the cooperative group work produced more words than did the synthetic group' (Watson, 1928, p. 332).

couraged, quantity emphasized, etc.). The groups and individuals were then given three problems: how to increase tourist travel in the United States, difficulties of having two thumbs, and steps to meet the teacher shortage. Group members were then asked to list as many suggestions as they could. Note that group members did not have to choose a correct solution or evaluate the proposals in any way.

Under these conditions, the four-man groups produced *more* unique suggestions than a *single individual*, but the interacting groups produced significantly *fewer* suggestions than a group synthesized from four individuals who had worked separately. There was some evidence to indicate that the suggestions from the interacting group were superior in quality to those from the synthetic group.

In a brief overview of their research, Parnes and Meadow (1959) reported that they failed to replicate the basic Taylor *et al.* study. Parnes and Meadow also reported that brainstorming groups (groups with instructions stressing creativity) are superior to synthetic groups without the instructions. Furthermore, brainstorming groups are superior to non-brainstorming groups.

Implications. We should emphasize that these particular studies do *not* offer evidence that the group of interacting individuals is inferior to a group of individuals working separately. The products of the two types of groups are not comparable directly. In the first place, the *experimenter* combines the products of the synthetic group. Thus the comparison in the Faust experiment should be: four individuals working together with no help from Faust versus a group of four individuals working separately from each other *plus* Faust's (or his research assistant's) clerical aid in combining the lists and omitting duplicate ideas.

Data from studies on group and individual problem solving frequently reveal that one or two of the group members could have solved the problem without the aid of the rest of the group. These skilled members even may have been slowed down by the necessity of listening to the inferior contributions of other group members and of demonstrating the worth of their own ideas. Why, then, do we not assign the problem to these superior group members in the first place?

We frequently do not know which individual has the correct answer *before* the group conference. The experimenter may well know the 'correct' answer to a problem before he assigns it to a group of laboratory subjects. But, if the executive knows the correct answer to a problem, then he would not need to assign it to anyone, much less a decision-making group. And, if he knows that a single expert can solve the problem, the problem often is delegated directly to the expert. It may turn out *after* the decision-making conference that a certain individual or a group of individuals (specified by hindsight) working separately could have done the job more efficiently. In order to utilize an individual or synthetic group we must know *at the start* of the decision-making process which individual(s) to choose, how the work is to be divided, and how solutions are to be recombined as a synthetic solution of separate individuals.

If the task is relatively routine, if emphasis is on quantity rather than quality and if an administrative aide is available to combine the individual efforts, then an executive might well turn a problem over to a roster of separate individuals and an administrative assistant rather than forming them into a committee. Such an administrator would still have the task of communicating the final list of solutions to the individuals who had contributed them and then might have to persuade them that the additions from the other participants were worthwhile; but these obstacles may not be serious considerations in many situations, especially if the practice had become routine. In any event, the final group product of face-to-face groups will exclude some of the ideas and information available to each member.

Proposition 2.2–B. The accuracy and quality of the final group product will be increased through the elimination of inferior individual contributions.

Dashiell (1935) staged an incident in a classroom and then had two of the students present serve as 'witnesses' before a class in legal psychology. Shorthand accounts of the 'testimony' were taken and each member of the class prepared a written report. Then the 'jurors' from the legal class met in a group conference and produced a single unanimous report. This unanimous report was 'less complete [Proposition 2.2–A] than that of any individual witness or individual juror since everyone had to agree on each fact, but clearly *more accurate* [Proposition 2.2–B] than that of any individual witness or juror' (Dashiell, 1935, pp. 1135–6).

Omissions do not always improve the final group product. For example, Lorge, Tuckman, Aikman, Spiegel and Moss (1955) reported that untrained, newly formed discussion groups lost almost 80 per cent of the ideas contributed by individual members; and, as a result, 75 per cent of the individual decisions were superior to the best group decisions. Although training in staff techniques significantly improved group performance, these newly formed groups continued to omit important individual contributions from their group product.

Of course, it may be to the group's advantage to omit certain individual contributions, especially if these contributions are in error. In later propositions we shall see how this selective process in interaction works to improve the quality of the final group product. A group decision which finds a place for every individual contribution may turn out to be an unworkable conglomeration.

Utilization of information in the decision-making group. In these early propositions we made much of the differences in the amount of information available to the individual and to the group. We saw how access to an increased range of information increases the probability that the group will hit on an 'obvious' solution (Proposition 2.1–B); and we shall see how this same increased range of information will increase the total man-hours of time which the group members spend working toward the solution (Proposition 2.3). Even with the extra time, groups still do not use all of the information at their disposal, and these omissions sometimes can increase the quality of the group product (Proposition 2.2).

These propositions have examined group decision making from a rational or statistical perspective; little attention has been given to the psychology of group members as they listen to the presentation of information. Shaw (1963) examined the behavior of group members who were given access (by the experimenter) to different numbers of alternative solutions to the problem being discussed by the group. The groups were discussing human relations problems which demanded that the group reach agreement on one of several plausible solutions. These problems differ from the 'eureka' problems cited earlier in which the answers are 'obvious'. On these problems other group members usually do not agree as soon as one member hits on the correct solution.

When compared to other group members who were given no extra solutions, Shaw found that the task relevant contributions and the participant ratings of contributions to the decision by the 'informed members' was higher. This difference, however, *decreased* as they were given more information. The difference between the informed members and the other group members was greatest when the informed member was given two possible solutions, next greatest when given access to four solutions and least great when given access to six alternative solutions. Are these results caused by the fact that the informed members did not make use of the information available because they were less persuasive in their presentation of the information? Although Shaw reports no quantitative data, he suggests (1963, p. 77), 'from observing group processes', that the informed member

does not make use of six units of information in the same way that he does two units. With two units, he tended to mention both suggested solutions, but selected one of these to try to sell to the group. With six units, he tended to mention all six suggested solutions, but did not give the impression of being committed to one in particular.

It is possible that possession of the extra information caused the individual to change his role from an advocator to a provider of information. Whether or not this role change improves group productivity will depend on the critical demands of the task.

Extending the work on the behavior of an informed group member, Shaw and Penrod (1962) used a similar technique to study the impact of varying amounts of information on the quality of group solutions. The experimenters gave all participants the first paragraph of a human relations case. In some experimental conditions, a certain participant (the informed member) was given one or two additional paragraphs of the problem. Although this procedure manipulates the amount of information, it also changes the definition of the problem. Perhaps because of the fundamental nature of the information, it appears that the other group members were reluctant to accept the information presented by the informed member. Two separate experiments fail to demonstrate a significant improvement in the group solutions when a single member is given extra information. It is not enough that the information be present; it must also be presented persuasively and legitimately documented before the other group members are likely to accept it.

We shall have more to say about the influence process in later chapters [see original source]. For the time being, it is sufficient to stress the fact that the availability of information does not mean it will be effectively used. The contributor may fail to support his ideas and listeners may be skeptical. For that matter, we must not assume that increased information *always* improves the quality of the group product. We cited many studies which seem to demonstrate that the increased range of information available in a group makes the interacting group superior to the individuals working alone. These studies, however, utilized tasks which did not require extensive evaluation of the alternatives. The answers were usually 'obvious' in the sense that other members are likely to agree as soon as one member hits on the correct answer. But what about the problems without a single 'correct' answer? Is it not likely that group members could get so bogged down in alternatives that they never would choose a single 'best' answer? There are, of course, times when no answer is better than a wrong answer. There are other times when the important task is to reach agreement or consensus on any one of a large number of equally 'correct' alternative solutions. In the latter case, extra information, in the form of too many alternatives, could decrease productivity.

Proposition 2.3. A group of individuals working together will usually consume more man-hours when compared to an equal number of individuals working separately, and a group with fewer members.

Since this proposition compares the productivity of individuals and groups, it is relevant only in cases where both individuals and groups can complete the task. If the individual is unable to solve the problem at all, then a comparison between a group and an individual is meaningless. But, for those tasks which both individuals and groups can complete, we generalize that man-hours (number of hours spent times the number of members working) will be greater for interacting groups than for synthetic groups and greater for large groups than for small groups. It should be stressed that we do not know *in advance* what problems can be solved only by groups because individuals are unable to complete the task.

Davis and Restle (1963) make this same prediction – that groups take longer than individuals – from a mathematical model which assumes that the group product results from a combination of both the correct *and incorrect* contributions of each individual member. For the experimental data they collected, their model more closely predicts group solution times than does a modified Lorge–Solomon model which assumes that the group combines only the correct individual contributions.

It should be noted that Davis and Restle used an experimental procedure in gathering their empirical data which limited the superiority of the group over its individual participants. Davis and Restle did not specify any method by which the group was to reach a group agreement: 'any member was allowed to record the answer'. Furthermore, group members were instructed to talk 'freely among themselves' and out loud as much as possible. The first procedure means that the group must devote time getting organized; and the second may increase the tendency of a member to contribute an idea, even if he does not think the idea is particularly good. Both of these instructions may have placed the group at a disadvantage with respect to individuals.

Taylor and Faust (1952) used a modified version of the twenty questions parlor game in which the subjects had thirty questions to guess the name of an object which the experimenter (*E*) had in mind. *E* found that groups of two and four members required fewer questions and less time than single individuals to discover the correct answer. But when the experimenter multiplied the time taken to reach the solution by the number of members in each group, groups of two took significantly more *man*-hours than individuals; and groups of four took significantly more *man*-hours than groups of two to reach the correct solution.

In this case, the group considered as a whole produced solutions superior to individuals working alone (Propositions 2.1–B and 2.2–B), but the superiority was bought at the price of extra man-hours (Proposition 2.3). Although it may be true that the best group member could have solved the problem in fewer man-hours, we cannot always know which member is the 'best' until after all the members have tried to develop the solution.

Implications. When the solution must be closely coordinated and a few proposals must be carefully integrated into a single answer, the decision-making group should be small in size, perhaps of four or five persons. This kind of problem is least likely to benefit from a wide range of alternatives, the elimination of random error, and the elimination of inferior proposals. The small size minimizes the problems of interpersonal organization and the lost man-hours of duplicated effort. On the other hand, should the problem require a quantitative estimate where individual errors are likely to be random (Proposition 2.1–A), the generation of an unlikely association or 'obvious' solution (Proposition 2.1–B), increasing the number of members should improve the group's potential. This increased potential, however, is bought at the cost of greater man-hours (Proposition 2.3). The advantages of the group deliberation are particularly costly when the problem requires the group members to develop an elaborate pattern of interpersonal relations. Finally, it may be cheaper to tap the resources of many men by having them work in isolation and then delegating an administrative assistant to pool the individual efforts.

References

BRUCE, R. S. (1935), 'Group judgments in the fields of lifted weights and visual discrimination', *J. Psychol.*, vol. 1, pp. 117–21.

DASHIELL, J. F. (1935), 'Experimental studies of the influence of social situations on the behavior of individual human adults', in C. Murchison (ed.), *Handbook of Social Psychology*, Clark University Press, pp. 1097–158.

DAVIS, J. H., and RESTLE, F. (1963), 'The analysis of problems and prediction of group problem solving', *J. abnorm. soc. Psychol.*, vol. 66, pp. 103–16.

DE SOTO, C. B. (1960), 'Learning a social structure', *J. abnorm. soc. Psychol.*, vol. 60, pp. 417–21.

FARNSWORTH, P. R., and WILLIAMS, M. F. (1936), 'The accuracy of the median and the mean of a group of judgments', *J. soc. Psychol.*, vol. 7, pp. 237–9.

FAUST, W. L. (1959), 'Group versus individual problem-solving', *J. abnorm. soc. Psychol.*, vol. 59, pp. 68–72.

GIBB, J. R. (1951), 'The effects of group size and of threat reduction upon creativity in a problem solving situation', *Amer. Psychol.*, vol. 5, p. 324.

GORDON, K. H. (1924), 'Group judgments in the field of lifted weights', *J. exp. Psychol.*, vol. 7, pp. 398–400.

HOPPE, R. A. (1962), 'Memorizing by individuals and groups: a test of the pooling-of-ability model', *J. abnorm. soc. Psychol.*, vol. 65, pp. 64–71.

HUSBAND, R. W. (1940), 'Cooperative versus solitary problem solution', *J. soc. Psychol.*, vol. 11, pp. 405–9.

KLUGMAN, S. F. (1945), 'Group judgment for familiar and unfamiliar materials', *J. genet. Psychol.*, vol. 32, pp. 103–10.

KNIGHT, H. C. (1921), 'A comparison of the reliability of group and individual judgments', unpublished M.A. thesis, Columbia University.

LORGE, I., FOX, D., DAVITZ, J., and BRENNER, M. (1958), 'A survey of studies contrasting the quality of group performance and individual performance, 1920–1957', *Psychol. Bull.*, vol. 55, pp. 337–72.

LORGE, I., and SOLOMON, H. (1955), 'Two models of group behavior in the solution of eureka-type problems', *Psychometrika*, vol. 20, pp. 139–48.

LORGE, I., TUCKMAN, J., AIKMAN, L., SPIEGEL, J., and MOSS, G. (1955), 'Solutions by teams and by individuals to a field problem at different levels of reality', *J. educ. Psychol.*, vol. 46, pp. 17–24.

PARNES, S. J., and MEADOW, A. (1959), 'University of Buffalo research regarding development of creative talent', in C. W. Taylor (ed.), *The Third University of Utah Research Conference on the Identification of Creative Scientific Talent*, University of Utah Press.

ROBY, T. B., and LANZETTA, J. T. (1957), 'A laboratory task for the study of individuals or groups', *Res. Rep. AFPTRC-TN-57-124, ASTIA Document No. AD 134 256, Lackland Air Force Base, Texas.*

ROBY, T. B., and LANZETTA, J. T. (1958), 'Considerations in the analysis of group tasks', *Psychol. Bull.*, vol. 55, pp. 88–101

SCHONBAR, R. A. (1945), 'The interaction of observer-pairs in judging visual extent and movement: the formation of social norms in "structured" situation', *Arch. Psychol.*, vol. 299, p. 95.

SHAW, M. E. (1955), 'A comparison of two types of leadership in various communication nets', *J. abnorm. soc. Psychol.*, vol. 50, pp. 127–34.

SHAW, M. E. (1963), 'Some effects of varying amounts of information exclusively possessed by a group member upon his behavior in the group', *J. gen. Psychol.*, vol. 68, pp. 71–9.

SHAW, M. E., and GILCHRIST, J. C. (1956), 'Intra-group communication and leadership choice', *J. soc. Psychol.*, vol. 43, pp. 133–8.

SHAW, M. E., and PENROD, W. T., JR, (1962), 'Validity of information, attempted influence, and quality of group decisions', *Psychol. Rep.*, vol. 10, pp. 19–23.

SHAW, M. E., ROTHSCHILD, G. H., and STRICKLAND, J. F. (1957), 'Decision processes in communication nets', *J. abnorm. soc. Psychol.*, vol. 54, pp. 323–30.

SMITH, M. (1931), 'Group judgments in the field of personality traits' *J. exp. Psychol.*, vol. 14, pp. 562–5.

STROOP, J. R. (1932), 'Is the judgment of the group better than that of the average member of the group?', *J. exp. Psychol.*, vol. 15, pp. 550–60.

TAYLOR, D. W., BERRY, P. C., and BLOCK, C. H. (1958), 'Does group participation when using brainstorming facilitate or inhibit creative thinking?', *Admin. Sci. Quart.*, vol. 3, pp. 23–47.

TAYLOR, D. W., and FAUST, W. L. (1952), 'Twenty questions: efficiency in problem solving as a function of size of group', *J. exp. Psychol.*, vol. 44, pp. 360–68.

THORNDIKE, R. L. (1938), 'On what type of task will a group do well? *J. abnorm. soc. Psychol.*, vol. 33, pp. 409–13.

TUCKMAN, J., and LORGE, I. (1962), 'Individual ability as a determinant of group superiority', *Hum. Rel.*, vol. 15, pp. 45–51.

WATSON, G. B. (1928), 'Do groups think more efficiently than individuals?', *J. abnorm. soc. Psychol.*, vol. 23, pp. 328–36.

YUKER, H. E. (1955), 'Group atmosphere and memory', *J. abnorm. soc. Psychol.*, vol. 51, pp. 17–23.

5 Marvin E. Shaw

Communication Networks

Excerpt from Marvin E. Shaw, 'Communication networks',
in L. Berkowitz (ed.), *Advances in Experimental Social Psychology*, vol. 1,
Academic Press, 1964, pp. 111-28.

1 Introduction

Communication lies at the heart of the group interaction process. No group, whether an informal or formal organization such as an industrial unit, governmental body or military group, can function effectively unless its members can communicate with facility. One major function of a chain of command is to provide channels of communication extending from the top downward throughout the group structure. The free flow of information (factual knowledge, ideas, technical know-how, feelings) among various members of a group determines to a large extent the efficiency of the group and the satisfaction of its members.

Administrative personnel often assume that the optimum pattern of communication for a given group or organization can be derived from the requirements of the task. Bavelas (1948, 1950) noted this assumption and raised several questions about the effects of fixed communication patterns upon group process. Do some communication networks have structural properties that limit group efficiency? What effects can such structural properties have upon problem-solving effectiveness, organizational development, leadership emergence, the ability of the group to adapt successfully to sudden changes in the environment? Bavelas also suggested a technique for investigating these questions in the laboratory. As a consequence of his work, extensive research has been carried out to analyse the relationships among structural properties of groups (communication networks) and group process variables.

This paper reviews several of these studies and attempts an integration by means of certain theoretical constructs. Section 2 reviews the methodology employed in the research on communication networks and considers some of the structural properties of these networks. Section 3 summarizes the major findings of experimental investigations of the effects of networks on group process. Section 4 explicates theoretical constructs advanced to explain network effects.

2 Research methodology
Methods of imposing communication patterns

Although the experimental method suggested by Bavelas is simple, it allows for maximum control of the communication structure. Group members are placed in cubicles which are interconnected by means of slots in the walls through which written messages can be passed. Slots may be closed to create any selected communication structure. Each cubicle is fitted with a silent switch which controls a signal light and a timer located at the experimenter's desk. The most common procedure has been to permit free (continuous) communication within limits imposed by the network. However, some investigators (Christie, Luce and Macy, 1952; Schein, 1958) have used an 'action quantization' procedure that restricted each subject to single, addressed messages transmitted at specified times. Also, some investigators substituted an intercom system for the slots – written messages system (Heise and Miller, 1951).

Network characteristics

Figure 1 shows communication networks that have been studied experimentally. The circles represent persons or positions in the network, and the lines represent communication channels (slots) between positions. Most channels are symmetrical (two-way); asymmetrical (one-way) channels are indicated by arrows. The labels are arbitrary designations, intended only to facilitate identification. It will be noted that the same label is used for similar networks for groups of different sizes, although there has been some criticism that networks of different sizes are not comparable. For example, Glanzer and Glaser (1961) asked why the three-person 'wheel' could not be called 'chain' and compared to the four- and five-person chains. They apparently could see no difference between the three-person wheel and the larger chains. Actually, there is good reason to label it 'wheel' and compare it

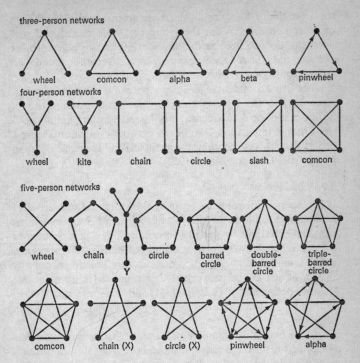

Figure 1 Communication networks used in experimental investigations.
Dots represent positions, lines represent communication channels
and arrows indicate one-way channels

with the larger wheels rather than chains. The essential characteristic of a wheel network is that one person communicates with all others, whereas all other members communicate only with this central person.

The three-person wheel in Figure 1 clearly fits this description. In a chain, on the other hand, there are two isolates (end-persons) who communicate with only one other (but different) person in the group and two or more persons in the group must serve as message relayers in order to disseminate information throughout the group. The three-person wheel does not have these features and, therefore, is clearly more comparable to the larger wheels than to the larger chains. Similar considerations are involved in the labeling of other networks. When the group size is decreased, different networks do not necessarily coalesce into a single pattern, as Glanzer and Glaser suppose; rather, certain networks found with larger groups cannot be formed with smaller groups.

One further comment regarding the networks shown in Figure 1. According to the Bavelas analysis, the spatial arrangement of positions is of no consequence; it is the relationships among positions that is important. Two of the networks shown in Figure 1 depart from this conception: the chain (X) and the circle (X) used by Christie, Luce and Macy (1952).

Structural indices

It has seemed desirable to quantify the structural properties of networks to facilitate the analysis of their effects on group behavior. Bavelas (1950) suggested a 'centrality index' as a measure of the differences between networks and positions within networks, based upon the distance, in communication links, between any two positions in the network. Other suggested indices include 'relative peripherality' (Leavitt, 1951) and 'independence' (Shaw, 1954a). Each of these indices merits consideration.

Centrality indices. In formulating the centrality measures, Bavelas (1950) first defined the *sum of distances* $(d_{x,y})$ for a given position as the minimum number of communication links that must be crossed in order for that position to communicate with all other positions in the group. The individual sums of distances in a network may be summed to obtain a sum of distances for the network $(\sum d_{x,y})$. Comparisons among networks may then be made on the basis of $\sum d_{x,y}$. However, to make comparisons among positions within a network, a relative measure (called relative centrality) was suggested. This measure is computed as the ratio of the network sum of distances to the sum of distances for the given position. Thus,

$$\text{Relative centrality} = \frac{\sum d_{x,y}}{d_{x,y}}.$$

Leavitt (1951), working with Bavelas, computed a centrality

index for the group by summing the relative centralities of all positions in the network.

In general, total centrality for networks has been found to correlate poorly with group performance and satisfaction (Shaw, 1954a, b), although relative centrality has been found to account moderately well for positional differences in performance and satisfaction (Leavitt, 1951; Shaw, 1954b). However, relative centrality does not reflect differences among positions in similar networks of different sizes, nor does it permit easy comparisons among positions in different networks. Leavitt (1951) noted the first inadequacy and proposed an index of relative peripherality as an alternate to relative centrality; Shaw (1954a) pointed to the second difficulty and attempted to overcome it by an independence index. These indices are described below.

Peripherality indices. The relative peripherality of any position in a network is the difference between the relative centrality of that position and the relative centrality of the most central position in that network. A total peripherality index for the network may be computed by adding all the individual peripheralities in the network.

Leavitt believed peripherality is related to group behavior variables via differences among positions in answer-getting potentials which structure group members' perceptions of their roles in the group. The relative peripherality index reflects differences in position independence, which in turn determine behavioral differences.

Since relative peripherality and relative centrality are perfectly correlated (negatively) within a given network, the two indices relate equally well to positional differences in performance and satisfaction. The advantage of peripherality over centrality lies in the greater comparability among positions in networks of different sizes. However, two positions in different networks having the same relative peripherality index do not necessarily produce the same behavior. Nor do two positions having different peripherality indices necessarily give rise to different behaviors. Likewise, the total peripherality index does not adequately reflect differences among networks. (The same statements hold, of course, for the centrality indices.) The independence index was developed in an attempt to overcome some of these shortcomings.

The independence index. Since the centrality–peripherality indices are imperfectly correlated with behavioral measures, there clearly are some important characteristics of networks and positions that are not reflected by these measures. Shaw (1954a) proposed that it is necessary to determine what characteristics do contribute to position independence. On a logical basis these features seemed to be (a) the number of channels available to a given position, (b) the total number of channels in the network, and (c) the number of positions for which a given position must relay information. The independence index (I index) for any one position was designed to reflect the weighted contributions of these various characteristics, as shown by the formula:

$$I = n + \left[n \left(1 - \frac{n}{N} \right) \right] + \log R_d + \log R_i,$$

where n = number of channels available to the given position,
N = number of channels in a completely interconnected network of the same size,
R_d = number of positions for which the particular position must serve as a direct relayer (i.e. directly connected to the position served) and
R_i = number of positions for which the position must serve as an indirect relayer (i.e. one or more links removed from the position served).

The I index has been shown to be better than either the centrality or the peripherality index in the sense that it makes possible direct comparisons among positions in different networks (Shaw, 1954a). However, no satisfactory method of computing the total independence in a network has been found, since the mere summation of positional values does not correlate highly with behavioral differences among networks.

In summary, the various structural indices described thus far have some explanatory value with regard to differences among positions within networks, but are inadequate to predict or explain differences among different networks.[1] Consequently, more general processes have been invoked as explanatory concepts. Although

1. For other mathematical analyses see Flament (1958a), Glanzer and Glaser (1959) and Luce *et al.* (1953).

several such concepts have been described by various writers, this paper will attempt to explain group behavior in communication networks in terms of two underlying processes which have been labeled 'independence' and 'saturation'. Before describing these concepts, however, a consideration of the effects of networks upon group process is helpful.

3 Effects of networks upon group process

This section reviews the initial studies conducted in the Group Networks Laboratory at MIT and selected follow-up experiments to demonstrate that communication networks are related to group behavior in systematic ways.

The MIT experiments

The initial studies are reported in articles by Bavelas (1950), Bavelas and Barrett (1951), Leavitt (1951), and Christie, Luce and Macy (1952). The experiment reported by Leavitt is representative of the approach described in the first three articles. He carried out his investigation in order to explore the relationship between the behavior of small groups and the patterns of communication in which the groups operate. Leavitt examined the effects of the five-man circle, chain, Y and wheel (Figure 1) on problem-solving effectiveness, satisfaction and organization characteristics of the group. The tasks were extremely simple symbol-identification problems. Each member in the group was given a card containing a number of symbols such as a square, a diamond, an asterisk, etc. Only one symbol appeared on each and every member's card. The task was to identify this commonly held symbol. Measures of performance were time taken to solve the problem, errors and number of messages sent. Networks did not differ in average time to solve, but the circle was slower than the other patterns when the measure was the single, fastest, correct trial. The circle groups made the greatest number of errors (16·6), the Y the smallest number (2·6) and the chain and wheel an intermediate number (9·8 in each case). The circle required considerably more messages than did the other networks.

Satisfaction of members was determined by means of a questionnaire. Circle members reported greatest satisfaction, wheel members least, with chain and Y members intermediate. Leadership emergence was also measured by questionnaire. The total frequency of persons named as leaders and the unanimity of opinion as to who was the leader, increased in the order: circle, chain, Y, wheel. For example, twenty-three of the twenty-five persons in the wheel named a leader and all agreed that he was the person in the most central position, whereas only thirteen of the twenty-five persons in the circle named a leader, and those named were scattered among all positions in the circle.

Operational methods (i.e. organizational patterns) used by the wheel, Y and chain were such that the information was funneled to the central position, where the decision was made and sent out to the peripheral positions. (Hereafter this organizational pattern will be referred to as a centralized organization.) The circle showed no consistent, operational organization.

With regard to individual positions in the network, persons in the more central positions generally required less time to solve the problem, sent more messages, made fewer errors, were better satisfied and were named leader more often than persons in the more peripheral positions.

Leavitt's findings clearly demonstrated a systematic relationship between the communication network imposed upon the group and the behavior of the group members. The experiments reported by Bavelas (1950) and by Bavelas and Barrett (1951) were carried out for essentially the same purpose, and their findings generally agree with those obtained by Leavitt. The experiments conducted by Christie, Luce and Macy (1952, 1956), however, had a rather different purpose. They were concerned with the effects of networks upon the information-handling process, learning in networks, and the testing of mathematical models.

Christie, Luce and Macy (1952) investigated the effects of five-person networks: circle, circle (X), chain, chain (X), pinwheel, barred circle, wheel, comcon and alpha (see Figure 1). The tasks assigned to the groups were number-identification problems, similar to the symbol-identification task used by Leavitt. An action quantized procedure was used; that is, all subjects prepared messages simultaneously and transmitted them at specified times. On a given exchange, each group member was permitted to send a single message to one other group member. In this experiment, the investigators were interested primarily in testing certain mathematical models; hence, not all data were presented. However, it is clear that the geometrical arrangement of the circle and chain networks had little or no effect on the group process; no differences in time scores and other behavioral measures between the circle and circle (X) or between the chain and chain (X) were observed. With regard to time, networks were ordered (from fastest to slowest) as follows: chain, pinwheel, circle, comcon. The probability of minimum solution (task completion with the smallest number of message exchanges possible in a given network) was found to be greatest in the chain and smallest in the pinwheel. The alpha, barred circle and wheel networks were about the same on this measure, while the circle was somewhat better and the comcon worse than this group of networks.

In a separate publication, Christie (1954) reported data concerned with the effects of learning in the comcon, circle, chain and pinwheel networks. The task was reconstruction of a number list, and the performance criterion was number of communication acts (i.e. message exchanges) required for solution. All networks did better than chance from the beginning, but only the chain and the circle showed significant learning. Since task solution required a minimum of five message exchanges in the chain, its absolute performance was poor in comparison with each of the other networks. The circle groups, on the other hand, achieved a high level of efficiency in comparison with other networks.[2]

These early experiments demonstrated quite clearly that the pattern of communication imposed upon a group is an important determinant of the behavior of that group. However, the findings also indicated that the particular relationship between communication pattern and group behavior depends in part upon other variables. The MIT studies stimulated a considerable amount of research designed to examine the effects of these other variables upon network/group behavior relationships and to test various theoretical interpretations of the underlying processes. A review of selected experiments will reveal the general conclusions that may be drawn from these follow-up investigations.

2. It is interesting to note that Leavitt and Knight (1963) recently concluded, on purely theoretical grounds, that the circle should be the most efficient network.

Selected follow-up investigations

The experiments described in this section were selected to demonstrate two general conclusions that can be drawn from the many communication network studies: (a) the major differences in group performance and satisfaction are between the centralized (wheel, Y, chain) and decentralized (comcon, circle) networks; and (b) the direction of these differences in group performance depends upon the kind of task assigned to the group.

Leavitt's experiment demonstrated differences among networks on the completion of one kind of task (symbol identification) under noise-free conditions. Heise and Miller (1951) extended this design by varying the intelligibility of the message and the type of problem given the group. They studied the three-person networks shown in Figure 1, using as tasks word-construction problems, sentence-construction problems and anagrams. Each problem was attempted in each network under three conditions of intelligibility. Speech, instead of written messages, was the method of communication. Intelligibility of the message was manipulated by controlling the relative intensities of speech and noise. Their results showed that for the word-construction problems the comcon was the most efficient, the wheel was intermediate, and the pinwheel was by far the least efficient network. For the sentence-construction problems, the results were similar except that the wheel replaced the comcon as the most efficient network. There were no marked differences in efficiency for the anagram problems. Noise generally accentuated differences for the first two kinds of tasks but not for the anagram problems.

Unfortunately, Heise and Miller used only three undergraduate subjects who went through all conditions for the word problem. Two of these subjects continued through the sentence problem with a new recruit as the third member, while the subjects for the anagram problems consisted of two groups of three graduate students each. Therefore, no statistical tests of the reliability of the obtained differences was possible. Since there are individual differences in group performance, we do not know to what extent the observed differences were due to the experimental variables or to individual differences. The large differences in the relationship between networks and group-effectiveness measures (time and errors) as a function of the task, however, suggest strongly that the kind of network that is most efficient depends upon the kind of task faced by the group.

This conclusion is also indicated by the findings in two experiments by Shaw (1954a, b). Leavitt, it will be recalled, interpreted his results in terms of centrality–peripherality indices which were supposed to reflect each position's accessibility to information. The first experiment reported by Shaw was designed to test this interpretation. On the basis of Leavitt's argument, it seemed reasonable to suppose that increasing the information input from external sources (i.e. the experimenter) should have the same effect upon a position as increasing the centrality of that position. For this purpose, the effects of four-person wheel, slash and circle networks (see Figure 1) on group effectiveness in solving arithmetic problems were examined. Although quite simple, these problems required more than the mere collation of information required by the symbol-identification task used by Leavitt. For half of the groups in each network the necessary information was distributed equally among group members (as Leavitt did), whereas for the other groups, the information was distributed unequally. In the unequal distribution condition, one of the most peripheral positions in each network was given five units of information, whereas all other positions were given one unit of information each.

Leavitt's measure of performance, the single fastest correct trial, indicated no differences among networks. However, the total time required to complete the task did reveal significant differences, although in a complicated manner. Analysis of variance revealed a significant trials $\times$ networks $\times$ distribution interaction; analysis of the interaction means showed that significant differences among networks occurred only on the third (and last) trial. The circle was fastest, the slash next fastest and the wheel the slowest of the three patterns, with the difference between the circle and the other patterns being greatest with unequal distribution of information. For over-all situational conditions the order was circle, slash, wheel – just the opposite of that expected from Leavitt's results. There were no differences among networks in number of errors, although the ability to correct errors (corrective power of the network) was greatest for the circle, next for slash and least for the wheel network – again contrary to expectations.

Findings with respect to number of messages, satisfaction, and leadership emergence were in general agreement with Leavitt's results.

All groups used either the centralized or 'each-to-all' organization (all information sent to all group members and then each member solved the problem independently). Centralized organization was used by 73 per cent of the wheel, 7 per cent of the slash, and 7 per cent of the circle groups. Each-to-all organization was used by 27 per cent of the wheel, 93 per cent of the slash and 93 per cent of the circle groups.

The most striking result of the unequal-distribution-of-information experiment was the reversal of effectiveness of the wheel and circle networks as compared with Leavitt's results. The most obvious difference in the two experiments was the greater complexity of the problems employed in the later study. Two observations suggested that task differences probably accounted for the reversal. First, the central person in the wheel was overloaded by the many communication demands of the situation, and second, persons in the peripheral positions were unwilling merely to accept a solution offered by the central person. Both of these effects presumably were more likely to occur with complex than with simple tasks. However, since there were several other differences between the Shaw and Leavitt experiments, an experiment (Shaw, 1954c) was carried out to demonstrate the effects of the task variable in which the three-person wheel and comcon (Figure 1) were compared using symbol-identification and arithmetic problems as tasks. Although the difference was not statistically reliable, the wheel groups required less time than did the comcon with the relatively easy symbol identification problems, whereas the comcon required less time than did the wheel with the more complex arithmetic problems. There were no differences in number of errors on the identification problems, but the wheel made more errors than did the comcon on the arithmetic problems.

Numerous other investigators have reported results which support the general conclusions that the major differences are between the centralized and decentralized networks, and that the direction of such differences is contingent upon the kind of task. First, let us consider studies employing fairly simple group tasks. Using symbol identification problems, Guetzkow and Simon

(1955) investigated the five-person wheel, circle and comcon networks shown in Figure 1. They were interested primarily in the effects of free communication between trials for organizational purposes (discussed later), but they also reported that the wheel was faster than the circle, with the comcon intermediate in speed.

Many other investigations using the symbol identification task might also be mentioned. Cohen, Bennis and Wolkon (1961) found that five-person wheel groups took less time to solve identification problems, made fewer answer changes and fewer final errors, sent fewer messages and recognized a leader more frequently than did circle groups. Both groups improved with practice, but wheel groups improved more than circle groups did. Networks did not produce over-all differences in satisfaction, but central positions were better satisfied than peripheral positions. Hirota (1953) repeated Leavitt's experiment using Japanese subjects. The wheel required less time to solve, followed by the Y, circle and chain, in that order; however, differences were not statistically reliable. Hirota also reported positional differences in frequency of communication and leadership emergence which agreed with Leavitt's findings. In a cross-cultural study, Mohanna and Argyle (1960) repeated the portion of Leavitt's experiment that made use of the wheel and circle networks. Leavitt's results were confirmed in that the wheel was found to be superior to the circle in time required, number of messages required, and errors made.

Studies using more complex problems usually found the decentralized networks more effective. In Holland, Mulder (1960) examined the effects of four-person wheel and circle networks on the solution of arithmetic problems. Over all, but especially in their early trials, the circle groups required less time per problem than the wheel groups. However, contrary to findings reported in this country (Shaw and Rothschild, 1956), with practice the wheel groups became relatively more efficient than the circle networks. The studies using sentence- and word-construction tasks (Heise and Miller, 1951) and those using noisy marbles (Macy, Christie and Luce, 1953) also showed that more decentralized networks are more efficient than centralized networks when solving even moderately complex problems (Flament, 1956, 1958b; Shaw, Rothschild and Strickland, 1957).

Some general conclusions concerning the effects of networks upon group processes

The evidence strongly supports the generalization that the major network difference is between centralized (e.g. wheel, chain, Y) and decentralized (e.g. circle, comcon) networks, and that the direction of this difference is determined in part by the degree of complexity of the task. It is instructive to tabulate the number of comparisons showing specified differences between centralized and decentralized networks with simple and with more complex problems. The results of one such tabulation are shown in Table 1. The 'simple problems' classification includes tasks that re-

Table 1 Number of Comparisons Showing Differences between Centralized (Wheel, Chain, Y) and Decentralized (Circle, Comcon) Networks as a Function of Task Complexity

	Simple problems[1]	*Complex problems*[2]	*Total*
Time			
Centralized faster	14	0	14
Decentralized faster	4	18	22
Messages			
Centralized sent more	0	1	1
Decentralized sent more	18	17	35
Errors			
Centralized made more	0	6	6
Decentralized made more	9	1	10
No difference	1	3	4
Satisfaction			
Centralized higher	1	1	2
Decentralized higher	7	10	17

1. Simple problems: symbol- , letter- , number- and color-identification tasks.
2. Complex problems: arithmetic, word arrangement, sentence construction and discussion problems.

quire the mere collation of information (symbol-, letter-, color-identification tasks). The 'complex problems' classification includes tasks that require some data operation procedures after the information has been collected in one place (arithmetic, word arrangement, sentence construction and discussion problems).[3] A comparison is a single difference in means (as reported in the literature) between a centralized and a decentralized network, without regard to level of significance. For example, if an experiment involved three centralized and one decentralized network (as did Leavitt's study), three comparisons were made.

Examination of Table 1 shows that with simple problems the more centralized network required less time than the decentralized network on fourteen of the eighteen comparisons, whereas, with more complex problems, the decentralized required less time than the centralized network on every comparison made.[4] Errors show the same pattern, but differences are less consistent than for time scores. With very few exceptions, individuals in decentralized networks are more active (send more messages) and are better satisfied than are persons in centralized networks, regardless of kind of task. Differences in activity are probably due merely to the fact that centralized have fewer channels than decentralized networks, as suggested by Glanzer and Glaser (1961). Organizational differences were not included in Table 1 because relatively few investigators examined this aspect in any systematic way. In most instances, however, centralized networks develop centralized organizations (i.e. all members send their information to one member who solves the problem and sends the answer to other members). Decentralized networks develop either each-to-all or centralized organizations about equally.

Numerous other variables have been examined in relation to group behavior in communication networks. The effects of these other variables generally raised or lowered the behavioral level

3. This is a rough classification and admittedly does not do justice to the complexity variable. The categorical grouping of tasks is not intended to deny the essential continuity of the complexity dimension.

4. Eighteen different experiments were involved in this tabulation. Since a single experiment sometimes contributed more than one comparison, there is some lack of independence among scores in Table 1. To overcome this, one comparison was drawn from each experiment. The results of this procedure showed the centralized network faster than the decentralized in six of eight experiments using simple problems, whereas the decentralized network was faster in ten of ten experiments using complex problems. This difference is highly reliable ($\chi^2 = 11\cdot26$, $p < 0\cdot001$).

of groups across all networks, either equally or in a manner which increased the differences among networks. For this reason, it is believed that these effects can be interpreted in terms of the same explanatory concepts used to explain the results presented thus far. Therefore, the independence and saturation constructs will be explained more fully before considering the effects of additional variables.

4 Explanatory concepts

It has been suggested (see p. 81) that the various effects of communication networks upon group behavior can be accounted for by two general processes labeled 'independence' (Leavitt, 1951; Shaw, 1954a) and 'saturation' (Gilchrist, Shaw and Walker, 1954).[5] Further, it is believed that the various explanations advanced by other investigators can be subsumed under one of these two more general processes.

Independence

The concept of independence was introduced by Leavitt (1951) to account for differences among network positions. He pointed to the differences in answer-getting potential among positions and suggested that the group members' perceptions of these differences structure their perceptions of their own roles in the group. In the wheel, for example, group members readily perceive the degree of information accessibility and the nature of their own roles. The central person is autonomous and controls the group. In the circle, on the other hand, any given group member is not exclusively dependent upon anyone else in the net, and his role is not clearly different from anyone else's role. Thus, his action is not as greatly controlled by others. Morale is higher with greater independence because independence permits the gratification of the culturally supported needs for autonomy, recognition and achievement. Independence bears a more direct relationship to group performance via its organizational influences upon the group. Leavitt

5. The labels applied to these two classes of intervening processes are unimportant. Independence and saturation were chosen because of the author's familiarity with them; however, 'autonomy' or 'self-realization' would be just as acceptable as independence, and 'vulnerability' or 'demands' as acceptable as saturation.

concluded: 'In summary, then, it is our feeling that centrality determines behavior by limiting independence of action, thus producing differences in activity, accuracy, satisfaction, leadership, recognition of pattern and other behavioral characteristics' (Leavitt, 1951, p. 49).

While the general notion of independence of action is useful, it has become clear that the original formulation is too limited. As stated earlier, structural indices such as centrality, relative peripherality and the I index do not appear to be highly valid measures of independence as reflected by measures of performance and satisfaction. As a consequence of the experimental results obtained from many studies, it is now clear that the concept of independence must be expanded to include freedom from all restrictions on action. We shall use the term 'independence', then, to refer to the degree of freedom with which an individual may function in the group. A person's independence of action may be influenced not only by accessibility of information but also by the actions of others in the group, by situational factors (such as communication 'noise', reinforcement, kind of task), and by the person's own perceptions and cognitions regarding the over-all situation. The concepts of 'autonomy' (Trow, 1957) and 'exercise of power' (Mulder, 1958, 1959a) are similar to independence.

The author's own view is that independence, as defined above is related to both performance and satisfaction; however, independence probably has a greater effect on satisfaction than on performance. We agree with Leavitt (1951) that its effect on member satisfaction probably is due to the fulfilment of culturally approved needs for autonomy, recognition, and achievement. This paper will try to show, however, that the effect of independence upon performance is due, not to its organizational influences, but to the individual's willingness and ability to perform under the more autonomous conditions. That is, lowered independence not only directly limits the possibilities for action (hence performance), but also reduces the person's willingness to perform at his optimum level.

Saturation

In addition to independence, a second process operates in group situations to influence group performance and satisfaction. This process, called 'saturation', was first described by Gilchrist, Shaw and Walker (1954). They observed that when the number of required messages for a given position passed a certain optimal level, communication requirements began to counteract the effects of position centrality. Two kinds of saturation were distinguished: 'channel saturation', which refers to the number of channels with which a position must deal, and 'message unit saturation', which refers to the number of messages the position must handle. These two kinds of saturation, of course, are correlated. Each of these main classes may be broken down further into 'input' and 'output' saturation. Total saturation experienced by a position is the sum of all the input and output requirements placed upon that position.

Like the original formulation of independence, this notion of saturation is too limited. The requirements placed upon the position, from whatever source, call for action by the individual who occupies that position. Therefore, the total saturation of a position is the result not only of the communication requirements, but also of the other requirements in the situation, such as data manipulation procedures that are necessary for task completion. Requirements of this sort are essentially those referred to as 'task demands' by Lanzetta and Roby (1956a and b, 1957). Saturation, then, refers to the total requirements placed upon an individual in a given position in the network. It varies with communication demands and task demands. Communication demands are determined by the number of channels available to the position, the task information to be transmitted and the demands imposed by the vagaries of the other members who have access to that position's channels. Task demands are determined by the requirements of the task *per se* and by interferences that must be overcome in the process of task solution.

Several explanatory concepts have been suggested by other investigators that are similar to saturation. The notion of 'vulnerability' (Mulder, 1959b, 1960) is essentially the same as saturation; organizational arrangements (Guetzkow and Dill, 1957; Guetzkow and Simon, 1955), task demands (Lanzetta and Roby, 1956a and b, 1957; Roby and Lanzetta, 1956), and 'inadequation' (Flament, 1958b and c) may be regarded as special cases of saturation.

Group effectiveness varies inversely with saturation. The greater the saturation the less efficient the group's performance.

Network and task effects in terms of independence and saturation

It is proposed, then, that independence and saturation processes jointly determine group behavior; variables such as the communication network and kind of task influence group performance and satisfaction through their effects upon these two underlying processes. On page 88 evidence was presented indicating that centralized networks are more effective for simple problems, whereas decentralized networks are more effective for complex problems. To what extent can the concepts of independence and saturation help explain these results?

The effects of networks on independence have already been discussed. Persons in peripheral positions in centralized networks have limited freedom of action (hence low independence), while persons in central positions have relatively great freedom (hence high independence). In decentralized networks, by contrast, all positions have approximately equal freedom of action (hence moderate to high independence). Generally speaking, independence is greater in decentralized than in centralized networks. Task complexity has relatively little effect upon independence.

Saturation is determined in part by the communication channels available to a position. Therefore, the central position of a centralized network is more vulnerable to saturation than any position in the decentralized network. Whether this potential saturation occurs, however, depends upon task demands and member demands. When the task is a complex one, the demands upon the central person are greater than when the task is less complex, not only because the communication demands are increased by complexity, but also because data manipulation procedures are more demanding with the more complex tasks. Therefore, the probability that the network will become saturated is greater with complex than with simple tasks, and greater for the centralized than for the decentralized network.

Further, if our assumptions about the effects of independence are correct, this difference in saturation as a function of task complexity should be enhanced by the unwillingness of group members to accept the dictates of the central person when the task is a complex one. With simple identification problems, needs for achievement and recognition can hardly be satisfied by the simple act of noting that the same symbol appears on each of several cards; hence, subjects in a centralized network are typically willing to accept the report of the central person. This should actually reduce saturation in centralized networks relative to decentralized networks because of decreased message requirements. When the task requires data manipulation, however, needs for achievement and recognition can attain some degree of satisfaction through the problem solution process; members therefore are less likely to accept the solution arrived at by the central person. For example, they ask for the information upon which his solution was based. This increases communication demands and, hence, saturation. In decentralized networks the willingness or unwillingness of members to accept the solution of another has relatively little effect on saturation, since each person typically has all the information for solution and often achieves the solution through his own efforts.

In summary, independence is greater in the decentralized than in the centralized network, regardless of the kind of task. Saturation should be less in the centralized than in the decentralized network with simple tasks, but greater in the centralized network with complex tasks. Therefore, member satisfaction should be greater in more centralized positions, but over-all satisfaction should be higher in decentralized networks. With simple tasks, the centralized should be more effective than the decentralized networks; whereas with complex tasks, the decentralized should be more efficient than the centralized networks. As we have seen, the experimental data generally agree with these expectations.

The author's feeling is that the effects of network and task variables upon group behavior are adequately accounted for by independence and saturation processes.

References

BAVELAS, A. (1948), *Appl. Anthropol.*, vol. 7, pp. 16–30.

BAVELAS, A. (1950), *J. Acoust. Soc. Amer.*, vol. 22, pp. 725–30.

BAVELAS, A., and BARRETT, D. (1951), *Personnel*, vol. 27, pp. 366–71.

CHRISTIE, L. S. (1954), *J. Oper. Res. Soc. Amer.*, vol. 2, pp. 188–96.

CHRISTIE, L. S., LUCE, R. D., and MACY, J. JR (1952), 'Communication and learning in task-oriented groups', *Research Laboratory of Electronics, MIT, Technical Report*, no. 231.

CHRISTIE, L. S., LUCE, R. D., and MACY, J., JR (1956),
in J. F. McCloskey and J. M. Coppinger (eds.), *Operations Research for Management*, vol. 2, Johns Hopkins Press, pp. 417–537.

COHEN, A. M., BENNIS, W. G., and WOLKON, G. H. (1961), *Sociometry*, vol. 24, pp. 416–31.

COHEN, A. M., BENNIS, W. G., and WOLKON, G. H. (1962), *Sociometry*, vol. 25, pp. 177–96.

FLAMENT, C. (1956), *Année Psychol.*, vol. 56, pp. 411–31.

FLAMENT, C. (1958a), *Année Psychol.*, vol. 58, pp. 119–31.

FLAMENT, C. (1958b), *Année Psychol.*, vol. 57, pp. 71–89.

FLAMENT, C. (1958c), *Bull. Centre d'Etudes Rech. Psychotech.*, vol. 7, pp. 97–106.

GILCHRIST, J. C., SHAW, M. E., and WALKER, L. C. (1954), *J. abnorm. soc. Psychol.*, vol. 49, pp. 554–6.

GLANZER, M., and GLASER, R. (1959), *Psychol. Bull.*, vol. 56, pp. 317–32.

GLANZER, M., and GLASER, R. (1961), *Psychol. Bull.*, vol. 58, pp. 1–27.

GUETZKOW, H., and DILL, W. R. (1957), *Sociometry*, vol. 20, pp. 175–204.

GUETZKOW, H., and SIMON, H. (1955), *Manag. Sci.*, vol. 1, pp. 233–50.

HEISE, G. A., and MILLER, G. A. (1951), *J. abnorm. soc. Psychol.* vol. 46, pp. 327–35.

HIROTA, K. (1953), *Japan. J. Psychol.*, vol. 24, pp. 105–13.

LANZETTA, J. T., and ROBY, T. B. (1956a), *J. abnorm. soc. Psychol.*, vol. 53, pp. 307–14.

LANZETTA, J. T., and ROBY, T. B. (1956b), *Sociometry*, vol. 19, pp. 95–104.

LANZETTA, J. T., and ROBY, T. B. (1957), *J. abnorm. soc. Psychol.*, vol. 55, pp. 121–31.

LEAVITT, H. J. (1951), *J. abnorm. soc. Psychol.*, vol. 46, pp. 38–50.

LEAVITT, H. J., and KNIGHT, K. E. (1963), *Sociometry*, vol. 26, pp. 260–67.

LUCE, R. D., MACE, J., JR, CHRISTIE, L. S., and HAY, H. D. (1953), 'Information flow in task-oriented groups', *Research Laboratory of Electronics, MIT, Technical Report*, no. 264.

MACY, J., JR, CHRISTIE, L. S., and LUCE, R. D. (1953), *J. abnorm. soc. Psychol.*, vol. 48, pp. 401–9.

MOHANNA, A. I., and ARGYLE, M. (1960), *J. abnorm. soc. Psychol.*, vol. 60, pp. 139–40.

MULDER, M. (1958), *Groepsstructuur, Motivatie en Prestatie*, Nederlands Instituut veer Praeventieve Geneeskunde, Leiden.

MULDER, M. (1959a), *Acta Psychol.*, vol. 16, pp. 178–225.

MULDER, M. (1959b), *Acta Psychol.*, vol. 16, pp. 356–402.

MULDER, M. (1960), *Sociometry*, vol. 23, pp. 1–14.

ROBY, T. B., and LANZETTA, J. T. (1956), *Sociometry*, vol. 19, pp. 105–13.

SCHEIN, E. H. (1958), *The Development of Organization in Small Problem-Solving Groups*, MIT Press.

SCHUTZ, W. C. (1958), *FIRO: A Three-Dimensional Theory of Interpersonal Behavior*, Holt, Rinehart & Winston.

SHAW, M. E. (1954a), *J. Psychol.*, vol. 38, pp. 139–49.

SHAW, M. E. (1954b), *J. abnorm. soc. Psychol.*, vol. 49, pp. 547–53.

SHAW, M. E. (1954c), *J. exp. Psychol.*, vol. 48, pp. 211–17.

SHAW, M. E., and ROTHSCHILD, G. H. (1956), *J. appl. Psychol.*, vol. 40, pp. 281–6.

SHAW, M. E., ROTHSCHILD, G. H., and STRICKLAND, J. C. (1957), *J. abnorm. soc. Psychol.*, vol. 54, pp. 323–30.

TROW, D. B. (1957), *J. abnorm. soc. Psychol.*, vol. 54, pp. 204–9.

Part Three Interpersonal Models

In this Part we consider models of behaviour which are based essentially on motivational concepts. While Lewinian thinking dominated the field of small group study in the early 1950s, more recently other approaches have become equally salient. One landmark was the theoretical formulation of Thibaut and Kelley (1959) which analyses relationships between two people in terms of their ability to reward or punish one another. It is not at all easy to render Thibaut and Kelley's concepts directly measurable but Thibaut's paper (Reading 6) illustrates one direction in which such work has developed.

Newcomb's work (Reading 7) attempts to account for the way in which friendship patterns develop in terms of the individual's needs to experience balance or similarity between himself and those with whom he associates. Balance theories are becoming increasingly important in a number of areas of social psychology. They have great potential for unifying areas which are currently treated as quite separate, such as interpersonal attraction, conformity and attitude change.

The contributions of Borg (Reading 8) and of Exline (Reading 9) are in a less theoretically oriented vein. Borg shows that there is considerable correlation between an individual's scores on personality tests and the way in which his behaviour is perceived by others in the group. Exline's works emphasizes that the bases on which such perceptions are formed are likely to include not only what a person says but also his non-verbal behaviours.

Reference

THIBAUT, J. W., and KELLEY, H. H. (1959), *The Social Psychology of Groups*, Wiley.

6 John Thibaut

The Development of Contractual Norms in Bargaining:
Replication and Variation

John Thibaut, 'The development of contractual norms in bargaining:
replication and variation', *Journal of Conflict Resolution*, vol. 12, 1968,
pp. 102–12.

Although a great deal of research has been done during the past
decade and a half on the processes associated with conforming to
norms (e.g. Deutsch and Gerard, 1955; Hollander, 1960; Jones,
Jones and Gergen, 1963), very little work has been done on the
prior processes through which the norms come into existence. In
understanding these processes and conditions which produce
norms it may be useful to begin by inquiring into the ways in
which norms provide adaptive solutions or functional advantages
that are superior to other forms of social control.

Such a functional approach has been suggested by Thibaut and
Kelley (1959, pp. 130–42) in discussing the consequences of substituting normative control for control by interpersonal power.
For example, in the A–B (dyadic) relationship, suppose A is in
the act of exercising power over B. The substitution of normative
control for the use of raw power may be advantageous to A as it
enables him to regularize and stabilize his control over B. At the
same time, the substitution reduces A's costs of surveillance and
eliminates the ostentation of his power usage. The advantages to
B of this substitution are less apparent but may consist of protecting him from any whimsical or arbitrary uses of power by A and
of shifting the control of his behavior from a personal locus in A
to the impersonal locus of the norm.

The foregoing approach implies that for a norm to be adaptive
and hence acceptable there must exist an over-all advantage in
outcomes to the participants in the relationship that is created or
maintained by the operation of the norm. The various parties in
the interaction must be in some sense better off within the normative constraints than without them. But even though norms, if
they existed, might provide advantages over alternative solutions,

it remains to identify more specifically the conditions and processes under which norms actually develop. This paper will attempt to outline some of these more specific conditions under which at least some types of norms may be expected to emerge.

The present research is particularly concerned with formal (contractual) agreements governing (a) the equitable distribution of outcomes between the participants and (b) the maintenance of loyalty to the relationship through forbidding withdrawal from it. We have chosen to study the emergence of such formal norms in the context of a 'mixed-motive' relationship (Schelling, 1960) which must be maintained if both participants are to obtain their best outcomes. In the relationship studied here, one participant (A) is given the opportunity to exploit the other (B), whose principal resource for countering such exploitation is to withdraw from the relationship. If, in the mixed-motive relationship, the conflict of interest between the interacting parties is relatively high (i.e. a competitive component is dominant), A's opportunity and motivation to exploit B will be relatively great.[1] If at the same time the attractiveness of alternatives to the relationship is also high, B's motivation to abandon the relationship (thereby reducing A's outcomes) will also be great.

Thus a high degree of conflict of interest is likely to tempt A to become exploitative, thereby threatening B, and highly attractive alternatives are likely to tempt B to become disloyal, thereby threatening A. How can these mutual threats[2] be resolved? First it is to be expected that under high conflict of interest, B (in order to protect himself against serious reductions in his share of the outcomes) will attempt to invoke rules of 'equity' and 'fair sharing'. And as alternatives to the relationship become highly attractive, A (in order to maintain the relationship within which he holds an advantage) will attempt to invoke rules of 'loyalty' and the like.

1. In the absence of conflict of interest, i.e. where the outcomes accruing to the parties are perfectly and positively correlated, no exploitation can occur, since one could hurt the other only by hurting himself.

2. The term 'threat' is used here and throughout this discussion in a very general sense. Thus, the term may refer to any of the following possibilities in which one party (X) has the capability of reducing the outcomes of another party (Y): X may attempt to control Y's behavior by communicating that he intends to reduce Y's outcomes unless a certain behavior is performed or

When *both* conflict of interest and attractiveness of alternatives are high, each party is threatened by behaviors which the other is tempted to perform, and each party may be expected to appeal to a rule of behavior which will forbid the actualization of such threats. Thus a type of 'interdependence' may be expected to develop in which each party's acceptance of the other's appeal is compensated for by a reduction in threat. B's agreement to inhibit his 'disloyalty' is compensated for by A's willingness to impose restraint on the exercise of his capacity for exploitation. This argument can be put in another way. Only when both threats are present in a relatively high degree are both parties motivated to evolve a formal agreement, and furthermore it is only under these conditions that B is provided with sufficient 'counter-power', through the existence of an attractive alternative to the relationship, to bargain effectively with A. If this reasoning is correct, strong mutual threats may establish the conditions that permit the emergence of formal norms of behavior (contracts) which incorporate adaptive mechanisms capable of supporting the maintenance of the relationship.

Experiment 1: Paris study

Four experiments have been conducted to evaluate the foregoing theoretical formulation. The original experiment has been reported in detail elsewhere (Faucheux and Thibaut, 1964; Thibaut and Faucheux, 1965) and hence it will be described here only in outline. Forty-eight pairs of fourteen-year-old boys recruited from two schools in the suburbs of Paris played a mixed-motive game. At the beginning of each experimental session, one member of each dyad was randomly assigned to the high-power position (A) and the other to the low-power position (B). The subjects remained in the same power position throughout the experiment. The subjects in each dyad were instructed not to compete with one another in the ensuing bargaining (for 'points') but rather to compete with

---

inhibited (contingent punishment); without a prior signal, X may reduce Y's outcomes simply to illustrate his power or to gain revenge for some earlier damage inflicted on him by Y or to attempt to increase the difference between the outcomes of the two parties (non-contingent punishment); X may also reduce Y's outcomes without really intending to do so, as when Y's outcomes suffer as a side-effect of X's pursuit of his own best outcomes (epiphenomenal punishment). For a theoretical analysis of the use of threats in interpersonal negotiatio n see Kelley (1965).

the other subjects who were in the same power position, i.e. all As were in competition, and all Bs were in competition.

The procedure for playing the game was as follows. By open discussion, the two subjects arrived at a tentative agreement about their joint behavior. When this tentative agreement was reached, A recorded it on a printed form provided for this purpose. Each subject then recorded privately his actual decision about what he would play. In this decision he was not obliged to honor the tentative agreement reached earlier; duplicity was thus possible. When the actual decisions were reached, they were announced publicly and recorded by A.

In playing the game, each subject had to decide, in effect, whether to attempt a negotiation with the other or to retreat to a non-contingent alternative value which guaranteed him a fixed outcome. If both subjects decided to negotiate, the subject assigned to the high-power position (A) was permitted to determine how the points would be allocated, within specified limits. If one of the subjects decided to play the alternative value, he received the number of points specified for that value and the other subject received zero points. If both subjects played the alternative value on any given trial, each received the points specified by the value.

The experimental treatments consisted of varying both the level of the external alternative and the degree of conflict of interest in the dyadic situation. The experiment was a 2×2 design, with two levels of external alternative and two degrees of conflict of interest. The high level of external alternative was set at thirty-five points and the low level at ten points. This means that in the high-alternative variation, either of the subjects could decide to receive an outcome of thirty-five points quite independently of the other's behavior. In the low-alternative variation, either subject could assure himself of ten points. If the other subject did not also on that trial decide to play the alternative, he would receive zero points. Conflict of interest was introduced in the following way. When, on any given trial, both subjects decided to attempt to negotiate (i.e. neither subject played the external alternative), the subject in the high-power position (A) was responsible for the distribution of outcomes. High conflict of interest was created by permitting subject A to determine the allocation of ninety-eight points between the limits of ten and eighty-eight; i.e. he could take for himself any number of points from ten to eighty-eight, leaving the remainder of the ninety-eight for B. Low conflict of interest was created by restricting A's allocation of the ninety-eight points to those ranging from forty-five to fifty-three; i.e. A could take for himself any number of points from forty-five to fifty-three, leaving the remainder for B.[3]

This game not only encourages the temptations to exploitation and disloyalty required by the theoretical formulation, but also permits various threats of punishment and acts of duplicity and revenge.

When the subjects had been instructed in the rules of play and had played three practice trials of a somewhat simplified version of the game described above, the actual experiment commenced. After six trials of the game had been played, an opportunity was introduced to form contractual agreements that would govern their behavior over a final set of three trials. (The number of trials to be played was never communicated to the subjects.) The experimenter emphasized that contracts were entirely voluntary and that they need not be formed unless the subjects wanted them. On each of the final three trials each subject recorded privately (a) whether or not he wanted a contract to be formed, and (b) if in fact he wanted a contract to be formed, the single rule (among three presented to him) that he would most prefer to have incorporated in the contract and the type and amount of sanction that he would like to have applied to violations of any contractual rules.

The three rules among which each subject wanting a contract had to choose were as follows:

EA-rule: it is prohibited to play the external alternative on this trial if a tentative agreement has been reached to attempt to negotiate (i.e. to work out a division of the ninety-eight points).

3. This arrangement created widely different degrees of conflict of interest, as measured by the correlation of outcomes potentially available to the two subjects. The product-moment correlation of the pairings of points to the two subjects over the array of all such possible allocations (including the values associated with the external alternatives) was -0.80 as the average value for the two High-Conflict conditions and $+0.76$ as the average value for the two low-conflict conditions. Though all of the possible allocations are surely not equally salient, they represent the objective situation confronting the bargainers.

D-rule: if on this trial a tentative agreement has been reached concerning the division and distribution of points between the bargainers, it is prohibited in the actual play to take more than has been agreed upon.

A *'dummy'* rule of no functional significance for the present situation.

It will be apparent that the first two rules are designed to prohibit the kinds of behavior which on theoretical grounds may be expected to threaten differentially the two partners. The two types of sanction afforded the subjects were indemnities and fines. Indemnities referred to payments (in points) the violator of a rule must make to the injured party. Fines referred to payments (in points) to be made by the violator to the experimenter. In the private recording of his preference for aspects of a contract, each subject could indicate any number of points between zero and 100 to be applied as an indemnity and/or as a fine.

After recording their individual preferences, the subjects discussed the matter and decided whether to form a contract, and, if a contract were to be formed, the rules and sanctions to be incorporated. The subjects were permitted to include in their contracts as many of the three rules as they liked and either or both types of sanctions. This procedure was repeated for three trials. Adherence to the various provisions of contracts was monitored and enforced by the experimenter.

Twelve dyads were assigned to each of the experimental conditions: high conflict and high alternative (HH), high conflict and low alternative (HL), low conflict and high alternative (LH), and low conflict and low alternative (LL).

Throughout the following presentation of results the term 'contract' will be reserved for written agreements specifying at least one rule to be observed and including a sanction for violations in the form of an indemnity. (Fines were so infrequently attached to contracts that we will omit any consideration of them in this discussion.) From the theoretical considerations raised earlier, it would be expected that, in comparison with dyads in the three other conditions, the HH dyads would form a greater number of written contracts governing their interaction. From the first row of Table 1, it can be seen that dyads in the HH condition formed on the average 2·75 contracts (the absolute limit being 3·00), as compared with means of less than 2·00 contracts in the other three conditions. An analysis of variance yields an F for interaction of 5·51, which is significant at the 0·05 level.

From row two of Table 1, it can be seen that all twelve of the HH dyads formed at least one contract, while only 64 per cent of the dyads in the remaining conditions did so. This difference between HH and the other conditions combined is significant by chi-square (4·26) at the 0·05 level.

The same pattern is revealed (in the third row of Table 1) by the frequency with which dyads included both the rule prohibiting the playing of the external alternative and the rule protecting agreements concerning the division of points. In all, 75 per cent of the HH dyads formed such contracts, but only 19 per cent of the remaining dyads did so. This difference yields a chi-square of 10·13, which is significant at well beyond the 0·01 level.

Experiment 2: double dyads[4]

To evaluate the generality of the findings of the first experiment (with Parisian schoolboys), a second experiment was performed using male undergraduates at the University of North Carolina. In all respects except two, the second experiment was a replication of the first. In pretesting the second experiment, it was discovered that a considerable increase in the vigor of bargaining occurred when two subjects were assigned to each of the positions occupied by single subjects in the original experiment. Accordingly, the procedure of the second experiment was changed so that, instead of individual A playing against individual B, dyad A played against dyad B, with the requirement that one member of each dyad must represent his dyad as spokesman in the face-to-face bargaining. The second member of each dyad remained physically concealed in the background, able to communicate only with his spokesman.

The second change incorporated in the procedure of Experiment 2 was calculated to depress somewhat the absolute number of contracts formed. (Since in the Paris experiment all twelve dyads in the HH condition formed at least one contract, it seemed advisable to avoid what might be a 'ceiling' effect.) To this end, a

4. The assistance of Charles Gruder and Roger Wells in the planning and execution of the experiment is gratefully acknowledged.

charge of two points was levied on each side for each contract formed.

Rows 4, 5 and 6 in Table 1 show the main results of this replication. In general, the pattern of contractual activity resembles that of the first experiment. Again the HH groups formed more contracts than did groups in the remaining conditions: the mean number of contracts formed in HH is greater (by t-test, $p < 0.05$) than the combined mean of the remaining conditions. Further, while 75 per cent of the HH dyads formed at least one contract, only 36 per cent of the dyads in the remaining conditions did so, a difference significant at the 0.05 level by chi-square (4·03). Finally, two-thirds of the HH dyads, as compared with 28 per cent of the remaining dyads, formed at least one contract incorporating the two relevant rules, and again this difference is significant at the 0.05 level by chi-square (4·10).

Though the results of the second experiment are in general agreement with those of the first, the replication showed an unexpectedly high rate of contractual activity in the HL condition. The processes responsible for this high rate in the second experiment are by no means clear. In the HL condition, the relatively unattractive alternative value would ordinarily lend little credibilty to any threats of disloyalty from the low-power position. It is conceivable, though, that the low-power position in the HL condition may have been sufficiently strengthened, by substituting a dyad for an individual, to compensate for its weak bargaining position. A comparable strengthening of the low-power positions in LH and LL, where the conflict of interest is low, would not be expected to produce the condition necessary for contract formation.

Experiment 3: personal attributes[5]

A third experiment was performed to explore further the limits of generality of the earlier results. The modification of design in this experiment concerns mainly the method of manipulating the

5. This experiment was conducted by Peter Murdoch and a detailed account of it is being published separately (Murdoch, 1967). In addition to the variables discussed here, Murdoch's study involved the variable of 'precision of control'. The present summary reports data only from that part of his experiment (the 'precise control' treatment) which is comparable with the data of the other experiments reported herein.

Table 1 Mean Numbers of Contracts, Frequencies of Groups Forming at least One Contract and Frequencies of Groups Forming at least One Contract Containing Both Relevant Rules (N = Twelve Groups in Each Condition in all Experiments)

Experiment		Experimental treatment				Row number
		Hi Con Hi Alt (HH)	Hi Con Lo Alt (HL)	Lo Con Hi Alt (LH)	Lo Con Lo Alt (LL)	
1. Paris study (N=48 dyads)	Mean contracts formed	2·75	1·33	1·67	1·92	1
	N groups forming at least one contract	12	6	9	8	2
	N groups forming at least one contract with both rules	9	2	2	3	3
2. Double dyads (N=48 quartets)	Mean contracts formed	1·58	1·25	0·67	0·08	4
	N groups forming at least one contract	9	8	4	1	5
	N groups forming at least one contract with both rules	8	7	3	0	6
3. Personal attributes (N=48 dyads)	Mean contracts formed	1·00	0·25	0·42	0·17	7
	N groups forming at least one contract	6	3	2	2	8
	N groups forming at least one contract with both rules	6	1	1	2	9
4. Dependency variation (N=48 dyads)	Mean contracts formed	0·92	0·25	0·33	0·58	10
	N groups forming at least one contract	7	2	3	4	11
	N groups forming at least one contract with both rules	6	1	2	3	12

mutual threats in the dyads. In the first two experiments reliance was placed on structural aspects of the game situation (conflict of interest and attractiveness of external alternatives) to produce perceptions that the other party was tempted in one degree or another to be exploitative or disloyal. In the present experiment the game situation used uniformly throughout all variations was that of the HH condition: all dyads were confronted with a high conflict of interest and highly attractive alternatives. The variables of perceived exploitativeness and disloyalty were directly manipulated by presenting each member of the dyad with (fictitious) information about the other. Thus A was provided with evidence that B was either disloyal or loyal, and B was provided with evidence that A was either exploitative or fair. Finally, in contrast to the earlier experiments, in this one when a subject played his alternative value, the other player did not receive zero points but instead received the alternative value.

It is assumed that dyads composed of an 'exploitative' A and a 'disloyal' B will behave in a manner similar to the HH dyads, those composed of an 'exploitative' A and a 'loyal' B will be like HL dyads, those composed of a 'fair' A and a 'disloyal' B will be like LH dyads, and those composed of a 'fair' A and a 'loyal' B will be like LL dyads. The experimental game was essentially the same as that used previously. As in Experiment 2, a charge was levied on each party for each contract formed; in this experiment the charge was seven points to each side. The contract provisions permitted the levying of fines but not indemnities as sanctions for rule violations. Again twelve dyads, composed of male undergraduates, were assigned to each of the four conditions.

Although (from rows 7, 8 and 9 of Table 1) the over-all level of contract formation appears to be somewhat lower than in the first two experiments, the pattern of results remains similar. The HH condition is again the most active. With respect to the average number of contracts formed, however, this experiment yields inconclusive results. Because the majority of dyads outside the HH condition formed no contracts at all, the variances between conditions are markedly non-homogeneous, and hence parametric tests do not seem appropriate. Frequencies of forming at least one contract and of forming at least one contract embodying the two relevant rules are again higher in HH than in the remaining conditions, with significance by chi-square at the 0·05 and 0·02 levels respectively.

Experiment 4: dependency variation[6]

In the three studies previously described, A's power was created and 'legitimized' by the experimenter's definition of A's role as that endowed with superior power and by assigning to A the function of making final decisions about the division between the two parties of their joint outcomes. In the present experiment, an attempt was made to manipulate power by creating within the dyad differential degrees of dependence on the relationship. This was done by setting different values of the external alternative for the two parties. As in the first two experiments, two levels (high and low) of attractiveness of the external alternative were maintained. However, *within* each of these levels member A was assigned a higher value of alternative than B. Hence, the level of alternative value was higher in the high-alternative treatment than in the low, and within each of those treatments, the alternative value for A was higher than for B. These alternative values were announced publicly. Instructions to the subjects contained no suggestion that any power differential existed or should exist between the two parties.

Conflict of interest was manipulated, as in the first two experiments, by restricting the bargaining to a narrow range of possible allocations in the low-conflict treatment and permitting a much larger range of allocations in the high-conflict treatment. In the present experiment, however, since power was based on differential dependency (and not on A's prerogative to determine the allocation of points), the actual distribution of points was decided jointly by the players on each trial of the game. Hence it was not possible, as in the earlier experiments, for A to exercise duplicity through allocating the points in a way that violated the prior tentative agreement, nor for either A or B to play the alternative after having tentatively agreed not to do so.

A further feature of Experiment 4 was the imposition of a charge (in points) to both players for each unit of time taken to reach agreement on each trial. In addition, though a player was permitted at any time to play his alternative value (thus terminating the trial),

6. The assistance of Robert Colman, James Kahan and Mickay Miller in the planning and execution of this experiment is gratefully acknowledged.

John Thibaut 109

both players were automatically given their alternative values if they had failed to take any action before a prescribed time limit ran out. Finally, in contrast to the earlier experiments, in this one when a subject played his alternative value, the other subject did not receive zero points but instead received *his* alternative value.

As in all of the earlier experiments, the possibility of forming written contracts was introduced for the last three trials of the game, and (as in Experiment 2) a two-point charge was levied on each party for each contract formed. Because of the changed nature of the game, the rules made available for possible inclusion in contracts also differed from those in the earlier experiments. The three rules, any or all of which could be included in any contract, were as follows:

An *EA-rule*: this rule is identical with that included in the earlier experiments; it prohibits playing the external alternative on a specified trial.

An *allocation rule*: this rule enables the players to agree on a specified narrowing of the range of possible allocations of points.

A *time rule*: this rule permits the fixing of a time limit shorter than that imposed by the experimenter.

Before proceeding to the results of this experiment, it may be worth commenting on the way in which the theoretical formulation given at the outset of this paper is relevant to the altered plan of this experiment. It is proposed that, as in the previous experiments, the pressures to form written contracts will be maximal in the HH condition. For in the HH condition, the com-presence of a wide range of possible allocations and a high alternative value is likely to induce player A to aspire toward a very large share of the points. It is also likely, on the other hand, that player B will be motivated and able to threaten and frustrate A's attainment of a large number of points by consuming time in the negotiation, though he thereby also reduces his own outcomes.[7] In the HL condition, B's ability to counter A's aspirations is much reduced, since (given the generally low level of alternative values) he shares a common interest

7. Admittedly, player B has less counter-power in this experiment than in the previous ones, and both the nature of his resources and the strategy of his approaches to A are somewhat unclear. It is distinctly possible that B is concerned in the HH condition not so much with delaying the negotiation as with desperately attempting to improvise (time-consuming) arguments that will produce concessions from A.

with A in avoiding delays that would ultimately lead to the alternative values. In the LH and LL conditions, the range of possible allocations is so narrow that B's freedom from exploitation is sufficiently protected without his being required to take the costly action of prolonging the negotiation.

From the foregoing considerations it is suggested that in the HH condition there exists between the players a mutuality of threat composed of (a) A's temptation to play his (extremely high) alternative value in the face of any resistance to his aggrandizing demands in the bargaining and (b) B's willingness to resort to the counter-controlling tactics of delaying the negotiation. These interpretations receive support from an analysis of the private preferences for contract provisions recorded by the players on each of the contract trials. Not only in the HH condition, but in general, the rule most favored by player A and least favored by player B was the time rule and the rule least favored by player A and most favored by player B was the rule prohibiting the play of the external alternative.

Hence the theoretical expectations about rates of contract formation remain the same as for the earlier experiments. The 'relevant' rules for maximizing mutual protection, however, are in this experiment the time rule and the alternative rule.

Twelve dyads, six composed of male undergraduates and six of female undergraduates at the University of North Carolina, were assigned to each of the four experimental conditions. The results are shown in the last three rows of Table 1. The over-all pattern of findings is similar to that obtained in the earlier experiments. As in Experiment 3, however, the data for mean numbers of contracts are inconclusive as a result of non-homogeneity of variance among the conditions. Frequencies of forming at least one contract and of forming at least one contract incorporating the two relevant rules are again higher in the HH condition than in the remaining ones, although in both cases the chi-squares yield significance only at the 0·10 level.

Discussion and conclusions

The four experiments appear to establish a dependable relationship between mutuality of threat and the formation of written agreements that provide normative protection against the actualization of these threats. In the first three experiments reported, the content of the threats consisted of the (perceived) temptation of the stronger party to become exploitative and of the weaker party to become disloyal to the relationship. Though the latter party (B) is empirically weaker, in the sense that in all three experiments his outcomes were significantly lower than A's even when the alternative was attractive, he does have considerable power. In fact, from the point of view of the structure of the game itself, B's position is at least as powerful as A's, since by disloyalty each can reduce the other's outcomes in the same large degree. However, we may speculate that B's power, though it is real enough both to himself and to A, is to an extent inhibited in its use by its radical and subversive character (Smith, 1965). Not only does its use deprive B of the opportunity to attain his best outcomes through the negotiation process, but it abruptly and drastically reduces A's outcomes and attacks the legitimate power vested in A's position by the experimenter. Though B is by no means ineffectual, his power may be too revolutionary to be fully effective. The results of the fourth experiment suggest that the theoretical formulation may be extended to include other sorts of threats so long as the threat from each side of the negotiation is substantial enough to create a balance of strong threat.

Though the relationship between mutuality of threat and contract formation appears to hold across the various subject samples and procedural differences studied here, there are a number of conditions under which the relationship would not be expected to hold. The mutual willingness to inhibit the performance of the behaviors that threaten and damage the other party depends crucially on the mutual perception by the parties that there exists some degree of commonality of interest which can be served by the adoption of formal agreements. If the competitiveness of the relationship becomes so severe that this component of common interest no longer exists or cannot be perceived, a normative resolution of the conflict would become impossible to achieve. Hence the relatively high rate of contractual activity obtained in the HH conditions in the four experiments reported here would not be expected to occur if any additional factors were introduced to produce irreconcilable competitiveness.[8]

8. Of course, if the commonality of interest is so great that very little competitiveness exists, then *contractual* norms are unnecessary.

One such factor concerns the levels of aspiration of the negotiating parties. Kahan (1966) has studied the effects of various levels of aspiration on the bargaining behavior of dyads in a game like that used in the present experiments. He has shown that, as the sum of the experimentally induced levels of aspiration of the two parties becomes progressively larger, the degree of competitiveness in the bargaining increases; and when the sum of the two aspiration levels significantly exceeds the joint outcome available for allocation, competitiveness indeed becomes extreme.

Another factor that may so exacerbate competitiveness that no basis for mutual accommodation remains has been studied by Miller (1966) in an experimental situation like that of our present studies. Miller found that when each of the negotiating parties knew only his own alternative value, as compared with the public knowledge of alternatives characteristic of the experiments reported here, deception and distrust (and, in general, the level of competitiveness) increased markedly. Such factors, then, as extremely high aspiration levels and privacy of alternative resources, if they act to obscure or remove any last vestiges of common interest will be expected to overwhelm the relationships obtained in the studies reported here.

There is another kind of factor not considered in the present research which may be of critical importance in producing the findings outlined in this paper. This factor, which is currently being studied by Roger Wells (personal communication), concerns the role of the third party in inducing written agreements. A uniform feature in all of the four experiments described here is the active presence of the experimenter, who introduces the possibility of contract formation and suggests the structure of its provisions. The experimenter thus functions as an active third party to the negotiations. The work being done by Wells suggests that the presence of such a third party is at least highly facilitative, if not indispensable, to the formation of formal norms.

According to Wells's analysis, formal norms (contracts) emerge under certain conditions in mixed-motive relationships experiencing a relatively high degree of conflict of interest, while informal norms arise when commonality of interest is dominant. The mutual distrust characteristic of relationships experiencing high conflict of interest is likely to make it extremely difficult for either party to introduce a normative overture without its being (and being perceived to be) a somewhat manipulative and self-aggrandizing tactic. And even if a beginning were made toward working out a formal agreement, the conflicted parties may rapidly become pessimistic about the possibilities for objective monitoring and sanctioning of contract violations. The critical advantage of the third party in introducing contractual negotiation is that he has no conflict of interest with either party.

Because they require the conflicted parties to inhibit the behaviors that are mutually threatening, formal norms are typically proscriptive. Informal norms, on the other hand, emerging from relationships dominated by common interests, are mainly prescriptive. The common interest insures that each party can help the other while still helping himself. Hence neither party is tempted nor very much able to hurt the other. Only simple prescriptions to perform the mutually accommodative behaviors are required, and the interventions of the third party are unnecessary.

References

DEUTSCH, M., and GERARD, H. B. (1955), 'A study of normative and informational social influence upon individual judgment', *J. abnorm. soc. Psychol.*, vol. 51, pp. 629–36.

FAUCHEUX, C., and THIBAUT, J. (1964), 'L'approche clinique et expérimentale de la genèse des normes contractuelles dans différentes conditions de conflit et de menace', *Bull. Centre d'Etudes Rech. Psychotech.*, vol. 13, pp. 225–43.

HOLLANDER, E. P. (1960), 'Competence and conformity in the acceptance of influence', *J. abnorm. soc. Psychol.*, vol. 61, pp. 365–9.

JONES, E. E., JONES, R. G., and GERGEN, K. J. (1963), 'Some conditions affecting the evaluation of a conformist', *J. Personal.*, vol. 31, pp. 270–88.

KAHAN, J. P. (1968), 'The effects of level of aspiration in an experimental bargaining situation', unpublished master's thesis, University of North Carolina.

KELLEY, H. (1965), 'Experimental studies of threats in interpersonal negotiations', *J. conflict. Resol.*, vol. 9, pp. 79–105.

MILLER, M. D. (1966), 'The effects of privacy or publicity and symmetry or asymmetry of alternative on bargaining in the interdependent dyad', unpublished master's thesis, University of North Carolina.

MURDOCH, P. (1967), 'The development of contractual norms in a dyad', *J. Personal. soc. Psychol.*, vol. 6, pp. 206–11.

SCHELLING, T. C. (1960), *The Strategy of Conflict*, Harvard University Press.

SMITH, W. P. (1965), 'Precision of control and the use of power in the triad', paper read at meeting of Eastern Psychological Association, 22–4 April.

THIBAUT, J., and FAUCHEUX, C. (1965), 'The development of contractual norms in a bargaining situation under two types of stress', *J. exp. soc. Psychol.*, vol. 1, pp. 89–102.

THIBAUT, J. W., and KELLEY, H. H. (1959), *The Social Psychology of Groups*, Wiley.

7 Theodore M. Newcomb

Stabilities Underlying Changes in Interpersonal Attraction

Theodore M. Newcomb, 'Stabilities underlying changes in interpersonal attraction', *Journal of Abnormal and Social Psychology*, vol. 66, 1963, pp. 376–86.

It is a safe prediction that individuals who are initially strangers to one another will, under conditions assuring that they will become well acquainted, experience many changes in the degree of their attraction toward one another. Such changes, like any others that scientists investigate, presumably occur in orderly ways, and the principles governing both change and non-change correspond to constancies. Lewin (1947), paraphrasing Cassirer (1923), notes that 'throughout the history of mathematics and physics problems of constancy of relations rather than of constancy of elements have gained importance and have gradually changed the picture of what is essential' (p. 5). The present report points to a few such constancies of relations that have been observed on the part of two populations of initial strangers over a four-month period, while their attitudes (elements involved in the relations) toward one another were characterized by a good deal of inconstancy.

As reported more fully elsewhere (Newcomb, 1961), two sets of seventeen male students served in two successive years as subjects in an investigation of the phenomena of getting acquainted. They had been successfully selected as total strangers to one another, and lived and took their meals together in a house reserved for them. During each of sixteen weeks they responded to a selected set of questionnaires, attitude scales or other instruments, many of which were repeated from time to time. In particular, they rated or ranked each other as to favorability of interpersonal attitudes (henceforth referred to as *attraction*) during almost every week. In addition, they frequently estimated one anothers' attitudes of various kinds. The present paper partially summarizes and also supplements findings reported in the original monograph, for the specific purpose of noting constancies that underlie inconstancies.[1]

The theoretical considerations from which the investigation stemmed were direct descendants from Heider's (1958) theory of 'balanced states'. For the purposes of this study, the elements among which a balanced relationship may exist for an individual are: his degree of attraction, positive or negative, toward another individual; his attitude, favorable or unfavorable, toward some object (in the inclusive sense, referring to persons, issues, and abstractions like general values); and the second individual's attitude, as perceived by the first individual, toward the same object. A balanced state exists among these elements in so far as attraction is positive and the individual perceives that his own and the others' attitudes are similar. Perceived dissimilarity together with positive attraction represents an imbalanced state; negative attraction (with which this paper does not specifically deal) together with perceived similarity of attitudes may be either imbalanced or merely nonbalanced (a matter of indifference); together with perceived dissimilarity, negative attraction may be either balanced of merely non-balanced.[2] These rules of balanced relationships include the specification of certain conditions, most important of which are that the attitude objects be of relatively high importance and be considered to have common impact upon self and others, in similar ways.[3]

The significant feature, for present purposes, of Heider's (1958) words is that 'if a balanced state does not exist, then forces toward this state will arise. If a change is not possible, the state of imbalance will produce tension' (p. 201). Thus balanced

1. There were, of course, individual instances of non-change, but as population variables most of the attitudes here considered were highly inconstant.

2. This description of balance as associated with negative attraction differs from Heider's position, according to which negative attraction together with dissimilarity is balanced and imbalanced together with perceived similarity. Theoretical considerations suggest that the former combination need not be rewarding nor the latter distressing; and empirical findings from the investigation here reported indicate that the former combination often does not have the stability that is characteristic of balanced relationships, while the latter does not necessarily have the instability characteristic of imbalanced relationships.

3. For a fuller statement concerning this theoretical approach see Newcomb (1953, 1959).

states tend to be stable and imbalanced ones unstable. In either case we are dealing with relations, in Lewin's terms, and not merely with elements of attitudes.

Individuals' attitudes

It is to be expected that individuals' attraction to the remaining group members will at first be unstable, because initial attraction responses (made on the third day) are necessarily based upon first impressions only; and that week-to-week changes should be in the direction of increased stability – that is, that the rate of change will be a declining one, because in successive weeks the amount of 'new' information that individuals receive about one another will decline. The kinds of information about another person that are relevant to attraction toward him are, in general, those that result in the attribution to him of properties that are regarded as rewarding. These are not necessarily persistent or 'inherent' personal properties; they may equally well include properties that are elicited only in interaction with specific other persons and they may, of course, be idiosyncratically attributed. Changes in attraction result not only from new discoveries of what characteristics another person already has, but also from observing qualities that, whether one knows it or not, one has oneself helped to elicit in him.[4]

Table 1 presents means of week-to-week 'reliability coefficients'; each subject's rank ordering of the other sixteen subjects in attraction at each week was correlated with his rank ordering for the following week. Table 2 shows similar coefficients, computed over longer intervals. The two tables together provide strong support for both predictions: initial responses have little predictive value even for so short a period as five weeks, whereas week 5 responses predict almost as well to week 15 as to week 10 ($p < 0.001$ in either case). Change continues throughout the entire period, but the rate of change declines hardly at all after the first five or six weeks. Except for very unpopular subjects, whose high attraction choices are not reciprocated and continue to be relatively erratic, attraction choices show comparatively little change after the first six weeks.

Such changes should occur, hypothetically, in spite of the indivi-

4. Certain distinguishable sources of interpersonal reward, and thus of attraction, have been elsewhere described by Newcomb (1960).

Table 1 Means of Seventeen Individual Correlations (rho) for Pairs of Adjacent Weeks

Weekly interval[1]	Year I	Year II
0–1	0·51	0·65
1–2 through 4–5[2]	0·82	0·84
5–6 through 9–10[2]	0·86	0·91
10–11 through 14–15[2]	0·88	0·90

Note: In rank ordering attraction toward other sixteen subjects.
1. Week numbers refer to the number of preceding weeks of acquaintance.
2. Variations within these sets of adjacent weeks are so slight that values for the pairs of weeks have been averaged, rather than presenting each one.

Table 2 Means of Seventeen Individual Correlations (rho) over Varying Intervals of Time

Weekly interval	Year I	Year II
0–15	0·29	0·31
0–10	0·32	0·35
0–5	0·38	0·43
5–15	0·66	0·70
5–10	0·82	0·84
10–15	0·83	0·85

Note: In rank ordering attraction toward other sixteen subjects.

dual's tendency to maintain a constant relationship between degree of perceived agreement and attraction to others concerning objects of importance to himself. If it may be assumed that the self is such an object, and in general a positively valued one, then it is to be expected that high attraction toward others will be associated with the perception of reciprocation of high attraction toward oneself. Table 3 supports this prediction for year I, and results for year II are almost identical. All estimates of reciprocation by rank 1 choices are at all times in the upper half of the distribution, and most of them in the upper eighth. There is a very strong tendency (not necessarily warranted) to assume that one's highest ranked associates return the compliment.

Table 3 Relationship Between Giving High Attraction and Perception of Receiving High Attraction from Same Persons (Year 1)

Estimated rank of reciprocated attraction	Number of subjects estimating reciprocation from their rank 1 choices at level indicated		
	Week 1	Week 5	Week 15
1–2 (very high)	14	14	12
3–4 (high)	3	2	2
5–8 (second quarter)	0	1	3
9–16 (lower half)	0	0	0
Total	17	17	17

Table 4 Summary of Relationships Found Between Level of Attraction to Other Subjects and Perceived Agreement with Them about Attractiveness of Remaining Subjects

Time of response	χ^2	df
Year I, Week 1	55·81***	2
Year I, Week 5	31·13***	2
Year I, Week 14	38·94***	2
Year II, Week 2[1]	17·54***	1
Year II, Week 5[1]	6·73*	1
Year II, Week 12[1]	9·95**	1

1. In year II only 5 per cent of all possible estimates, based on a randomly drawn sample, were made. The somewhat lower significance levels in year II result, in part at least, from the smaller Ns in that year.

* $p < 0·01$.
** $p < 0·005$.
*** $p < 0·001$.

It is to be expected, on similar grounds, that attraction to other individuals will be paralleled by perceived agreement with them as to the relative attractiveness of the remaining House members. As shown in Table 4, which summarizes relationships between level of attraction to others and degree of perceived agreement with them about the relative attractiveness of other House members, there is in both populations, at all stages of acquaintance, a significant relationship between these two variables.

Table 5 Summary of Significance Levels at which Two Highest Ranking Choices by all Subjects are Judged to be Highly Attracted to Each Other (Year 1, Week 5)

Category of estimated attraction	Number of estimates		χ^2	df
	Obtained	Expected		
Highest quarter	22	8·5	26·51*	1
Upper half	33	17·0	28·30*	1
'Favorable'	34	23·6	13·68*	1

* $p < 0.001$.

A special instance of this tendency is to be found in the almost universal tendency to assume that one's two most preferred sociometric choices are highly attracted toward each other. (In view of the fact that reciprocated attraction from rank 1 and rank 2 choices is also perceived as very high, this set of phenomena may be labeled 'the perception of perfect triads'.) According to the year I data, which for this purpose are more complete than in year II, but which are well supported by the latter, the relationships shown in Table 5 are typical of all stages of acquaintance. It seemed to be almost unthinkable to these subjects that their two most preferred choices should be hostile to each other, and almost so that they should be merely 'neutral'. Early estimates to this effect were in several cases quite inaccurate; lack of information invites autistic judgements. Later ones were highly accurate; as earlier perceptions of perfect triads were discovered to be erroneous, preferences shifted in such manner as to justify the perception of perfect triads.

Balance inducing forces should also result, at all times, in the perception of closest agreement with most attractive others with respect to objects other than the self and House members. The data most suitable for testing this prediction are subjects' rankings of the six Spranger values[5] in year II, together with their estimates of how each other subject would rank them. Both at week 2 and at week 14 the relationships between attraction toward other subjects and estimates of agreement with them were highly significant; χ^2 values are 17·19 and 11·63, respectively, corresponding p values being < 0.001 and < 0.005, $df = 2$. The slight decline in this relation, from week 2 to week 14, is also found in other tests of the same prediction; it reflects in part the countereffects of greater accuracy with increasing acquaintance.

Thus the data show a continuing increase, though at a rapidly declining rate, in the stability of attraction toward others. They also show that at all times, to about the same degree, attraction toward others is related to perceived agreement with them concerning a variety of things.

Dyad relationships: mutual attraction and actual agreement

In so far as subjects were alert to increments of information about one another with continued interaction among them, it is predictable that estimates of others' attitudes will become increasingly accurate with continued acquaintance; and that actual relationships between mutual attraction and agreement will increasingly approach the perceived relationships. The latter prediction presumes that, with increasing accuracy, subjects will discover that some of their assumptions about agreement with attractive others are not justified, and will tend either to modify their own attitudes or to shift their attraction preferences to individuals with whom they are in fact more closely in agreement.

With respect to the self as an object, the data do not support the first prediction: estimates of others' attraction toward oneself do not become more accurate with increasing acquaintance, and this is true at all levels of expressed attraction. Frequencies and magnitudes of inaccuracies are quite constant, although they are at all times predominantly in the direction of overestimating the true

5. 'Spranger values' were classifications proposed by Edouard Spranger in his *Types of Men* (Niemeyer, Halle, 1928) which later formed the basis of Allport and Vernon's 'study of values' ('A test for personal values', *J. abnorm. soc. Psychol.*, vol. 26, 1931, pp. 231–48). Their test (which Newcomb utilizes in this extract) was designed to measure an individual's relative standing on six types of value or evaluative attitude: theoretical, economic, aesthetic, social, political, religious. [*Ed.*]

level of reciprocated attraction. Estimates are in general fairly accurate, especially at the extremes of expressed attraction. Most subjects, apparently, are rather sensitive to others' indications of attraction toward themselves, at all times, and at all times there is a constant tendency to exaggerate the degree to which one's own attraction toward another person is reciprocated at about the same level.

The accuracy with which subjects estimate each others' attraction preferences toward other House members does increase. During the early period (weeks 0–5) this increase is significant only for the estimator's highest attraction ranks, representing individuals with whom he is likely to have associated frequently enough after five weeks to estimate their preferences reasonably well. By week 15 the trend is unmistakable at all attraction ranks: in year I (the population in which these data are most nearly complete) fifteen of seventeen subjects were more accurate than at week 1 – the binomial probability of which is beyond 0·001.

Subjects' accuracy in estimating others' rank ordering of Spranger values increases at a high level of significance, as shown in Table 6, in which the indices of accuracy represent rank-order correlations between each subject's estimated rank ordering of each other subject's responses and the latter responses as actually made. The mean accuracy of 272 estimates, according to this index, is 0·25 at week 2 and 0·49 at week 14.

Table 6 Relative Accuracy of Estimating Other's Rank Ordering of Spranger Values, Early and Late

Accuracy level[1]	Number of estimates at indicated levels of accuracy		
	Week 2	Week 14	Total
≥0·60	66	110	176
<0·60, >0·14	103	95	198
<0·14	103	67	170
Total	272	272	544

Note: $\chi^2 = 17·92$, $p = 0·001$, $df = 2$.
1. Rho between each estimated rank with actual rank.

Turning now to actual dyadic relationships, it is to be expected that sensitivity to others' responses to oneself will increasingly result in similar levels of attraction on the part of dyad members, whatever that level may be. In so far as forces toward balance with regard to the self are tempered with considerations of reality, dyad members should come to assign about the same degree of attraction to one another. Table 7 shows that this is indeed the case. A large proportion of the dyads whose members accord very different levels of attraction to each other include a very popular or a very unpopular individual, or both. Apart from this consideration, the tendency toward increasing reciprocation of attraction by dyad members at closely similar levels is almost universal. This fact about objective dyadic relationships, combined with the unchanging tendency to perceive favorably reciprocated attraction, reflects shifts in actual attraction preferences: changes are such that increasingly accurate judgements of others' attraction toward oneself result in increasingly close reciprocation.

Table 7 Ns of Dyads Whose Members' Attractions to Each Other Differ by Three (of Sixteen) Ranks or Less

Time of response	Obtained	Expected	χ^2	df
Year I, week 0	51	50	0·00	1
Year II, week 0	59	53	0·61	1
Year I, week 15	77	53	10·61**	1
Year II, week 15	72	53	6·46*	1

* $p < 0.02$.
** $p < 0.002$.

With respect to Spranger values, also, the effects of increased accuracy in judging others, together with constant forces toward balance, are that actual agreement is increasingly associated with high mutual attraction. At week 2, when these responses were first obtained, there was no relationship between pair agreement and mutual pair attraction ($\chi^2 = 1.17$, $p < 0.50$, $df = 1$). At week 14, however (when responses were last obtained), the relationship had become highly significant, as shown in Table 8. The χ^2 value of this distribution, with both variables equally dichotomized, is 9·52, $df = 1$, and $p < 0.001$ by a one-tailed test.

It happened that there were almost no changes in subjects' ranking of the six Spranger values between early and late acquaintance; it was therefore possible to predict later dyad attraction from initial agreement nearly as well from early as from late agreement; early agreement did not, however, predict to early attraction. Similar results were obtained with two other sets of attitude items, each quite wide-ranging in content, from which indices of dyad agreement were computed; first responses to these items were made on the third day of acquaintance in year I, and by mail one month before subjects arrived at the university in year II. As shown in Table 9, in neither case did preacquaintance agreement bear any relationship to early scores of mutual attraction, but high preacquaintance agreement in each year predicted significantly to high mutual attraction four or five months later.

Table 8 Relationship Between Degree of Agreement about Spranger Values and Mutual Pair Attraction (Week 14, Year 11)

Level of agreement	Number of dyads at attraction level indicated				Total
	Highest quarter[1]	Second quarter[1]	Third quarter[1]	Lowest quarter[1]	
Highest quarter	12	6	9	6	33
Second quarter	10	16	6	4	36
Third quarter	9	4	8	11	32
Lowest quarter	7	4	10	14	35
Total	38	30	33	35	136

1. For reasons described in the full report, dyad scores are routinely categorized according to proportions of *expected*, not obtained, frequencies, which typically show slight differences.

In view of the general increase in accuracy of estimating others' attitudes and in view of the constant tendency to prefer balanced to unbalanced states, it follows that with increasing acquaintance there should be an increasing tendency toward relationships that are balanced not merely phenomenologically but also in fact. This means that, except in the case of attitudes that show little or no change, change in mutual attraction between dyad members should be accompanied by change in their actual agreement. This prediction is best tested with respect to agreement about the relative attractiveness of House members. As shown in Table 10, the early relationship between mutual dyad attraction and agreement about House members approached zero in both populations, and increased to a significant level in the later weeks. Typically, there was a good deal of shifting about during the earlier weeks, both with respect to mutual attraction and to preferences among other House members, with the result that the relationship between attraction and actual agreement becomes a highly significant one. It can also be shown, by more detailed analysis, that among dyads at a high level of mutual attraction in early weeks there is significantly higher agreement three months later on the part of dyads whose mutual attraction remains at the same high level than on the part of dyads whose mutual attraction has decreased. Change or non-change in these two respects proceeds together and interdependently.

High attraction structuring within populations

Both a rationale and supporting evidence have been presented for the expectation that with increasing acquaintance subjects will shift their attraction preferences in such manner as to satisfy constant preferences for balance (that is, agreement with attractive others about objects of importance), and to take into account considerations of reality, with continuing increments of information about one another. With specific reference to dyad members' agreement about the attractiveness of other House members, this expectation leads to the prediction of increasing numbers of high attraction triads and larger subgroups, for the following reasons. Dyad members will tend to find one or more other individuals toward whom each of them is strongly attracted; dyads in which this does not occur will tend to be unstable. It is likely, as has been shown, that this high attraction will be reciprocated in kind by a third individual; if so, a high attraction triad has been formed, composed of the three mutually attracted pairs; if not, in the case of some particular person, it is likely to occur with a different one. Once a high attraction triad has been formed, similar processes

Table 9 Predictive Value of High Attitudinal Agreement at Early Periods for High Mutual Attraction at Early and Late Periods

Nature of attitudes	Year	Week of attitude response	Week of attraction response	χ^2	df
Miscellaneous	I	0	0	0·46	1
Miscellaneous	II	−4	0	0·00	1
Spranger values	II	2	2	1·17	1
Miscellaneous	I	0	13	8·78*	1
Miscellaneous	II	−4	13	11·68**	1
Spranger values	II	2	14	9·52**	1

* $p < 0.005$.
** $p < 0.001$.

tend toward further accretion, with the attendant formation of high attraction tetrads and larger subgroups.

With respect to triads, such processes did occur, in both populations. Since our principal interest lies in stable triads we took, as a criterion of stability, triads all three of whose component dyadic relationships maintained a high level of mutual attraction for three consecutive weeks. During the first three weeks of acquaintance only two of seventeen possible triads remained stable by this criterion in year I and three of thirteen in year II. During the last three weeks, however, seven of thirteen in year I and fourteen

Table 10 Summary of Mean Correlations Between Mutual Attraction and Actual Agreement about Other House Members on the Part of 136 Dyads

Week	Year I	Year II
0–1	0·15	0·18
2–5	0·45	0·37
6–9	0·52	0·40
10–13	0·50	0·43
14–15	0·46	0·58

of nineteen in year II remained stable; the respective p values, by exact test, based on Ns of early and late triads that were stable and that were unstable, were 0·036 and 0·017. Numbers of stable triads do increase with acquaintance; there were too few high attraction tetrads and pentads at any time to be studied.

The attraction structuring of the total populations can be described in various ways, which might include numbers of high attraction subgroups of various sizes, the attraction relationships among them, and the number of isolates (individuals who have no mutually high attraction relationships at all). The two population structures did not differ in important ways at first, but interesting differences later appeared, as suggested by the sociograms presented in Figure 1, which show all subgroups of two or more whose

year I, week 15   year II, week 15

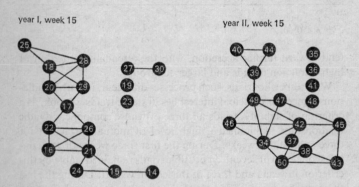

Figure 1   High attraction structure of two populations on final acquaintance. Circles represent individuals; connecting lines represent mutual attraction at high levels

members' levels of mutual attraction reached a rather high criterion. The visual appearance of these two sociograms, together with certain other evidence not here reported, suggests differences along a dimension that might be called centrality versus divisiveness – a difference not predicted on the basis of any theoretical considerations. A rather simple index of divisiveness confirmed the appearance, and a *post hoc* hypothesis was formulated concerning the sources of this difference. This hypothesis rests upon the contribution of two variables to centrality: the degree of interconnectedness among high, mutual attraction dyads on the part of the individuals having the highest attraction power ('popularity'), and the amount of attraction power concentrated in these individuals. It was found that among the most popular six individuals in each population, who together accounted for somewhat more than half of the attraction power in each population, 20 per cent of all such dyads met the criterion of interconnectedness in year I as compared with 53 per cent in year II. Moreover, there was more attraction power concentrated in the six most popular individuals in year II than in year I. Thus each variable contributes to the greater centrality in year II. It is, in fact, an artifactual necessity that whichever of two populations of the same size has these characteristics will be the more centrally structured: great interconnectedness at high levels of mutual attraction among individuals having most attraction power; and greater attraction power on the part of the same number of popular individuals. These are not necessarily the only variables that contribute to centrality, but they do necessarily contribute to it, for the following reasons. Popular individuals who are multiply connected by high mutual attraction constitute a triad or larger subgroup that serves as a core substructure, each of whose members brings with him several 'hangers-on' who are thus added onto the core structure. And the more 'hangers-on' thus added, the larger the substructure becomes.

Our *post hoc* hypothesis as to why so few popular subjects were multiply interconnected in year I and so many in year II is simply that there was more agreement among the six popular individuals in the latter than in the former year; the evidence abundantly supports it.

1. The most nearly comparable attitude responses made by both populations were to miscellaneous batteries of items; in year I the fifteen dyads among the six popular subjects agreed with each other no more closely than did all other pairs, whereas in year II their agreement was significantly closer than that of other pairs ($p < 0.05$).

2. In authoritarianism (*F*-score), five of the six popular subjects in year II were extremely low, ranking 1, 2, 3, 4 and 5 in a low scoring population; in year I, on the other hand, the six popular subjects covered nearly the entire range, from 2 to 17.

3. Although no comparable data are available for year I, five of the six popular subjects in year II were in extraordinarily close agreement in Spranger values – and they knew it: the mean of their ten intercorrelations in actual response was 0·72, and the mean of their estimated agreements with each other was 0·75. (The sixth, who disagreed with all of the others both in *F*-score and in Spranger values, was number 39, the only one of the six not having high mutual attraction with more than one of the others.) Thus the central proposition concerning balance accounts for the close interconnectedness of six popular subjects in one year and for the absence of it in the other year, and thus accounts for the different attraction structurings in the two populations. It does not, of course, account for the fact that in year II but not in year I popularity was pretty much concentrated among a set of five closely agreeing individuals. Our general theory has nothing to say about the characteristics which led to popularity in these populations, and we can only say that our random methods of selecting subjects had this consequence.

Individual characteristics of subjects

Several theoretically derived expectations have been shown to be supported by empirical findings. Our tests, however, have been statistical ones, pertaining to populations or subpopulations and not to individuals. There are two relevant questions concerning the manner in which individuals' characteristics contribute to the findings.

First, it is possible that a comparatively few individuals contribute all or most of the variances that account for the statistically significant findings; if so, the generalizability of the findings is severely limited. The findings depend rather heavily on assumptions concerning two kinds of individual tendencies: to prefer balanced to imbalanced relationships; and at the same time to take account of 'reality' in the form of accretions of information that may disturb existing states of balance. Individual indices of both of these tendencies (sensitivity to balance, and accuracy in judging others) were therefore constructed. Results of intensive analyses of all thirty-four subjects may be summarized as follows:

1. Individual differences are clearly apparent, with respect to both balance and accuracy.
2. In estimating others' attitudes toward varying kinds of objects there are in each population typically one or two individuals who show little or no sensitivity to balance, or no greater than chance accuracy in making estimates.
3. The subjects who are deviant in these ways with respect to one attitude object at a particular stage of acquaintance are not necessarily deviant with respect to other attitude objects, or at other times.

In sum, the tendencies to be sensitive to balanced relationships and to judge others' attitudes more accurately with increasing acquaintance, which underlie our theoretically derived predictions, appear to be present, at least in some degree, in all of our subjects.

As to measured individual characteristics, authoritarianism (as measured by the F-Scale) seemed most likely to be relevant to the problems of this investigation. Our expectations concerning authoritarianism stem from several studies suggesting that F-Scale scores (Adorno *et al.*, 1950) are related to 'perceptiveness of others' (Christie and Cook, 1958, in a review of the relevant evidence on this point, pp. 180–83). Such evidence leads to the expectation that low F-scorers should be relatively accurate in estimating others' attitudes. With one exception (estimates of others' ordering of attraction toward House members in year I), the prediction is supported with respect to various attitude objects, and according to different indices of accuracy, in both populations. The data that best lend themselves to detailed analysis of accuracy consist of estimates of others' rank ordering of Spranger values, made in identical manner at weeks 2 and 14 of year II. These data show that on the rather difficult task of ranking other subjects according to agreement with the estimator, the non-authoritarians excel the authoritarians in accuracy on late but not on early acquaintance; the correlation of 0·56 between F-score and accuracy at the later time is significant at $<0·01$.

Inaccurate estimates of others' attitudes may represent distortions either in the balance promoting direction or in the opposite direction; the former may be considered autistic, and if we assume that imbalanced relationships represent a form of ambiguity, of which authoritarians are relatively intolerant (cf. Adorno *et al.*,

1950), then it is to be expected that high F-scorers' inaccuracies will be in the autistic direction, relative to low F-scorers. No difference in this respect appears at week 2, when autistic errors are relatively frequent at all F-score levels; but the prediction is well supported at week 14: comparisons of autistic, accurate and contra-autistic estimates for low, intermediate, and high F-scorers yield a χ^2 of 13·02 in the predicted direction, significant at $< 0·01$, $df = 4$, by a one-tailed test.[6]

These and other findings are consistent with the following interpretation. The greater sensitivity of the very low F-scorers enables them to select as most attractive those with whom they are in fact most closely in agreement about a rather wide range of values. The non-authoritarians' characteristic solution to imbalance is non-autistic: they tend to achieve balance not by exaggerating actual agreement with those to whom they are attracted (on other grounds), but by judging rather accurately who is in agreement with them and letting their highest attractions be determined accordingly. The characteristic solution of the more authoritarian subjects tends to be just the reverse: instead of letting their personal preferences be determined by accurate perceptions of agreement, they tend to perceive more agreement than actually exists with those toward whom they are already attracted.

Nature of constant relations

Three kinds of elements, in Lewin's (1947) sense, have been considered: an individual's attraction toward another person; his attitude toward some object other than that person; and that person's attitude, as he perceives it, toward the same object. Under the conditions of the investigation here reported, the stability curves of these three kinds of elements were quite different: attitudes toward nonperson objects (especially toward general values) showed little change from first to last acquaintance; attraction toward other House members, on the part of most subjects, became relatively stable by the end of the first six weeks or so; and estimates of others' attitudes were relatively slow in stabilizing,

6. If the 'accurate' estimates are ignored, in order to compare autistic and contra-autistic responses only, the inverse relationship between autism and authoritarianism is still significant at the 0·05 level.

though with individual differences. If the study had been concerned only with subjects' own attitudes and attractions, it might well have been terminated after six rather than sixteen weeks. But in view of the crucial place, in the present formulation, of perceptions of others' attitudes and in view of the relatively slow and continuing changes in estimates of others' attitudes, it might be argued that the study should have been continued for another several weeks.

What does remain relatively constant, in spite of these differential rates of stability and change, is the second-order relationship between the relationship of two of them (own and other's perceived attitude) and attraction. With regard to such diverse attitude objects as the individual subject himself, other group members, and a range of nonperson objects, such a relationship, described as a balanced one, is found at all stages of acquaintance. This constant relationship is maintained despite the fact that all of the related elements are changing, or some of them are changing while others are not. Eventually, the single elements tend to become stable, but the level at which they do so is governed by the same constancy of relationships that prevailed throughout the earlier periods of change.

The psychological processes by which intra-personal states of balance are maintained may be described as follows. As group members interact with one another, each of them selects and processes information – about objects of common interest, about one another as sources of attitudes toward those objects, and about one another as objects of attraction – in such ways that the inconsistencies and conflicts involved in imbalanced relationships tend to be avoided. Both autistic processes ('balance at all costs') and realistic ones ('the truth, whatever it costs') are involved, their respective weightings being determined both by individual differences and by the strength of the attitudes involved. When interaction begins with total strangership, increments of information are inevitable; attitude change results from the necessity to adapt simultaneously to increments of information and to constant preferences for balanced relationships.

Interacting members of dyads and larger groups necessarily make such adaptations to one another simultaneously. In so far as they do so realistically, the consequence of reciprocal adaptation is a mutual relationship that is in fact maximally satisfying to both or all of them – that is, maximally within the limits of what is possible. Realism tends to increase with acquaintance and, combined with constant tendencies toward balance, the inevitable trend is toward mutuality of attraction. Stable relationships tend to persist, and relationships that are in fact balanced tend to be stable because they are mutually rewarding and not likely to be disturbed by increments of information with continued interaction.

Viewed intrapersonally, the generalizable constancies underlying changes in interpersonal attraction that apply to all individuals – regardless of their differences in preferring some personal properties to others and regardless of the personal traits that others present – are preferences for balanced relationships, and tendencies to adapt to information regarded as valid. Viewed interpersonally, the generalizable constancies are the necessities (which may become internalized as preferences) confronting each of a set of interacting persons to make successive adaptations to one another, simultaneously and reciprocally, in the direction of establishing relationships that are both realistic and balance promoting for each. It is relationships that are simultaneously rewarding to each and realistically apprehended by each that tend to be stable. Such relationships are both psychologically (intrapersonally) balanced and objectively (interpersonally) balanced.

Attitude changes that are governed by these constancies stem from a triple confrontation that is characteristic of *la condition humaine*. Each of us must somehow come to terms, simultaneously, with the other individuals and groups of which our interpersonal environment is constituted; with the world that we have in common with those persons and groups; and with our own, intrapersonal demands, including the preference for balanced states. In so far as the individual's confrontation is characterized by changing input of information, the elements that correspond to his attitudes are subject to inconstancy, but the lawfulness with which they change corresponds to certain constancies in relationships among the elements. It is such constancies that make possible viable adaptations, simultaneously, to multiple confrontations.

References

ADORNO, T. W., FRENKEL-BRUNSWIK, E., LEVINSON, D. J., and SANFORD, R. N. (1950), *The Authoritarian Personality*, Harper & Row.

CASSIRER, E. (1923), *Substance and Function*, Open Court, Chicago.

CHRISTIE, R., and COOK, P. (1958), 'A guide to published literature relating to the authoritarian personality through 1956', *J. Psychol.*, vol. 45, pp. 171–99.

HEIDER, F. (1958), *The Psychology of Interpersonal Relations*, Wiley.

LEWIN, K. (1947), 'Frontiers in group dynamics: concept, method, and reality in social science, social equilibria and social change', *Hum. Rel.*, vol. 1, pp. 5–41.

NEWCOMB, T. M. (1953), 'An approach to the study of communicative acts', *Psychol. Rev.*, vol. 60, pp. 393–404.

NEWCOMB, T. M. (1959), 'Individual systems of orientation', in S. Koch (ed.), *Psychology: A Study of a Science*, vol. 3, McGraw-Hill, pp. 384–422.

NEWCOMB, T. M. (1960), 'Varieties of interpersonal attraction', in D. Cartwright and A. Zander (eds.), *Group Dynamics: Research and Theory*, Row, Peterson, 2nd edn, pp. 104–19.

NEWCOMB, T. M. (1961), *The Acquaintance Process*, Holt, Rinehart & Winston.

8 Walter R. Borg

Prediction of Small-Group Role Behaviour from Personality Variables

Walter R. Borg, 'Prediction of small group role behavior from personality variables', *Journal of Abnormal and Social Psychology*, vol. 60, 1960, pp. 112–16.

This study explores the degree to which a person's role in a small-group problem-solving seminar can be predicted from a battery of group administered tests which attempt to measure skills and personality characteristics observed to be important in small group situations. The specific hypothesis to be tested is that a person's scores on tests selected to give measures of assertiveness, rigidity, self orientation, and sociability will predict his role in a problem-solving seminar.

Method
Subjects

The *S*s included 819 Air Force Majors and Lieutenant-colonels in the Command and Staff School of the Air University, Class 1957. They were divided into sixty seminars of twelve to fourteen officers each, and worked in the same seminar group for a period of two and a half months. A large portion of the curriculum of the school is devoted to problem-solving activities and discussions in the seminar groups. The problems dealt with by the seminars vary considerably in nature but, for the most part, involve practical Air Force problems of a sort that might be encountered by a Wing Staff.

Variables and measures

The first step in the research was the selection of tests to go into the predictor battery, which was to contain tests to measure variables related to patterns of behavior that had been found in observations of small-group activity. A careful survey was made in order to identify variables that had occurred repeatedly in studies based on observations of small-group interaction (Bass, 1951;

Bass *et al.*, 1953; Carter, 1951, 1954; Carter, Haythorn, and Howell, 1950; Carter *et al.*, 1951; Cattell and Stice, 1953; Haythorn, 1953; Sakoda, 1952; Schutz, 1955). The variables that appeared most frequently in these studies were:

Sociability. This variable, under different names, such as Personal Orientation, Group Sociability and Social Adjustment, has been reported frequently in studies concerned with small-group interaction.

Self-orientation. Variations of this measure have appeared repeatedly under such names as Power Orientation (Schutz, 1955) and Individual Prominence, (Carter, 1954; Carter and Nixon, 1949).

Rigidity. Rigidity and related variables such as Authoritarianism, Conformity and Dogmatism have been investigated in a number of relevant studies of small-group behavior (Greer, 1955; Haythorn *et al.*, 1956; Lippitt, 1940; McCurdy and Eber, 1954; Medalia, 1955).

Assertiveness. This variable has been employed with considerable success by Schutz (1955) and is somewhat similar to variables employed in other small-group research such as Forceful Leadership, Surgency (Cattell, 1951), Ascendance (Bass *et al.*, 1953), Physical Energy (Sakoda, 1952) and Individual Prominence (Carter, 1954).

The tests selected to supply predictive measures of these characteristics included the following:

The FIRO Test. This test was developed by Schutz (1955) and has been used by him with considerable success for predicting leadership behavior and organizing compatible groups. The form of the test employed in this research consisted of seven items, each of which was regarded as a separate score on the suggestion of Schutz. These items attempt to measure degree of power orientation, as compared with personal orientation and degree of assertiveness.

The California F-scale, Form 40. This form of the *F*-scale employs the items that were found to be most discriminating in the original research at the University of California (Adorno *et al.*, 1950).

The Anxiety to Achieve Battery. This battery consisted of six group tests from the Cattell Objective Analytic Personality Battery (Cattell, 1955) and yielded a single factor score.

The Social Extroversion Score, from the Inventory of Factors STDCR (Guilford, 1945).

Eight factor scores from the Guilford Opinion Inventory (Guilford, 1951). This test was developed by Guilford from his factor analysis of the 'interests' of Air Force officers. Factors used included: need for variety, orderliness, need for attention, physical drive, aggression, resistance to restriction, cultural conformity, self-reliance. The entire predictor battery yielded eighteen scores.

Derivation of factor scores

After the battery was administered, results were subjected to centroid factor analysis. A total of four orthogonal rotations were made, yielding four factors. Rotated factor loadings may be found in Table 1. The factors were interpreted as follows:

Table 1 Rotated Factor Loadings Employed in Developing Weighted Factor Scores

Variable	Loading
Factor 1: Assertiveness	
Schutz G-H, Assertiveness	0·61
Schutz 5, Assertiveness	0·66
Schutz 6, Success in Attaining Leadership	0·57
Schutz 7, High Self-Estimate of Leadership Ability	0·43
S Factor from Guilford's STDCR, Social Extroversion	0·58
P Factor from Guilford's Opinion Inventory, High Level of Physical Drive	0·36
Factor 2: Power Orientation	
Schutz A-B, Power Orientation	0·43
G Factor from Guilford's Opinion Inventory, Self-Reliance	0·40

Table 1 (cont.)

Variable	Loading
Factor 3: Rigidity	
California F Scale, Authoritarianism	0·56
S_0 Factor from Guilford's Opinion Inventory, Tendency toward Orderliness	0·39
F Factor from Guilford's Opinion Inventory, Cultural Conformity	0·53
Factor 4: Aggressive Non-Conformity	
V_0 Factor from Guilford's Opinion Inventory, Need for Variety	0·45
L Factor from Guilford's Opinion Inventory, Need for Attention	0·54
Q Factor from Guilford's Opinion Inventory, Aggression	0·62
M Factor from Guilford's Opinion Inventory, Resistance to Restriction	0·43

Factor 1, Assertiveness, was loaded heavily on Schutz's Assertiveness scores, as well as Guilford's Physical Drive score and Social Extroversion score. A separate Sociability Factor, mentioned as an important variable in several studies, did not emerge. If additional Sociability measures had been included in the predictor battery, the factor may have emerged or may have loaded under Assertiveness as did Guilford's Social Extroversion score.

Factor 2, Power Orientation, had loadings on Schutz's Power Orientation score, as well as Guilford's Self-Reliance variable.

Factor 3, Rigidity, seems clearly indicative of Rigidity, being loaded most heavily on the California *F*-scale. Other significant loadings include Guilford's Cultural Conformity score and Orderliness score.

Factor 4, Aggressive Non-Conformity, is more difficult to interpret. The heaviest loading on this factor was in Guilford's Aggression scores. Other variables loading on this factor included Guilford's Need for Variety score, Need for Attention score and Resistance to Restriction score. Several interpretations of this factor were considered. In some respects it appeared quite similar to Cattell's

Hypomanic Aggression. Another possible interpretation was that the factor was indicative of social immaturity, while a third interpretation was that it reflected frustration in the military environment. For several reasons, an interpretation of the factor as Aggressive Non-Conformity seemed most plausible. First, the heavy weighting of Aggression and Need for Attention seemed to point in this direction. The loadings on Need for Variety and Resistance to Restriction suggest a negative reaction to the restrictions and conformity demands found in the military environment. Observations of the Command and Staff School, secondly, reveal that a significant number of students display overt aggressive attitudes toward the school. Some students also displayed considerable negativism concerning the testing itself. This negativism might well have been reflected in some of the test scores where it could have come to the surface. For example, some of the items on the Aggression test, such as those advocating punitive action, could give the S an indirect means of expressing aggression or negativism aroused by the testing situation. Weiss and Fine's (1956) research dealing with the effect of the individual's immediate mood on attitude measures indicates that the individual's mood may be reflected to a significant degree in items where aggression can be displayed.

Weighted factor scores were computed including all variables loading over 0·30 and most heavily loaded on the given factor. These personality factor scores constituted the predictors against which to compare small-group role scores (see Table 2).

Small-group role scores

The small-group role scores were based on two peer nominations completed in the second and fifth weeks after the groups were organized. The first peer nomination contained six brief paragraphs describing typical small-group behavior patterns. These paragraphs described popular-social behavior, good followers, assertive behavior, rigid behavior, creative behavior and leadership. Each seminar member nominated the person (by code number) who best fitted each description and checked a five-point scale to indicate the degree to which the selected individual fitted the description. Each seminar member received a score for each of the six roles which was the sum of his nominations weighted for degree of fit. These scores were then converted to standard scores.

The second peer nomination used the same six role descriptions but required the individual to select three seminar members most fitting the description and three least fitting the description. The individual's score for each role was the algebraic sum of his best fit and least fit nominations. Scores on the second peer nomination were converted to standard scores and combined with first peer nomination scores to give six composite role scores for each S.

Results

In order to determine the degree to which the personality factor scores predicted small-group role scores, samples of individuals who had made either high or low role scores were selected. The four individuals in each seminar who received the highest scores on a given role were selected as well as the four individuals with the lowest role scores. These cases were further screened to eliminate individuals from the top group who were not at least 0·6 σ above the mean on both peer nominations and eliminating individuals from the bottom group who were not at least 0·6 σ below the mean on both peer nominations. Thus the persons chosen were not only at the extreme within their group but were at the extreme with respect to the entire sample on the role score under consideration.

Table 2 Correlations Between Predictor Factors and Small-Group Role Scores

Factor Scores	Popular Social	Good Follower	Assertive	Rigid	Creative	Leader
	1	2	3	4	5	6
1. Assertive	0·245*	−0·221*[1]	0·422*[1]	0·216*[1]	0·423*[1]	0·389*[1]
2. Power Orientation	−0·044	0·066	0·012[1]	0·008[1]	0·020[1]	0·020
3. Rigidity	0·065[1]	0·026[1]	−0·114*	0·012	−0·176*[1]	−0·158*[1]
4. Aggressive Non-Conformity	0·108	−0·060	0·141*[1]	−0·020	0·207*[1]	0·175

* Significant beyond 0·01 level.
1. Results as hypothesized.

A total of twenty-four hypotheses were then developed. The relationship of each of the four predictor factors to each of the six small-group roles was hypothesized to be either positive, negative or zero (see Table 2) based upon psychological theory and previous research results. Fourteen of these hypotheses were supported by the data. In all, twelve of the twenty-four widespread biserial correlations computed between the small-group roles and the personality factors were significant at the 0·01 level.

It may be seen, however, in Table 2 that although many of the correlations were significant they were too small to permit prediction of the role of a given individual from his personality scores. By far the most promising of the predictor scores is factor 1, Assertiveness. This score correlated significantly with all six role scores and yielded correlations around 0·40 with Assertiveness, Creativity and Leadership roles. As Table 3 indicates, these three

Table 3 Correlations Between Different Peer Roles on the Second Rating

Variable	1	2	3	4	5	6
1. Popular-social	0·000	0·139	0·255	−0·348	0·264	0·252
2. Good follower	0·139	0·000	−0·251	−0·404	0·065	0·105
3. Assertive	0·255	−0·251	0·000	0·452	0·710	0·599
4. Rigid	−0·348	−0·404	0·452	0·000	0·207	0·177
5. Creative	0·264	0·065	0·710	0·207	0·000	0·817
6. Leader	0·252	0·105	0·599	0·177	0·817	0·000

roles are moderately intercorrelated, suggesting that they are measuring a single broad leadership role. A combination of these three role scores correlates 0·46 with Factor 1. This correlation is sufficiently high to permit reasonably good selection for small-group leadership if it is established that this role is stable from situation to situation.

Discussion

The results shown in Table 2 generally support the findings of earlier research. Several studies have been reported that are concerned with relationships between personality and small-group behavior. Some of these have analysed small-group observational data so as to yield personality factors. Some have explored relationships between peer or supervisor evaluations and small-group behavior. Only a few, however, have attempted to predict small-group behavior from personality test scores.

Leadership ratings of twenty sorority girls in a leaderless group discussion situation were compared with their scores on the Rorschach, Guilford–Zimmerman Temperament Survey and F-scale by Bass et al. (1953) in one study of this type. Bass found no significant results with the F-scale, but did find that Ascendence and Sociability scores on the Guilford–Zimmerman and High Verbal Output on the Rorschach were significantly correlated with Leadership ratings. The Rorschach result is in all likelihood an artifact of Bass's L G D rating system, which depends to a considerable degree on Verbal Output (Bass, 1951). The correlation between Ascendency and Leadership in Bass's study, however, is almost identical to the correlation between Assertiveness and Leadership found in the research reported in this paper.

In another study of small-group leadership (Cattell and Stice, 1953) leaders in thirty-four groups were compared in terms of scores on the 16 PF Test. They found four variables that differentiated between leaders and non-leaders at the 0·05 level. These were Super Ego Strength, Adventurousness, Self Confidence and High Self-Sentiment Formation. These variables, as described by Cattell, are similar in many respects to the Assertiveness and Power Orientation factors used as predictors in this paper. Richardson and Hanawalt (1944) compared two types of leaders and non-leaders on the basis of their scores on the Bernreuter Personality Inventory. They found their leader groups to be more dominant, extraverted and self-sufficient than the non-leaders.

Thus, the few studies that have been done, despite the use of different personality measures, different leadership measures and different types of Ss, all agree to a considerable extent that leaders are significantly more assertive, self confident and extraverted than non-leaders.

Studies employing other personality variables as predictors of small-group roles are much less conclusive.

Several workers have employed the F-scale and related measures in small-group research with varying results. The rigidity factor used in the research reported in this paper was correlated negatively to the variables in the broad leadership role, but the correlations, although significant, are too low to have much meaning. Some work has indicated that authoritarian leaders function effectively in authoritarian groups (McCurdy and Eber, 1954). There is also evidence that different types of individuals emerge as leaders in authoritarian and equalitarian groups (Adorno *et al.*, 1950; Haythorn *et al.*, 1956). Some work has demonstrated a positive relationship between Authoritarian Leadership and Group Cohesiveness (Medalia, 1955), while other research has found a negative relationship between these variables (Lippitt, 1940). Unlike Assertiveness, which appears to be an important leadership variable in most groups, the importance of authoritarianism varies greatly with the group, the task and the leader.

Four of Schutz's items loaded heavily in the Assertiveness factor and one in the Power Orientation factor identified in this research. The results of Schutz's experimental battery, particularly the Assertiveness items, were impressive but indicated a need for further development. Schutz's scores have rather low reliability as they are each based on only one item. The items aimed at measuring Assertiveness were found to correlate with each other from 0·19 to 0·47. Items measuring Power *v.* Personal Orientation, however, correlated with each other −0·09 to +0·09, indicating little common variance. As Schutz's technique becomes more highly developed, the Power Orientation variable might become useful in role prediction.

Summary and conclusions

A sample of 819 Air Force officers was administered a test battery designed to predict the individual's role in small-group situations. This battery was factor analysed, yielding four factors: Assertiveness, Power Orientation, Rigidity and Aggressive Non-Conformity. The sample was then divided into sixty small groups of twelve to fourteen members and rated with respect to six small-group roles. Twenty-four widespread biserial correlations were computed between the four predictor factors and the six small-group roles. Twelve of these correlations were significant at the 0·01 level. The predictor factor 'Assertiveness' was most successful, correlating 0·46 with a composite leadership role.

With regard to significance of these results for future work, it seems reasonable to conclude from the success in predicting the leadership composite that prediction of certain roles and behavior patterns in small-group activity can be achieved by further developing predictor instruments along the lines indicated by this study. Further research may make it possible to analyse changes in the individual's role behavior that are attributable to differences in certain measurable characteristics of other group members in problem-solving groups.

References

ADORNO, T. W., FRENKEL-BRUNSWIK, E., LEVINSON, D. J., and SANFORD, R. N. (1950), *The Authoritarian Personality*, Harper & Row.

BASS, B. M. (1951), 'Situational test: 2. Leaderless group discussion variables', *Educ. psychol. Meas.*, vol. 2, pp. 196–207.

BASS, B. M., MCGEHEE, C. R., HAWKINS, W. C., YOUNG, P. C., and GEBEL, A. S. (1953), 'Personality variables related to leaderless group discussion behavior', *J. abnorm. soc. Psychol.*, vol. 8, pp. 120–28.

CARTER, L. F. (1951), 'Some research on leadership in small groups', in H. Guetzkow (ed.), *Groups, Leadership and Men*, Carnegie Press.

CARTER, L. F. (1954), 'Evaluating the performance of individuals as members of small groups', *Pers. Psychol.*, vol. 7, pp. 477–84.

CARTER, L. F., and NIXON, M. (1949), 'An investigation of the relationship between four criteria for leadership for three different tasks', *J. Psychol.*, vol. 27, pp. 245–61.

CARTER, L. F., HAYTHORN, W., and HOWELL, M. A. (1950), 'A further investigation of the criteria of leadership', *J. abnorm. soc. Psychol.*, vol. 45, pp. 350–58.

CARTER, L. F., HAYTHORN, W., SCHRIVER, B., and LANZETTA, J. (1951), 'The behavior of leaders and other group members', *J. abnorm. soc. Psychol.*, vol. 46, pp. 589–95.

CATTELL, R. B. (1951), 'Determining syntality dimensions as a basis for morale and leadership measurement', in H. Guetzkow (ed.), *Groups, Leadership and Men*, Carnegie Press.

CATTELL, R. B. (1955), *Handbook for the Objective-Analytic Personality Test Batteries*, Institute for Personality and Ability Testing, Champaign, Illinois.

CATTELL, R. B., and STICE, G. S. (1953), *Four Formulae for Selecting Leaders on the Basis of Personality*, University of Illinois.

GREER, F. L. (1955), *Small Group Effectiveness, Series 1955*, Institute for Research in Human Relations, Philadelphia.

GUILFORD, J. P. (1945), *Manual. An Inventory of Factors STDCR*, Sheridan Supply, Beverly Hills.

GUILFORD, J. P. (1951), *Opinion Inventory*, Air Research and Development Command, San Antonio, Texas.

HAYTHORN, W. (1953), 'The influence of individual members on the characteristics of small groups', *J. abnorm. soc. Psychol.*, vol. 48, pp. 265–84.

HAYTHORN, W., COUCH, A., HAEFNER, D., LANGHAM, P., and CARTER, L. (1956), 'The behavior of authoritarian and equalitarian personalities in groups', *Hum. Rel.*, vol. 9, pp. 57–74.

LEWIN, K., LIPPITT, R., and WHITE, R. (1939), 'Patterns of aggressive behavior in experimentally created social "climates"', *J. soc. Psychol.*, vol. 10, pp. 271–99.

LIPPITT, R. (1940), 'An experimental study of authoritarian democratic group atmospheres', *Univ. Iowa Stud. Child Welf.*, vol. 16, pp. 43–195.

MCCURDY, H. E., and EBER, H. W. (1954), 'Democratic vs. authoritarian: a further investigation of group problem solving', *J. Personal.* vol.22, pp. 258–69.

MEDALIA, N. Z. (1955), 'Authoritarianism, leader acceptance, and group cohesion', *J. abnorm. soc. Psychol.*, vol. 51, pp. 207–13.

RICHARDSON, H. M., and HANAWALT, N. G. (1944), 'Leadership as related to the Bernreuter Personality Measures: III. Leadership among adult men in vocational and social activities', *J. appl. Psychol.*, vol. 28, pp. 308–17.

SAKODA, J. M. (1952), 'Factor analysis of OSS situational tests', *J. abnorm. soc. Psychol.*, vol. 47, pp. 843–52.

SCHUTZ, W. C. (1955), 'What makes groups productive?', *Hum. Rel.*, vol. 8, pp. 429–65.

WEISS, W., and FINE, B. J. (1956), 'The effect of induced aggressiveness on opinion change', *J. abnorm. soc. Psychol.*, vol. 52, pp. 109–14.

9 Ralph V. Exline

Explorations in the Process of Person Perception:
Visual Interaction in Relation to Competition, Sex and
Need for Affiliation

Ralph V. Exline, 'Explorations in the process of person perception: visual
interaction in relation to competition, sex and need for affiliation',
Journal of Personality, vol. 31, 1963, pp. 1–20.

We need not subscribe to the view that 'the eyes are the window
to the soul' to recognize that the action of another's eyes can be
interpreted as expressive movement from which information both
about the transmitter and his reaction to outside events may be
derived (Reusch and Kees, 1959). But what kinds of information do
we obtain from observation of another's visual behavior? Do
people who differ in personality type differ in the manner in which
they visually interact with others? Are there systematic relationships to be found in the visual behaviors of those who occupy
different but related positions in an organization or social hierarchy? Knowing that we use others' visual behaviors as cues to
their internal states or unexpressed motives, do we also try to communicate such states and/or motives to others through our own
visual behavior? Although we often act as if we assume to know the
answers to the above questions,[1] little in the way of systematic
investigation of these phenomena has been reported. With the
exception of studies of judgement of emotional expression (Ruckmick, 1921; Woodworth, 1938) and eye-blink rates in relation to
anxiety states (Doehring, 1957; Kanfer, 1960), psychologists have
tended to leave the study of such behavior to the poets and novelists.

This study represents the first of a series of investigations into
the role of visual interaction in interpersonal communication.
It is exploratory, designed in part to test the feasibility of collecting
reliable data about visual interaction, and in part to test hypotheses,

1. Krasner, for example, would seem to assume some such shared understanding when, in a study of social reinforcement, he instructs *E* not to look
at *S* who is being given low social reinforcement (1958).

hopefully heuristic, about visual interaction in relation to selected personality and situational variables.

Variables to be studied were selected on both empirical and theoretical grounds. In an earlier study of interpersonal perception (Exline, 1960), the investigator observed that groups composed of persons high in n-affiliation were characterized by visual inter-action of a quite different order than were groups composed of persons low in n-affiliation. In high affiliation groups the speaker, whether man or woman, would be likely to sweep the group with a glance or, alternatively, to focus first upon one and then another group member until he or she had spoken to all, or most, of the group. Low affiliation persons would either content themselves with glancing at one or two others, fix their gaze on a spot over the heads of co-workers, or focus upon work materials while speaking. Similarly, the high affiliation listener appeared to be more prone to look at the speaker than was his low affiliation counterpart. Crude hand-kept records of the extent to which those high and low in n-affiliation looked at a speaker showed differences significant beyond the 0·001 level.

Such data, while admittedly primitive, suggest that n-affiliation may well be a personality variable systematically related to differences in visual style. As such it would seem to be related to a function of representation (or consciousness of another) which Heider (1958) has termed communion. A similar view has been stated by Simmel (1921), who sees willingness to engage in visual interaction as a means of establishing communion with others. According to Simmel it is the mutual, as distinct from the one-way, glance which signifies union; and whether we seek or avoid such visual contact depends upon our desire for union with another. Simmel, however, implies that for some there are risks in visual communion, for he writes that: 'By the glance which reveals the other, one discloses himself.... The eye cannot take unless at the same time it gives.' Such risks are more directly stated by Sartre (Scheutz, 1948), who argues: 'Either the other looks at me and alienates my liberty, or I assimilate and seize the liberty of the other.' Sartre would seem to suggest that to look at another encroaches upon his autonomy, and that when two glances meet a wordless struggle ensues until one or the other succeeds in establishing dominance. A dominance which is, perhaps, signaled by the lowered glance of the loser? Thus, while both Simmel and Sartre point to the intimate nature of a mutual glance, Simmel would seem to emphasize its potential for facilitating communion while Sartre stresses the invitation to interpersonal conflict which may be read into such a glance. Sartre's position reminds us of Heider's (1958) suggestion that representation also functions to help one gain control over that part of the environment which is represented.

The above arguments suggest that simultaneous (or mutual) visual interaction signifies the momentary establishment of a personal, very intimate, relationship. If so, those aspects of personality or social context which encourage the development and maintenance of such intimacy should be reflected in predictable patterns of visual interaction between and among the parties concerned.

With respect to personality differences which should be systematically related to mutual visual interaction, it appears reasonable to assume that those desiring to affiliate with others desire intimacy, while those desiring to control others shy away from the reciprocity implied by an intimate relationship. For the former, the mutual glance could represent communion – the act of looking being akin to an act of sharing, or association, or of participation in a wordless exchange. As such it would seem to be a moment to be prolonged. A recent finding that one's degree of n-affiliation is inversely related to his attempts to exert control over a group's decision (Exline, 1962) suggests that to low affiliators, the relationship could be one of combat, a clash of wills, a struggle for dominance. To such persons, perhaps, the mutual glance simultaneously acts as challenge and arena for a momentary struggle of wills. The term momentary is used advisedly, for it would seem that the costs of maintaining such a conflict would insure the brevity of mutual glances. Personal predilections toward relationships of communion or control would, in short, seem to lead to differential evaluation of, and hence differential tendencies to engage in, such activity.

The effects of personal predilections also may be influenced by the composition of the group. In a triad, for example, two persons who share a common trait may concentrate their attention on each other to the eventual exclusion of the third.[2] In view of the explor-

2. The author wishes to thank Martin Wallach (personal communication) for this suggestion.

atory nature of this study, however, a simpler design was preferred to one which permitted investigation of the effects of composition variables. Groups were composed of persons who were relatively similar in the degree of their affiliation orientation, and whether high or low, mutual visual interaction was compared across the affiliation category.

In summary, it was hypothesized (Hypothesis 1) that: groups composed of persons more disposed toward relationships of communion than control (groups of persons composed of high n-affiliators) engage in more mutual visual interaction than groups not so disposed.

Let us consider next the social context in which interaction occurs. The general knowledge that one's set toward another affects one's behavior toward him suggests that situational factors affecting sets toward communion should predictably affect the incidence of mutual glances between members of a group. In a situation of rivalrous competition, for example, both affiliative and non-affiliative persons could be assumed to feel less like entering into a communion-based intimacy with others than would be the case in non-rivalrous situations. Returning to the earlier assumption that, for affiliative persons at least, the mutual glance signifies a communion-oriented intimacy, it is expected that such persons would curtail their mutual glances as the situation becomes more competitive and rivalry increases. Thus it is hypothesized (Hypothesis 2) that: the incidence of mutual glances in groups composed of persons high in n-affiliation is lower in competitive than in less competitive situations.

No predictions concerning the effect of competition on mutual glances of persons low in n-affiliation were incorporated into the second hypothesis. The omission reflects the investigator's opinion that several plausible but contradictory assumptions can be invoked to explain the meaning which the mutual glance has for low n-affiliation persons in competitive situations.

On the one hand, we have suggested that low affiliative persons are more ascendant than their more affiliative counterparts. If correct, this assumption suggests that competitive conditions may cause ascendant persons to view a mutual glance as a challenge to assert control rather than as an invitation to commune. Should a challenge be assumed, an ascendant person might well feel that to avert his or her gaze would be an indication of submission. We would expect such an interpretation to lead the low affiliation person to maintain the glance longer than would be the case when the glance would not be likely to be interpreted as a challenge. More mutual glances would thus be recorded in groups of low affiliation persons under competitive than under less competitive conditions.

While the finding that less affiliative persons write more control-oriented messages (Exline, 1962) would seem to support the assumption that low n-affiliation is coordinate with high ascendancy, it is possible that other motives, e.g. greater task orientation, may have contributed to the low affiliation persons' more marked attempts to influence or exert control over their groups' decisions. Thus it is possible that low n-affiliation persons are not more ascendant than are high affiliators, and we could assume that lows differ from highs mainly in that they have less desire for warm and friendly relations with others. We could then argue that the meaning of the mutual glance would, regardless of the competitive nature of the situation, signify only a shared desire to establish warm personal relations. We would not expect a person who does not generally desire warm relationships to be much affected by whether or not the situation is competitive, and thus would not predict that the competitiveness of the situation affects the number of mutual glances observed in low n-affiliation groups.

In view of the above considerations, prediction as to the effects of competitiveness was restricted to the effects of such a situation on the behavior of affiliative persons only. The visual data of non-affiliative groups were studied, however, in order to develop data about the effect of competition on mutual glances in such groups.

The hypotheses presented above were tested by means of data collected in a $2 \times 2 \times 2$ variance design in which the variables were n-affiliation, competition and sex. The latter variable was incorporated into the design to permit exploration of the effect of an interesting and readily controlled variable upon mutual visual interaction.

Method
Procedures

From a large number of persons given a test of n-affiliation prior to the experiment, sixteen groups of three men and sixteen groups

of three women were formed. Each group comprised persons whose
n-affiliation score fell in the same half of a distribution split at the
median affiliation score. In the laboratory phase, each group was
given the same problem to discuss but discussed it under conditions
which were systematically varied to create one of two different
degrees of competition. Observers seated behind a one-way mirror
recorded visual interaction among group members throughout the
discussion. Upon termination of the discussion, *S*s filled out scales
to describe feelings of satisfaction and the degree to which they
were acquainted with one another.

n-Affiliation

Affiliation scores were obtained through a content analysis of
responses made to the items in Elizabeth French's Test of Insight
(1955). This test consists of ten single-sentence descriptions of
behavior typical of hypothetical individuals. It is assumed that the
respondent reveals certain of his own basic motivations when asked
to 'explain' the behavior and describe the actor. A typical item is:
'Joe (or Frances) is always willing to listen.' French provides
criteria which can be used to determine the individual's degree of
n-affiliation, *n*-achievement and positive or negative orientation.
Examples follow: *n*-affiliation (negative): 'because he is afraid that
others won't like him if he doesn't'; *n*-achievement (positive):
'because he is trying to learn how to listen well'.

Analysis of an *S*'s ten descriptions provide indications of both
affiliation and achievement orientation. It is theoretically possible
that one's motivation to achieve a high standard of performance in
non-social activities could generalize to a desire to achieve a
dominant position *vis-à-vis* other persons in social situations. Thus
if a person gives many affiliation and many achievement responses,
it is not clear how an induction designed to have differential effects
on each motive (e.g. instructions to compete) would affect the
behavior of that person. In order to eliminate the above unclarity,
an affiliative (communion) orientation was defined in terms of the
ratio of affiliation to achievement responses; thus, a high *n*-affilia-
tion to *n*-achievement ratio was assumed to signify an affiliative
orientation which was clearly more communion- than control-
oriented and vice versa.

To summarize, the eight groups of each sex drawn from a pool of Ss whose ratios fell above the median affiliation–achievement ratio were assumed to represent communion-oriented groups, whereas the eight groups of each sex drawn from a pool of Ss whose ratios fell below the median were assumed to be relatively more control-oriented.

The group task and the induction of competition

All groups were given a task in which group members privately named a hypothetical, newly developed soap product for automatic washers, then discussed their idea with the others. Half of the group in each affiliation–sex subcategory, however, were instructed to decide upon one of the three names, whereas the other half of the groups were instructed to discuss the names without attempting to decide among them. It was assumed that the instruction to agree upon one of the three names would introduce a competitive element which would be missing from the situation of those groups instructed only to discuss the names. To further stress the competitive aspect of the situation, it was implied to the competitively instructed groups, that a considerable reward would go to that individual who suggested the one best name among those agreed upon by the groups.

An attempt was made to insure a minimum spread of participation by instructing the groups to follow a clockwise order of presenting their ideas until each person had spoken twice, after which a free discussion was permitted. Finally, E designated one person to start the discussion and left the room. The groups waited for a signal to begin and their discussion was observed as described below.

Visual interaction

Patterns of visual interaction were recorded by two observers seated behind a one-way mirror. Observers specified the target and duration of each person-oriented visual fixation by manipulating push-button switches which activated the pens of an Esterline-Angus twenty Pen Operations Recorder. A third observer also identified each speaker and recorded the duration of each speech on the recording chart. By this means, synchronized records of visual and verbal behavior durations were obtained. A schematic representation of the observation arrangements is presented in Figure 1.

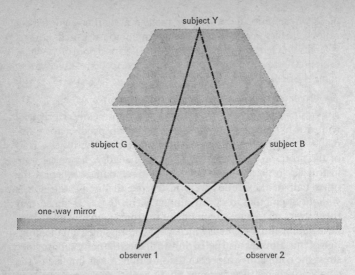

Figure 1 Schematic representation of arrangements for the observation of visual interaction

Several indexes of visual behavior can be derived from data obtained by the methods just described. Individuals can look at others while speaking to them, while being spoken to by them, or while the other is speaking to a third party. In addition, an index of mutual glances can be derived by dividing the number of seconds any two persons simultaneously look at one another by the total interaction time available to them. While all of the various aspects of visual interaction were explored, it is the index of mutual glances which was particularly relevant to the present investigation. This index, when transformed to arc sine coefficients, provided the data used to test the hypotheses suggested in the previous section.

Results
Reliability of observation

The operations recorder was wired so that the two observers' recordings of the common S's behaviors were located on adjacent channels. (A representative recording is depicted in Figure 2.) This arrangement permitted computation of the extent to which the

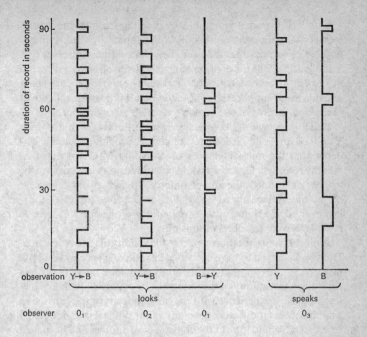

Figure 2 Sample (ninety seconds) of visual interaction between two persons recorded by two observers

two observers agreed as to the direction and duration of the *S*'s glances. Evidence concerning observer agreement was obtained by correlating the number of seconds which the two observers recorded for each common *S*'s focus on each other group member in ten randomly selected groups. The two recordings of Y's focus on B correlated 0·98, while the two recordings of Y's focus on G correlated 0·97; both correlations being significant beyond the 0·01 level. Additional and more precise evidence as to inter-observer agreement was obtained by comparing the recorded profiles. If the two observers simultaneously recorded that Y looked at B for a given period of time, the tracings on adjacent channels would show identical profiles (see Figure 2). An index of agreement was derived for each common S by dividing the total number of seconds that the adjacent profiles overlapped[3] by the maximum number of seconds that the combined observations indicated that Y looked at B. The index of agreement between observers averaged 81 per cent over the ten groups checked. The above data are taken as evidence to support the conclusion that it is possible reliably to record judgements of one person's visual focus upon another.

Reliable records of observers' judgements of the extent to which Y looked at B and G does not, of course, provide conclusive evidence that the mutual glances of Y–B and Y–G were just as reliably recorded. Observers could have erred more in recording the activity of B and G, the non-common Ss, than they did in the case of Y, the commonly observed S. For purposes of this study, however, it is assumed that observations of the other Ss were as reliable as were the observations of subject Y.

A more serious question concerns the validity of the observation. Did the Ss judged to have exchanged a mutual glance indeed look directly at one another? This study provides no data to test rigorously the validity of the observations of mutuality. Nevertheless, extensive experience with the method leads to the conviction that the observations were generally valid. While it is undoubtedly true that a S could look at the chin or ear of another and be judged as looking the other in the eye, it was found in practice that Ss seated as depicted in Figure 1, noticeably turned their heads to directly face another when looking him in the eye. Observers also noted that the angle at which they sat enabled them to use the position of the S's irises to estimate with confidence whether or not Ss focused their glance in the region of the others' eyes.[4] In any event, errors of measurement which did occur would be just as likely to occur in one experimental condition as in another. There is, then, no reason to expect the data to be biased systematically for or against any hypotheses under consideration.

3. To correct for slight variations in reaction time, a gap of two seconds (one space on the graph represented in Figure 2) between the two profiles was ignored.

4. It was also assumed that an S could reliably and validly judge when another S was actually looking into his eyes. This assumption has since proven to be well-founded, as was shown in a well-designed, rigorously executed study by Danielson and Gibson (1961).

Visual interaction

Mean mutuality index scores categorized by sex, affiliation ratios and competitive conditions are listed in Table 1, and the results of the analysis of variance in Table 2. It is immediately apparent that there are significant sex differences in mutual visual interaction. Women are significantly more prone to engage in such activity than are men. The possibility that such differences were due to different degrees of acquaintance was rejected when low and non-significant correlations were found between being acquainted with and tending to look at the other.[5]

The data also suggest that sex and n-affiliation interact to affect the amount of mutual visual interaction in a given dyad. Highly affiliative females look more at one another relative to less affiliative females than is the case for males, who, in fact, show the opposite tendency.

Additional data listed in Table 1 and analysed in Table 2 show that when visual interaction is categorized in terms of total looking, looking while speaking and looking while listening, women look significantly more than do men in each case. This, of course, is consistent with the mutuality analysis, a fact which is not surprising since mutuality, looking while speaking, and looking while listening, could not very well be independent of total visual activity. It is of interest to note, however, that when actual mutuality scores are compared to those expected from a chance model, women still engage in significantly more mutual visual interaction than do men. This latter analysis was accomplished by first obtaining an expected value for the mutuality of each dyad (percentage of time that Y looked at B × percentage of time B looked at Y), then rank-ordering within each sex the difference between expected and actual mutuality recorded for each dyad, and, finally, comparing the differences found for each sex by means of the Mann–Whitney U-statistic (1947). A critical ratio of 1.80 ($0.05 > p > 0.01$ – one-tailed test) showed that actual female mutuality exceeded the chance model to a significantly greater degree than did male mutuality scores. Women, it seems, not only look more and achieve higher mutuality scores than do men, but also exhibit

5. Pearson product-moment rs were figured independently for all eight subcells. Average value of $r = 0.147$, and the χ^2 test did not permit rejection of the hypothesis that the rs came came from a common population of rs.

Table 1 Means[1] of Various Indexes of Visual Activity
Categorized by Sex, *n*-Affiliation and Salience of Competition

Independent variables		N per categories	Visual activity indexes (in % of total time available)			
			Mutuality	Listening	Speaking	Total time
Sex:	males	48	3·0[2]	29·8	25·6	23·2
	females	48	7·5	42·4	36·9	37·3
n-Affiliation:	high (A)	48	5·6	36·9	31·5	29·9
	low (a)	48	4·9	35·3	30·9	30·6
Competition:	salient (C)	48	4·3	33·1	28·8	28·2
	subdued (c)	48	6·2	39·1	33·7	32·4
Dyad:	Y–G	32	5·4	*43·9*	35·0	*39·2*
	Y–B	32	5·9	*37·9*	33·2	*29·2*
	B–G	32	4·5	*26·5*	25·9	*24·4*
Interactions	male A	24	*2·2*	28·7	*21·6*	19·8
Sex ×	male a	24	*3·8*	31·0	*29·5*	26·6
Affiliation:	female A	24	*9·0*	45·0	*41·5*	40·0
	female a	24	*6·1*	39·7	*32·3*	34·6
Sex ×	male C	24	2·8	29·3	27·3	24·6
Competition:	male c	24	3·1	30·4	23·8	21·9
	female C	24	5·8	36·9	30·3	31·8
	female c	24	9·2	47·8	43·5	42·8
Affiliation ×	AC	24	4·3	33·9	26·6	27·6
Competition:	Ac	24	6·9	39·8	36·4	32·3
	aC	24	4·4	32·3	30·9	28·8
	ac	24	5·4	38·4	31·0	32·4
Sex ×	male AC	12	1·8	25·2	22·0	19·0
Affiliation ×	male Ac	12	2·6	32·2	21·2	20·6
Competition:	male aC	12	3·9	33·3	32·6	30·0
	male ac	12	3·6	28·6	26·5	23·2
	female AC	12	6·8	42·5	31·3	36·1
	female Ac	12	11·2	47·6	51·6	44·0
	female aC	12	4·9	31·2	29·2	27·5
	female ac	12	7·2	48·1	35·4	41·7

greater mutuality when the sheer amount of looking is itself held constant. Men's looking, it would seem, is more likely to be characterized by the one-way (stolen?) glance.

When visual interaction is considered in relation to personality and situational variables, the data support neither of the hypotheses presented earlier. Means in Table 1, while showing slight effects in the direction of the *n*-affiliation hypothesis (Hypothesis 1), did not reach significance (Table 2). Similarly, the differences in means of highly affiliative persons in the two competitive conditions were in the direction predicted in Hypothesis 2, but the differences did not reach significance at the 0·05 level.

It is, of course, possible that affiliative tendencies are unrelated to visual behavior. It is also possible that the definition of communion orientation in terms of the ratio of affiliative to achievement responses has confounded the affiliation variable. In actual fact some persons classified as low affiliators had given twice as many affiliation responses than had other persons classified as high affiliators. Indeed, some 15 per cent of the *S*s would have been reclassified if only the median number of affiliation responses had been used as the basis for classification.

Post hoc analyses

In order to explore the possibility that the communion variable was confounded by the operations used to classify *S*s, *S*s were reclassified as follows: (a) *S*s were classified as being affiliatively communion-oriented only if both the number of their affiliation responses and ratio of their affiliation to achievement responses were above the median values recorded for all *S*s. (b) If *S*s fell below the median of both measures, they were located in the non-affiliative group. (c) *S*s who fell in different halves of the two distributions were eliminated from consideration, as were dyadic relationships where both members of the dyad did not meet the revised criterion of communion.

Mean mutuality scores based on the revised method of categorizing *n*-affiliation scores are listed in Table 3. Statistical treat-

1. To simplify presentation, interaction means involving the dyads (or positions) were not listed (no significant interaction effect).

2. Groups of italicized means are those associated with significant effects in the analysis of variance.

Table 2 Analyses of Variance of Various Indexes of Visual Activity[1] Categorized by Sex *n*-Affiliation and Salience of Competition

Variable	df	Mutuality MS	Mutuality F	Listening MS	Listening F	Speaking MS	Speaking F	Total time MS	Total time F
A(sex)	1	688·30	12·73**	1428·97	7·44*	1698·74	11·24**	1246·68	6·05*
B(*n*-affil.)	1	7·85	n.s.	25·31	n.s.	50·79	n.s.	17·60	n.s.
C(competition)	1	134·73	n.s.	398·70	n.s.	590·49	n.s.	271·45	n.s.
D(dyad)	2	21·64	n.s.	998·53	9·75**	318·81	n.s.	525·89	12·40**
A×B	1	285·59	5·28*	189·22	n.s.	776·40	5·14*	660·41	n.s.
A×C	1	71·90	n.s.	253·76	n.s.	774·35	5·12*	314·11	n.s.
A×D	2	18·76	n.s.	40·05	n.s.	123·28	n.s.	88·91	n.s.
B×C	1	9·97	n.s.	0·01	n.s.	160·66	n.s.	28·18	n.s.
B×D	2	8·50	n.s.	25·34	n.s.	19·54	n.s.	69·28	n.s.
C×D	2	21·88	n.s.	49·53	n.s.	22·82	n.s.	2·51	n.s.
A×B×C	1	1·89	n.s.	394·31	n.s.	7·29	n.s.	242·92	n.s.
A×B×D	2	8·29	n.s.	40·88	n.s.	26·29	n.s.	8·69	n.s.
A×C×D	2	6·51	n.s.	10·64	n.s.	55·76	n.s.	15·70	n.s.
B×C×D	2	32·86	n.s.	6·84	n.s.	248·98	n.s.	15·42	n.s.
A×B×C×D	2	1·49	n.s.	282·48	n.s.	207·80	n.s.	29·83	n.s.
E, ABC[2]	24	54·06		192·14		151·10		206·16	
DE, ABC[3]	48	14·68		102·44		105·22		42·41	

1. Percentages listed in Table 1 were given the inverse *sine* transformation (Edwards, 1960).
2. Error term for all A, B, C effects only.   3. Error term for all D effects.
* *p* < 0·05.   ** *p* < 0·01.

Table 3 Mean Index of Mutual Visual Interaction Categorized by Revised *n*-Affiliation Scores, Sex and Salience of Competition (Index = % MVI of total time available)

Affiliation	Sex	Competitive set					
		Salient		Subdued		Mean	N
		$\overline{X}$	N	$\overline{X}$	N		
High	males	1·5	7	3·4	7	2·4[3]	14
	females	4·8	8	11·8	10	8·7[3]	18
	means: comp. by affil.	3·3	15	8·4	17	6·0[1]	32
Low	males	3·0	8	2·8	8	2·9[3]	16
	females	7·6	6	4·5	5	6·2[3]	11
	mean: comp. by affil.	4·9	14	3·5	13	4·2[1]	27
Means for sex by competition	male	2·3	15	3·1	15	2·7[2]	30
	female	6·0	14	9·4	15	7·8[2]	29
Means for competitive set		4·1	29	6·2	30		

1. Means for Affiliation.
2. Means for Sex.
3. Means for Sex by Affiliation.

ment of these data was complicated by the difficulty in carrying out a complex variance analysis given the unequal and disproportionate subcell *n*s resulting from the revised categorization. In addition, in some groups the recategorization eliminated two of the three possible dyadic comparisons, thus making it impossible to calculate the variance attributable to groups within conditions.

In view of the above considerations, the analysis can only be considered suggestive. The graphic method of depicting the nature of an interaction (Edwards, 1960) is admirably suited to such a purpose. By this method, significance is indicated if lines representing the dependent variable means of each level of a given variable cannot be said to be within the limits of random sampling. In Figure 3, the means of Table 3 represent graphically the affiliation × competition interaction, while Figure 4 represents the interaction of *n*-affiliation, sex and competition variables.

In Figure 3 the graphic representation of the effect upon mutual glances of the interaction of two levels of *n*-affiliation and two levels of competition results in lines which are far from parallel. This finding points to the existence of a significant interaction effect, which in fact was found when correction for disproportionality was used in a 2×2 analysis of variance.[6]

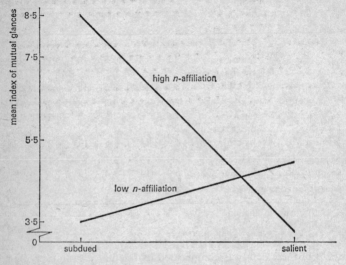

Figure 3   Mean percentage of time spent in mutual visual interaction for each of two levels of *n*-affiliation at two levels of competition

Figure 4 strongly suggests the existence of still a higher order interaction based on the effect of sex. The nature of the deviation from the parallel observed in Figure 3 more closely resembles the deviation characteristic of the female means graphed in Figure 4. The lines representing male means, while certainly not parallel, deviate much less from the parallel than do those for women. Means in Table 3 and the graphs in Figure 4 also demonstrate that sex differences in the amount of mutual visual interactions were not changed by eliminating those persons whose *n*-affiliation scores

6. *F* for *n*-affiliation $\times$ competition $= 7 \cdot 80$, $0 \cdot 01 > p$, *df* 1 and 55.

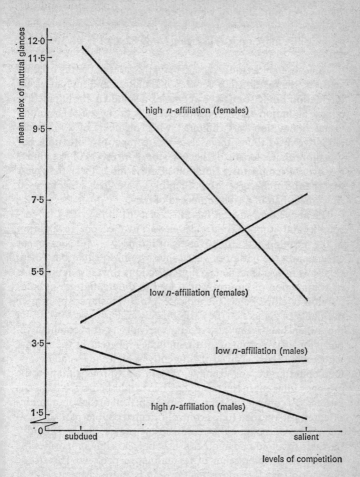

Figure 4   Mean percentage of time each sex spends in mutual visual interaction for each of two levels of *n*-affiliation at two levels of competition

did not meet the revised criteria of classification. A mean index of 7·8 per cent mutuality for women compared to one of 2·7 per cent for men shows that women's behavior is still characterized by significantly more mutual glancing ($t = 9·82, 0·01 > p > 0·001, df$ 57).

Thus, though sex differences remain the same as per the original analysis, the relationship between n-affiliation and mutual visual interaction would seem to be a complex resultant of the interaction of sex, affiliation and competition. The data suggest that mutual visual interaction was inhibited when members of a relatively affiliative dyad found themselves in a competitive situation, but was more characteristic of the behavior of members of less affiliative dyads in competitive situations. Furthermore, the data suggest that the above effects were considerably greater in dyads composed of women than in dyads composed of men.

The above data suggest that there is merit in the view that personality and situational variables *interact* to affect one's evaluation of the meaning and attractiveness of intimacy – with subsequent effects upon the nature of visual interaction. In situations where rivalry is not salient, personal predilections toward relationships of communion or control would lead to differential use of communion-oriented behaviors indicated, in this instance, by greater mutuality of glances on the part of highly affiliative persons. If, on the other hand, the task requires rivalrous (or competitive) behavior, it is possible that the intimacy inherent in the mutual glance would be conceived of differently by high and low affiliators. One could argue, for example, that in a rivalrous situation the intimacy inherent in the mutual glance would be perceived as the intimacy of combat, an intimacy more repellent to the communion-oriented person than to his control-oriented counterpart. In summary, one speculates that competition causes highly affiliative partners to avoid one another's gaze but, possibly, intensifies the mutual visual interaction of less affiliative persons. The strong indication that the above relationship is more characteristic of women than men would serve to underline the basic differences already noted in the visual activity of the two sexes.

Discussion

This study has shown that various aspects of the visual behavior of persons engaged in free discussion can be systematically and accurately recorded. Various patterns of visual interaction were identified and there seems to be considerable evidence to support the view that men and women differ markedly in their visual behavior. Women look at one another more than do men and, once contact has been made, also hold the other's gaze longer than do men. The above findings, plus data which suggest that the interaction of *n*-affiliation and situational factors may well affect the visual behavior of women more than of men, lead one to speculate that the two sexes generally give different weight to the importance of visual phenomena in their social fields. Witkin (1949), for example, has shown women to be consistently more affected than are men by visual cues in establishing their bodily orientation in space. He has also shown that women, more so than men, are affected by the visual structure of the field in which a figure is embedded (1950). The results of the present study suggest that Witkin's findings with respect to sex differences in visual dependence on a physical field may be paralleled by similar sex differences in visual dependence upon objects in a social field. Women, that is, may look at other persons more than do men because they value more highly the kinds of information they can obtain through such activity.

The *post hoc* findings concerning the relatively greater reduction in activity of female high affiliators in a competitive condition do not contradict the above interpretation. They suggest, rather, that women's visual activity is not only more likely to be oriented toward social stimuli than men's, but that it is also more affected by relevant social field conditions. If we assume that competitive situations result in the production of cues of rejection and antagonism, that such cues are often communicated via facial expressions and that highly affiliative persons would be disturbed by the recognition of such cues, then the greater dependence of women on visual stimuli would increase the probability of receiving undesirable stimuli unless the *S* acts to reduce the reception of such. Reduction in the degree to which one engages in mutual glances would seem to be an effective way of cutting down on the reception of such unpleasant information.

The less affiliative person, on the other hand, would seem to respond to the challenge of the competitive situation in a more assertive fashion. Under such conditions the increased visual behavior could be interpreted as reflecting either greater self-assertiveness, greater utility of the information to be gained by looking, or both. These latter points are speculative and will remain so until more data are available. Let us confine ourselves to the observations that men and women differ in the behavior here studied, and to the suggestion that these differences are related to differential dependency on the social field.

This study barely scratches the surface of the meaning of visual interaction in interpersonal relations. While the methodological feasilibity of recording visual interaction seems to have been established, many questions of interpretation exist. Studies toward learning more about the affects on visual interaction of such factors as sex, cultural norms and motives to conceal information are already under way. From these and other studies to follow we may one day see as through a glass, but less darkly, the ramifications of the subtle, yet important, technique of nonverbal communication.

Summary

This study represents an exploratory investigation of patterns and correlates of visual interaction in face-to-face groups. Sixteen groups of three men and sixteen groups of three women, categorized by degree of n-affiliation and further differentiated by the competitiveness of the group setting, were compared along various dimensions of visual interaction recorded while they worked on a group discussion task. Special attention was given the phenomenon of mutual visual interaction, which was assumed to be coordinate with a momentary intimacy. Interrelationships among personal attributes, competitive situations, and mutual glances were tested by visual interaction data which observers recorded on a multichannel operations recorder.

The results showed (a) a rather high degree of agreement among observers who recorded patterns of visual interaction; (b) that women looked significantly more at one another than did men, while speaking, while being spoken to, and when simultaneous glances were measured; and (c) that a first analysis showed sex and n-affiliation interacted to affect mutual glances.

When the bases of assigning persons to n-affiliation categories were revised, the data, while not permitting a ready analysis of interrelations among sex, affiliation and competition effects, strongly suggested that the above three variables interacted to affect the amount of mutual visual interaction recorded. Competition seemed to inhibit mutual glances among high affiliators and increase it among low affiliators. Moreover, the preceding effect appeared to be markedly stronger in the female groups. A *post hoc* analysis suggests that the original method of deriving *n*-affiliation categories disguised the true relationships among the variables cited above.

Sex differences in visual interaction were discussed in relation to Witkin's findings that the availability of visual cues differentially affects the two sexes in their manner of orienting themselves in a physical field. In addition, it was suggested that competitive atmospheres interact with affiliative need to qualify the perceiver's tendencies to seek or avoid communion or challenge.

References

DANIELSON, A., and GIBSON, J. J. (1961), 'Acuity for the perception of being looked at', unpublished manuscript, Cornell University.

DOEHRING, D. G. (1957), 'The relation between manifest anxiety and rate of eyeblink in a stress situation', *USN Sch. Aviat. Med. res. Rep.*, no. 6.

EDWARDS, A. L. (1960), *Experimental Design in Psychological Research*, Holt, Rinehart & Winston, rev. edn.

EXLINE, R. V. (1960), 'Effects of sex, norms, and affiliation motivation upon accuracy of interpersonal preferences', *J. Personal.*, vol. 28, pp. 397–412.

EXLINE, R. V. (1962), 'Effects of need for affiliation, sex, and the sight of others upon initial communications in problem-solving groups', *J. Personal.*, vol. 30, pp. 541–56.

FRENCH, E. G. (1955), 'Development of a measure of complex motivation', unpublished manuscript, Personnel Research Laboratory, Lackland Air Force Base, Texas.

HEIDER, F. (1958), *The Psychology of Interpersonal Relations*, Wiley.

KANFER, F. H. (1960), 'Verbal rate, eye blink, and content in structured psychiatric interviews', *J. abnorm. soc. Psychol.*, vol. 61, pp. 341–7.

KRASNER, L. A. (1958), 'A technique for investigating the relationship between the behavior cues of the examiner and the verbal behavior of the patient', *J. consult. Psychol.*, vol. 22, pp. 364–6.

MANN, H. B., and WHITNEY, D. R. (1947), 'On a test of whether one o two random variables is stochastically larger than the other', *Ann. Math. Stat.*, vol. 18, pp. 50–60.

REUSCH, J., and KEES, W. (1959), *Nonverbal Communication*, University of California Press.

RUCKMICK, C. A. (1921), 'A preliminary study of the emotions',
Psychol. Monogr., vol. 30, no. 3, pp. 30–35.

SCHEUTZ, A. (1948), 'Sartre's theory of the alter ego', *Philos. Phenomenol.
Res.*, vol. 9, pp. 181–99.

SIMMEL, G. (1921), 'Sociology of the senses: visual interaction',
in R. E. Park and E. W. Burgess (eds.), *Introduction to the Science
of Sociology*, University of Chicago Press.

WITKIN, H. A. (1949), 'Sex differences in perception', *Trans. N. Y. Acad.
Sci.*, vol. 12, pp. 22–6.

WITKIN, H. A. (1950), 'Individual differences in ease of perception of
embedded figures', *J. Personal.*, vol. 19, pp. 1–15.

WOODWORTH, R. S. (1938), *Experimental Psychology*, Holt.

Part Four Social Roles

The concept of 'role' has a very long history, being one of those terms which the social sciences have taken over from everyday usage. Even by social scientists the term has been used in a number of distinguishable ways as Reading 10, by Gross, Mason and McEachern, shows. Clarification of the kind provided by Gross has been a high priority, since almost any model of group behavior is built around the notion that different group members behave in different ways in response to one another.

The research reported by Kahn *et al.* (Reading 11) examines the bases upon which managers attempt to influence one another's role performance. Their findings confirm Gross's view that role consensus is not always high and they go on to examine what managers do when faced with role conflict and ambiguity.

Slater's paper (Reading 12) reports part of a project initiated by R. F. Bales, whose goal was to examine the differentiation of roles in small temporary laboratory groups. The results show that, as expected, two sorts of role were differentiated in the group, one concerned with achieving the group's task and the other with maintaining harmonious relations in the group. Bales and his co-workers hypothesized that such differentiation occurs in all groups, including for example the husband–wife role differentiation in family groups. Later work has shown that task–social role differentiation is not always found in natural groups, but it is certainly true that the degree to which 'task' and 'socio-emotional' roles are differentiated are fundamental to how the groups operate. This has proved particularly true in the study of leadership, with which Reading 13 is concerned.

The experiment by Lewin, Lippitt and White (1939) concerning the effects of different leader roles on boy's clubs has led to a great deal of empirical research. But not all workers have obtained results showing that participative or democratic leadership roles are more effective. In particular, Fiedler has shown that the effectiveness of a leader's role depends on several factors. After a reading of earlier selections it need be no surprise that the nature of the task looms large among these factors. The Fiedler model improves on the participative model not by proving it wrong, but by specifying the boundaries of its applicability.

De Charms, Carpenter and Kuperman (Reading 14) show that the existence of role consensus in a group in fact makes it more difficult to describe a group member, since one has less information available concerning him. Where a group member acts 'out of role', i.e. as an 'origin' of his behaviour rather than as a 'pawn' of his role specification, others feel they know him better. Such findings may help to account for the superiority of participative leadership under some conditions.

Reference

LEWIN, K., LIPPITT, R., and WHITE, R. K. (1939), 'An experimental study of leadership and group life', reprinted in H. Proshansky and B. Seidenberg (eds.), *Basic Studies in Social Psychology*, Holt, Rinehart & Winston, 1965.

10 N. E. Gross, W. S. Mason and A. W. McEachern

The Postulate of Role Consensus

Excerpt from N. E. Gross, W. S. Mason and A. W. McEachern, *Explorations in the School Superintendency Role*, Wiley, 1958, pp. 21–47.

Involved in many, but not all, formulations of the role concept in the social science literature is the assumption that consensus exists on the expectations applied to the incumbents of particular social positions. It is this postulate that we now propose to examine in the fields of cultural anthropology, social psychology and sociology.

The interest anthropologists have in 'roles' and 'role expectations' is to a large extent dependent on their interest in 'cultures'. Since their treatment of the concepts of 'culture' and 'role' are similarly interdependent, it is necessary in examining the postulate of role consensus to consider initially some aspects of the treatment anthropologists have given the culture concept. 'Culture' has been a central conceptual tool of anthropologists in their description and analysis of ethnographic data. Some have been concerned primarily with the dynamics of culture, an interest which is evidenced by the nineteenth century theories of unilinear cultural and social evolution and by the current interest in such problems as innovation in culture (Barnett, 1953), difficulties involved in introducing cultural change (Spicer, 1952), and the analysis of changing values (Vogt, 1951).

A growing emphasis in recent anthropological work, however, tends to be on culture as a variable exerting an impact on other phenomena such as personality, national character, motivation, perception, cognition, language, sexual behavior and abnormal behavior.[1] Culture is most frequently viewed as an independent variable whereas the other listed phenomena are treated as dependent. These problems suggest the increasing liaison between cultural anthropology and psychology, especially psychoanalytic psychology.

1. For a review of each of these research areas see C. Kluckhohn (1954).

In addition to being central in these special problem areas, culture is the key construct overlying the continuing descriptive ethnological work of anthropologists. As Murdock (1954, p. 21) says,

whatever special problems he may go to the field to investigate, [the anthropologist] is expected to bring back and publish, not only an answer to his special problem, but also a descriptive account, as complete as he can make it, of the entire culture of the people studied.

It can be said that the concept of culture is embedded in nearly every major problem that has attracted the attention of cultural anthropologists since Klemm.

Cultural anthropology, like sociology and psychology, has its semantic problems. Just as sociologists disagree among themselves about the meanings of such terms as 'group' and 'institution', and just as psychologists engage in semantic disputes over the denotation of 'personality', so have anthropoligsts quarreled among themselves over the definition of culture. C. Kluckhohn, in quoting from his and Kroeber's extensive and critical review of the concept of culture (1954, p. 923) says that,

most social scientists now formulate the concept of culture approximately as follows: culture consists of patterns, explicit and implicit, of and for behavior acquired and transmitted by symbols, constituting the distinctive achievement of human groups, including their embodiments in artifacts; the essential core of culture consists of traditional (i.e. historically derived and selected) ideas and especially their attached values; culture systems may, on the one hand, be considered as products of action, on the other hand as conditioning elements of further action.

In elaborating on this formulation Kluckhohn notes that anthropologists are concerned with pattern analysis, '... the interrelation of parts and of their relation to the whole' in addition to a listing of cultural traits. It is emphasized that 'culture is not behavior ...' but that it emerges from and returns to behavior. He distinguishes two related but different ways in which anthropologists use 'culture (1954, p. 924)'.

On the one hand, 'culture' denotes a logical construct, the network of abstracted patterns generalized by the anthropologist to represent the regularities distinctive of the group in question. On the other hand, 'culture' designates these patterns or 'norms' as internalized by the individuals making up the group.

Kluckhohn also describes three parts of aspects of culture (1954, p. 925):

Part of culture consists in norms for and modalities in behavior. Another part consists in ideologies justifying or rationalizing certain ways of behaving. Finally, every culture includes broad general principles of selectivity and ordering ('highest common factors') in terms of which patterns *of* and *for* behavior are reducible to parsimonious generalizations.

Smith (1954, p. 40), from the viewpoint of psychology, has also noted certain consistencies in the anthropologist's usage of culture:

'Culture' in the abstract is a generalization from 'cultures', while a culture is itself an abstract concept ascribed to some identified social group. The important components of current usage would seem to include (a) a conception of shared ways of behaving, predispositions to behavior, and (perhaps) products of behavior, and (b) the restriction that if something is a part of culture, it is learned – transmitted socially rather than biologically.

According to Smith (1954, p. 40), culture is not a theory, but simply a concept.

The term itself [culture] embodies no articulated propositions from which consequences can be drawn and put to test. It asserts nothing about reality. The psychologist who turns to anthropology after studying his lessons in the logic of science may therefore show some surprise when he encounters statements about the importance of the concept as an anthropological contribution.

Why has the construct of culture, then, had an impact on the sciences concerned with social man? Smith's observation on its influence in psychology is cogent (1954, pp. 40–41):

With the *concept* of culture goes an *orientation*, if not a theory, that a very wide range of human phenomena is cultural in nature. The importance of the concept rests, then, in the host of assertions in which it occurs, to the effect that phenomena x, y, z, etc. are cultural in origin, or are influenced in specific ways by culture.

The concept of culture has forced psychologists to broaden their frame of reference to include extrapersonal, in addition to intrapersonal forces, in explanations of personality and individual behavior. Although Murdock has observed that the concept of culture is as indigenous to sociology as to anthropology, as seen, for example, in Sumner's (1906) concepts of *folkways* and *mores*, certain ideas in anthropology such as cultural relativism have had considerable impact through their destruction of many social science ethnocentric and monolithic theories. The anthropologist's emphasis on variability in cultures in different societies has also resulted in a growing recognition among sociologists that, usually, their generalizations may be limited to, at most, a single culture.

Deeply embedded in the 'culture' or ideology of anthropologists is the belief that one of their major tasks, if not their primary one, is to uncover the covert behavior patterns or 'blueprints for behavior' of the society they study. Just as a detective feels he must find the motive if he is to resolve a crime, so the anthropologist feels he must isolate culture patterns if he is to make sense out of the myriad bits of behavior he observes in a particular society. It is for these regularities in social behavior that he searches. To state that anthropologists are concerned with isolating the culture or behavior patterns for a society is not, however, to present an unequivocal description of what a specific anthropologist does.

That 'culture' is frequently used by anthropologists in ambiguous ways is pointed out by Linton in his warning to psychologists about the pitfalls to be avoided in using the concept. He says (1945, pp. 42–3; Gross, Mason and McEachern's italics):

In their attempts to use this concept [culture] as a tool for research even the anthropologists sometimes become confused. Thus they frequently fail to distinguish even in their descriptive studies between cultures as they exist through time and cultures as they exist at a particular point in time, although these two aspects of the concept present different problems and call for somewhat different methods of approach. ... Of much greater importance to the psychologist is the anthropologist's almost constant failure to distinguish clearly between the *reality of a culture as a configuration of behaviors*, and so on, and *the construct which he develops on the basis of this reality* and uses as a tool for the description and manipulation of cultural data. The lack of a terminology which will serve to distinguish clearly between these two aspects of the culture concept has been a source of endless trouble not only to psychologists and anthropologists but also to those logicians and philosophers who have attempted to deal with the culture concept.

To distinguish among these ideas Linton (1945, p. 43) introduced the terms *real culture, real culture patterns, culture construct* and *total culture construct*. The real culture of a society '... consists of the actual behavior, and so on, of its members. It includes a vast number of elements, no two of which are identical.'

Despite this uniqueness, however, Linton suggests that there is a patterning among the multitude of behavioral items that constitute the real culture of a society. They can be initially categorized by the situations in which they usually occur, and they fall within a definable range (1945, pp. 44–5):

Moreover, the variations in such a series will ordinarily be found to fall within certain easily recognizable limits. ... Behaviors which fall within the effective range [bring the desired results] will be considered normal, while those which fall outside of it will be regarded as queer and, frequently, as reprehensible.

These ranges of normal behaviors to given situations he designates as 'patterns within the real culture'. A real culture '... may be conceived of as a configuration composed of a great number of such patterns all of which are, in greater or less degree, mutually adjusted and functionally interrelated.' (Linton, 1945, p. 45). Linton then makes a statement which has been unfortunately overlooked by many students who have been concerned with culture patterning in a society (1945, p. 45): 'The important thing to remember is that each of the *real culture patterns* is not a single item of behavior but a series of behaviors varying within certain limits.'

After observing that it would be impossible to list or describe all the behavioral items which make up the real culture and pointing out that anthropology needs some type of summary device for descriptive and analytic purposes, he introduces the concepts of *culture construct* and *total culture construct*. The former

establishes the *mode* of the finite series of variations which are included within each of the real culture patterns and then uses this mode as a symbol for the real cultural patterns. ... The *total culture construct* is developed by combining all the culture construct patterns which have been developed in this way. ... Although the culture construct may not be in exact correspondence with the real culture at any point, it provides a brief and convenient approximation of the conditions existing within the real culture (1945, pp. 45–6; Gross, Mason and McEachern's italics).

Cultural constructs are modal behaviors and a total culture construct is a series of *modes* abstracted from a series of real culture patterns. Both ignore the variance in the distribution of behaviors found in particular situations.

Linton, then, was certainly aware, as are most anthropologists, that in any given situation the observer will probably find a range of behaviors. He apparently assumed, however, that the distribution of behaviors for a specific situation in a society usually has a single mode, and this assumed mode he defined as a cultural construct. For many situations this assumption of unimodality is undoubtedly reasonable, but to maintain, as Linton apparently does, that most real culture patterns are unimodal is to state a tenuous assumption. It minimizes the importance of the possibility that for some situations there may be bimodal, trimodal or multimodal behavioral distributions. In a society with clearly differentiated social strata such as castes, classes, ethnic or religious social categorizations, one might expect to find with some regularity multimodal distributions. In a society undergoing rapid social change unimodal tendencies might not be expected in many real culture patterns. In one characterized by sharp internal cleavages bimodalities might be anticipated. These hypotheses are clearly as tenable on a priori grounds as the unimodal one.

The emphasis on unimodality also tends to dismiss variable behavior surrounding the modal category or categories, assuming they exist, as simply deviant behavior. Such behavior *may* represent evidence for the existence of subcultures. It may be indicative of the existence or the emergence of cleavages, strains or conflicts in the social structure. It may provide clues for the prediction of social and cultural change in the society. As Inkeles and Levinson (1954, p. 1015) suggest for national character studies, it may reveal that a particular society contains multimodal personalities or no modal personalities at all, in contrast to a single modal personality.

The postulate of unimodal behavioral distributions is a hypothesis that can be and should be empirically examined, not a 'given' to be taken for granted. Perhaps major advances in anthropological theory may result from a shift in focus from 'central tendencies' in behavior to variability in behavior *within* a single society.

Deriving from the basic conception of 'culture' is the anthropological treatment of consensus on evaluative standards in a society. Although Linton, for example, recognized variability in the behavior of position incumbents he assumed that there was consensus among the members of a society on the behavior *expected* for at least some position incumbents. These he termed *ideal patterns*. Whereas *real culture patterns* refers to a distribution of behaviors of the members of a society in a particular situation and a *culture construct* has reference to the mode of that distribution, *ideal culture patterns*

are abstractions which have been developed by the members of a society themselves. They represent the consensus of opinion on the part of the society's members as to how people should behave in particular situations.... The extent to which such ideal patterns have been developed will vary greatly in different societies.... However, no group ever develops ideal patterns of behavior corresponding to all situations.... *In general, ideal patterns appear to be developed most frequently with respect to those situations which a society regards as of primary importance and particularly with respect to those involving the interaction of individuals in different positions in the social system* (Linton, 1945, pp. 52–3; Gross, Mason and McEachern's italics).

Culture, then, could be said to include the patterning of actual behavior and the patterning of evaluative standards for behavior. In C. Kluckhohn's words (1954, p. 924):

'*Patterns of* and *for* behavior' means that both what people do and what they say they do or should do are taken into account. Culture encompasses both 'designs for living' and the abstracted patterns of regularities in actual living.

For Murdock, however, patterned behavior apparently refers only to ideal behavior patterns. In discussing what an outside observer in a foreign culture must do to understand the behavior of the people, he says (1954, p. 22; Gross, Mason and McEachern's italics):

His first task is to make those norms explicit. The inevitable result has been that anthropologists have devoted their primary attention to *patterned behavior*, i.e. *to those norms which are verbalized as the ideals to which behavior should conform*, are taught to each oncoming generation, and are enforced by the formal and the informal punishment of deviation.

How do anthropologists go about isolating these 'ideal patterns' (Linton), or 'patterned behavior' (Murdock), or 'patterns for behavior' (Kluckhohn)? Whereas the real culture constructs or the modes of behavioral distributions are found by observing actual behavior, these 'ideal patterns', since they are presumed to be in people's heads, are isolated by asking people what they are. According to Murdock (1954, p. 22):

Any member of the society knows a large proportion of these norms, whether or not they govern his own behavior, for the norms incumbent upon persons in other statuses constitute an aspect of his expectations in his social interaction with them. To gain an accurate account of patterned behavior, therefore, an ethnographer needs only a few competent informants, selected judiciously but not necessarily in accordance with any standard sampling technique.

That there are difficulties in such interviews is suggested by Linton's observation on operational procedures (1945, p. 52):

Even in the most analytically minded and culture conscious societies the investigator finds again and again that informants are quite unable to tell what the proper behavior in a particular situation would be and have to fall back on relating what happened on various occasions when this situation arose.

Kluckhohn's comments on the methods used to isolate implicit patterns suggest that the anthropologist engage in 'inference' to invoke them (1954, p. 924; Gross, Mason and McEachern's italics).

Here the anthropologist *infers* least common denominators which seem, as it were, to underlie a multiplicity of culture content. Only in the most sophisticated and self-conscious of cultures will his attention be called directly to these by the carriers of the culture, and then only in part.

A statistically oriented social scientist might be upset by Murdock's description of his procedure, especially in view of the following comment by Linton on the anthropologist's problems in psychological testing and recording covert culture (1945, pp. 39–40; Gross, Mason and McEachern's italics):

The problem of establishing the covert patterns within a culture is much the same as that of ascertaining the content and organization of an individual's personality, and investigations are subject to the same sources of error....It is almost impossible to make this a true random sample. The individuals with whom the field worker is brought into contact are not mere units in a statistical table but *actual people whose reactions to the investigator will be as varied as those of persons in our own society.* ... There is thus a very real, if unconscious, selection of subjects which introduces a margin of error when one attempts to refer the test results to the society as a whole.

Some interesting consequences are suggested by considering the conceptualization of ideal culture patterns in conjunction with operations used to isolate them. In the first place, the concept of ideal culture patterns implies that the members of a society have in actuality developed a 'consensus of opinion' in regard to some situations 'involving the interaction of individuals in different positions in the social system' (Linton, 1945, p. 53). This is simply accepted as a postulate by many anthropologists and, since they assume that there is a 'consensus' they invariably isolate 'agreed upon' ideal culture patterns. But the idea of consensus on the evaluative standards for the incumbents of a position is clearly subject to empirical examination. Whether or not there is consensus on the behavior expected of position incumbents, or how much consensus there is, are evidently empirical questions, since 'consensus' describes an empirical condition of agreement among a number of people.

Linton indicates that age, sex and family positions of a society are those on which we can typically expect to find agreement. But the few empirical studies on the degree of agreement on the evaluative standards applicable to the female position in American society all conclude that there is a high degree of disagreement among the role definers used.[2] If it is argued that the demonstrated lack of consensus on this position is a function of a complicated industrialized society, then we might consider anthropological studies of less complicated societies. Lewis in his study of Tepoztlan (1949, p. 610) concludes that:

The picture of village life which emerges from our material is therefore quite different from the idealized, almost Rousseauan version of Tepoztlan conveyed by the earlier study of the village by Robert Redfield and later elaborated by Stuart Chase.

2. The relevant studies are Komarovsky (1946), Rose (1951) and Wallin (1950).

Lewis interprets his data as revealing a wide disparity between actual and ideal behavior. It is suggests that an equally if not more acceptable interpretation of Lewis' data is that there is a lack of consensus on ideal patterns on the role definition of husband and wife among older and younger women and between women and men in the village.

Murdock, assuming consensus, makes the following statement (1954, p. 22; Gross, Mason and McEachern's italics):

The situation is quite otherwise when a scientist is studying his own society and is writing up his results for other members of the same society. He and his readers, as participants, already *know* the major norms of the culture, and it would be trite to detail them.

This is a remarkable assertion in view of the manifold 'subcultures' in American society, its high divorce rate, union–management conflict, North–South differences concerning desegregation in schools and housing, and the conflicting views found in most 'readers' columns' in newspapers on the roles of the husband, wife, and child in American society. Perhaps these differences are incidental to the 'major norms' to which Murdock was referring, but they can hardly be considered incidental to American society.

Just as the concept of the 'culture construct' has tended to focus attention on modal behavior with the result that non-modal behaviors are ignored, so has the postulate of consensus on ideal culture patterns tended to result in the ignoring of the possible complexities in the evaluative standards that the members of a society have internalized. The result has been lack of concern for the possibility of pluralistic ideal patterns and for those situations which position incumbents face that are characterized by incompatible standards. The possible reality of subcultural patterning has been overshadowed by the assumed actuality of a unicultural patterning. The concept of ideal pattern has similarly tended to block the use of 'normative data' to penetrate dynamic problems of cultures – their inconsistencies, their cleavages and their internal strains.

Smith has observed that the usual anthropological analysis of an entire culture is conducted by one or two field workers who live in the society a relatively short period of time and that, in consequence, '... the field worker is forced into bold extrapolations if he aspires to any synthetic characterization of the culture as a whole' (Smith, 1954, p. 37). We referred earlier to the differences between Lewis' and Redfield's description of the culture of Tepoztlan. Margaret Mead observes (quoted in C. Kluckhohn, 1954, p. 965), concerning the anthropologist's interviewing skills, 'Each informant is evaluated individually against a wide knowledge (on the part of the interviewer) of the culture of the informant, the social structure of which the informant is a part, and the particular subject about which the informant is being interviewed.'

Margaret Mead's comments suggest a possible compounding of the bias of initial nonrandom selection of respondents through the addition of the bias of pre-judgement of their responses. Waller (1932) tells us that if we ask teachers and mothers how a teacher should behave toward a child we will obtain different responses. If we ask principals and teachers the same question, we probably would obtain more similar responses. The population of role definers may be a significant factor in the degree of consensus on evaluative standards an investigator finds.

In view of these methodological difficulties it is not surprising that intuitively plausible accounts of the ideal patterns of a society by anthropologists are sometimes viewed as artistic rather than scientific formulations. If ideal patterns are internalized norms then it is reasonable to expect that investigators will use as their basic source of data the responses of the individuals who have presumably internalized them. But Linton and Kluckhohn suggest that respondents frequently cannot verbalize them even though the investigator can. Although intuition and reconstruction have their place in science, they are acceptable only when consistent with reliable and valid empirical evidence. It is frequently difficult to accept inferred ideal patterns as valid. Plausible findings and valid findings deserve to be distinguished from one another.

If these critical observations are reasonable, they imply the need for systematic research on the degree of consensus on evaluative standards in a society – especially for the examination of consensus on role definition. Linton's formulation of the role concept blocks such inquiries because built into its definition is the postulate that there is role consensus. It will be recalled that he defines a role as '... the sum total of the culture patterns associated with a particular status. It thus includes the attitudes, values and behavior ascribed by the society to any and all persons occupying this status' (Linton, 1945, p. 77). It is the phrase 'ascribed by society' that contains the postulate of consensus. The untested assumption is that the members of a society hold the same expectations for incumbents of the same position.

This conceptualization of role does not allow for the investigation of the impact of variant and dominant orientations on role definition which Florence Kluckhohn (1953) suggests operate in any society. If individuals hold variant orientations this should be expressed in variant definitions of a role as well as in different behavior. This implies that one of the factors accounting for different role behavior may be variant role definitions, a possibility completely ignored by the postulate of role consensus. Nor is this postulate compatible with some of Roberts's empirical findings (1951, p. 77):

It can be concluded that, in so far as this survey of three closely similar Ramah Navaho households is concerned, the hypothesis that every small group defines an independent and unique group-ordered culture has been supported.

For certain types of anthropological problems purposive sampling procedures are, of course, appropriate. However, for the isolation of the ideal culture patterns of a society it is suggested that random samples of the members of a society may be needed to investigate the degree of consensus on the evaluative standards applied by the *members* of the society to the behavior of position incumbents.

The concept of ideal cultural patterns implies a hypothesis which, like all hypotheses, deserves testing, not the manipulation of operational procedures to insure that it cannot be rejected. Perhaps organism-centered as well as culture-centered conceptual schemes are needed in cultural anthropology which embrace the role definitions of particular individuals rather than, or as well as, the assumed consensus of a population of individuals.[3]

3. See Whiting and Child (1953), for a conceptual scheme that attempts to bring 'culture' down to the individual level. For the implication of the analysis of consensus on culture patterns for personality and culture studies, see Inkeles and Levinson (1954). It is of further interest to note that Clyde Kluckhohn raised the sampling and variability in culture pattern problems as early as 1939. See C. Kluckhohn (1939).

Such an orientation to the problem of role consensus suggests a series of theoretical questions that anthropologists have tended to ignore: how much consensus on what behaviors is required for a society to maintain itself? How much disagreement can a society tolerate in what areas? To what extent do different sets of role definers hold the same role definitions of key positions in a society? On what aspects of role definition do members of different 'subcultures' in a society agree and disagree? To what extent is deviant behavior a function of deviant role definitions? Why do members of a society differ in their role definitions? Each of these questions suggests that systematic research on role consensus may be of importance for the development of cultural anthropology.

Acceptance of the postulate of consensus on role definition has not been restricted to the discipline of cultural anthropology but may also be found in the writings of social psychologists and sociologists, especially those who have been influenced by Linton. An examination of its involvement in the work of certain social psychologists and the background from which it developed is instructive. We shall consider two psychologists who have made substantial contributions to the area of social psychology.

The development of 'psychological' social psychology was largely a consequence of a recognition that the inclusion of only intrapersonal variables in the analysis of personality and individual behavior limited the phenomena for which adequate theories could be developed. Although there were numerous obstacles to the diffusion of sociological and anthropological insights, theoretical ideas, and empirical findings to psychology, gradually some of them permeated the frameworks of certain influential psychologists (Newcomb, 1954). The most important general contribution of sociology was perhaps, as Newcomb has suggested, '... nothing less than the necessity of coming to terms with the ineluctable fact of groups' (1954, p. 233).

That human behavior is in part a function of the actions and reactions of other members of the multiple social systems in which the individual lives and behaves and that it is influenced by normative or evaluative standards are basic notions of sociology and anthropology. The diffusion of these ideas, found in the writings of such men as Cooley (1922), Linton (1936, 1945), Mead (1934),

Sapir (see Mandelbaum, 1949) and Thomas and Znaniecki (1918), into psychology was greatly facilitated by the research and writings of such psychologists as Lewin (1935, 1951), Newcomb (1943), Piaget (1932), and Sherif (1936). The formulations they proposed for examining the phenomena of personality and individual behavior included, explicitly or implicitly, the ideas of social structure and culture. They recognized that extrapersonal influences had to be taken into account. These psychologists were influential in pointing out the importance for many problems of treating the actions of an individual as *interactions*, that the 'social self' was largely derivative of the history of interactions of the individual, and that human behavior is influenced by the 'norms' of the society and the groups of which the individual is a member.

From the standpoint of the postulate of role consensus perhaps one of the most significant aspects of this diffusion process was that with it went the acceptance by some psychologists of the notion of ideal cultural patterns in the conceptual scheme of Linton, and especially of his concepts of status and role. The reason for the acceptance of Linton's concepts is not surprising. As Murdock has said (1954, p. 19), Linton clearly and concisely articulated the key idea of the 'functional' school in anthropology '… that cultures and subcultures are organically related to the structured social groups and subgroups that carry them, which has been axiomatic in sociology at least since the days of Sumner.'

Murdock (1954, pp. 19–20) also makes the point that: 'Utterly incredible as it must seem to the psychologist and sociologist, it is nevertheless almost literally true that no work by an American anthropologist recognized this fact until the appearance of Linton's *The Study of Man* in 1936.' In addition, in his collaboration with Kardiner and in his analysis of the relationship between culture and personality (Linton, 1945), Linton demonstrated that his concepts were useful for the study of personality.

In short, Linton's conceptualization of status and role related the basic ideas of social structure and culture in a form in which they could be readily assimilated into existing socio-psychological conceptual schemes. It brought culture and social structure down to the individual level, to the level of analysis at which the psychologist feels most comfortable in developing theory and treating data. The relevance of the broad, and to many psychologists the vague, ideas of culture and social organization to their problems became more evident.

One of the psychologists who has clearly recognized the potential contributions of sociology and anthropology to the analysis of an individual's values, attitudes, and behavior is Newcomb. He views social psychology as a quasi-separate discipline focusing on the individual and his behavior in a sociocultural matrix. Although he recognizes that for some problems it is relevant for the psychologist to study human behaviors as 'functions of persons' (Newcomb,1954) without regard to interpersonal and cultural influences, and that for others it is meaningful to study individual behavior without regard to intrapersonal influences, it is his position that many human behavior problems demand a frame of reference containing both sets of factors. For him, this is the special province of social psychology. In developing a framework for this synthetic point of view, Newcomb thinks of the term role as a central concept. Since he has developed one of the most carefully designed sets of 'role' concepts in social psychology and since his constructs are based on Linton's conceptualization, it is instructive to examine how role consensus is treated in his work.

That Newcomb's conceptual formulation is based on Linton's definitions of status and role is clear (Newcomb, 1950, p. 280):

The ways of behaving which are expected of any individual who occupies a certain position constitute the *role* (or, as many writers use the term, social role) associated with that position. ... A position, as Linton's term 'status' implies, is something static; it is a place in a structure, recognized by members of the society and accorded by them to one or more individuals. A role, on the other hand, is something dynamic; it refers to the *behavior* of the occupants of a position – not to all their behavior, as persons, but to what they do *as occupants of the position.*

It is of parenthetical interest to observe that in this quotation from Newcomb there is an example of the ambiguity frequently found in the literature over the differentiation between expected behavior and actual behavior of position incumbents [see ch. 2 of *Explorations in the School Superintendency Role*, pp. 11–15]. In the first sentence 'role' is defined as 'expected ways of behaving'. In the last one it is defined as actual behavior of position incumbents, 'to what they do *as occupants of the position*'.

Newcomb's treatment of the consensus problem in his *Social*

Psychology might best be described as one of ambivalence toward the postulate of role consensus. At one point he says: 'Both behavior standards and norms for perceiving people are shared by *all* members of any group, but they apply in distinctive ways to different members of the group, depending upon how these members are classified' (Newcomb, 1950, p. 276; Gross, Mason and McEachern's italics). This would seem to imply that he assumes consensus on role definition. A similar implication might be taken from his discussion of Merton's analysis of the bureaucratic structure (1950, p. 278; Gross, Mason and McEachern's italics, except for last example),

each position carries with it *definite prescriptions* toward behaving toward other persons in related positions. Thus, the position of mother carries with it the implication of *certain ways of behaving* toward children, just as the position of store clerk carries with it certain ways of behaving toward customers, toward employers, and toward other clerks. Such ways of behaving toward others, which are *defined* for different positions, are called *roles*. ...

Yet, on the other hand, at certain points in Newcomb's discussion he appears to be aware of the possibility of lack of consensus on positional expectations. In introducing the concept of role prescription ('a limited set of behaviors, "tied together" by a common understanding of the functions of a position', Newcomb, 1950, p. 282) he says: 'Roles thus represent ways of carrying out the functions for which positions exist – ways which are *generally agreed upon* within whatever group recognizes any particular position and role' (1950, p. 281). In this statement there would seem to be at least some room for disagreement among group members, and therefore, one could infer, recognition of the possibility of imperfect consensus.

In his discussion of possible operational definitions of a prescribed role, Newcomb (1950, p. 282) most clearly gives recognition to the possibility of lack of consensus among role definers:

For example, determining what is included in a mother's prescribed role in a specific society would involve obtaining the following kinds of information from a representative sample of all the people in that society who recognize that particular position: (a) a list of behaviors which are expected of mothers – such as nursing infants, protecting children from danger, or teaching them table manners; (b) information as to whether each behavior on the list is demanded or is merely permitted of mothers. A criterion of 50 per cent agreement that any given behavior is demanded of all mothers ... might be set up. In that case, the prescribed role would consist of all the behaviors which were considered by at least half of the respondents to be demanded of all mothers.

Although this is only an illustration of an operational definition of a prescribed role, one could maintain that 50 per cent is as good a criterion of disagreement as agreement. It would also seem reasonable to at least consider what the other 50 per cent felt before defining a role according to the 50 per cent of respondents who agree.

On the next page of his discussion, however, he says that roles are 'ready made'. The following quotation suggests the postulate of consensus.

Very few young men in any society have to use an encyclopedia to learn about either their future roles as husbands or those of their future wives. Their brides are similarly familiar, long before marriage, with most aspects of their roles as wives, as well as those of their husbands. If the marriage of any particular couple 'fails', it is not likely to be merely because of the strangeness of their prescribed roles. It is apt to be, as Burgess and Cottrell have shown, because the personality of one or both of them is such that special demands, not necessarily included in the prescribed role are made which the other spouse is unable or unwilling to meet.

In this statement we see an example of the reasoning that is likely to follow the assumption of consensus. The assumption is that there is consensus among the members in the society who recognize the positions of husband and wife. The reason a marriage breaks up is 'apt to be' that one or both of the position incumbents because of 'personality reasons' have 'inappropriate' expectations for the other's behavior to which the marriage partner will not conform.

But another explanation of the 'break-up' might be that there is a lack of consensus between the position incumbents as to what constitutes the 'prescribed roles' of wife or husband. The position incumbents themselves are part of 'the population' of the definers of the position. Furthermore, one of the reasons for this lack of consensus could be that the husband comes from a religious-ethnic segment in the society in which there is consensus on the expectation that a husband should be the only breadwinner in the family, regardless of the size of the loaf. On the other hand, his wife's religious-ethnic 'group' might be one in which a wife is expected to work the first few years of marriage. In short, there may be a lack of consensus on the expectations attached to the positions of husband and wife between different segments of a population of role definers.

It is interesting that the postulate of consensus seems to enter into Newcomb's discussion primarily when he is considering the phenomena of social structure and culture at a fairly abstract level. In his consideration of possible operations to delineate a role or a prescribed role the postulate of consensus appears to assume lesser importance.

It should be emphasized that we have examined Newcomb's formulation of role in his *Social Psychology* (1950) only from the viewpoint of his treatment of role consensus. It is only fair to state that from other vantage points his formulation represents a clear advance over earlier schemes. For example, his concepts of *prescribed role* and *role behavior* distinguish clearly between the expected and the actual behavior of a position incumbent. He also emphasized that to divorce a position from other positions with which it is related is to lose much of the potential heuristic value of the concept.

One other example of the treatment of role consensus by a psychologist is worthy of consideration in illustrating the more or less uncritical acceptance of the postulate of role consensus. Sherif, under the influence of Sapir, Kroeber and Rivers, was one of the first psychologists to argue for the inclusion of the concept of norms in psychological theory. His research on the influence of social interaction on perception and on the development of social norms was of considerable importance in diffusing socio-cultural ideas in psychology. Sherif appears not only to have accepted the postulate of consensus in role definition but also to have gone a long way beyond most anthropologists in assuming absolute conformity. In discussing the individual's 'role' in society, he says (Sherif, 1936, pp. 187–8):

Every kind of *status* places the individual in definite relationship to other individuals, whereby his duties, responsibilities and privileges are prescribed within that social order. Once he is *there*, in a particular status, he has no choice, but fulfils the requirements demanded of the status. And he may (this is the general case) fulfil the requirements with the good natured complacency typical of many a bourgeois gentleman, even with an air of originality, as if he were the first one to accomplish those things.

There are signs, however, that there is growing recognition that the analysis of role consensus is an important theoretical area of inquiry for social psychology. In a statement on research that is needed to achieve better articulation between sociology and psychology, Newcomb (1954, p. 255) emphasized the need for 'conceptual and operational refinement' of the concept 'consensus' in role and communication research. In their review of 'psychological aspects of social structure', Riecken and Homans (1954, p. 788) consider certain hypotheses in which consensus on norms is and is *not* assumed. For example, in discussing factors possibly related to the development of group consensus they observe: 'The norms of members probably become more similar with time, but there seem to be no empirical studies of this relationship.' The different role definitions of stewards held by workers, foremen, and shop stewards, and the implications of these differences for strains in occupational positions have been investigated by Jacobson, Charters and Lieberman (1951).

Considering consensus on role definition as an empirical problem, not a 'given', raises serious questions with respect to Sullivan's concept of the 'consensually validated' (see Foote and Cottrell, 1952) and Cameron's concept of 'public verification' (Cameron, 1947a) and suggests the potential theoretical importance of introducing role consensus as a variable in studies of psychopathology. Of perhaps even more potential utility for the study of pathological behavior is the notion of perceived role consensus. For example, how does an actor's perception of the degree of consensus on expectations held by 'significant others' on evaluative standards applicable to his position affect his role behavior?

Although there is not now a systematic body of literature concerned with the determinants and consequences of consensus on role definition for individual behavior and group functioning, these and other recent developments suggest that such a body of literature will probably emerge.

An examination of role formulations in the sociological literature reveals that the postulate of role consensus has been as embedded in sociology as in anthropology and social psychology. Recently, however, some writers have recognized the theoretical importance of consensus as a problem and have suggested the need for systematic research in this area. In the sociological formulations in which the postulate of consensus is involved, it is usually implied, just as in anthropology and psychology, by the way in which the term role is defined.

A number of formulations of this kind lean heavily on Linton's definition. Bennett and Tumin (1948, p. 96), for example, say: 'By role, then, we have reference to what the society expects of an individual occupying a given status. This implies that any status is *functionally* defined by *the role attached to it*.' Linton's influence is also apparent in L. Wilson and Kolb's formulation (1949, p. 208):

Culture generally organizes these exceptions regarding behavior into an articulated whole, composed of the interrelated *norms* (social rules) defining the basic *social positions* in the group. ... As indicated, it is the function of the person occupying the position to carry out the rights and obligations associated with it. This collection of rights and duties is a social *status* ... and in carrying them out the person is playing a social *role*. A *role* is defined as a pattern of behavior corresponding to a system of rights and duties and associated with a particular position in a social group. Since we have already spoken of these patterns as being articulated with one another, it is only necessary to add that such organization of social roles makes it possible for the group to function as a unit and the members to realize their individual and collective goals.

These definitions illustrate the kind most frequently found in the sociological literature. Another formulation of role, found primarily in the writings of the 'sociological' social psychologists, is usually derived from Mead (1934), who used the term role with considerably less precision than the social scientists whose definitions were considered in chapter 2 [not included here]. Mead was not attempting to develop a set of concepts to embrace social structural and cultural elements, but was primarily interested in a description of the developmental sequence through which a child moves in the process of socialization.

For Mead, to take the role of another is to 'put one's self in place of the other', adopting attitudes appropriate to the other's 'role', thereby providing one's self with the appropriate stimuli (attitudes) for the particular responses associated with another's role.

It is generally recognized that the specifically social expressions of intelligence, or the exercise of what is often called 'social intelligence', depend upon the given individual's ability to take the roles of, or 'put himself in place of', the other individuals implicated with him in given social situations; and upon his consequent sensitivity to their attitudes toward himself and toward one another (Mead, 1934, p. 141).

And again: 'When a child does assume a role he has in himself the stimuli which call out that particular response or group of responses' (p. 150).

Cottrell's emphasis on the interactional and self-other basis of role in one of his formulations [see ch. 2 of *Explorations in the School Superintendency Role*, p. 15] may be thought of as a lineal descendant of Mead's interpretation of the concept. In this definition, the postulate of consensus is not involved, since roles are considered to be elements of concrete interaction situations, and its referent, as we suggested earlier, could be considered nonnormative stimuli and responses.

Other 'descendants' of Mead in their attempts, apparently, to link his with Linton's definition, seem to accept the postulate of consensus. Cameron's (1947b, p. 90) definition illustrates the result of this fusion:

[A role is]...a comprehensive and coherent organization in behavior of functionally related, interlocking attitudes and responses ... a product of social learning which has been *culturally defined* by the behavior of others. . . .

Lindesmith and Strauss have an essentially similar definition in which the postulate of consensus seems to be involved. They say (1956, pp. 383–4, 385):

The concept of role refers to the most intricately organized patterns of response of which the human organism is capable, i.e. to verbally organized systems of response to an organized, subdivided and patterned environment.

And in elaboration they add:

In the enactment of roles the following are essential:

1. An identification of self;

2. Behavior in given situations which is appropriate to this identification;
3. A background of related acts by others (counter-roles) which serve as cues to guide specific performance;
4. An evaluation by the individual, and by others, of the role enactment.[4]
The postulate of consensus may be inferred from the phrase, 'behavior, in given situations, which is appropriate to this identification'.

In contrast to these formulations are another of Cottrell's and those of Parsons and Stouffer. Cottrell was one of the first sociologists who recognized the theoretical utility of treating role consensus as a variable. In a paper concerned with an individual's adjustment to age and sex roles (Cottrell, 1942) he presented a series of hypotheses concerning the degree of adjustment to these roles. Several of them are concerned with 'role' adjustment as a function of such variables as 'the clarity with which such roles are defined' (p. 618), and 'the consistency with which others in the individual's life situations exhibit to him the response called for by his role' (p. 619). Here, then, is a clear recognition of role consensus as a useful variable in the analysis of social behavior. Similarly, in suggesting a series of hypotheses concerning social disorganization and 'cultural roles', Warren (1949, p. 84), distinguishes among cultural, social, and personal roles and one of his hypotheses is: 'Social disorganization varies inversely with the clarity of definition of cultural roles.'

From an examination of Parsons's definition of a social system one might infer that he assumes consensus on the evaluative standards applicable to group members. He says that (Parsons, 1951, pp. 5–6; Gross, Mason and McEachern's italics),

a social system consists in a plurality of individual actors interacting with each other in a situation which has at least a physical or environmental aspect, actors who are motivated in terms of a tendency to the 'optimization of gratification' and *whose relation to their situations, including each other, is defined and mediated in terms of a system of culturally structured and shared symbols.*

The italicized part of the quotation with its reference to the

4. In the first edition (1949) of *Social Psychology*, Lindesmith and Strauss view 'behaviour, in prescribed situations, *which is appropriate to this identification*' as a basic feature of role behavior (pp. 165–6).

'culture' or symbolic interaction in a social system might suggest the consensus postulate.

In his elaboration of the elements of a social system, however, it becomes clear that consensus on evaluative standards is assumed only for *stable* interaction systems. After noting that an actor's orientation to another includes evaluative standards, he says (Parsons, 1951, p. 37; Gross, Mason and McEachern's italics):

Stability of interaction in turn depends on the condition that the particular acts of evaluation on both sides should be oriented to *common standards* since only in terms of such standards is 'order' in either the communication or the motivational contexts possible.

Although Parsons defines an institution as 'a complex of patterned elements in role-expectations which may apply to an indefinite number of collectivities' (1951, p. 39), (collectivities are viewed as systems 'of concretely interactive specific roles') he recognizes that, empirically, the degree of agreement on evaluative standards is problematic, falling on a continuum ranging from 'full institutionalization' to 'anomie'.

The institutionalization of a set of role expectations and of the corresponding sanctions is clearly a matter of degree. This degree is a function of two sets of variables; on the one hand those affecting the actual sharedness of the value orientation patterns, on the other those determining the motivational orientation or commitment to the fulfilment of the relevant expectations.... The polar antithesis of full institutionalization is, however, *anomie*, the absence of structured complementarity of the interaction process or, what is the same thing, the complete breakdown of normative order in both senses (Parsons, 1951, p. 39).

These passages from Parsons indicate not only his recognition of role consensus as a variable but also his recognition of the importance of the theoretical linkage between the 'evaluative standards' of groups, of larger systems in which they are involved, and the degree of their internalization in the individual.

Stouffer, in an analysis of conflicting social norms, has demonstrated that college students may perceive that authorities and students hold variant or incongruent expectations. In addition, his analysis makes clear that the '*range of* approved or permissible behavior' (Stouffer, 1949, p. 708) must be taken into account in describing social norms and that this range may be necessary for continuing social behavior. His concluding comments are (1949, p. 717):

From the theoretical standpoint, the most important implication of this paper may stem from its stress on variability. In essay writing in this field it is common and convenient to think of a social norm as a point, or at least as a very narrow band on either side of a point. This probably is quite unrealistic as to most of our social behavior. And it may be precisely the ranges of permissible behavior which most need examination, if we are to make progress in this realm which is so central in social science. For it may be the very existence of some flexibility or social slippage – but not too much – which makes behavior in groups possible.

Cottrell and Parsons suggest that consensus on role definition would be related in a positive and linear manner to the stability of social system and to personal gratification, whereas the inference might be drawn from Stouffer's conclusions that it may be curvilinear.

Homans, in *The Human Group*, is also aware that the degree of consensus among group members on positional expectations may vary. After defining a role as norms that state '... the expected relationships of a person in a certain position to others he comes into contact with ...' (Homans, 1950, p. 126) in his discussion of norms, he says: 'No doubt the norms accepted in a group vary somewhat from one person to another ...' and '... the more frequently men interact with one another, *the more nearly alike they become in the norms they hold*, as they do in their sentiments and activities' (p. 126; Gross, Mason and McEachern's italics).

His proposition that '... *the members of the group are more often more alike in the norms they hold than in their overt behavior*' (1950, p. 126) presents degree of consensus as a variable. Homans's suggested explanation of this proposition is that since an individual's perception of a norm is subject to a 'less immediate influence than his social activity, itself', it will vary 'less than his social activity' (1950, p. 127). On an *a priori* basis, reasoning leading to the opposite conclusion can easily be developed: since overt behavior is visible and therefore more amenable to social sanctions than norms, individuals will be more alike in their behavior than in their norms.

Despite Homans's awareness of the possibility of imperfect role consensus, he tends to think of consensus on norms among group members in *The Human Group* as a *given* 'in social systems' and in consequence explores only conformity to norms, not their variability, as a factor affecting the interaction, sentiments, activities or rankings of group members.

In the small-group research of Bales and his associates consensus on rankings of group members is sometimes treated as a variable, although consensus on role definition is not. This is the case partly because Bales is usually working with contrived groups at a 'prenormative stage' and with those that do not contain differentiated positions [see ch. 2 of *Explorations in the School Superintendency Role*, p. 15].

Recently, there has been a handful of empirical studies in which differential role definitions by sets of role definers have been investigated. Davis has attempted to test certain hypotheses originally suggested by Cottrell concerning clarity of role definition and adjustment in 'official leader' military 'roles' (Davis, 1954). Hall (1955) investigated the relationships between 'cohesiveness' and role consensus, and between 'cohesiveness' and the role behavior of incumbents of the position of aircraft commander.

Borgatta's (1955) finding that incumbents of different military positions held different attitudes in a number of different scalable areas and Henry and Borgatta's (1953) report of incongruent attitudes of commissioned and enlisted air force personnel toward the punitiveness of sanctions for deviant military behavior both suggest that there are empirical disparities in the evaluative standards applicable to incumbents of the same position.

Several investigations of the existence or correlates of types of marriage 'roles' have been concerned with the degree of consensus on role definition among some population of role definers. The hypothesis of lack of consensus is involved in, or may be inferred from, several studies of sex roles, for example, those of Komarovsky (1946), Rose (1951) and Wallin (1950). The studies of Chartier (1950), Wardwell (1952) and R. N. Wilson (1952) of the 'roles' of the chiropractor, the poet and the 'literary élite', respectively, and Reismann's (1949) differentiations of four subtypes of the bureaucratic role suggest directly or indirectly the importance of different expectations for occupants of the same position.

Finally, mention must be made of Williams's (1951, pp. 347–71) incisive analysis of institutional variation and 'cultural fictions' in a society. In summarizing his consideration of these problems he says (1951, p. 370):

It has been repeatedly stressed in this chapter that social norms vary considerably in the way individuals conceive of and conform to them. In addition, we suggested the crucial point, in connexion with cultural fictions, that shared assumptions and expectations can play an essential part in behavior, even when regarded by the actors as fictional or when so described. . . .

In attempting to place the problem of role consensus in its social science setting we observed that the postulate of consensus is still enmeshed in the analyses of many students of social behavior. Since their analyses assume consensus on role defintions among members of a group or 'society', they have ignored its possible significance as a variable for social science inquiry. We also observed, however, that during the past decade there has been an increasing tendency to consider role consensus an important variable for the study of individual social behavior, the functioning of social systems and cultural organization.

That the members of a social system, whether a dyad or a total society, must agree among themselves to *some extent* on values or expectations is a matter of definition. The point we have been trying to underscore is that the degree of consensus on expectations associated with positions is an empirical variable, whose theoretical possibilities until recently have remained relatively untapped.

In our examination of the anthropological definitions of culture we suggested a number of questions that deserve investigation. If cultural anthropologists follow Murdock's suggestion and give greater emphasis to variations in normative patterns, they will be forced to deal directly with the theoretical implications of differential role definitions by members of a society.

From the standpoint of individual behavior, research on role consensus is required in order to investigate, for example, the propositions suggested by Cottrell regarding individual adjustment or the utility of Sullivan's and Cameron's notions concerning the therapist-client relationship and the etiology of pathological behavior.

In sociological inquiry a number of questions deserves systematic investigation. For example, what are the determinants of high and low consensus on role definition in social systems? What types of interaction tend to facilitate or block the development of consensus in different kinds of social systems? What impact does differential consensus have on the functioning of social systems, on group effectiveness, group equilibrium, and on the gratification of its members?

This is a very small sample of questions that are open to examination when the postulate of consensus is abandoned. In contrast to the holistic approach so frequently found in social science literature, that is, that a role is an indivisible *unit* of rights and duties ascribed by a group or society, theoretically grounded empirical inquiries are needed to determine how much agreement there is on the expectations for the behavior of position incumbents. Conceptual schemes for role analysis that preclude the investigation of the basic question of role consensus are distinctly limited.

References

BARNETT, H. G. (1953), *Innovation: The Basis of Cultural Change*, McGraw-Hill.

BENNETT, J. W., and TUMIN, M. M. (1948), *Social Life, Structure and Function*, Knopf.

BORGATTA, E. F. (1955), 'Attitudinal concomitants to military statuses', *Social Forces*, vol. 33, pp. 342-7.

CAMERON, N. (1947a), *Psychology and the Behavior Disorders*, Houghton Mifflin.

CAMERON, N. (1947b), *The Psychology of Behavior Disorders*, Macmillan Co.

CHARTIER, B. (1950), 'The social role of the literary élite', *Social Forces*, vol. 29, pp. 179-86.

COOLEY, C. H. (1922), *Human Nature and the Social Order*, Scribner.

COTTRELL, L. S. (1942), 'The adjustment of the individual to his age and sex roles', *Amer. soc. Rev.*, vol. 7, pp. 617-20.

DAVIS, F. J. (1954), 'Conception of official leaders roles in the air force', *Social Forces*, vol. 32, pp. 253-8.

FOOTE, N. N., and COTTRELL, L. S., JR (1952), *The Contributions of H. S. Sullivan*, Hermitage House.

HALL, R. L. (1955), 'Social influence on the aircraft commander's role', *Amer. soc. Rev.*, vol. 20, pp. 292-9.

HENRY, A. F., and BORGATTA, E. F. (1953), 'A comparison of attitudes of enlisted and commissioned air force personnel', *Amer. soc. Rev.*, vol. 18, pp. 669-71.

HOMANS, G. C. (1950), *The Human Group*, Harcourt, Brace & World.

INKELES, A., and LEVINSON, D. J. (1954), 'National character: the study of modal personality and sociocultural systems', in G. Lindzey (ed.), *Handbook of Social Psychology*, vol. 2, Addison-Wesley, pp. 977–1020.

JACOBSON, E., CHARTERS, W. W., JR, and LIEBERMAN, S. (1951), 'The use of the role concept in the study of complex organization', *J. soc. Iss.*, vol. 7, pp. 18–27.

KLUCKHOHN, C. (1939), 'Theoretical bases for an empirical method of studying the acquisition of culture by individuals', *Man*, vol. 39, pp. 1–6.

KLUCKHOHN, C. (1954), 'Culture and behavior', in G. Lindzey (ed.), *Handbook of Social Psychology*, vol. 2, Addison-Wesley, pp. 921–76.

KLUCKHOHN, F. R. (1953), 'Dominant and variant value orientations', in C. Kluckhohn and H. A. Murray (eds.), *Personality in Nature, Society and Culture*, Knopf, pp. 342–57.

KOMAROVSKY, M. (1946), 'Cultural contradictions and sex roles', *Amer. J. Sociol.*, vol. 52, pp. 184–9.

LEWIN, K. (1935), *A Dynamic Theory of Personality*, McGraw-Hill.

LEWIN, K. (1951), *Field Theory in Social Science*, Harper & Row.

LEWIS, O. (1949), 'Husbands and wives in a Mexican village: a study of role conflict', *Amer. Anthropol.*, vol. 51, pp. 602–10.

LINDESMITH, A. R., and STRAUSS, A. L. (1956), *Social Psychology*, rev. edn, Dryden.

LINTON, R. (1936), *The Study of Man*, Appleton-Century-Crofts.

LINTON, R. (1939), 'Foreword', in A. Kardiner, *The Individual and his Society*, Columbia University Press.

LINTON, R. (1945), *The Cultural Background of Personality*, Appleton-Century-Crofts.

MANDELBAUM, D. G. (ed.) (1949), *Selected Writings of Edward Sapir in Language, Culture and Personality*, University of California Press.

MEAD, G. H. (1934), *Mind, Self and Society*, University of Chicago Press.

MURDOCK, G. P. (1954), 'Sociology and anthropology', in J. Gillin (ed.), *For a Science of Social Man*, Macmillan Co., pp. 14–31.

NEWCOMB, T. M. (1943), *Personality and Social Change*, Dryden.

NEWCOMB, T. M. (1950), *Social Psychology*, Dryden.

NEWCOMB, T. M. (1954), 'Sociology and psychology', in J. Gillin (ed.), *For a Science of Social Man*, Macmillan Co., pp. 230–40.

PARSONS, T. (1951), *The Social System*, Free Press.

PIAGET, J. (1932), *The Moral Judgement of the Child*, Harcourt, Brace & World.

REISMANN, L. (1949), 'A study of role conception in bureaucracy', *Social Forces*, vol. 27, pp. 305–10.

RIECKEN, H. W., and HOMANS, G. C. (1954), 'Psychological aspects of social structure', in G. Lindzey (ed.), *Handbook of Social Psychology*, vol. 2, Addison-Wesley.

ROBERTS, J. M. (1951), 'Three Navaho households: a comparative study in small group culture', *Pap. Peabody Mus. Amer. Arch. Ethn.*, vol. 40, no. 3, Peabody Museum, Cambridge, Massachusetts.

ROSE, A. M. (1951), 'The adequacy of women's expectations for adult roles', *Social Forces*, vol. 30, pp. 69–77.

SHERIF, M. (1936), *The Psychology of Social Norms*, Harper & Row.
SMITH, M. B. (1954), 'Anthropology and psychology' in J. Gillin (ed.), *For a Science of Social Man*, Macmillan Co., pp. 32–66.
SPICER, E. H. (ed.) (1952), *Human Problems in Technological Change*, Russell Sage Foundation.
STOUFFER, S. A. (1949), 'An analysis of conflicting social norms', *Amer. soc. Rev.*, vol. 14, pp. 707–17.
SUMNER, W. G. (1906), *Folkways*, Ginn.
THOMAS, W. I., and ZNANIECKI, F. (1918), *The Polish Peasant in Europe and America*, vols. 1 and 2, Badger.
VOGT, E. Z. (1951), 'Navaho veterans: a study of changing values', *Pap. Peabody Mus. Amer. Arch. Ethn.*, vol. 41, no. 1, Peabody Museum, Cambridge, Massachusetts.
WALLER, W. (1932), *The Sociology of Teaching*, Wiley.
WALLIN, P. (1950), 'Cultural contradictions and sex roles: a repeat study', *Amer. soc. Rev.*, vol. 15, pp. 288–93.
WARDWELL, W. (1952), 'A marginal professional role: the chiropractor', *Social Forces*, vol. 30, pp. 339–48.
WARREN, R. L. (1949), 'Social disorganization and the interrelationship of cultural roles', *Amer. soc. Rev.*, vol. 14, pp. 83–7.
WHITING, J. W. M., and CHILD, I. (1953), *Child Training and Personality*, Yale University Press.
WILLIAMS, R. M., JR (1951), *American Society*, Knopf.
WILSON, L., and KOLB, W. L. (eds.) (1947), *Sociological Analysis*, Harcourt, Brace & World.
WILSON, R. N. (1952), 'The American poet: a role investigation', unpublished Ph.D. dissertation, Harvard University.

11 R. L. Kahn, D. Wolfe, R. P. Quinn, J. D. Snoek and R. A. Rosenthal

Power, Influence and the Role-Sending Process

Excerpt from R. L. Kahn, D. Wolfe, R. P. Quinn, J. D. Snoek and R. A. Rosenthal, *Organizational Stress: Studies in Role Conflict and Ambiguity*, Wiley, 1964, pp. 185–205.

Expectations held by members of a role set have an impact on the focal person through various processes of social interaction and influence. The specific process, of course, differs from one issue to another and from one situation to another, but each interpersonal relationship involves a characteristic set of influence processes.

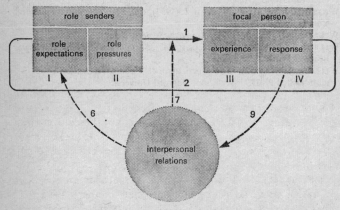

Figure 1   Partial model of factors involved in role conflict and ambiguity

The core of the theoretical model presented [see ch. 2 of *Organizational Stress*], represents a circular process of influence and counterinfluence (see Figure 1). This chapter deals with the effects of interpersonal relations on the role-sending process itself. Arrow 9 represents the effects of coping techniques upon the focal person's interpersonal relations. Arrow 7 represents two clusters of implicit hypotheses: (a) various kinds of interpersonal relations affect the kinds of influence techniques that are used in exerting role pressures, and (b) the nature of the relationship between the focal person and a role sender mediates the effects of the sent pressures on the focal person's experience of and response to the situation. The former hypothesis is the subject of the present chapter.

Role pressures and psychological forces

Role theory is predicated on the general assumption that a person's behavior is determined in part by the expectations held for him by certain significant others in related positions. There are, of course, other influences on one's behavior, which have yet to be dealt with in terms commensurate with the influence of role expectations. A more powerful role theory must handle such questions as these: how do role pressures from others create psychological forces on the person? How do these forces combine with other forces to determine the person's behavior?

At the present time these questions can be answered only in general and approximate terms, but it is clear that a distinction must be made between forces that exist in the person's psychological space and conditions or events that exist in his objective environment. What others expect him, want him or even urge him to do is not necessarily what he will do. In fact, the impact of others' attempts to influence him is often quite different from that intended. This is quite clear when role senders' expectations or desires are in conflict; when a person cannot logically comply with all the pressures upon him, he must reject some.

The concepts of influence and power are central to the questions just raised. How do people influence one another's behavior? What are the bases or preconditions for influence? Under what conditions will the influence yield a result desired by the influencer? What other effects does it have? These are questions which must be faced if we are to form an adequate understanding of the role-sending process.

Effective and attributed power

The present study treats power in two ways: in terms of the extent to which a given role sender can get the focal person to do what he

R. L. Kahn, D. Wolfe, R. P. Quinn, J. D. Snoek and R. A. Rosenthal

wants him to do – called *effective power*; in terms of how much the focal person feels that the role sender influences his behavior on the job – called *attributed power*.

In estimating the effective power of a role sender, data were drawn from several sections of the role-sender interview: open-ended questions on what the role sender would do were the focal person to fail to perform his job activities; questions concerning what the role sender had done in the past when he had trouble getting the focal person to do something; a question asking what the role sender could do as a last resort if the focal person failed to comply with his wishes; and a series of fixed-alternative questions covering various bases of power which the role sender could use or had used in the past. From these several sources and from descriptions and outcomes of past conflicts between role sender and focal person, each role sender was assigned a position on a five-point scale indicating his over-all power over the focal person rather than his intentions for him. Inter-coder reliability of this over-all power code was 0·90.

Data for attributed power were elicited from the focal person. He was asked about each of his role senders: *how important is this person in determining how you do your job?* Responses were given on a five-point scale ranging from *not at all* to *extremely*.

The correlation between the measures of effective and attributed power is a modest but significant 0·20; however, this should not be taken as an estimate of the validity of either measure. These variables are quite distinct conceptually, one dealing with influence from the point of view of the influencer, the other from the point of view of the one influenced. There is reason to expect these correlations to be modest. One role sender may be able to influence the focal person in desired directions quite readily, but seldom feel called upon to exert such influence. Another sender may have a major impact on the focal person in spite of difficulties in getting him to go along with his wishes. Although a sender may not obtain compliance with his expectations, these expectations may none-theless have considerable impact upon the focal person in terms of tension and emotional turmoil.

The distinction between effective and attributed power is based on the following theoretical assumptions: role pressures are conceived as specific attempts to influence the behavior of a person in a given position. Under most circumstances they generate a set of pyschological forces on the person, only some of which are in the direction intended by the influencer. Other forces are generated by the sender's behavior even when he intends no particular influence. Attributed power reflects the effects of all these forces, whereas effective power reflects only those which are in the intended direction and only when they result in the desired behavior.

Bases of power and varieties of influence techniques

French and Raven (1959) propose five general types of interpersonal power – legitimate, reward, coercive, expert and referent – each of which is based on a kind of relationship between two persons and each of which is associated with a set of influence techniques. A sixth general type might be called indirect power, that in which one person influences another by inducing a third party to apply the influence directly. For any given pair of persons several types of power may be available, and a variety of influence techniques are generally used singly or in combination.

Data on specific techniques of influence were obtained with the use of both closed and open-ended questions. Two sets of questions elicited scalar responses about the availability and use of different techniques representing all six types of power. In addition, senders were asked a series of open-ended questions asking each one what he would do if the focal person failed to perform his job activities properly, what he had done in the past when he had trouble influencing the focal person and what he could do as a last resort to influence him. Responses to these questions were coded into *a priori* categories, representing a wide variety of ways in which one person might influence another. That a given response was coded into a particular category did not necessarily mean that the role sender had ever actually used this technique – only that he 'might' use it. This 'might' indicates that the respondent felt that the technique was available to him and that he was not constrained from using it if necessary.

All types of power are potentially relevant to the role-sending process, but they are not equally distributed within the role set and probably are not equally effective in creating the desired forces in the focal person. The relationship between the focal person and any given role sender determines in large measure the kinds of influence techniques available to the sender.

Functional dependence and the necessity for power

When one asks who in a large-scale organization should be able to influence any particular member, the answer is by no means simple. A basic principle in traditional theories of organization is unity of command. This principle holds that each member should have just one boss, a supervisor to whom the member is totally responsible and who has a legitimate right to control his behavior. In the extreme this would mean that each member has just one role sender. This state of affairs is in general realistically impossible even if it were desirable.

But more important, where the functions and technology of an organization are varied and complex, an intricate pattern of inter-dependence is almost always found. A person's behavior on the job is not a matter of concern to his supervisor alone. Many others need to have him perform in (more or less) specified ways if they are to carry out their functions and meet their objectives adequately. They have a vested interest in what he does and how he does it. This fact stems largely from the formal division of labor and the resultant requirement for coordination and integration of effort. It also grows out of the more personally defined needs and objectives of each of the person's immediate associates.

The concept of *functional dependence* between positions reflects the fact that one person's task can be accomplished adequately only if certain others perform their jobs in a satisfactory manner. It can well be argued that given the necessarily imperfect specification of responsibilities, the greater one's functional dependence on another, the more one needs to have available reasonably effective techniques for influencing that other. In the intensive study the measure of functional dependence [see ch. 10 of *Organizational Stress*] indicated the total scope of the focal person's activities on which the role sender was functionally dependent.

Presumably some communication with role senders is required for the performance of any focal role. This requirement increases under conditions of high functional dependence. A moderate but highly significant correlation ($r = 0.35$, $p < 0.001$) is found between frequency of communication and functional dependence:

the greater the need for coordination, the more frequent the communication. The correlation is not higher, of course, because the two parties often talk about many things in addition to required coordination of activities.

If one speaks more to those on whom he is functionally dependent, does this also mean that he can influence them more? The correlations here between functional dependence and power are even more modest though still significant: $r = 0.28$ with effective power and $r = 0.27$ with attributed power ($p < 0.01$) in each case). There is thus a tendency for those who most need to influence the focal person to have the power to do so, but that power may not always be adequate and there are others who also have power over him.

Functional dependence, communication and the formal authority structure

The authority hierarchy is the organization's official mechanism of coordination and control. Let us turn now to the question of whether this mechanism generally fits the requirements of the functional dependencies. Table 1 shows the mean degree of functional dependence on the focal person for each of the nine categories of relative authority-status.

It is clear first of all that the focal person's immediate superiors are most dependent on him; they are able to perform their jobs only if the focal person performs virtually all parts of his job properly. The dependence of the supervisors derives not so much from the technological interconnectedness of their jobs with those of their subordinates as from the fact that these superiors are held accountable for the actions of their subordinates.

Immediate subordinates constitute the group with the second highest degree of functional dependence. If the focal person does not make the appropriate decisions or take facilitating actions, the work of his subordinates may become difficult or meaningless. But here, too, some of their concern centers around supervisory responsibilities, for example, the fairness with which the focal person allocates tasks among or takes disciplinary action with his subordinates. Nevertheless, in spite of and because of his authority over them, the focal person's own direct subordinates tend to have a high degree of functional dependence on him. We will consider later the extent to which they have power commensurate with this dependence.

Table 1 Functional Dependence of Role Senders on the Focal Persons[1] in Relation to Relative Status and Authority (from the intensive study)

| | Direct | | Indirect | |
	Percentage of activities concerning role sender	*N*	*Percentage of activities concerning role sender*	*N*
Superior (2)	95	25	47	7
Superior (1)	96	52	72	23
Peer			51	73
Subordinate (1)	81	138	62	38
Subordinate (2)	81	10	36	12

1. Mean percentage of focal office activities concerning role sender at least 'Somewhat'. F-test of over-all differences among means is significant at $p < 0.001$.

Note also in Table 1 that those who are not in a direct line of command with the focal person are much less dependent on him. Two other trends are also evident. First, at any given distance from the focal person, his superiors tend to be more dependent on him than his subordinates. Second, the greater the organizational distance of the role sender, the less dependent he is on the focal person. The correlation between functional dependence and organizational proximity is 0.31 ($p < 0.01$), but the moderate size of this correlation suggests that the functional division of the organization into departments and work sections is not always as adequate as it might be.

Table 2 indicates that communication patterns within the role set match the functional dependencies fairly well.[1] Communication

1. The results presented in Table 2 are based on the focal person's estimates of frequency of communication. A virtually identical pattern is found when the role sender's estimates are used, except that in all categories other than the direct subordinate, the senders estimate a slightly higher frequency of communication.

Table 2 Mean Frequency of Communication with Role Senders in Relation to Relative Status and Authority (from the intensive study)

	Direct			Indirect		
	Percentage having daily contact[1]	Mean[2]	N	Percentage having daily contact[1]	Mean[2]	N
Superior (2)	64	5·1	23	14	2·7	6
Superior (1)	82	5·1	50	44	4·7	22
Peer				61	5·1	69
Subordinate (1)	95	6·2	133	47	4·6	32
Subordinate (2)	70	5·0	8	42	4·2	12

1. A score of five or more. Test of association significant at $p < 0.001$.
2. Scale: 7. Almost constantly; 6. Several times a day; 5. Once or twice a day; 4. Several times a week; 3. About once a week; 2. A few times a month; 1. Less often.

frequencies are highest with those who are in a direct line of command with the focal person, particularly with his immediate subordinates, virtually all of whom he talks to at least once a day. Some of this talk, of course, is fairly superficial. The opportunities for coordination are present, but this probably should not be taken as evidence that it is successfully accomplished.

Three additional findings in Table 2 are worthy of note. First, there is a fairly high frequency of communication with peers in spite of their relatively low average functional dependence. It is among peers that one tends to find the strongest friendships; however, so much of their talk may be irrelevant to the work of either party. Second, individuals report communicating more with their surbordinates than with their superiors in either the direct or indirect category ($p < 0.05$). Finally, there is a rather sharp correlation between organizational proximity and frequency of communication ($r = 0.52$, $p < 0.001$). This suggests that the organizationally (and perhaps geographically) distant role sender who does happen to have high functional dependence upon the focal person may find opportunities for coordination somewhat difficult. We noted earlier [see ch. 10 of *Organizational Stress*] that one solution to this problem by the distant, functionally dependent role sender is for him to insist that the focal person adhere strictly to organizational rules, thereby insuring the predictability of the focal person's behavior.

Power and formal authority relationships

Formal organizational charts are at best idealized representations of the channels through which control over organizational activities is exercised. Their divergence from the actual power structure of organizations is notorious. Among the several bases of social power, only that of legitimate authority is wholly implied by the formal structure. Even this base depends in practice on the degree to which members adopt the values of the organization which confers such legitimacy. Other power differentials are typically conferred along with formal authority, for example, differential access to information or resources for rewarding or coercing. Yet the extent to which formal authority relationships imply such differentials is an open issue, and their implications for such 'informal' power bases as appeals to personal friendship have been even less explored.

To what degree do the formal authority relations in organizations correspond to the observed power relations? For the organizations included in the intensive study, this question is answered in Table 3. This table shows relative status and formal authority in relation to the independently obtained code of effective power. When role sender and focal person are in the same direct line of command, the effective power of the role sender increases monotonically with his status relative to the focal person. This increase is not, however, linear; a gross power differential occurs between the focal person's direct superiors and subordinates, with considerably smaller differences occurring *within* these two groups. Among role senders not in a direct line of command with the focal person, the effective power of the role sender over the focal person is also a monotonic function of relative status. The power of 'indirect' role senders is generally less than the power of senders in a direct line of authority with the focal person, particularly where his status superiors are concerned. The power of peers over the focal person is less than that of any superior status groups, but greater than that of any of his subordinates.

If this table presents no surprise, it probably should arouse some concern. For although direct superiors who have perhaps the greatest need to influence also have the power to do so, others who need to influence the focal person in order to do their jobs are relatively powerless. They have a vested interest in his performance but generally lack the ability to put power into the role pressures they exert on him. Some organization theorists will find this table reassuring; the concept of unity of command has some empirical confirmation. The focal person himself might see this as a desirable state of affairs. Few of us want more than one boss. But most of

Table 3 Mean Effective Power of Role Sender over Focal Person in Relation to Relative Status and Authority (from the intensive study)[1]

	Direct		Indirect	
	Mean	N	Mean	N
Superior (2)	4·5	25	3·5	6
Superior (1)	4·1	52	2·7	23
Peer			2·4	70
Subordinate (1)	2·0	137	2·3	37
Subordinate (2)	1·8	10	1·3	12

1. F-test of over-all differences among means is significant at $p < 0.001$.

us would like to be able to influence those on whom we are dependent and those who influence us. These findings indicate that subordinates are largely frustrated in this respect. Although coordination between their jobs and that of the superior (i.e. the focal person) is required, they must generally do the adjusting. They are typically unable to elicit adjustments from him.

But let us consider this situation with respect to the power the focal person attributes to his associates. Table 4 presents the findings for each of the nine relative status–authority categories. There is, indeed, a tendency to attribute more power to superiors than to subordinates in the direct line of command, but the sharp differential between them is not found here. Subordinates and peers alike have a substantial impact on the focal person in spite of the fact that they may encounter difficulty in gaining his overt compliance with their requests. It seems that their role pressures do induce significant forces on him and he feels they must be taken seriously. But they less often result in the intended consequences. Thus the unity of command may well exist with respect to overt action (effective power), but the focal person does not feel that he has just one boss. In fact he feels pressures coming from all sides even if he does not comply with them.

Table 4 Mean Power Attributed to Role Senders in Relation to Relative Status and Authority (from the intensive study)[1]

	Direct		Indirect	
	Mean	N	Mean	N
Superior (2)	4·5	23	3·2	6
Superior (1)	4·6	50	3·7	22
Peer			3·9	70
Subordinate (1)	3·9	133	3·9	32
Subordinate (2)	4·1	8	3·8	12

1. F-test of over-all differences among means is significant at $p < 0.001$.

The dilemma here stems in part from the high magnitude of the direct superior's power. If one must conform to the supervisor's every demand, there may be little latitude for compliance with pressures from others. When those others have what they consider to be legitimate requests and they are denied, they often return with renewed pressure, at which time they might use more extreme (but perhaps no more successful) influence techniques. To the extent that the focal person feels this added pressure and finds it stressful, he will attempt to cope with it in the best way he knows how; and if there are interpersonal repercussions, for example, rejection or counterattack, they are apt to be directed toward the (weaker) subordinates rather than the (stronger) superiors.

The answer may as often lie in reducing the power (or at least the pressure) from superiors so that the focal person can be more responsive to the needs of his subordinates and peers. Coordination generally needs to involve a process of mutual influence with some adjustment on both sides. Certainly both parties will be more motivated to coordinate their activities in this kind of give-and-take atmosphere.

Authority relations and influence techniques

The results discussed so far represent only in a very global way the complex associations between an organization's authority and power structures. Let us turn now to a more detailed consideration of particular interpersonal influence processes. If every effective role sending involves some power implication, that is, some consequences of compliance or non-compliance, what are the bases of that power? What influence techniques are available and under what conditions are they used? The various influence techniques people use to enforce their role expectations are closely related to matters of formal status and authority.

Formal authority and legitimate power

The most conspicuous among influence techniques based on formal authority are direct orders and commands. Table 5 presents the association between relative status and the percentage of role

Table 5 Percentage of Role Senders Reporting Being Able to Order the Compliance of the Focal Person in Relation to Relative Status and Authority[1] (from the intensive study)

	Direct		Indirect	
	%	Base N	%	Base N
Superior (2)	60	25	0	6
Superior (1)	24	52	4	23
Peer			4	70
Subordinate (1)	3	137	3	37
Subordinate (2)	0	10	0	12

1. Test of association significant at $p < 0.001$.

senders replying to the open-ended power questions that they might order or command the focal person to comply with their expectations. Clearly those most able and willing to exercise this legitimate authority over the focal person are his superiors in the direct chain of command. The entries of near zero in the remaining cells indicate that the hierarchical plan is well actualized. Even the touch of organizational anarchy implied by the entries of 3 and 4 per cent in the indirect column may be spurious; a response that 'I tell him to do it' would have been coded as an order, even if it were intended as a request.

Particularly interesting in Table 5 is the fact that less frequent references to legitimate authority are made by immediate superiors, direct superiors (1), than by those more remote in the hierarchy, direct superiors (2). Since a person works more closely with his immediate superior than with the person two or more levels above him, it is likely that affective relations become more important. The desire of an immediate superior to develop and maintain these affective ties might reduce his willingness to use such naked influence techniques as direct commands.

Table 6 Mean Ability to Use One's Authority over Decisions in Relation to Relative Status and Authority[1] (from the intensive study)

	Direct		Indirect	
	Mean	N	Mean	N
Superior (2)	4·6	24	3·7	7
Superior (1)	4·3	51	2·9	23
Peer			2·3	69
Subordinate (1)	1·6	136	2·0	36
Subordinate (2)	1·0	10	1·5	12

1. F-test of over-all differences among means significant at $p < 0.001$. Tables 6, 7 and 8 employ five-point scales ranging from 'never' or 'not at all' to 'usually' or 'a great deal'.

A similar pattern is found in response to the question: *To what extent could you use the authority you have to make the final decision when taking up a question with (the focal person)?*

Table 6 indicates that this also is almost entirely a base of power for superiors, but peers rarely and indirect superiors sometimes also feel this is something they can fall back on. Note the similarity of these means to effective power for each of the nine categories (Table 3). A correlation of 0.74 is found between the effective power index and the question on use of one's authority. But before concluding that this *is* the effective power base, let us consider other influence techniques.

Reward and coercive power

Another implication of organizational status is differential access to resources for rewarding compliance or punishing lack of compliance with one's expectations.

Table 7 indicates the mean extent to which role senders feel they

Table 7 Mean Reward Power of Role Senders over the Focal Person in Relation to Relative Status and Authority[1] (from the intensive study)

	Direct		Indirect	
	Mean	N	Mean	N
Superior (2)	4·0	25	2·3	7
Superior (1)	3·7	51	2·4	23
Peer			2·2	73
Subordinate (1)	1·5	135	1·8	37
Subordinate (2)	1·0	10	1·0	12

1. *F*-test of over-all differences among means significant at $p < 0.001$.

can reward the focal person in some way, for example, by recommending him for a promotion or raise. As with legitimate authority, control over both these rewards is concentrated in the hands of one's direct superiors. Seventy per cent of the direct superiors replied to open-ended questions that they might offer the recommendation of a raise as a means of influence, whereas no more than 11 per cent in any other category suggested they might do so. Reward power is also highly correlated ($r = 0.63$) with the over-all index of effective power.

For the most part, the reins of coercive power – the ability to

Table 8 Coercive Power of Role Senders over the Focal Person in Relation to Relative Status and Authority (from the intensive study)

a. Mean ability to make things difficult on the job[1]

	Direct		Indirect	
	Mean	N	Mean	N
Superiors (2)	4·5	24	4·8	6
Superiors (1)	4·0	50	3·4	22
Peers			3·0	67
Subordinates (1)	2·6	132	2·9	36
Subordinates (2)	2·3	10	1·4	11

b. Mean ability to take disciplinary action[2]

	Direct		Indirect	
	Mean	N	Mean	N
Superiors (2)	4·1	24	2·8	6
Superiors (1)	3·6	50	1·7	23
Peers			1·3	70
Subordinates (1)	1·3	135	1·4	36
Subordinates (2)	1·1	10	1·0	12

1. *F*-test of over-all differences among means significant at $p < 0.01$.
2. *F*-test of over-all differences among means significant at $p < 0.001$.

punish – are also in the hands of direct superiors. Table 8a indicates the extent to which people in various positions feel that they 'could make things difficult for (the focal person) on the job if he refused to do something'. Here superiors in both the direct and indirect categories feel that they can take recourse to coercion. The most legitimate form of coercive power is represented in the phrase *disciplinary action*. Table 8b indicates that the threat of official punishments as an influence technique is almost exclusively available to direct superiors.

Other, more specific kinds of coercion are also generally controlled by superiors in the status hierarchy. Tables 9a – c indicate that while these are seldom used, threat of transfer, of dismissals, and of blocking promotion or salary increase is the virtually exclusive domain of superiors.

There is one source of coercive power, in marked contrast, which one's superiors are relatively reluctant to use – that of withholding aid, information, or cooperation (Table 9d). Such reluctance is very likely a function of the extent to which the performance of the unit would be jeopardized were such cooperation withheld. In the extreme such behavior would amount to organizational suicide for the superior, since he is directly accountable for failures of the focal person. Consistent with this finding, superiors declared themselves more willing than any other group to remedy the performance deficiencies of the focal person by 'working with him and helping him'. Thirty per cent of superiors indicated they would work with and help the focal person in this eventuality; the

Table 9 Availability of Coercive Influence Techniques in Relation to Relative Status and Authority[1] (from the intensive study)

	Superiors	Peers	Sub-ordinates
(a) Percentage of role senders indicating they might threaten the focal person with transfer in order to influence him[2]	28	4	2
b. Percentage indicating they might threaten dismissal[2]	24	1	1
c. Percentage indicating they might threaten blocking salary increase or promotion[2]	12	1	0
d. Percentage indicating they might withhold aid, information or cooperation[2]	19	32	44
Base N	106	70	196

1. Status-authority categories have been combined to simplify the table. Data are based on coded responses to the open-ended power questions.

2. Test of association significant at $p < 0.001$.

comparable figure for peers was 18 per cent and that for subordinates only 11 per cent. Not only are one's superiors most unwilling to risk loss of performance by withholding help; they are also most ready to give help should performance problems arise.

On the other hand, the status group most ready to withhold aid, information, or cooperation are the subordinates two levels below the focal person and in the same chain of command. Eighty per cent of this group mention withholding as a means of controlling the focal person, and they are ideally situated to exercise such control. They are sufficiently removed from the focal person that they do not suffer the immediate repercussions of his difficulties. At the same time, they (unlike the indirect subordinates of the same status) are sufficiently close to the departmental machinery to know exactly where and how to throw the monkey wrench so that it will create maximum difficulty for the focal person and minimum difficulty for themselves.

It seems likely that threats of withholding aid and the like must be implicit except under unusual circumstances. An overt threat of such a kind would generally leave the threatener quite vulnerable to retaliation unless he controlled all the power, and this clearly is not the case for subordinates. The responses in this category of influence seem to indicate what the role sender might resort to if he became sufficiently dissatisfied with the focal person's behavior. Responding in this uncooperative fashion is unlikely to gain compliance with one's requests, but the implicit threat of such a reaction may lead the focal person to maintain at least minimal satisfaction for his subordinates.

Expert and referent power

The one type of power that seems to be in virtually universal use is that which French and Raven (1959) refer to as expert power. It is conceived as that power which stems from the one person's respect for another's knowledge and judgement. The role senders were asked: *To what extent could you rely on the confidence (the focal person) places in your special knowledge or advice as a means to getting him to do something?* The average answer for the total sample was 4·2, on a scale for which 4 represents *quite a bit* and 5 is *a great deal*. Interestingly, in none of the nine status-authority categories is the mean less than 4·0.

These findings smack of more than a little vanity, but in fact the focal persons report having that much respect for their role senders' knowledge and judgement. Moreover, the influence techniques associated with expert power – bringing new information about the situation, explaining, clarifying, reasoning, arguing, talking it over in a general attempt to persuade the other to one's point of view – are used more commonly than are any others. Eighty-six per cent of the superiors, 81 per cent of the peers and 72 per cent of the subordinates report using such techniques. These techniques are available to virtually everyone and with proper tact can be used without fear of retaliation. Of course, they are not always effective. One is often less persuasive than he would like to be; listening is not the same as hearing or believing.

Referent power, based on one person's attraction or to identification with another is less often used overtly. Few respondents indicated spontaneously that they would use personal friendship as a means of influencing the focal person. Some interesting intergroup differences are apparent, however, in the admitted use of such friendship appeals on past occasions. Table 10 indicates that

Table 10 Percentage of Role Senders Reporting the Use of Friendship Appeals in Influencing the Focal Person in Relation to Relative Status and Authority[1] (from the intensive study)

	Direct		Indirect	
	%	Base N	%	Base N
Superior (2)	17	25	33	6
Superior (1)	18	52	48	23
Peer			37	70
Subordinate (1)	20	137	27	37
Subordinate (2)	0	10	42	12

1. Test of association significant at $p < 0.01$.

such appeals are most characteristic of role senders who are *not* in the same line of command with the focal person. Only the remote subordinates, direct subordinates (2), report that they never have

R. L. Kahn, D. Wolfe, R. P. Quinn, J. D. Snoek and R. A. Rosenthal 217 used such appeals; and, consistently enough, 80 per cent of these people have already declared themselves willing to withhold aid, information or cooperation for the sake of influencing the focal person. That for each relative status level the indirect line of command groups are the more likely to use friendship appeals suggests that in formal organizations such appeals are used largely to compensate for deficiencies in other types of power. This finding substantiates an assumption made in the discussion of boundaries [see ch. 6 of *Organizational Stress*]: namely, that individuals interacting across departmental lines must rely heavily on personalized friendship appeals as a means of influence. Their abilities to modify each other's behavior as best suits their individual needs are based on affective bonds – bonds which are often chronically strained by the demands of others in their respective departments.

Perhaps the most interesting aspect of these findings is that overt appeals to friendship seem often to be made where the bonds of friendship appear weakest. One may rely on friends for cooperation and personal favors, but calling his attention to the friendship in the midst of an influence attempt is often distasteful to the other person. Friendship seems to 'wear thin' with such reminders. But this should not be taken as an indication that referent power does not operate in large scale organizations. Affective bonds of trust, respect and attraction are formed with close associates, and cooperative attitudes generally go along with them. But the influence process is often more subtle and less overt. Direct influence attempts, other than making one's wishes known, often are not necessary. There seems to be a general tendency to identify with one's supervisor (perhaps because of his power and status), and it is likely that much of his influence is based on this identification process rather than on direct orders, promises of reward, or threats of punishment.

Indirect power

Indirect processes of influence (i.e. those using a third party intermediary) are very common in large-scale organizations. In chapter 10 data were presented indicating that those in the direct superior (2) groups frequently rely on indirect influence, with direct superiors (1) being the third parties. A similar relationship holds for the subordinate groups as well, 50 per cent of the direct subordinate (2) group using intermediaries and only 25 per cent of the direct subordinate (1) group doing so. The availability of intermediaries who might intervene in their behalf may be the saving grace of peers and subordinates. Eighty-eight per cent of the peers, 77 per cent of the subordinates and 54 per cent of the superiors mention they could go to his or their superiors or to 'higher management' as a means of influencing the focal person.

For many subordinates this is a last resort kind of action only to be used on very important issues. There are strong standards against going over a superior's head even when one has nowhere else to turn. Peers may do so with relatively greater impunity, especially those who share a direct supervisor with the focal person.

In general indirect influence is the primary tactic of those who are organizationally distant – two or more levels above or below the focal person. Its availability is very significant to all those who are not in a direct line of command with him; although they may prefer to go directly, the fact that they can go through channels to his boss gives them power they may not have directly.

We should bear in mind that role pressures exerted through a third party are usually filtered by that person's frame of reference. The intermediary can distort or elaborate the message, soften or strengthen the pressure and change its direction altogether. Indirect role sendings may be seen as originating in the intermediary. Conversely, direct influence attempts are often presented as if they had been initiated by others, for example, as if it were a grass roots movement and a majority of the department members stand behind it. The possibilities of 'political' manipulation are legion. Indirect influence may be quite open and innocent or Machiavellian in its complexity and deceptiveness. Nevertheless it is quite a different process from the direct sending of role pressures.

Effectiveness of influence techniques

An evaluation of the effectiveness of various influence techniques is difficult if not considered in the context of a specific situation. Probably one would be well advised to limit almost all of his influence efforts to simple requests and persuasion attempts, in which the decision will presumably be made rationally. But the fact is that this is generally effective to the extent that the role sender has available other kinds of power to back up his requests. One need not threaten massive retaliation very often to have his modest requests taken seriously. 'Walk softly and carry a big stick' may be a useful adage in organizational life as well.

Table 11 presents the correlations between the index of effective

Table 11 Correlations between Effective Power and the Availability of Various Influence Techniques[1] (from the intensive study, $N = 381$)

Influence techniques	Correlation (r) with effective power
Legitimate power:	
1. Use one's authority to make the final decision	0·74*
2. Direct order or command	0·31*
Reward power:	
3. Recommend for promotion or raise	0·63*
Coercive power:	
4. Disciplinary action	0·80*
5. Make things difficult on the job	0·61*
Expert power:	
6. Rely on his confidence in one's knowledge	0·18*
7. Bring new information about the situation	0·01
8. Convince him it is right for company	0·07
Referent power:	
9. Appeal to friendship	0·22*
10. Ask personal favors	0·04
11. Appeal to company loyalty	0·19*
Indirect power:	
12. Go through channels or some other person	0·06

1. Based on responses to fixed alternative questions.
* $p < 0.001$.

power and various power bases or influence techniques. There is an impressive cluster of legitimate, reward and coercive techniques which contribute significantly to the role sender's effective power. These are available almost exclusively to the focal person's organizational superiors. The power cards are indeed stacked in favor of the formal authority structure. This does not mean, of course, that superiors spend much of their time ordering or bribing or threatening. But their ability to do so is well known, so that role pressures from above generally result in the desired action. In contrast the types of power available to subordinates and peers – expert, referent and indirect for the most part – tend not to be so highly associated with effective power.

The futility of subordinate role senders is demonstrated in the results in Table 12. In response to the question: *What would you*

Table 12 Percentage of Role Senders Avoiding Influence Efforts[1] in Relation to Relative Status and Authority (from the intensive study)

	Superiors	Peers	Subordinates
(a) Do it myself[2]	36	46	66
(b) Drop it, do nothing[2]	6	17	34
(c) Turn it over to someone else[3]	24	10	19
Base N	106	70	196

1. In response to query: *What would you do if (focal person) failed to do this?* percentages can add to more than 100 per cent because the question is asked with regard to each of the focal person's activities, each of which could elicit a different response.
2. Test of association significant at $p < 0.001$.
3. Test of association significant at $p < 0.10$.

do if (the focal person) failed to do this?, asked about each of his activities, many role senders indicated alternatives to continued influence efforts. Their general lack of power is reflected in the subordinates' and to lesser extent the peers' turning away from continued role pressures in favor of *dropping it* or *doing it themselves*. That superiors sometimes do it themselves or assign it to others probably indicates not a lack of effective power but rather a recognition of the focal person's inability to perform the task. Superiors also tend to indicate the further consequences of the focal person's hypothetical failure, for example, reprimand him, get rid of him, fire him. But it is the subordinates who frequently report that they can do nothing to get the focal person to do the task.

Summary

Role pressures are exerted through social influence processes and techniques which are based primarily in the formal role relations between the role sender and the focal person. Although the functional dependence of role senders on the focal person – an indication of the need for influence over him – is distributed throughout the role set, power is highly concentrated in the hands of his direct superiors. Legitimate power, reward power, and coercive power are almost exclusively theirs.

Peers and subordinates must fall back on expert, referent, and indirect influence techniques. Even when they are dependent on the focal person's performance of certain activities, if he should fail to do them, subordinates and peers frequently can do nothing or must perform the activities themselves. But in spite of their general inability to gain the focal person's compliance with their requests (they lack effective power), they do have an impact on him. The focal person does attribute power to them as well as to superiors, and finds that role pressures from any direction can be a source of stress.

Reference

FRENCH, J., and RAVEN, B. (1959),'The bases of social power', in D. Cartwright (ed.), *Studies in Social Power*, Research Center for Group Dynamics.

12 Philip E. Slater

Role Differentiation in Small Groups

Philip E. Slater, 'Role differentiation in small groups', *American Sociological Review*, vol. 20, 1955, pp. 300–310.

Small-group research provides a most fruitful meeting-ground for psychological and sociological thinking. Few fields of study lend themselves so easily to this dual perspective. The concept of 'role' holds a potentially strategic position in this rapprochement, but its use in empirical studies has thus far left this potentiality unexploited.

We might define a role as a more or less coherent and unified system of items of behavior. With even this minimal definition it becomes apparent that role performance in the small-group situation will have both consequences which are important to the functioning of the group in which the role is performed and personal consequences of importance to the individual who performs it. Similarly, an individual may be motivated to perform a role both by specific inducements offered by the group and by more general needs operating within the individual himself.

The rather general failure to consider simultaneously both of these aspects of role performance has constituted a very real stumbling-block in small-group research. This paper will attempt to illustrate the way in which consideration of both psychological and sociological factors may aid in the interpretation of tendencies for members of small experimental groups to behave in systematically differentiated ways.

Our research in this area[1] has been centered around five problems:

1. To what extent do group members distinguish between different *kinds* of favorable evaluations of their fellow group members, or,

1. For the theoretical assumptions underlying this research see Bales (1953) and Bales and Slater (1955).

conversely, to what degree do they tend to rank fellow members similarly on criteria assumed to be different? A consistent tendency for subjects to rate one man high on one criterion and another man high on a second criterion would constitute prima facie evidence for the existence of a set of differentiated roles, at least in the minds of the subjects themselves.

2. What effect do repeated interactions have upon such discriminations? Since randomly composed laboratory groups are rather ephemeral organizations, it might be assumed necessary for some time to elapse before even a crude prototype of the elaborate kind of differentiation found in permanent groups would appear.

3. How do individuals differentiated by their fellow group members differ in their behavior? How can we characterize this behavior and how do these characterizations relate to the criteria upon which the individuals were rated?

4. How do such individuals respond to each other? Do differentiated 'specialists' cooperate or compete with each other?

5. What is the relationship of personality factors to role differentiation? Are there factors which predispose an individual to assume a particular role? What is the effect upon the group as a whole of variations in the motivations of various 'specialists'?

Procedure

The sample consisted of twenty groups of from three to seven men each, with four groups of each size. Each group met four times, so that a total of eighty meetings were studied. The groups were composed of paid male undergraduates at Harvard who knew each other only casually, if at all, prior to the first meeting. They were told that we were engaged in the study of group discussion and decision making, and that we would observe them through a one-way mirror. Each subject was given a five-page factual summary of an administrative problem which the subjects were asked to solve as a group, assuming the role of administrative staff to the central authority in the case under discussion. They were given forty minutes to discuss the case and decide (a) why the persons involved in the case were behaving as they did and (b) what the central authority should do about it. A new case was used for each meeting. The subjects' remarks during the discussion were classified according to Bales's set of interaction categories (see Bales, 1951).

Following each session the subjects filled out a questionnaire which included the following questions:

1. Who contributed the best ideas for solving the problem? Please rank the members in order. *Include yourself.*
2. Who did the most to guide the discussion and keep it moving effectively? Please rank the members in order. *Include yourself.*
3. How well did you personally like each of the other members? Rate each member on a scale from 0 to 7 where zero means, 'I feel perfectly neutral toward him', and seven means 'I like him very much.'[2]

At the end of the fourth session an additional question was asked:

4. Considering all the sessions, which member of the group would you say stood out most definitely as a leader in the discussion? How do you rank the others. *Include yourself.*

These questions, along with the Bales interaction scores, constituted the major source of data for this study.

Prior to analysis of the data, each of the twenty groups was assigned to one of two classes, according to whether the members showed high or low agreement on their responses to questions 1 and 2 above. This procedure was followed on the basis of findings by Heinicke and Bales (1953) that these two types of groups showed different development characteristics. It was felt that role differentiation might take different forms in groups with varying degrees of agreement on status ratings.

The measure used to represent agreement on status ratings is based on Kendall's 'coefficient of concordance'[3] which he calls 'W'. It is obtained from a matrix of rankings, each individual (placed in vertical order on a series of rows) ranking each individual (placed in horizontal order on a series of columns). In Kendall's formula:

$$W = \frac{12S}{m^2 (n^3 - n)}$$

where S equals the sum of the squares of the deviations of the column totals from the grand mean, and n equals the number of

2. A different form of question was used for some of the earlier groups, but both forms were reduced to rank orders for the present study.
3. See Kendall (1948), pp. 160 ff. See also F. Kraüpl Taylor (1951).

individuals ranked by *m* observers. In our rankings $n = m$, since everyone in the group ranks everyone, including himself. When agreement is perfect, *W* is equal to one; when there is no agreement, *W* is equal to zero.

W indices obtained from the rankings made on questions 1 and 2 were averaged, and the resulting mean called the 'index of status consensus'. When the average Index of a group over all four meetings was 0·500 or above, the group was classified as a 'high' group. When the index was below 0·500, the group was classified as a 'low' group.

Specialization as perceived by subjects

Subjects in this sample may be ranked in five different ways for each session. From the interaction scores it was possible to assign rank order to the men according to who talked the most and who *received* the most interaction. From the post-meeting questions it was possible to rank the men on the perceived quality of their ideas, their perceived ability to guide the discussion, and their personal popularity. Our interest in role differentiation stemmed from the relationships of these rank orders to each other.

A simple method of seeking out tendencies toward specialization consists of counting the number of times a man with top rank on any one of these five measures holds top rank on none of the other measures. Such a man might be considered a 'specialist', and if such 'specialists' are found in one characteristic more often than in the others, this characteristic might be considered a specialized one.

Table 1 indicates that there are more cases in which the best-liked

Table 1 Number of Sessions[1] Out of a Possible Eighty in Which a Given Person Holds Top Position in One and Only One Rank Order Out of Five Possible Rank Orders

Talking	11·0
Receiving	10·5
Ideas	12·0
Guidance	11·6
Liking	30·4
Total	75·5

1. The decimals arise from ties in rankings.

man holds top ranking in only that one characteristic than cases of any other sort of isolated prominence. The difference between this characteristic and the other four is significant at the 0·001 level, using a chi-square test. Popularity is apparently a relatively specialized achievement.

Further information may be obtained by proceeding in the reverse manner and asking rather, how often does the same person in a particular group hold top position on two characteristics? Table 2 shows, for each pair of characteristics, the percentage of cases in which such coincidence occurs.

Table 2 indicates that for both high and low status-consensus

Table 2 Percentage of Total Number of Sessions (Eighty) in Which the Same Person Holds Top Position in Two Rank Orders at the Same Time

High status-consensus groups

	T	R	I	G	L
Talking		51·3	63·3	36·5	20·5
Receiving			53·3	39·0	34·3
Ideas				56·3	32·0
Guidance					45·5
Liking					

Low status-consensus groups

	T	R	I	G	L
Talking		52·5	43·7	40·0	32·0
Receiving			28·7	42·5	37·0
Ideas				50·0	16·5
Guidance					20·0
Liking					

groups, popularity is least often associated with other characteristics. The difference is significant at the 0·01 level in both cases, using a chi-square test. Marked differences between high and low groups appear, however, when we examine the table further. The two participation measures, talking and receiving, are significantly less often associated with ideas in the low groups than in the high

(0·01 level), and ideas and guidance are significantly less often associated with liking (0·01 level). In other words, in the high groups high participation (talking and receiving) is associated with high rated task ability (ideas and guidance), but neither is strongly associated with popularity. In the low groups the association of high rated task ability with popularity is even lower (less in fact than chance expectancy), while the association of high participation with high rated task ability tends to break down.

Note that talking and receiving are strongly associated in both high and low groups, as are ideas and guidance. This fact perhaps justifies the groupings made above, which will be used throughout this section wherever they seem to be appropriate.

These techniques for determining the amount of specialization among these various characteristics are not entirely satisfactory, since they deal only with the top man on each rank order. To meet this problem, mean rank order correlations between all pairs of characteristics were computed, and are shown on Table 3.[4]

First, as we might expect from Tables 1 and 2, the correlations between liking and the other four characteristics are the lowest correlations in both the high- and low-group matrices. Second, the tendency for amount of participation and rated task ability to be highly correlated in the high groups and poorly correlated in the low groups is even more sharply outlined in Table 3 than in Table 2.[5]

4. The use of rank order correlations here involves serious statistical problems, due to the small sizes of our groups. Clearly a rho drawn from a three-man group means very little, and rhos from even the larger sizes are not too reliable. In dealing with this problem two different techniques were used: (a) median values were computed; (b) means based on the raw rhos of all but the three-man groups were computed. While these methods yielded identical results, neither is entirely satisfactory, and we suggest that the reader accept these findings with reserve.

5. All of the correlations in the low groups are, in fact, lower than those in the high groups, a result which is not surprising in view of the fact that low agreement between raters is equivalent to low reliability of measures, which would tend to produce lower correlations in the low groups. All of the differences between high and low groups in Table 3 are significant at the 0.05 level or better, with the exception of the talking–receiving correlations (which are not based on ratings), the ideas–guidance correlations and the guidance–liking correlations. It is notable, however, that ideas and guidance are very highly correlated even in the low groups, and this fact, along with the

Table 3 Intercorrelations between Talking, Receiving and Ratings on Ideas, Guidance and Liking. Mean Rank Order Correlations of Sixty-Four Sessions (size 3 excluded)

High status-consensus groups

	T	R	I	G	L
Talking		0·88	0·80	0·75	0·38
Receiving			0·74	0·74	0·46
Ideas				0·83	0·41
Guidance					0·49
Liking					

Low status-consensus groups

	T	R	I	G	L
Talking		0·69	0·48	0·51	0·10
Receiving			0·44	0·52	0·16
Ideas				0·71	0·14
Guidance					0·27
Liking					

Differences between the correlations in Table 3 were tested in the following manner: the ten correlations in each matrix were divided into three sets, with the talking – receiving and ideas – guidance correlations in the first set, the four correlations between the participation measures and the rated task ability measures in the second set, and the four correlations between liking and the other measures in the third set. The three sets were then tested against each other by means of sign tests. Note that in the first set the correlations are high in both high and low groups, in the second set they are high in the high groups and relatively low in the low groups, while in the third set they are relatively low in both.

In the high groups there was no significant difference between the first two sets. The first set was significantly higher than the third set, at the 0·01 level, and the second set was significantly higher than the third at the 0·05 level. In the low groups the first set

existence of several high group/low group differences which are not based upon ratings, suggests that unreliability of low group measures plays little part in the creation of qualitative differences between high and low groups.

was significantly higher than the second and the second significantly higher than the third, both at the 0·01 level.

Popularity, then, again appears to be the most specialized characteristic, regardless of the degree of status consensus in the group. In low status-consensus groups, however, the tendency for liking to separate itself from other characteristics is stronger, and seconded by the dissociation of rated task ability from amount of participation.

In summary, role differentiation in the high groups seems to be bipartite, with an active 'task specialist' and a best-liked man. In the low groups, it tends to be tripartite (as well as more extreme), with an active participator who is neither well liked nor highly rated on task ability, a more passive task specialist who is not well liked, and a popular individual who is neither active nor highly rated on task ability.

Changes over time

Common sense and sociological folk-lore would lead us to expect that any tendency toward role specialization in these groups would increase over time, as the group became more highly 'organized' or 'structured'. This expectation is fulfilled. Table 4 shows the

Table 4 Percentage of Cases in Which the Same Man Holds Top Position on Like Ranking and Idea Ranking at the Same Time, by Sessions[1]

Sessions			
1	2	3	4
56·5	12·0	20·0	8·5

1. The trends for high and low groups are identical.

number of times in each meeting in which the top man on ideas is also best liked. Table 5 shows the number of times in each meeting in the low groups in which the top man on either participation measure is also top man on either task ability rating. The trend in Table 4 is significant at the 0·01 level, the trend in Table 5 at the 0·05 level, using chi-square tests.[6]

6. Computations using mean rhos, in the manner of Table 3, yield similar results.

The selection of ideas as the task ability measure in Table 4, rather than guidance, is based upon the fact that it is in general less highly correlated with liking, and thus in some sense 'purer'. Guidance and liking do tend to correlate less with the passage of time, but the trend is more gradual, as we might expect.

Table 5 Percentage of Cases in Low Status-Consensus Groups in Which the Same Man Holds Top Position on a Participation Measure (Talking or Receiving) and a Task Ability Measure (Ideas or Guidance) at the Same Time,[1] by Sessions

Sessions			
1	2	3	4
55·0	28·7	41·3	30·0

1. Using the mean of the four possible combinations.

Role differentiation and leadership

At the end of the fourth session, after differentiation has become well developed, our subjects are asked to rank each other on the most generalized of criteria, leadership. What is the relationship of this ranking to the five more specialized ones?

This relationship may be determined by finding the top man on each measure for all four sessions taken together, and then computing the percentage of cases in which top rank on leadership coincided with top rank on each of the five other measures. The results were as follows: guidance 80 per cent, receiving 65 per cent, ideas 59 per cent, talking 55 per cent and liking 25 per cent.[7] A chi-square test shows liking to coincide significantly less often (at the 0·01 level) with leadership than the other four characteristics. The best-liked man is in fact chosen leader no more often than would be expected by chance.[8]

Yet, strangely enough, leadership is most *strongly* associated

7. There were no important differences between high and low groups.
8. Computations using mean rank order correlations between leadership and the five other characteristics yield the same results.

with those measures which are in turn most strongly correlated with popularity, namely, receiving and guidance (see Tables 2 and 3). This fact seems less strange if we consider the generalized character of leadership. Subjects choosing a leader must take into account a wider range of abilities and virtues than in deciding who has the best ideas or whom they like best. The chosen leader of a group is perhaps the man who has the highest hypothetical *combined* rating on all possible characteristics related to the group's purposes and needs. The man so chosen is not likely to be *dis*liked, nor to have unacceptable ideas nor to be unable or unwilling to participate in the discussion. Hence those measures which are themselves more general, that is, related to a wider range of abilities, will correlate more highly with leadership. Tables 2 and 3 suggest that guidance and receiving are more general in this sense than their counterparts, ideas and talking.

Behavioral differences between idea men and best-liked men

Thus far we have dealt with the differentiation of task ability and popularity primarily as perceived by the subjects. We might now ask, is this trend a reflection of actual behavioral differences between the perceived 'specialists', or have our subjects merely been gripped by some sort of sociological delusion while making their ratings? What, for example, does a best-liked man *do*?

In order to compare the Bales's interaction profiles of idea men and best-liked men, the following procedure was followed: (a) all sessions in which the best liked man also held top rank on ideas were eliminated; (b) all sessions in which ties for top rank occurred in either ranking were eliminated. The raw profiles of the remaining forty-four matched pairs of idea men and best-liked men were added together, and percentage profiles computed, as shown in Table 6.[9]

The most salient general difference in Table 6 is the tendency for the idea man to initiate interaction more heavily in Area B (problem-solving attempts) and the best-liked man in Area A (positive reactions). The idea man also seems to disagree somewhat more, and shows a little more antagonism, while the best-liked asks more

9. Although some suggestive variations in these differences appear when the sample is divided into high- and low-group pairs, the major outlines are the same.

Table 6 Composite Profiles in Percentages of Forty-Four Top Men on Idea Ranking and Forty-Four Top Men on Like Ranking for the Same Sessions

		Initiated		Received	
	Interaction category	Idea men	Best-liked men	Idea men	Best-liked men
Area A:	1. Shows solidarity	3·68	4·41	2·57	3·15
Positive	2. Shows tension release	5·15	6·98	7·95	9·20
reactions	3. Shows agreement	14·42	16·83	23·29	18·27
Area B:	4. Gives suggestion	8·97	6·81	7·01	7·22
Problem solv-	5. Gives opinion	32·74	28·69	25·52	31·09
ing-attempts	6. Gives orientation	18·54	17·91	14·06	14·54
Area C:	7. Asks orientation	3·04	3·71	3·62	2·80
Questions	8. Asks opinion	1·84	2·94	1·94	1·74
	9. Asks suggestion	0·93	1·33	0·85	0·84
Area D:	10. Shows disagreement	8·04	7·60	10·65	9·35
Negative	11. Shows tension increase	1·92	2·16	1·59	1·35
reactions	12. Shows antagonism	0·73	0·63	0·95	0·45

questions and shows more tension. On the receiving end, the situation is largely reversed, with the idea man receiving more agreement, questions, and negative reactions, while the best-liked man receives more problem-solving attempts and more solidarity and tension release. The general picture is thus one of specialization and complementarity, with the idea man concentrating on the task and playing a more aggressive role, while the best-liked man concentrates more on social-emotional problems, giving rewards and playing a more passive role.

The problem of testing the significance of these differences is a vexing one, in view of the interdependence of the categories. Several different techniques have been utilized, the most satisfactory of which has been the use of category indices based upon the raw profiles of each man.[10] If, for example, we wish to test the apparent

10. Such a technique gives equal weight to each man, contrary to the composite profiles in Table 6, which, since they lump together all acts of all men, give greater weight to those men whose total rate of participation is higher. As a result, some differences which seem negligible in Table 6 are actually very consistent, and vice versa.

tendency for idea men to interact more in Area B and best-liked men in Area A, we simply divide the number of scores each man has in Area A by his score in Area B, and compare the resulting indices of the two types of men. Best-liked men should and do have significantly higher indices than idea men (at the 0·01 level, using a sign test).

Another index may be constructed by simply placing in the numerator all categories in which the best-liked man initiated more interaction and in the denominator all categories in which the idea man initiated more. The same procedure may be followed for the receiving profiles. On both of these indices the best-liked man is significantly higher (at the 0·01 level).

The principal drawback of these indices is that they fail to show us which categories are most crucial in differentiating idea from best-liked men. Unfortunately, there is no satisfactory solution to this problem, in view of the statistical difficulties mentioned above. Comparing raw scores in each category would be fruitless, since the idea men have a somewhat higher total rate of participation and will therefore tend to show larger scores in every category. Percentage profiles for each man may be computed, and percentage scores in each category compared, but this exacerbates problems of interdependence and distribution. In order to give some clue, however, to the relative importance of the various categories in differentiating idea men from best-liked men, sign tests were performed on individual percentage profiles, category by category, for interaction initiated by each type of man. These showed categories 2, 3, 4, 5, 8 and 11 as the strongest differentiating categories.[11] Grouping categories by area, however, produces differences stronger than those generated by any of the component categories, with the single exception of Area D. In other words, Area A differentiates idea men from best-liked men better than categories 1, 2 and 3 taken individually, Area B better than categories 4, 5 and 6 taken individually, and Area C better than categories 7, 8 and 9 taken individually. In Area D, grouping does not seem meaningful, since

11. A study by Richard Mann, performed on a different sample, showed almost identical results for a slightly different type of comparison. Mann used not top men, but all men, comparing those who had higher ratings on task ability than on liking with those who had higher liking ratings than task ratings. See Mann (1954).

the three categories do not tend in the same direction. The tendency for the idea men to initiate more in categories 10 and 12, however, is so weak that it may almost be discounted.

These findings indicate that qualitative differentiation in the subjects' ratings of each other is accompanied by qualitative differentiation in the overt behavior of the subjects rated, such that idea men tend to specialize in active problem-solving attempts, and best-liked men in more reactive, less task-oriented behavior. The apparent complementarity of these two patterns suggests that a large share of the group's interaction may take place directly between the two 'specialists'. Since both are by definition highly valued in one way or another by the group, a high rate of interaction between them would be an indication that this relationship constitutes some sort of focal point in the group, and that the welfare of the group may be to some extent dependent upon the strength of this relationship. It would, therefore, be useful to know whether or not the two men interact more with each other than with other members.

Table 7 shows the extent to which this interaction preference existed. The tendency seems sufficiently marked, especially in the High groups, to justify the conclusion that the relationship is quantitatively important, though not always dominant in the group. Since the total amount of participation of the best-liked man averages no more than the average for all men, the findings in Table 7 suggest that his interaction is concentrated around the idea man to a greater extent than that of the other group members. In other words, although there may be men in the group who interact in general more heavily than the best-liked man, they do not engage the idea man in interaction to the same degree.

Some evidence also exists indicating that the relationship between the two 'specialists' tends on the whole to be the most positive in the group, especially in the high groups. Comparing the ratings each subject gave to each other subject on the question 'How well did you personally like each of the other members?' we find that:

1. The best-liked man tends to give the idea man a rating higher than the average of the other group member ratings of the idea man. This difference is significant at the 0·01 level, using a sign test.

Table 7 Interaction between Top-Ranking Men on Ideas (I) and Top-Ranking Men on Being Liked (L)

Characteristic of interaction observed	Percentage of cases in which characteristic occurred		Significance level for high and low groups combined
	High groups	Low groups	
I interacted with L more than he did with any other member	44·7	48·0*	**
I interacted with L more than any other member interacted with L	52·6*	50·0*	***
L interacted with I more than he did with any other member	73·7***	52·0**	***
L interacted with I more than any other member interacted with I	57·9*	30·0	*
Percentage expected by chance	28·9	26·0	

Level of significance: no asterisk, not significant; *, 0·05; **, 0·01; ***, 0·001.

2. The best-liked man gives the idea man a rating higher than his mean rating of other group members (significant at the 0·05 level).
3. The idea man gives the best-liked man a rating higher than the average of the other member ratings of the best-liked man in the high groups (significant at the 0·05 level) but not in the low.
4. The idea man gives the best-liked man a rating higher than his mean rating of other group members (significant at the 0·01 level).

We thus have the rather interesting picture of a respected task-oriented group member who is at best only moderately well liked, receiving strong support from a perhaps more socially oriented member who is the most popular man in the group, and with whom the task-oriented member forms a close and active relationship. Qualitative differentiation seems to be associated, then, with cooperation. Quantitative differentiation, i.e. differentiation along any single status dimension, may well be associated with more competitive responses.

Personality factors in differentiation

The data from which this study was drawn include little material which bears directly upon analysis of personality characteristics. An indirect source of material, however, appears in the subjects' ratings of each other on the question 'How well did you like each of the other members'. Many subjects tend to give all other members the same rating on this question. Since these subjects also tend to rate highly, they are saying, in effect, 'I like everyone'. Such undifferentiated ratings constitute about one-fifth of all the ratings in the sample, but they are not by any means divided equally among different types of subjects. Best-liked men are the most frequent non-differentiating members, idea men the least frequent. The difference between them is significant at the 0·05 level, using a chi-square test. Top guidance, talking and receiving men fail to differentiate about as often as the sample as a whole.

There is also a striking difference between high and low status-consensus groups on the distribution of undifferentiated ratings. In the high groups, subjects who refuse to differentiate their ratings tend to be persons with low status, i.e. persons who do not hold top rank on any of the five characteristics mentioned above. In the low groups, non-differentiating persons tend to be high status persons. This tendency is significant at the 0·01 level, using a chi-square test.

The meaning of this tendency to make undifferentiated ratings will perhaps become more clear if we examine its relationship to the only direct measure of personality characteristics available, i.e. subject scores on the California F-Scale. A thirty item F-scale was given to sixty-two of the 100 subjects in the sample, with differentiating raters receiving a mean F-score of 85, and non-differentiating raters a mean score of 103. The difference is significant at the 0·001 level, using a standard t-test.

High F-scores would thus be expected to distribute themselves much as do the undifferentiated liking ratings. Mean F-scores of all top-ranking men in high and low groups are shown in Table 8, and three types of differences are immediately apparent. First, top men in high groups generally have lower F-scores than top men in

Table 8 Mean Scores on Thirty-Item *F*-Scale for Top Men on Five Characteristics and Leader, in High and Low Groups

	High groups	Low groups	All groups
Leader	76·2	85·2	80·7
No. 1 guidance	88·7	79·2	83·9
No. 1 receiving	83·3	94·2	88·7
No. 1 talking	74·9	103·8	89·3
No. 1 ideas	82·3	101·2	91·7
No. 1 liking	91·1	99·9	95·5

low groups. This tendency is significant (at the 0·01 level) only in the case of talking and ideas, however. Second, idea men have significantly lower scores than best-liked men (0·05 level) in the high groups, though not in the low. Third, there is a tendency for top men on what have been described as more generalized characteristics, namely, leadership, guidance and receiving, to have lower *F*-scores than top men on the more specialized characteristics, talking, ideas and liking. This difference is significant at the 0·05 level.

Both relatively high *F*-scores and undifferentiated ratings may be interpreted as reflecting a tendency toward a rigid and over-simplified approach to interpersonal relations. Fine perceptual discriminations, or flexible and situationally determined behavior, are perhaps not to be expected from subjects falling into this category.[12] Their behavior will be determined rather by chronic, compulsive responses to inner needs, such as the need to be accepted and loved, the need to deny negative feelings toward members of one's own group, and so forth.

When we recall that low groups are more sharply specialized than high groups, and that the best-liked role is the most specialized of all our measures, it becomes clear that the common factor in all these findings is a strong relationship between this personal rigidity and specialization. The sharper the role differentiation in the group, or the more specialized the role played by the individual, the greater the rigidity in the personality or personalities involved.

12. An inference which might also be made on the basis of the high negative correlation between *F*-score and intelligence.

Discussion

According to Barnard (1938, pp. 55 ff.), the survival of any organization depends upon its ability to solve two problems: the achievement of the purposes for which the organization was formed and the satisfaction of the more immediate needs of the members of the organization. On the small-group level, Bales (1951, p. 10) makes a related distinction between the problems of the group involving goal achievement and adaptation to external demands, and problems involving internal integration and the expression of emotional tensions. The first group of problems he calls adaptive–instrumental problems, the solution of which demands activity in the task area. The second he calls Integrative–Expressive problems, the solution of which demands activity in the social-emotional area. Bales goes on to emphasize the difficulties inherent in attempting to solve both groups of problems at the same time.

Similar difficulties arise when the same *individual* attempts to take an active lead in solving these problems simultaneously. In large organizations the solution of integrative-expressive problems is in large part left to the leaders of informal groups, the importance of which Barnard (see 1938, pp. 223–4) and others (see Homans, 1950, pp. 48 ff.) have emphasized.

We have found that the most fundamental type of role differentiation in small experimental groups is the divorcing of task functions from social-emotional functions. Presumably, the ideal leader of a small group would be sufficiently skilful and flexible to alternate these types of behavior in such a way as to handle both problems, and maximize his status on all possible dimensions. He would be able to make both an active, striving response to the task and a sympathetic response to the individual needs of group members. He would be a high participator, well liked, rated high on task ability and eventually chosen leader.

Such individuals are rare. They appear occasionally in high status-consensus groups, almost never in low. It is possible that the absence in the low groups of anyone approaching this ideal type is responsible for their low status-consensus. Where a group must choose between individuals who are in different ways one-sided and limited in their capabilities, agreement on ratings will be difficult to attain.

There are at least two kinds of reasons for the rarity of such men. First, there are sociological factors, revolving around the non-compatibility of the task and social-emotional roles. Adaptation to pressures from outside the group, such as are created by a task which must be performed, involves, by definition, change. The individual who presses toward solution of a task inadvertently forces those around him to make continual minor adjustments in their behavior, and to re-examine continually their ideas and values in the light of these external demands. The individual who concerns himself with internal social-emotional problems, on the other hand, is supportive in his responses to the ideas and behavior of those around him and continually reaffirms their dominant values. The orientation of the task specialist is thus more techno-logical, that of the social-emotional specialist more traditionalistic. It is presumably the latter type of behavior which seems more appealing to members called upon to indicate whom they person-ally like best.

This is not to say that the task specialist will actually be disliked, but rather that his task emphasis will tend to arouse some negative feelings – feelings which may not be expressed, and which will never outweigh his value to the group in the minds of its members. Such feelings merely neutralize any strong positive feelings other members may hold toward him. Only in the low groups are task specialists actually *un*popular, and this phenomenon is perhaps expressive of the rigidity with which low-group task specialists perform their role.

The second set of reasons may be called psychological. These have to do with the individual's predisposition to assume a particular role. Men who are best-liked may 'have to be liked' and may achieve prominence in this role because of the ingrat-iating skills they have acquired during their lives in bringing this desired situation about. Avoidance of conflict and controversy may be a felt necessity for this type of person – hence, his behav-ior will show nothing that could be a source of disharmony. He will avoid even the thought that he might like some of his fellow members better than others. His rate of interaction will be average – not too high, not too low. He will in fact retire into the conven-tional safety of the 'average Joe'. He may even avoid the per-formance of task functions altogether, because of the personal threats which task activity might hold for him. Instead, he will express the group's feelings and questions and place its stamp of approval upon what has already come to pass.

The task specialist, on the other hand, may assume this role only because of an unwillingness or inability to respond to the needs of others. A compulsive concentration on an abstract problem will serve as an intellectual shield against the ambiguity of human feelings. Needs to express hostility may be channeled into aggressive and dogmatic problem-solving attempts.

When these motives determine the assumption of a specialized role in a group, the outlook for this group would seem to be poor. The F-score data suggest that such motives may in fact determine the behavior of specialists in low status-consensus groups.

It is even possible that the presence in a group of individuals with motives of this sort *creates* low status-consensus. The difficulty of choosing between inadequate specialists has already been mentioned. Furthermore, it seems reasonable to expect that rigidity in the personality structure will be associated with rigidity in the value structure of the individual concerned. The F-scale is in fact founded on this assumption. Such absolutistic value systems, rigidly held and zealously defended, will impede the formation of any kind of consensus, particularly consensus on the relative emphasis the group should place upon task and social-emotional activities.

The way in which this kind of consensus in turn determines the degree of consensus on a particular rating may be illustrated by considering again the process of choosing a leader. It was suggested above that the man chosen as leader is that individual who is felt to possess those qualities which best serve to satisfy *both* the task and social-emotional problems of the group. Since different groups emphasize task and social-emotional problems in varying proportions, the attribution of leadership will depend not only upon the choice of one person over another but also upon the differential stress placed upon these group problems by the group. The group problems might thus be conceived as factors, with weights assigned to them by the group according to some elementary kind of value consensus. One group, e.g. might attribute leadership on the basis say, of 0·7 task ability, 0·3 likeability; another might reverse the weights.[13] The fact that liking coincides so seldom with leadership suggests that in our sample social-emotional skills are not highly valued and are given a low weight. This may be due to the heavy task demands placed upon the group by the experimental situation or to the emphasis placed upon task ability and achievement by our culture.

In any case, leadership will be attributed to that member who has the highest combined rating on these and perhaps other factors. But if implicit agreement on weights is lacking, each rater will be making a qualitatively different evaluation, and leadership consensus becomes almost impossible.

Similarly, in making more specialized evaluations, a rater must decide what a specialist is supposed to do before deciding how well he does it. If there is no agreement in a group about what a given role should include, then roles will be performed in accordance with individual norms and will be evaluated in terms of personal criteria. Agreement on role definitions is thus hindered by rigid value systems at the very time when the inflexibility characteristic of specialists operating under these conditions makes this agreement all the more imperative.

In this discussion we have isolated three types of role structure.

1. The rare case in which a single leader performs all functions and differentiation does not occur. This is a high-group phenomenon.
2. The case in which moderate specialization arises simply because the specialists lack the exceptional talent necessary to counteract the sociological pressures toward differentiation. Choice of role is undoubtedly determined by personality factors as well as situational factors. Such preferences will not, however, be immutable. This is the more common case in high groups.
3. The case in which extreme specialization is brought about by psychological as well as sociological pressures. Specialization is sharp and disruptive, due to the fact that it springs from an over-determined response to inner needs rather than a flexible response

13. This discussion of leadership as a fused role is founded on suggestions by Arthur Couch. A factor analysis of leadership variables by Couch and Carter produced factors closely related to those discussed here. See Carter (1953).

to the needs of others, or to the demands of an ever-changing task situation. Specialists perform in a particular role because they 'have to' rather than because it is useful or desirable. This is a low-group phenomenon.

Thus while differentiation occurs in both high and low status-consensus groups, it seems to occur for different reasons. It is only the depth and breadth of the differentiation which will supply an immediate clue to which kinds of reasons are operating. One final example of this duality of meaning is the highest participator, who has not been considered in much of the foregoing analysis.

It will be recalled that in high groups, the highest participator usually receives the highest rating on task ability. Approval and acceptance of his ideas perhaps encourage him to participate more heavily and also generate his high rating. In low groups, the highest participator is far less often rated highly. He apparently does not adjust his amount of participation to the approval and acceptance he receives, but persists in interacting despite their absence. His participation time is determined by his own aggressiveness, by insensitivity rather than responsiveness to feedback from others. In keeping with the motivations of other low-group specialists, he talks, not because it is helpful to the group for him to do so, but because he has to.

In short, low-group specialists are going through many of the same motions as high-group specialists, but their needs and purposes differ. It would seem likely that *double entendres* of this sort constitute a major factor in obscuring the complexity of small-group relationships.

References

BALES, R. F. (1951), *Interaction Process Analysis*, Addison-Wesley.

BALES, R. F. (1953), 'The equilibrium problem in small groups', in T. Parsons, R. F. Bales and E. A. Shils (eds.), *Working Papers in the Theory of Action*, Free Press.

BALES, R. F., and SLATER, P. E. (1955), 'Role differentiation in small groups', in T. Parsons and R. F. Bales (eds.), *The Family: Socialization and Interaction Process*, Free Press.

BARNARD, C. I. (1938), *The Functions of the Executive*, Harvard University Press.

CARTER, L. F. (1953), 'Leadership and small group behavior', in M. Sherif and M. O. Wilson (eds.), *Group Relations at the Crossroads*, Harper & Row.

HEINICKE, C., and BALES, R. F. (1953), 'Developmental trends in the structure of small groups', *Sociometry*, vol. 16, pp. 7–38.

HOMANS, G. C. (1950), *The Human Group*, Harcourt, Brace & World.

KENDALL, M. G. (1948), *Rank Correlation Methods*. [Griffin edn 1962.]

KRAÜPL TAYLOR, F. (1951), 'Quantitative evaluation of psycho-social phenomena in small groups', *J. ment. Sci.*, vol. 97, pp. 690–717.

MANN, R. D. (1954), 'The relation of informal states to role behavior in small discussion groups', unpublished honours thesis, Harvard University.

13 Fred E. Fiedler

The Contingency Model:
A Theory of Leadership Effectiveness

Fred E. Fiedler, 'The contingency model: a theory of leadership effectiveness', in H. Proshansky and B. Seidenberg (eds.), *Basic Studies in Social Psychology*, Holt, Rinehart & Winston, 1965, pp. 538–51.

Leadership, as a problem in social psychology, has dealt primarily with two questions, namely, how one becomes a leader, and how one can become a *good* leader, that is, how one develops effective group performance. Since a number of excellent reviews (e.g. Bass, 1960; Gibb, 1954; Mann, 1959; Stogdill, 1948) have already dealt with the first question we shall not be concerned with it in the present paper.

The second question, whether a given leader will be more or less effective than others in similar situations, has been a more difficult problem of research and has received correspondingly less attention in the psychological literature. The theoretical status of the problem is well reflected by Browne and Cohn's (1958) statement that 'leadership literature is a mass of content without coagulating substances to bring it together or to produce coordination. . . .' McGrath (1962), in making a similar point, ascribed this situation to the tendency of investigators to select different variables and to work with idiosyncratic measures and definitions of leadership. He also pointed out, however, that most researchers in this area have gravitated toward two presumably crucial clusters of leadership attitudes and behaviors. These are the critical, directive, autocratic, task-oriented versus the democratic, permissive, considerate, person-oriented type of leadership. While this categorization is admittedly oversimplified, the major controversy in this area has been between the more orthodox viewpoint – reflected in traditional supervisory training and military doctrine that the leader should be decisive and forceful, that he should do the planning and thinking for the group, and that he should coordinate, direct and evaluate his men's actions – and the other viewpoint – reflected in the newer human-relations-oriented training and in the philosophy behind nondirective and brain-storming techniques – which stresses the need for democratic, permissive, group-oriented leadership techniques. Both schools of thought have strong adherents and there is evidence supporting both points of view (Gibb, 1954; Hare, 1962).

While one can always rationalize that contradictory findings by other investigators are due to poor research design, or different tests and criteria, such problems present difficulties if they appear in one's own research. We have, during the past thirteen years, conducted a large number of studies on leadership and group performance, using the same operational definitions and essentially similar leader attitude measures. The inconsistencies which we obtained in our own research program demanded an integrative theoretical formulation which would adequately account for the seemingly confusing results.

The studies which we conducted used as the major predictor of group performance an interpersonal perception or attitude score which is derived from the leader's description of his most and of his least preferred co-workers. He is asked to think of all others with whom he has ever worked, and then to describe first the person with whom he worked best (his most preferred co-worker) and then the person with whom he could work least well (his least preferred co-worker, or LPC). These descriptions are obtained, wherever possible, before the leader is assigned to his team. However, even where we deal with already existing groups, these descriptions tend to be of individuals whom the subject has known in the past rather than of persons with whom he works at the time of testing.

The descriptions are typically made on twenty eight-point bipolar adjective scales, similar to Osgood's Semantic Differential (Osgood, Suci and Tannerbaum, 1957), e.g.:

Pleasant 8 : 7 : 6 : 5 : 4 : 3 : 2 : 1 Unpleasant

Friendly 8 : 7 : 6 : 5 : 4 : 3 : 2 : 1 Unfriendly

These items are scaled on an evaluative dimension, giving a score of 8 to the most favorable pole (i.e. Friendly, Pleasant) and a score of 1 to the least favorable pole. Two main scores have been derived from these descriptions. The first one, which was used in our earlier studies, is based on the profile similarity measure D (Cronbach and Gleser, 1953) between the descriptions of the most and of the least preferred co-worker. This score, called the Assumed Similarity between Opposites, or ASo, indicates the degree to which the individual perceives the two opposites on his co-worker continuum as similar or different. The second score is simply based on the individual's description of his least preferred co-worker, LPC, and indicates the degree to which the subject evaluates his LPC in a relatively favorable or unfavorable manner. The two measures are highly correlated (0·80 to 0·95) and will here be treated as interchangeable.

We have had considerable difficulty in interpreting these scores since they appear to be uncorrelated with the usual personality and attitude measures. They are, however, related to the Ohio State University studies' 'Initiation of Structure' and 'Consideration' dimensions (Stogdill and Coons, 1957). Extensive content analyses (Julian and McGrath, 1963; Morris, 1964) and a series of studies by Hawkins (1962) as well as still unpublished research by Bass, Fiedler and Krueger have given consistent results. These indicate that the person with high LPC or ASo, who perceives his least preferred co-worker in a relatively favorable, accepting manner, tends to be more accepting, permissive, considerate and person-oriented in his relations with group members. The person who perceives his most and least preferred co-workers as quite different, and who sees his least preferred co-worker in a very unfavorable, rejecting manner tends to be directive, controlling, task-oriented and managing in his interactions.

ASo and LPC scores correlated highly with group performance in a wide variety of studies, although, as mentioned above, not consistently in the same direction. For example, the sociometrically chosen leader's ASo score correlated −0·69 and −0·58 with the percentage of games won by high-school basket-ball teams and −0·51 with the accuracy of surveying of civil-engineer teams (Fiedler, 1954), and the melter foreman's ASo score correlated −0·52 with tonnage output of open-hearth shops (Cleven and Fiedler, 1956). These negative correlations indicate that low ASo or LPC scores were associated with good group performance, i.e. that these groups performed better under managing, directive leaders than under more permissive, accepting leaders. However, while the ASo score of the sociometrically accepted company managers also correlated negatively (-0.70) with the net income of consumer cooperatives, the board chairman's ASo score under the same circumstances correlated $+0.62$ (Godfrey, Fiedler and Hall, 1959). Thus, groups with different tasks seemed to require different leader attitudes. In a more recent study of group creativity in Holland, the leader's LPC score correlated with performance $+0.75$ in religiously homogeneous groups with formally appointed leaders, but -0.72 in religiously heterogeneous groups; and while the correlation was $+0.75$ in homogeneous groups with appointed leaders it was -0.64 in homogeneous groups having emergent (sociometrically nominated) leaders (Fiedler, Meuwese and Oonk, 1961).

The results of these investigations clearly showed that the direction and magnitude of the correlations were contingent upon the nature of the group-task situation which confronted the leader. The problem resolved itself then into (a) developing a meaningful system for categorizing group task situations; (b) inducing the underlying theoretical model which would integrate the seemingly inconsistent results obtained in our studies; and (c) testing the validity of the model by adequate research.

Development of the model
Key definitions

We shall here be concerned with 'interacting' rather than 'co-acting' task groups. By an interacting task group we mean a face-to-face team situation (such as a basketball team) in which the members work *interdependently* on a common goal. In groups of this type, the individual's contributions cannot readily be separated from total group performance. In a co-acting group, however, such as a bowling or a rifle team, the group performance is generally determined by summing the members' individual performance scores.

We shall define the leader as the group member who is officially appointed or elected to direct and coordinate group action. In groups in which no one has been so designated, we have identified the informal leader by means of sociometric preference questions such as asking group members to name the person who was most influential in the group, or whom they would most prefer to have as a leader in a similar task.

The leader's effectiveness is here defined in terms of the group's performance on the assigned primary task. Thus, although a company manager may have, as one of his tasks, the job of maintaining good relations with his customers, his main job and the one on which he is in the final analysis evaluated, consists of the long-range profitability of the company. Good relations with customers, or high morale and low labor turnover may well contribute to success, but they would not be the basic criteria by this definition.

The categorization of group-task situations

Leadership is essentially a problem of wielding influence and power. When we say that different types of groups require different types of leadership we imply that they require a different relationship by which the leader wields power and influence. Since it is easier to wield power in some groups than in others, an attempt to categorize groups might well begin by asking what conditions in the group-task situation will facilitate or inhibit the leader's exercise of power. On the basis of our previous work we postulated three important aspects in the total situation which influence the leader's role.

Leader–member relations. The leader who is personally attractive to his group members, and who is respected by his group, enjoys considerable power (French, 1956). In fact, if he has the confidence and loyalty of his men he has less need of official rank. This dimension can generally be measured by means of sociometric indices or by group atmosphere scales (Fiedler, 1962) which indicate the degree to which the leader experiences the group as pleasant and well disposed toward him.

Task structure. The task generally implies an order 'from above' which incorporates the authority of the superior organization. The group member who refuses to comply must be prepared to face disciplinary action by the higher authority. For example, a squad member who fails to perform a lawful command of his sergeant may have to answer to his regimental commander. However, compliance with a task order can be enforced only if the task is relatively well structured, i.e. if it is capable of being programmed.

One cannot effectively force a group to perform well on an unstructured task such as developing a new product or writing a good play.

Thus, the leader who has a structured task can depend on the backing of his superior organization, but if he has an unstructured task the leader must rely on his own resources to inspire and motivate his men. The unstructured task thus provides the leader with much less effective power than does the highly structured task.

We operationalized this dimension by utilizing four of the aspects which Shaw (1962) recently proposed for the classification of group tasks. These are (a) decision *verifiability*, the degree to which the correctness of the solution can be demonstrated objectively; (b) *goal clarity*, the degree to which the task requirements are clearly stated or known to the group; (c) *goal path multiplicity*, the degree to which there are many or few procedures available for performing the task (reverse scoring); and (d) *solution specificity*, the degree to which there is one rather than an infinite number of correct solutions (e.g. solving an equation *v*. writing a story). Ratings based on these four dimensions have yielded interrater reliabilities of 0·80 to 0·90.

Position power. The third dimension is defined by the power inherent in the position of leadership irrespective of the occupant's personal relations with his members. This includes the rewards and punishments which are officially or traditionally at the leader's disposal, his authority as defined by the group's rules and bylaws, and the organizational support given to him in dealing with his men. This dimension can be operationally defined by means of a check list (Fiedler, 1964) containing items such as 'Leader can effect promotion or demotion', 'Leader enjoys special rank and status in real life which sets him apart from, and above, his group members'. The median interrater agreement of four independent judges rating thirty-five group situations was 0·95.

A three-dimensional group classification

Group-task situations can now be rated on the basis of the three dimensions of leader–member relations, task structure and position power. This locates each group in a three-dimensional space. A rough categorization can be accomplished by halving each of the

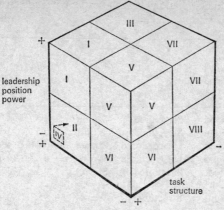

Figure 1 A model for the classification of group-task situations

dimensions so that we obtain an eight-celled cube (Figure 1). We can now determine whether the correlations between leader attitudes and group performance within each of these eight cells, or octants, are relatively similar in magnitude and direction. If they are, we can infer that the group classification has been successfully accomplished since it shows that groups falling within the same octant require similar leader attitudes.

A previous paper has summarized fifty-three group-task situations which are based on our previous studies (Fiedler, 1964). These fifty-three group-task situations have been ordered into the eight octants. As can be seen from Table 1, groups falling within the same octant show correlations between the leader's A S o or L P C score and the group performance criterion which are relatively similar in magnitude and direction. We can thus infer that the group classification has been accomplished with at least reasonable success.

Consideration of Figure 1 suggests a further classification of the cells in terms of the effective power which the group-task situation places at the leader's disposal, or more precisely, the favourableness of the situation for the leader's exercise of his power and influence.

Table 1 Median Correlation between Leader LPC and Group Performance in Various Octants

	Leader–member relations	Task structure	Position power	Median correlation	Number of relations included in median
Octant I	Good	Structured	Strong	−0·52	8
Octant II	Good	Structured	Weak	−0·58	3
Octant III	Good	Unstructured	Strong	−0·41	4
Octant IV	Good	Unstructured	Weak	0·47	10
Octant V	Mod. Poor	Structured	Strong	0·42	6
Octant VI	Mod. Poor	Structured	Weak		0
Octant VII	Mod. Poor	Unstructured	Strong	0·05	10
Octant VIII	Mod. Poor	Unstructured	Weak	−0·43	12

Such an ordering can be accomplished without difficulty at the extreme poles of the continuum. A liked and trusted leader with high rank and a structured task is in a more favorable position than is a disliked and powerless leader with an ambiguous task. The intermediate steps pose certain theoretical and methodological problems. To collapse a three-dimensional system into an unidimensional one implies in Coombs's terms a partial order or a lexicographic system for which there is no unique solution. Such an ordering must, therefore, be done either intuitively or in accordance with some reasonable assumptions. In the present instance we have postulated that the most important dimension in the system is the leader–member relationship since the highly liked and respected leader is less in need of position power or the power of the higher authority incorporated in the task structure. The second most important dimension is the task structure, since a leader with a highly structured task does not require a powerful leader position. (For example, privates or noncommissioned officers in the army are at times called upon to lead or instruct officers in certain highly structured tasks – such as demonstrating a new weapon or teaching medical officers close order drill – though not in unstructured tasks – such as planning new policies on strategy.) This leads us to order the group-task situations first on leader–member relations, then on task structure, and finally on position power. While admittedly not a unique solution, the resulting ordering constitutes a reasonable continuum which indicates the degree of the leader's effective power in the group.[1]

A contingency model for predicting leadership performance

As was already apparent from Table 1, the relationship between leader attitudes and group performance is contingent upon the accurate classification of the group-task situation. A more meaningful model of this contingency relationship emerges when we now plot the correlation between LPC or ASo and group performance on the one hand, against the octants ordered on the effective power or favourableness-for-the-leader dimension on the other. This is shown in Figure 2. Note that each point in the plot is a *correlation* predicting leadership performance or group effectiveness. The plot therefore represents fifty-three *sets of groups* totaling over 800 separate groups.

As Figure 2 shows, managing, controlling, directive (low LPC) leaders perform most effectively either under very favorable or under very unfavorable situations. Hence we obtain negative correlations between LPC and group performance scores. Considerate, permissive, accepting leaders obtain optimal group performance under situations intermediate in favorableness. These are situations in which (a) the task is structured, but the leader is disliked and must, therefore, be diplomatic; (b) the liked leader has an ambiguous, unstructured task and must, therefore, draw upon the creativity and cooperation of his members. Here we obtain positive correlations between LPC and group performance scores. Where the task is highly structured and the leader is well liked, nondirective behavior or permissive attitudes (such as asking how the group ought to proceed with a missile count-down) is

1. Another cell should be added which contains real-life groups which reject their leader. Exercise of power would be very difficult in this situation and such a cell should be placed at the extreme negative end of the continuum. Such cases are treated in the section on validation.

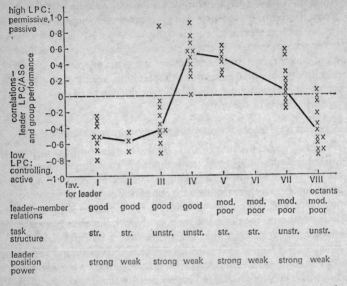

Figure 2 Correlations of leader LPC and group performance plotted against octants, that is, favorableness of group-task situation for leader

neither appropriate nor beneficial. Where the situation is quite unfavorable, e.g. where the disliked chairman of a volunteer group faces an ambiguous task, the leader might as well be autocratic and directive since a positive, nondirective attitude under these conditions might result in complete inactivity on the part of the group. This model, thus, tends to shed some light on the apparent inconsistencies in our own data as well as in data obtained by other investigators.

Empirical tests: extension of the model

The basic hypothesis of the model suggests that the directive, controlling, task-oriented (low LPC) leader will be most successful in group-task situations which are either very favorable or else very unfavorable for the leader. The permissive, considerate, human-relations-oriented (high LPC) leader will perform best under conditions which are intermediate in favorableness. This hypothesis was tested by reanalysing data from previous studies as well as by a major experiment specifically designed to test the model. Both are briefly described below.

Reanalyses of previous studies

As we indicated before, there is reason to believe that the relationship between the leader and his members is the most important of the three dimensions for classifying group-task situations. The problem of exercising leadership will be a relatively easy one in group-task situations in which the leader is not only liked by his crew and gets along well with his group, but in which the task is structured and the leader has a relatively powerful position. The situation will be somewhat more difficult if the leader under the latter circumstances has an only moderately good relationship with his group members, and it will be quite difficult if the leader-member relations are very poor, i.e. if the group members reject or actively dislike the leader. Ordinarily this does not occur in laboratory studies. It does happen, however, that real-life groups strongly reject leaders – sometimes to the point of sabotaging the task. Since such a situation would present a very difficult problem in leadership, we would expect better performance from the task-oriented, controlling leader, and hence a negative correlation between the leader's ASo or LPC score and his group's performance. This result appeared in one study of bomber crews for which we already had the appropriate data, and it was tested by new analyses in two other studies.

Bomber crew study. A study of B-29 bomber crews was conducted (Fiedler, 1955) in which the criterion of performance consisted of radar bomb scores. This is the average circular error or accuracy of hitting the target by means of radar procedures. The crews were classified on the basis of the relationship between the aircraft commander and his crew members. The crews were ordered on whether or not (a) the aircraft commander was the most chosen member of the crew and (b) the aircraft commander sociometrically endorsed his key men on his radar bombing team (the radar observer and navigator).

The results of this analysis are presented in Table 2. It can be seen that the correlations between ASo and crew performance are highly negative in crews having very good and very poor leader–

Table 2 Correlations between Aircraft Commander's (ACs) ASo Score and Radar Bomb Scores under Different Patterns of Sociometric Choices in B-29 Bomber Crews

	Rho	N
AC is most preferred crew member and chooses keymen (K)	−0·81	10
AC is most preferred crew member and is neutral to K	−0·14	6
AC is most preferred crew member and does not choose K	0·43	6
AC is not most preferred crew member but chooses K	−0·03	18
AC is not most preferred crew member and is neutral to K	−0·80	5
AC is not most preferred crew member and does not choose K	−0·67	7

group relations, but they tend to be positive in the intermediate range.

Anti-aircraft artillery crews. A second set of data came from a study of anti-aircraft artillery crews (Hutchins and Fiedler, 1960). The criterion of crew performance consisted of scores indicating the 'location and acquisition' of unidentified aircraft. These crews were subdivided on the basis of leader–crew relations by separately correlating the leader's LPC score with group performance (a) for the ten crews which most highly chose their crew commander, (b) the ten which were in the intermediate range and (c) the ten crews which gave the least favorable sociometric choices to their leader. Correlation coefficients (rho) of −0·34, +0·49 and −0·42 were obtained respectively for the three sets of artillery crews. Here again there is a clear indication that controlling and directive leaders perform most effectively under very favorable or unfavorable leader–group relations (negative correlations between LPC and group performance), whereas more permissive and accepting leaders obtain optimal group performance when leader–group relations are intermediate in favorableness (positive correlations between LPC and group performance).

Consumer cooperative companies. Finally we reanalysed data from a study of thirty-one consumer cooperatives (Godfrey, Fiedler and Hall, 1959) in which the criterion of performance consisted of the percentage of company net income over a three-year period. The companies were subdivided into those in which the general manager was sociometrically chosen (a) by his board of directors as well as by his staff of assistant managers, (b) by his board but not his staff, or (c) by his staff but not his board and (d) the companies in which the general manager was rejected, or not chosen, by both board of directors and staff. The findings shown in Table 3 are clearly

Table 3 Correlations between General Manager's ASo Score and Company Net Income

	Rho	N
Gen. Mgr is chosen by board and staff (ASo Perf.)	−0·67	10
Gen. Mgr is chosen by board, but rejected by staff	0·20	6
Gen. Mgr is rejected by board, but chosen by staff	0·26	6
Gen. Mgr is rejected by board and staff	−0·75	7

consistent with those reported above for the two studies of military personnel.

The results of these three investigations are summarized in Figure 3. It can be seen that the task-oriented, managing, low LPC leaders performed best under very favorable and under very unfavorable situations, while the permissive, considerate leaders performed best under conditions intermediate in favorableness. These data, therefore, clearly support the hypothesis derived from the model.

Experimental test of the contingency model

In cooperation with the Belgian naval forces we recently conducted a major study which served in part as a specific test of the model. Only aspects immediately relevant to the test are here described. The investigation was conducted in Belgium where the French- and Dutch-speaking (or Flemish) sectors of the country have been involved in a long-standing and frequently acrimonious dispute. This conflict centers about the use of language, but it also involves a host of other cultural factors which differentiate the 60 per cent Flemish- and 40 per cent French-speaking population groups in Wallonie and Brussels. This 'linguistic problem', which is rooted in the beginning of Belgium's natural history, has in recent years been the cause of continuous public controversy, frequent protest meetings and occasional riots.

Fred E. Fiedler 257

The linguistic problem is of particular interest here since a group consisting of members whose mother tongue, culture and attitudes differ will clearly present a more difficult problem in leadership than a group whose members share the same language and culture. We were thus able to test the major hypothesis of the model as well as to extend the research by investigating the type of leadership which linguistically and culturally heterogeneous groups require.

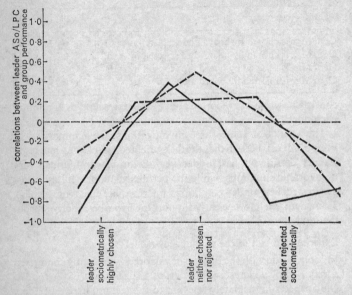

Figure 3 Correlations between leader LPC or ASo scores and group performance under three conditions of leader acceptance by the group in studies of bomber crews, anti-aircraft artillery crews and consumer cooperatives

Design

The experiment was conducted at the naval training center at Ste Croix-Bruges. It utilized forty-eight career petty officers and 240 recruits who had been selected from a pool of 546 men on the basis of a pretest in which we obtained LPC, intelligence, attitude and language comprehension scores.

The experiment was specifically designed to incorporate the three major group classification dimensions shown in Figure 1, namely, leader–member relations, position power, and task structure. It also added the additional dimension of group homogeneity v. heterogeneity. Specifically, forty-eight groups had leaders with high position power (petty officers) while forty-eight had leaders with low position power (recruits); forty-eight groups began with the unstructured task, while the other forty-eight groups began with the two structured tasks; forty-eight groups were homogeneous, consisting of three French- or three Dutch-speaking men, while the other forty-eight groups were heterogeneous, consisting of a French-speaking leader and two Flemish members, or a Dutch-speaking, Flemish leader and two French-speaking members. The quality of the leader–member relations was measured as in our previous studies by means of a group atmosphere scale which the leader completed after each task session.

Group performance criteria

Two essentially identical structured tasks were administered. Each lasted twenty-five minutes and required the groups to find the shortest route for a ship which, given certain fuel capacity and required ports of call, had to make a round trip calling at respectively ten or twelve ports. The tasks were objectively scored on the basis of sea miles required for the trip. Appropriate corrections and penalties were assigned for errors.

The unstructured task required the groups to compose a letter to young men of sixteen and seventeen years, urging them to choose the Belgian navy as a career. The letter was to be approximately 200 words in length and had to be completed in thirty-five minutes. Each of the letters, depending upon the language in which it was written, was then rated by Dutch- or by French-speaking judges on style, the use of language, as well as interest value, originality, and persuasiveness. Estimated reliability was 0·92 and 0·86 for Dutch- and French-speaking judges, respectively.

It should be noted in this connexion that the task of writing a letter is not as unstructured as might have been desirable for this experiment. The form of any letter of this type is fairly standardized, and its content was, of course, suggested by the instructions. The navy officers with whom we consulted throughout the study considered it unwise, however, to give a highly unstructured task, such as writing a fable or proposing a new policy, since tasks of this nature were likely to threaten the men and to cause resentment and poor cooperation. High and low task structure is, therefore, less well differentiated in this study than it has been in previous investigations.

Results

The contingency model specifies that the controlling, managing, low LPC leaders will be most effective either in very favorable or else in relatively unfavorable group-task situations, while the permissive, considerate, high LPC leaders will be more effective in situations intermediate in difficulty.

The basic test of the hypotheses requires, therefore, that we order the group-task situations represented in this experiment in terms of the difficulty which they are likely to present for the leader. Since there are sixteen cells in the design, the size of the sample within each cell (namely, six groups) is, of course, extremely small. However, where the conditions are reasonably replicated by other cells, the relationship can be estimated from the median rank-order correlations.

The hypothesis can be tested more readily with correlations of leader LPC and group performance in homogeneous groups on the more reliably scorable second structured task. These conditions approximate most closely those represented in Figure 3, on bomber and anti-aircraft crews and consumer cooperatives. We have here made the fairly obvious assumption that the powerful leader or the leader who feels liked and accepted faces an easier group-task situation than low-ranking leaders and those who see the groups as unpleasant and tense. Each situation is represented by two cells of six groups each. Arranging the group-task situations in order of favorableness for the leader then gives us the following results:

High group atmosphere and high position power ... $-0.77, -0.77$
High group atmosphere and low position power ... $+0.60, +0.50$
Low group atmosphere and high position power ... $+0.16, +0.01$
Low group atmosphere and low position power ... $-0.16, -0.43$

These are, of course, the trends in size and magnitude of correlations which the model predicts. Low LPC leaders are again most effective in favorable and unfavorable group-task situations; the more permissive, considerate, high LPC leaders were more effective in the intermediate situations.

Extending the model to include heterogeneous groups requires that we make a number of additional assumptions for weighting each of the group-task dimensions so that all forty-eight cells (i.e. sixteen cells × three tasks) can be reasonably ordered on the same scale. We have here assigned equal weights of three to the favorable poles of the major dimension, i.e. to homogeneity, high group atmosphere and high position power. A weight of one was assigned to the first structured task, and a weight of two to the second structured task on the assumption that the structured task makes the group-task situation somewhat more favorable than the unstructured task, and that the practice and learning effect inherent in performing a second, practically identical, task will make the group-task situation still more favorable for the leader. Finally, a weight of one was given to the 'second presentation', that is, the group task which occurred toward the end of the session, on the assumption that the leader by that time had gotten to know his group members and had learned to work with them more effectively, thus again increasing the favorableness of his group-task situation to a certain extent.

The resulting weighting system leads to a scale from 12 to 0 points, with 12 as the most favorable pole. If we now plot the median correlation coefficients of the 48 group-task situations against the scale indicating the favorableness of the situation for the leader, we obtain the curve presented in Figure 4.

As can be seen, we again obtain a curvilinear relationship which resembles the one shown in Figure 2. Heterogeneous groups with low position power and/or poor leader-member relations fall below point 0·00 on the scale, and thus tend to perform better with controlling, directive, low LPC leaders. Only under otherwise very favorable conditions do heterogeneous groups perform better with permissive, considerate, high LPC leaders, that is, in group-task situations characterized by high group atmosphere as well as high position power, four of the six correlations (66 per cent) are positive, while only five of eighteen (28 per cent) are positive in the less favorable group-task situations.

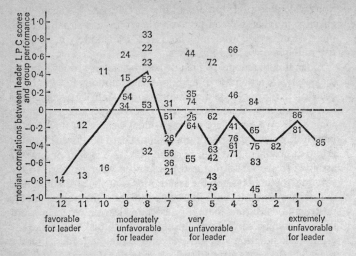

Figure 4 Median correlations between leader L P C and group performance scores plotted against favorableness-for-leader scale in the Belgian Navy study. The code is explained in Table 4

It is interesting to note that the curve is rather flat and characterized by relatively low negative correlations as we go toward the very unfavorable end of the scale. This result supports Meuwese's (1964) recent study which showed that correlations between leader L P C as well as between leader intelligence and group performance tend to become attenuated under conditions of relative stress. These findings suggest that the leader's ability to influence and control the group decreases beyond a certain point of stress and difficulty in the group-task situation.

Discussion

The contingency model seeks to reconcile results which up to now had to be considered inconsistent and difficult to understand. We have here attempted to develop a theoretical framework which can provide guidance for further research. While the model will undoubtedly undergo modifications and elaboration as new data become available, it provides an additional step toward a better

Table 4 Code in Figure 4

Composition	1st digit			2nd digit		
	Pos. pow.	High group atmos.	Low group atmos.	Task	1st pres.	2nd pres.
Homo.	High	1	5	Str. I	1	2
Homo.	Low	2	6	Str. II	3	4
Het.	High	3	7	Unstr.	5	6
Het.	Low	4	8			

understanding of leadership processes required in different situations. We have here tried to specify exactly the type of leadership which different group-task situations require.

The model has a number of important implications for selection and training as well as for the placement of leaders and organizational strategy. Our research suggests, first of all, that we can utilize a very broad spectrum of individuals for positions of leadership. The problem becomes one of placement and training rather than of selection since both the permissive, democratic human-relations-oriented and the managing, autocratic, task-oriented leader can be effectively utilized. Leaders can be trained to recognize their own style of leadership as well as the conditions which are most compatible with their style.

The model also points to a variety of administrative and supervisory strategies which the organization can adopt to fit the group-task situation to the needs of the leader. Tasks can, after all, be structured to a greater or lesser extent by giving very specific and detailed, or vague and general, instructions; the position power of the group leader can be increased or decreased and even the congeniality of a group and its acceptance of the leader can be affected by appropriate administrative action, e.g. increasing or decreasing the group's homogeneity.

The model also throws new light on phenomena which were rather difficult to fit into our usual ideas about measurement in social psychology. Why, for example, should groups differ so markedly in their performance on nearly parallel tasks? The model – and our data – show that the situation becomes easier for the leader as the group moves from the novel to the already known group-task situations. The leaders who excel under relatively novel and therefore more difficult conditions are not necessarily those who excel under those which are more routine, or better known, and therefore more favorable. Likewise, we find that different types of task structure require different types of leader behavior. Thus, in a research project's early phases the project director tends to be democratic and permissive: everyone is urged to contribute to the plan and to criticize all aspects of the design. This situation changes radically in the more structured phase when the research design is frozen and the experiment is under way. Here the research director tends to become managing, controlling and highly autocratic and woe betide the assistant who attempts to be creative in giving instructions to subjects, or in his timing of tests. A similar situation is often found in business organization where the routine operation tends to be well structured and calls for a managing, directive leadership. The situation becomes suddenly unstructured when a crisis occurs. Under these conditions the number of discussions, meetings, and conferences increases sharply so as to give everyone an opportunity to express his views.

At best, this model is of course only a partial theory of leadership. The leader's intellectual and task-relevant abilities, and the members' skills and motivation, all play a role in affecting the group's performance. It is to be hoped that these other important aspects of group interaction can be incorporated into the model in the not too distant future.

References

BASS, B. M. (1960), *Leadership, Psychology and Organizational Behavior*, Harper & Row.

BROWNE, C. G., and COHN, T. S. (eds.) (1958), *The Study of Leadership*, Interstate Printers and Publishers.

CLEVEN, W. A., and FIEDLER, F. E. (1956), 'Interpersonal perceptions of open hearth foremen and steel production', *J. appl. Psychol.*, vol. 40, pp. 312–14.

CRONBACH, L. J., and GLESER, G. C. (1953), 'Assessing similarity between profiles', *Psychol. Bull.*, vol. 50, pp. 456–73.

FIEDLER, F. E. (1954), 'Assumed similarity measures as predictors of team effectiveness', *J. abnorm. soc. Psychol*, vol. 49, pp. 381–8.

FIEDLER, F. E. (1955), 'The influence of leader–keymen relations on combat crew effectiveness', *J. abnorm. soc. Psychol.*, vol. 51, pp. 227–35.

FIEDLER, F. E. (1962), 'Leader attitudes, group climate, and group creativity', *J. abnorm. soc. Psychol.*, vol. 65, pp. 308–18.

FIEDLER, F. E. (1964), 'A contingency model of leadership effectiveness', in L. Berkowitz (ed.), *Advances in Experimental Social Psychology*, Academic Press.

FIEDLER, F. E., and MEUWESE, W. A. T. (1963), 'The leader's contribution to performance in cohesive and uncohesive groups', *J. abnorm. soc. Psychol.*, vol. 67, pp. 83–7.

FIEDLER, F. E., MEUWESE, W. A. T., and OONK, S. (1961), 'Performance of laboratory tasks requiring group creativity', *Acta Psychol.*, vol. 18, pp. 100–119.

FRENCH, J. R. P., JR. (1956), 'A formal theory of social power', *Psychol. Rev.*, vol. 63, pp. 181–94.

GIBB, C. A. (1954), 'Leadership', in G. Lindzey (ed.), *Handbook of Social Psychology*, vol. 2, Addison-Wesley.

GODFREY, E. P., FIEDLER, F. E., and HALL, D. M. (1959), *Boards, Management, and Company Success*, Interstate Printers and Publishers.

HARE, A. P. (1962), *Handbook of Small Group Research*, Free Press.

HAWKINS, C. (1962), 'A study of factors mediating a relationship between leader rating behavior and group productivity', unpublished Ph.D. dissertation, University of Minnesota.

HUTCHINS, E. B., and FIEDLER, F. E. (1960), 'Task-oriented and quasi-therapeutic role functions of the leader in small military groups', *Sociometry*, vol. 23, pp. 293–406.

JULIAN, J. W., and McGRATH, J. E. (1963), *The Influence of Leader and Member Behavior on the Adjustment and Task Effectiveness of Negotiation Groups*, Group Effectiveness Research Laboratory, University of Illinois.

McGRATH, J. E. (1962), *A Summary of Small Group Research Studies*, Human Sciences Research Inc., Arlington (litho).

MANN, R. D. (1959), 'A review of the relationship between personality and performance in small groups', *Psychol. Bull.*, vol. 56, pp. 241–70.

MEUWESE, W. A. T. (1964), 'The effect of the leader's ability and interpersonal attitudes on group creativity under varying conditions of stress', unpublished doctoral dissertation, University of Amsterdam.

MORRIS, C. G. H. (1964), 'The effects of leader attitudes on the behavior of problem solving groups and their leaders', unpublished MA thesis, University of Illinois.

OSGOOD, C. E., SUCI, G. A., and TANNENBAUM, P. H. (1957), *The Measurement of Meaning*, University of Illinois Press.

SHAW, M. E. (1962), 'Annual technical report, 1962', University of Florida (mimeo).

STOGDILL, R. M. (1948), 'Personal factors associated with leadership: a survey of the literature', *J. Psychol.*, vol. 25, pp. 35–71.

STOGDILL, R. M., and COONS, A. E. (1957), 'Leader behavior: its description and measurement', *Ohio State University Research Monograph*, no. 88.

14 Richard de Charms, Virginia Carpenter and Aharon Kuperman

The 'Origin–Pawn' Variable in Person Perception

Richard de Charms, Virginia Carpenter and Aharon Kuperman, 'The "origin–pawn" variable in person perception', *Sociometry*, vol. 28, 1965, pp. 241–58.

Albert Schweitzer is usually seen as a man who is voluntarily working for the good of mankind in Africa. Our perception of him is that of a man who is free, is pursuing what he has chosen as his contribution to humanity and is happy in doing it. If anything is seen as constraining him to this work it is his own dedication to the value of working for the good of mankind. We see Albert Schweitzer as the *origin* of his behavior.

John Doe has just been drafted into the army, preventing him from going to college as he had wished. He is peeling potatoes on KP while his buddies are out 'on the town'. Our perception of him is that of a man who is completely constrained, pursuing an activity not of his own choosing. He is probably miserable and finds little to value in the constraining force – the army. We see John Doe, not as the origin of his behavior, but as a *pawn*.

Behavior is readily interpreted along the 'origin–pawn' dimension, and the interpretation may have important effects. If we ask ourselves in a specific instance 'What made him do that?' the interpretation of the word 'made' can be very important. If force is implied, especially from an external personal source, we may absolve the person who was forced to behave in a socially disapproved way of all responsibility. We locate the 'cause' of his behavior as external to him and say he is 'merely a pawn in the game'.

If we interpret the question 'What made him do that?' in terms of intentions, we assume that the 'cause' or 'origin' of the behavior lies in the intention and a person is held personally responsible for his intentions. The motivational implications of the attribution of intention are developed by Urmson (1952) and by Anscombe (1957). The importance of such attribution in person perception probably derives from the personal experience of the person attributing intentions to another. In the past he may be assumed to have felt strongly under some conditions that he freely initiated his behavior, and under other conditions that he was constrained by direction from some external force. Thus, personal knowledge of being treated like a pawn or feeling like an origin enter into the attribution of intention.

It seems reasonable to assume that different external sources of influence on the behavior of a person will be seen as differentially constraining his behavior. A person who is caught in the web of a large organization which has absolute power to control his behavior in ways which he does not like or approve is a pawn. A pawn is relatively powerless compared to an origin, and power relationships are most certainly entailed when inferences are made along the origin-pawn dimension.

At the societal level alienation may be involved, for, as Seeman (1959), and Rotter, Seeman and Liverant (1962) have shown, feelings of powerlessness may reflect alienation from society. Alienation, in turn, may be a consequence to the worker of industrialization, as pointed out by Marx, or of bureaucratization as suggested by Max Weber.

In this connexion it is also relevant to mention Merton's (1957) analysis of Durkheim's concept of anomie which stresses the lack of overlap between values of an anomic individual and those of the culture or organization of which he is a part. The anomalous situation arises of a person who is a deviant from the norms of the group either as to the ends which he values or as to the approved means by which he seeks the ends. Under such conditions the person will not have access to the means of achieving his life goals, as Meier and Bell (1959) have shown, and will be perceived as a pawn.

The person who is seen as the origin of his behavior is assumed to be personally responsible for it. He has found means within his group of achieving some of his life goals, and has initiated the appropriate behavior. One example of such behavior in our culture is that of the entrepreneur. McClelland (1961) sees entrepreneurial behavior as most appropriate and conducive to the goal of economic development of the culture, and one of the major characteristics which McClelland attributes to entrepreneurs is the desire for individual responsibility for their actions.

Richard de Charms, Virginia Carpenter and Aharon Kuperman 267

Evidence presented by McClelland indicates that individual responsibility is not necessarily precluded in working for a group or an organization, as long as the individual can feel free to initiate action and make decisions contributing to group success. Clearly such innovative behavior would be seen as originating within the person. Apparently we cannot assume that all persons working in a bureaucratic structure will feel like or be seen as pawns. Overlap between the goals of the organization and those of the individual might lead to the inference that he is more of an origin despite the fact that he is working for a bureaucratic organization.

The 'origin–pawn' concept derives its social psychological roots from Heider's (1958) discussion of the perception of the locus of causality of behavior. Research showing the importance of the locus of causality concept has been reported by Thibaut and Riecken (1955a and b), Pepitone (1958), and Wilkins and de Charms (1962), among others. From these studies we can assume that when people attempt to infer motives from a person's behavior they often take into account to what extent the behavior may be considered to be 'his own' and to what extent he 'was forced' into it. They probably arrive at some estimate which reaches neither extreme of the origin–pawn dimension for the underlying concept involves a continuous dimension rather than a discrete dichotomy. The evidence from which one draws inferences probably has to do with such things as (a) whether or not an agent of persuasion is trying to get the person to act in a prescribed way; (b) whether the person likes or dislikes the agent; and (c) 'what's in it for him' (reward or punishment for the person). Ultimately the judgement is probably made in terms of an estimate of how the observer making the judgement would feel under such circumstances.

The purpose of this study is to investigate some of the personal and situational aspects which affect the perception that a person is acting as an origin or is being pushed around like a pawn. From the broader context sketched above we can derive the generalization that a large impersonal bureaucratic organization fosters a feeling of powerlessness in its members. From this we may predict that people involved in the network of a large bureaucratic organization may be seen as pawns *vis-à-vis* the organization. The perception may be tempered by information about the person's attitudes towards the organization. If overlap may be assumed between the individual's and the organization's goals, he will be seen as more of an origin.

Specifically, we presented our subjects with a series of stories in all of which the principal character (hero) is being influenced to do something by another character or group (the persuasive agent). The persuasive agent is presented as either very attractive or very unattractive to the hero, and is variously an individual, a small group or a large organization.

On the assumption that inferences about an observed person's behavior are affected by the perceiver's estimate of how *he* would feel in the situation, we have attempted to measure a generalized characteristic of the subjects along a dimension of feeling in control of fate or of being controlled by it. As an outgrowth of Rotter's (1954) social learning theory, Rotter, Seeman and Liverant have developed a scale to measure the perception of internal *v.* external control of reinforcements: 'External control refers to the perception of positive and/or negative events as being unrelated to one's own behaviors in certain situations and therefore beyond personal control' (Rotter, Seeman and Liverant, 1962, p. 499). A form of the internal–external control (I–E) scale developed by these authors was used here to measure a personal aspect of subjects which was hypothesized to be related to their perception of the hero along the origin–pawn dimension.

The choice of the independent variable of attractiveness of the persuasive agent was guided by the hypothesis (I) that the hero would be perceived more as an origin when he was being persuaded by an agent that he liked and more as a pawn when being persuaded by an agent that he disliked, when all other factors were held constant.

The type of persuasive agent was varied from individual to small group to large organization to test the hypothesis (II) that a hero reacting to a large organization would be seen as more of a pawn than a hero reacting to a small group or an individual. The feeling of control over fate (as measured in each subject) was included to test the hypothesis (III) that subjects who feel that they have internal control over the consequences of their own actions will perceive the hero as more of an origin than subjects who feel external control over their own behavior.

The variation of type of persuasive agent to test hypothesis II is really a composite variable. The agents used were an individual, a small group, and a large organization. The major difference may be seen as size of group, but as size of group increases several other aspects are also likely to change in real groups. The individual and the small group can be personally known, the large organization cannot, and the type of power wielded by an individual, a small group or a large organization may be quite different. In the present study, an attempt was made to select typical agents in the real world rather than to try to assure that the *only* difference between agents was the number of people included. Although it might be argued that it would be more precise to vary the size alone, we followed the assumption that it would be more meaningful and realistic to investigate the effects of typical agents despite their composite nature.

Method

Forty-two vignettes about seven different heroes were composed around a basic design which always presented a hero who was being persuaded to do something. Each vignette explained (a) who the hero was; (b) what his relationship with and attitude toward the persuasive agent was; (c) what the hero was being asked to do; and (d) what extra reward he would get for doing it well in each case. The seven different heroes varied as to occupation and social status, and each of them appeared in six different vignettes in which the major independent variables of positive *v*. negative agent by individual, small group, large organization appeared in all six combinations. This formed a 2×3 design.

Six of the heroes were being asked to do something which was over and above routine duty but not extreme – something which they would not do without some incentive. Thus, the army private was asked to stand 'extra' guard duty. These six heroes were considered examples of extrinsic incentive situations and constituted the major part of the study. As a comparison, one hero was presented who was to be intrinsically motivated. He was a professor who needed no help, but was vitally interested in studying cancer with the goal of 'helping mankind'. In this version he was encouraged to do it by the six types of agents contained in the independent variables. The six versions of this intrinsically motivated hero were 'tacked on' to the basic design.

The six extrinsic heroes and the six variations of the independent variables were arranged to form a 6^2 Latin Square. In such a design all subjects responded to six vignettes in which the hero was always different (plus the seventh of the intrinsic professor). Each subject reacted to each of the six independent variations paired with a separate hero. In order to get a complete replication, six subjects were needed since they produced thirty-six responses, one under each of the six variations of type and attractiveness of agent for each of the six different heroes. The 'intrinsic professor' vignette was 'tacked on' to the design to vary as one of the other heroes. The resulting data can be analysed for variance attributable to subjects, blocks of subjects (the specific combination of hero and independent variable they received), I–E score of a subject, the six heroes, attractiveness of agent and type of agent.

Table 1 condenses the content of the forty-two vignettes into the various relevant categories. All subjects reviewed the vignette containing the political party precinct worker first, etc., in the order of the first column, except that the professor was inserted in ordinal position three for all subjects. Table 2 presents the Latin Square design.

Table 2 Latin Square Design

Block of subjects	Order of presentation						
	1 Political	2 Army	4 Business	5 Government	6 Doctor	7 Union	3 Professor*
1	+L**	−s	−i	+s	−L	+i	+s
2	+i	+L	−s	−i	+s	−L	−i
3	−L	+i	+L	−s	−i	+s	−s
4	+s	−L	+i	+L	−s	−i	+L
5	−i	+s	−L	+i	+L	−s	+i
6	−s	−i	+s	−L	+i	+L	−L

* The professor was the same treatment as Government for any subject.
** L=large organization; s=small group; i=individual.
  +=positive attractiveness; −=negative attractiveness.

Table 1 Outline of Stimulus Materials

Hero	Persuasive agent			
	Individual	Small group	Large group	Reward
1. Political party precinct worker	Precinct committee-man	Fellow precinct workers	Republocrat party	Appointment in recorder's office
2. Army private	C.O. (Major)	Men in his platoon	The army	Special three-day pass
3. Salesman, General Machines, Inc.	Office sales manager	Other salesmen	The company	Paid delegate to convention
4. Clerk, U.S. Embassy Moscow (protocol sec.)	Chief of Protocol Section	Embassy Protocol Section	State department	'Hitch-hike' flight to Switzerland
5. Medical intern	Chief resident in pediatrics	His fellow interns	American Medical Association	Residency appointment
6. Member, Shoe Worker's Union	Union shop steward	His work crew	Amalgamated Shoe Worker's Union	Requested shift and slight pay increase
7. University professor	Another professor	A few colleagues	His university	None – hopes to help mankind
(a) Positive attractiveness	'a man whom he likes and admires very much'	'they are his friends off the job as well as on'	Hero has high regard for the record of the organization	
(b) Negative attractive-ness	'a man whom he considers an opportunist, and so does not respect'	'lazy and incompetent; not the kind of men he would want as close personal friends'	Hero is disgusted with the organization; feels that it does not accomplish anything worthwhile	

After each vignette the subject responded to six Likert-type items on a scale from strong agreement to strong disagreement. The responses were converted into a seven-point scale. The items were slightly reworded to adapt them to each vignette but the basic phrases were identical. Four of the items constituted the origin–pawn scale, two worded so that a high score indicated that the hero would feel like an origin. These items follow:

(The name of the hero) will feel that all decisions are being made for him by (the name of the agent).
In this situation (the name of the hero) will feel that (the name of the agent) is arbitrarily controlling him like a pawn.
(Hero) will feel that he is completely free to make his own decisions in carrying out (name of task).
In carrying out (name of task), (hero) will feel completely free.

Two of the items after each vignette constituted the Task Enjoyment Scale:

(Hero) will very much enjoy his (name of task).
(Name of task) will seem very unpleasant to (hero).

After giving responses to these six items after all seven vignettes, subjects completed a form of the I–E scale consisting of the twelve items given by Rotter, Seeman and Liverant (1962). Responses were again on a seven-point agree-disagree scale, and the items were in couplets of two (one to be reverse scored) from six diverse areas, namely (a) academic recognition; (b) social recognition; (c) love and affection; (d) dominance; (e) social-political; (f) general life philosophy. In each of these areas the items attempt to measure how much the subject feels in control of his reinforcement or how much he feels controlled by others. The total scale scores indicate a general attitude toward internal or external control in a broad spectrum of life situations. In our terms the scale may be said to measure how much the subject feels like an origin or a pawn of fate in many situations.

The total score was computed for each subject (possible range 12–84, actual range 38–80) and the scores within each of the six blocks of subjects were split at the median score of that block. The median within the blocks varied from 60·5 to 64·5 (over-all median = 63·5). The greatest discrepancy produced by this procedure was one subject who was classified as high who was 2·5 points below the over-all median. In all, ten subjects would have been classified differently by an over-all median split but only one varied from the over-all median by more than 1·5. The within-blocks split seems justified on these grounds and is necessary to maintain the advantages of the Latin Square.

The subjects were 216 college students enrolled in introductory psychology classes, who read the vignettes and responded to the scales in the classroom setting. Each block of subjects contained eighteen who were high on the I–E scale and eighteen who were low. Excluding the 'intrinsic professor' vignette, the basic analyses of variance were carried out on 1296 scores (one from each of the six vignettes for each subject representing his total on the origin–pawn or the task–enjoyment scales). The total represents eighteen complete replications of the design above the median I–E score and eighteen replications below the median.

Results

The appropriate error term

Table 3 presents the basic data from the origin–pawn scale, which takes the form of thirty-six means based on thirty-six scores in each cell formed by the $2 \times 3 \times 6$ design. The table is composed in such a way that the significant comparisons of means representing independent variables are displayed. Table 4 presents the results of the analysis of variance.

Of first concern is the fact that using the within cells variance (1050 df) as error variance results in a significant interaction ($p < 0.05$) between all three independent variables. Such a finding may be interpreted as indicating that the general pattern of the effects of attractiveness and type of persuasive agent is not constant across the six various themes. The amount of variance attributable to the interaction, however, is small ($F = 1.9$, $df\ 10/1050$) compared to the variance attributable to the major variables (Attractiveness $F = 347.8$, $1/1050\ df$; type of groups $F = 31.0$, $2/1050\ df$; theme $F = 23.3$, $5/1050\ df$). Statistically, it is feasible to use the variance attributable to the highest order interaction as the error term. In essence, this reduces the analysis of variance to one which treats the thirty-six means in Table 3 as the basic scores. The residual variance degrees of freedom reduces from 1050 to 10. Ordinarily

Table 3 Mean Scores in Origin–Pawn Scale

Persuasive agent		Theme						I–E score		
Attractiveness	Type	Political	Army	Business	Govern't	Doctor	Union	High	Low	Total
Positive	Individual	4·34	4·59	4·22	5·49	5·45	4·85	5·00	4·65	4·82
	Small group	4·58	4·85	5·38	5·42	5·59	4·94	5·38	4·87	5·12
	Large group	4·27	3·98	5·06	5·14	5·44	4·65	4·99	4·52	4·75
	Subtotal	4·40	4·47	4·89	5·35	5·49	4·81	5·12	4·67	4·89
Negative	Individual	3·43	3·23	3·58	3·75	3·93	3·19	3·58	3·44	3·51
	Small group	4·36	3·70	4·55	5·09	3·74	3·42	4·22	4·07	4·14
	Large group	2·87	2·26	3·97	3·73	3·60	3·14	3·26	3·26	3·26
	Subtotal	3·55	3·06	4·03	4·18	3·76	3·25	3·68	3·59	3·64
	Total	3·97	3·77	4·46	4·76	4·62	4·03	4·40	4·13	4·26

Note: N in each cell=36.

Table 4 Analysis of Variance of Origin–Pawn and Task-Enjoyment Scales

Source of variation	Origin–pawn				Task-enjoyment		
	df	Mean square	F	p	Mean square	F	p
Between subjects	215						
Between blocks	5	181·3	3·5	<0·01	32·4	2·5	<0·05
I–E level	1	371·6	7·1	<0·01	22·4	1·7	—
Blocks×I–E	5	86·2	1·6	—	10·9	0·8	—
Within block	204	52·3	—	—	12·9	—	—
Within subjects	1080						
1. Group attractiveness	1	8260·8	182·7	<0·0005	5492·5	337·0	<0·0005
2. Type of group	2	735·3	16·3	<0·001	64·3	3·9	<0·10
3. Theme	5	554·1	12·3	<0·001	94·8	5·8	<0·01
1×2	2	116·7	2·6	—	66·1	4·1	<0·05
1×3	5	107·7	2·4	—	25·1	1·5	—
2×3	10	97·7	2·2	—	17·6	1·1	—
1×2×3	10	45·2*	—	—	16·3*	—	—
Residual	1050	23·7	—	—	8·5	—	—

* Used as error term in computing F-ratios for within subjects comparisons.

this would be too stringent a restriction, but in the present case, the main effects remain highly significant.

Such a drastic curtailment of the analysis seems justified conceptually since it does not reduce below significance level any results which were involved in the major hypotheses. All results which lose significance are tenuous at best since they are reactions to specific aspects of the various themes or persuasive agents. For instance, the hero who disliked his position in the Moscow Embassy's protocol section was seen as an origin far out of proportion to any of the other comparable situations. The unique combination of the three independent variables (Moscow Embassy, disliked protocol section) contributed to the significant highest order interaction. Speculation about why this combination should be unique would seem to be useless theoretically. The danger of discarding theoretically meaningful results by the stringent analysis, therefore, seems slight.

Origin–pawn results

Results indicate that the hero is seen as more of a pawn when the persuasive agent is presented as unattractive. The hero is seen as reacting most as a pawn to large organizations and least to small groups. Subjects with scores below the median on the I–E scale (who perceive the control of their own reinforcements as primarily external to themselves) perceive the hero as more of a pawn under all conditions than do subjects above the I–E scale median. These findings confirm the major hypotheses of the study and are graphically presented in Figure 1.

Significant variation between the means representing the themes indicates that the hero who is seen as most like an origin is the U.S. Embassy clerk in Moscow. In descending rank order to the Army Private the order is as follows: (a) U.S. Embassy clerk in Moscow; (b) medical intern; (c) business salesman; (d) member of the shoe-worker's union; (e) political party precinct worker; (f) army private.

Task–enjoyment results

Table 5 presents the results from the task–enjoyment scale. The analysis of variance using the over-all interaction as the error term is again employed. The hero is seen as enjoying the task more

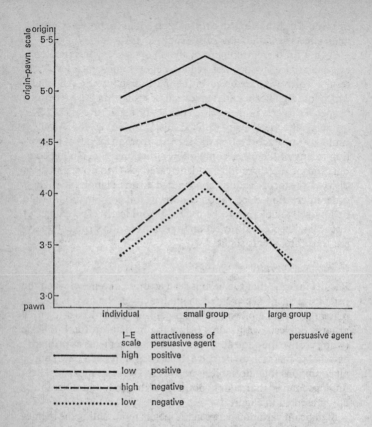

Figure 1 Mean rating on the origin–pawn scale for subjects high and low on the internal and external control (I–E) for various stimulus persons

when the persuasive agent is attractive. There is an interaction between attractiveness and type of agent. The task is enjoyed less when the attractive agent is an individual than when it is either a small group or a large organization. On the other hand, the task is enjoyed less when the unattractive agent is a large organization than when it is either a small group or an individual.

There is no significant relationship between the I–E scale and task-enjoyment. The significant relationship between task–

Table 5 Mean Scores on Task–Enjoyment Scale

Persuasive agent			Theme						I–E score		
Attractiveness	Type		Political	Army	Business	Govern't	Doctor	Union	High	Low	Total
Positive	Individual		6·12	5·67	4·38	6·10	6·10	5·33	5·73	5·51	5·62
	Small group		5·94	5·88	5·47	5·97	6·07	5·97	6·00	5·77	5·88
	Large group		5·54	5·99	5·72	6·22	5·94	5·55	6·00	5·66	5·83
	Subtotal		5·87	5·84	5·19	6·10	6·04	5·62	5·91	5·65	5·78
Negative	Individual		3·74	3·85	3·06	4·38	4·03	3·81	3·92	3·69	3·81
	Small group		4·35	4·17	3·68	4·88	3·72	3·36	4·00	4·05	4·03
	Large group		3·40	2·75	3·16	3·82	3·46	3·32	3·22	3·42	3·32
	Subtotal		3·83	3·59	3·30	4·36	3·74	3·50	3·71	3·72	3·72
	Total		4·85	4·72	4·25	5·23	4·89	4·56	4·81	4·69	4·75

Note: N in each cell = 36.

enjoyment and theme indicates the following descending order of task–enjoyment: (a) U.S. Embassy clerk; (b) medical intern; (c) political party precinct worker; (d) Army private; (e) member of the shoe-worker's union; (f) business salesman.

Intrinsic-professor results

Table 6 presents means on the origin–pawn scale for the 'tacked-on' theme involving the professor who was intrinsically motivated to work on cancer research. As was expected the ratings were extremely high on the origin–pawn scale. This resulted in a ceiling effect and consequent inhomogeneity of variance.[1]

Table 6 Mean Scores of the Origin–Pawn Scale for the Intrinsic Professor

| Attractiveness of agent | I–E level | Type of persuasive agent | | | |
		Individual	Small group	Large organization	Total
Positive	High	6·33	5·69	6·76	6·25
	Low	6·19	6·21	5·94	6·11
	Subtotal	6·26	5·95	6·35	6·18
Negative	High	5·39	6·03	5·91	5·77
	Low	5·49	5·60	4·92	5·35
	Subtotal	5·44	5·82	5·42	5·56
Combined	High	5·86	5·86	6·34	6·01
	Low	5·84	5·91	5·43	5·73
	Total	5·85	5·89	5·89	5·87

Note: N in each cell = 18.

It is clear without any resort to statistical analysis that the professor is seen as far more an origin than any of the other heroes. In addition, the analysis of variance indicates that when the

1. Analysis of variance in the face of inhomogeneity may be justified on two counts. In the present case; the danger is not that significant findings will be erroneous, but that findings will be masked by the ceiling effect. Statistically, the restriction of analysis of variance to cases where homogeneity obtains is no longer considered necessary. See, for instance, Box (1953) and Winer (1962).

attractive agent encourages him he is perceived as freer (more an origin) than when the unattractive agent does. The type of group and level of the I–E scale do not account for significant variance alone, but the I–E scale interacts with type of group significantly. This interaction may be seen at the bottom of Table 6 and indicates that when the persuasive agent is an individual or a small group, no differences are perceived by subjects high as opposed to low on the I–E scale. When the agent is a large organization, however, high I–E subjects see the hero as freer (more like an origin) whereas low I–E subjects see him as constrained (more like a pawn).

The task–enjoyment scale means were also extremely high for the intrinsic-professor, higher for the attractive agent than for the unattractive. Neither type of group nor level of I–E scale accounted for significant variance.

Discussion

This study was designed to demonstrate that a variable derived from Heider's (1958) concept of the perceived locus of causality is an important dimension in person perception. The results unambiguously support the conclusion that persons are perceived as acting more like pawns under certain conditions, and under others they are seen more as origins of their own behavior. Put another way, the perception that a person is 'pushed around' under certain conditions and more freely acting from his own volition under others is apparently an inference which subjects make reliably. The inference is a function of information given about the person, the situation, and the personal characteristics of the subject making the inference. The data are consistent with the assumption that the origin–pawn inference is a continuous bipolar variable although no attempt was made to test this assumption in contrast to some other alternative.

It is clear from the data that persons who are being persuaded to engage in 'extra-duty' activity are perceived as more the origin of their own behavior when they like and respect the persuasive agent than when the persuasive agent is disliked. The inference might be drawn that a person feels freer when working for an attractive agent than when working for an unattractive one, even when all other conditions more relevant to freedom are constant. This hypothesis may seem like common sense, but theoretically the connexion between the attractiveness of an agent who is attempting to control a person's behavior and the person's feeling of freedom is not immediately obvious. The reasoning which led to the present experiment was that a person who likes and respects another probably accepts the other's goals more readily than he would accept the goals of a disliked person, and he may assume more overlap between his and a liked person's goals. He will therefore feel that compliance to the persuasion of an attractive agent is behavior directed toward goals of his own choosing, i.e. that he is actually the origin of his own behavior. It could be said that in this situation he feels more intrinsically than extrinsically motivated, since the rather vague concept of intrinsic motivation probably has a strong component of the origin feeling. When a person is intrinsically motivated he feels like an origin.

The data show that the professor who freely chose the task and did not have to be persuaded is seen as the extreme case of an origin. If an attractive agent encourages him, he is seen as more an origin than if an unattractive agent encourages him. This is interesting in that the agent here was not presented as influencing or in a position to reward the behavior.

It was hypothesized that a persuasive agent consisting of a large organization would lead to the strongest inference that the hero was a pawn compared with small group or individual agents. According to Marx, Weber and Durkheim large organizations engender feelings of alienation, anomie and powerlessness, with the consequent feelings of being pushed around like a pawn. On the other hand, one might expect that the feeling of being an Origin *vis-à-vis* a large organization might be strong if the individual can use the power of the organization to attain his own goals. The evidence indicates that the large organization is seen as treating the individual more as a pawn than is the small group or the individual under all conditions where the job to be done is not chosen by the person but by the agent. When the task is freely chosen, however, as in the 'intrinsic-professor' vignette, subjects high on the I–E scale perceive the professor as more of an origin when encouraged by the university than when encouraged by his colleagues. The reverse holds for subjects low on the I–E scale.

In general, large organizations as compared to individuals or small groups are seen as tending to make pawns out of people.

There is some evidence, however, that subjects who feel that they can control their environment in order to gain reinforcements see a person who is pursuing something of his own choosing as freer when he is encouraged by a large organization. Perhaps these subjects feel that they can use the power of the organization to give them greater freedom.

When the persuasive agent is an individual the person is seen as slightly less a pawn than when the agent is a large organization. When the agent is a small group, however, the person is seen as least constrained (least like a pawn) even when the small group members are disliked.

The measure of task–enjoyment was included in the experiment to test the assumption that a person is perceived as not enjoying the task to the extent that he is seen as a pawn. A high relationship between the origin–pawn and the task–enjoyment scales was expected and found. As would be predicted, task–enjoyment is perceived as much higher when the persuasive agent is liked than when disliked. The hero is assumed to dislike the task most when working for a large disliked organization, but the task is not seen as so odious to the hero when he is working for a disliked small group. The more positive attitude toward the small group even when disliked as compared to the large organization is again in evidence.

The task–enjoyment scale may be used to check whether the origin–pawn scale merely reflects a general affective reaction to the various conditions or is measuring something unique. There are two pieces of evidence to indicate that the origin–pawn scale has validity in its own right. The results for the origin–pawn and the task–enjoyment scales are similar (but not identical) in the variables of type and attractiveness of group – as would be expected. The various situations or themes, however, are rated differently on the two scales. For instance, the army private induces the strongest inference that the person is a pawn whereas the salesman is seen as much less of a pawn. Task–enjoyment is lowest for the salesman and third from lowest for the army private. Statistical analysis of these themes indicates that the scales are giving significantly different results and can be considered to be measuring different things.[2]

2. The four means were tested for interaction using the largest error term, i.e. the highest order interaction variance for the task enjoyment scale ($F = 5.58$, $p < 0.05$, 1/10 df). This is the most conservative test.

Richard de Charms, Virginia Carpenter and Aharon Kuperman 283

Perhaps the most convincing evidence for the validity of the origin–pawn scale is the fact that results on it are predictable from the I–E scale, but the task–enjoyment results are not predictable by this scale. This result shows that subjects who themselves feel in control of their destinies (as opposed to those who do not) make greater distinctions along the origin–pawn scale, but do not differ on the task–enjoyment scale. Without such evidence the results with the origin–pawn variable might be attributable to a generalized 'halo' effect. With such evidence the variable appears to be validly related to the theoretical concepts attributed to it.

Finally, the fact that aspects of the hero and the personal characteristics of the perceiver both affect the responses on the origin–pawn variable needs elaboration. It is impossible to trace empirically exactly how a personal characteristic affects the perception of a person as an origin or as a pawn. Taking a lead from Polanyi's (1958) concept of personal knowledge, we felt it probable that in drawing inferences from the behavior of others, a person's personal knowledge of how he might feel in such a situation would affect his inference. Thus a person who feels that he has control over the valued outcomes in his life would assume that this kind of personal knowledge is an integral part of the person he is observing. He might then be expected to see other persons who are like him more as origins than would a person who feels little control of outcomes. The data presented here are consistent with this hypothesis.

To the extent that a person differentiates others from himself, however, he may not see them in ways congruent to his own feelings of control. A power-oriented person who feels little control may see himself as a pawn to others to whom he attributes origin characteristics, especially if they are of higher status than he (see Thibaut and Riecken, 1955a and b). Under conditions where power is of primary concern it may be possible to classify people as origins and pawns, but it would be a mistake to conceive of the origin–pawn variable as a general trait. Rather, it will probably be more useful to follow the assumption that under different conditions a person will perceive himself and/or others as more or less the origin of his behavior. It is even quite possible that some people conceive of themselves as origins only when they are subjugating others as pawns whereas other people conceive of themselves primarily as an origin only when they can treat others as origins.

References

ANSCOMBE, G. H. M. (1957), *Intention*, Blackwell.

BOX, G. E. P. (1953), 'Non-normality and tests on variance', *Biometrika*, vol. 40, pp. 318–35.

HEIDER, F. (1958), *The Psychology of Interpersonal Relations*, Wiley.

MCCLELLAND, D. C. (1961), *The Achieving Society*, Van Nostrand.

MEIER, D. L., and BELL, W. (1959), 'Anomie and differential access to the achievement of life goals', *Amer. soc. Rev.*, vol. 24, pp. 189–202.

MERTON, R. K. (1957), *Social Theory and Social Structure*, Free Press.

PEPITONE, A. (1958), 'Attributions of causality, social attitudes, and cognitive matching processes', in R. Tagiuri and L. Petrullo (eds.), *Person Perception and Interpersonal Behavior*, Stanford University Press, pp. 258–76.

POLANYI, M. (1958), *Personal Knowledge*, University of Chicago Press.

ROTTER, J. B. (1954), *Social Learning and Clinical Psychology*, Prentice-Hall.

ROTTER, J. B., SEEMAN, M., and LIVERANT, S. (1962), 'Internal versus external control of reinforcements: a major variable in behavior theory', in N. F. Washburne (ed.), *Decisions, Values and Groups*, vol. 2, Macmillan Co., pp. 473–516.

SEEMAN, M (1959), 'On the meaning of alienation', *Amer. soc. Rev.*, vol. 24, pp. 783–91.

THIBAUT, J. W., and RIECKEN, H. W. (1955a), 'Authoritarianism, status, and the communication of aggression', *Hum. Rel.*, vol. 8, pp. 95–120.

THIBAUT, J. W., and RIECKEN, H. W. (1955b), 'Some determinants and consequences of the perception of social causality', *J. Personal.*, vol. 24, pp. 113–33.

URMSON, J. O., PETERS, R. S., and MCCRACKEN, D. J. (1952), 'Symposium: motives and causes', *Aristotelian Society*, suppl. 26, pp. 139–94.

WILKINS, E. J., and DE CHARMS, R. (1962), 'Authoritarianism and response to power cues', *J. Personal.*, vol. 30, pp. 439–57.

WINER, B. J. (1962), *Statistical Principles in Experimental Design*, McGraw-Hill.

Part Five Norms and Behaviour Change

A group norm is an evaluation, shared by all or most of the members, of behaviour relevant to the group. All role prescriptions are thus, strictly speaking, norms. But the term 'norm' is usually restricted to those evaluations which apply more or less equally to the behaviour of all the members of the group. A great deal of experimental work has been done concerning the group member who is at odds with all other members of his group. The pioneer study was that of Asch (1956), and many later studies have followed a similar format. The subject is placed in a setting where all other members of his group purportedly make judgements which they believe correct on the task, but which are actually erroneous. The subject may or may not go along with the majority. Progress in the study of norms has not been so satisfactory as has that with roles. Reading 15 by Willis and Hollander indicates one reason why: conformity and deviance are not explicable as a single dimension. One must take into account not only pressures on the group member to conform or to deviate, but also the degree to which the member is dependent on the group. Where the member has other more attractive group memberships available his behaviour may be more readily explicable in terms of the norms of those other groups. Such groups have been termed reference groups. The paper by Schulman (Reading 16) shows how some of these extraneous variables may affect the Asch conformity studies. Studies of attitude change are equally relevant to this topic, and a number of such studies, are to be found in an accompanying Penguin Modern Psychology, *Attitudes* (Jahoda and Warren, 1966).

Tuckman's review (Reading 17) is concerned with the question of whether there are any universal norms which influence the development of any short-term group in parallel ways. It appears that there may be. The following two papers represent opposite viewpoints in a current controversy as to whether groups develop norms favouring more risky courses of action than those advocated by the members of the group individually. The controversy is far from resolved, but the answer may turn out to hinge on how far subjects are responding to real rather than hypothetical risks.

Finally, we return briefly to leadership. Hollander (Reading 20) shows that group members may be prepared to give leaders the benefit of the doubt when they violate group norms provided they have built up a previous credit of goodwill.

References

ASCH, S. E. (1956), 'Studies of independence and conformity:
I. A minority of one against an unanimous majority', *Psychol. Monogr.*, vol. 70, no. 9.

JAHODA, M., and WARREN, N. (eds.) (1966), *Attitudes*, Penguin Books.

15 Richard H. Willis and Edwin P. Hollander

An Experimental Study of Three Response Modes in
Social Influence Situations

Richard H. Willis and Edwin P. Hollander, 'An experimental study of
three response modes in social influence situations', *Journal of
Abnormal and Social Psychology*, vol. 69, 1964, pp. 150–56.

What are the alternatives to conformity? That is, what are the
possible ways of responding to felt social pressures? Despite the
great concern at present with phenomena of conformity and social
influence, this basic question has received insufficient attention in
terms of alternative modes of response. One attempt at specification in this area, departing from the traditional unidimensional
conformity–nonconformity conception, is presented in the model
developed and provided with preliminary experimental support
in two earlier papers by Willis (1963, 1965).

This particular specification can be described as a two-dimensional *response model*. It is concerned with an elaboration of the
response, or dependent variable, side of the picture, rather than
with the explication of relationships between independent and
dependent variables. Such a response model is in contrast with
process models (for example, Hollander, 1958; Kelman, 1961)
which are primarily concerned with dynamic processes which can
account for those relationships over time.

The present study sets out to provide additional experimental
data within the framework of the Willis response model, and
therefore is best considered a demonstration since several independent variables are manipulated simultaneously in order to observe
differences between experimental groups.

The more usual conceptualization of conformity–nonconformity response is illustrated in the recent work of Walker and
Heyns (1962, pp. 4–6) in which conformity and nonconformity are
represented as opposite poles of a single dimension, with perfectly
congruent normative behavior resting at one extreme and growing
magnitudes of discrepancy located at increasing distances beyond.
The end of the scale labeled 'nonconformity' is defined not directly,

but only by exclusion as deviation from the opposite end.

A variant of the unidimensional view has been suggested in the writings of Asch (for example, 1956), and by the theoretical analysis of Marie Jahoda (1959). Here 'independence', rather than nonconformity, is contrasted with conformity. This represents an improvement over the conceptualization of Walker and Heyns insofar as independence has a more precise meaning than does undifferentiated nonconformity. In fact, the Asch–Jahoda model cannot be said to be incorrect, but merely insufficiently general. We shall return to this point presently.

One or the other of these unidimensional response models has been employed, explicitly or implicitly, by virtually all workers in the areas of social influence and attitude change. As a departure from these, the Willis model employs two dimensions of response to adequately represent conformity and nonconformity behavior. The first of these dimensions is dependence–independence; the second is conformity–anticonformity. These are represented as orthogonal to one another, as shown in Figure 1.

Three basic modes of responding to felt social pressures are delineated – *conformity*, *independence* and *anticonformity*. Pure conformity behavior is defined as a completely consistent attempt on the part of the individual to behave in accordance with the normative expectations of a specified group, as he sees them. Pure independence behavior occurs whenever the individual perceives relevant normative expectations, but gives zero weight to them as guides to his behavior. This does not mean that the individual fails to 'weigh' the expectations, in the sense of evaluating their importance and relevance, but rather that, whatever the process, he rejects them for purposes of formulating his decisions. The person capable of acting independently is able to resist social pressures, rather than merely being unaware of them or ignoring them.

In the case of pure anticonformity, the response of the individual is directly antithetical to the norm prescription. Consider the individual faced with a decision between two alternatives, one of which has been socially defined as right, the other as wrong. If the two alternatives can be considered as diametrically opposed, then choosing the one defined as wrong would exemplify pure anticonformity behavior. Pure anticonformity behavior, like pure conformity behavior, is pure dependence behavior.

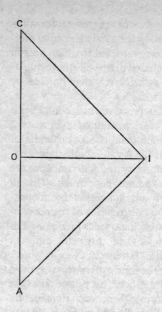

Figure 1 Relationships between conformity, independence and anti-conformity

In Figure 1, points C and A represent pure conformity and pure anticonformity, respectively. Point I represents pure independence behavior, while pure dependence behavior can fall anywhere along line CA. Line CI represents combinations of conformity and independence, with no trace of anticonformity. Points within triangle CIA represent various combinations of all three response modes.

Since this model is a response model, it of course says nothing about relationships between independent and dependent variables, nor about the processes underlying such relationships. It deals exclusively with the kinds of reactions to felt social pressures an individual might exhibit. It is felt, however, that such a response model is essential to the definition and understanding of mechanisms underlying social influence and conformity.

Returning to the Asch–Jahoda conformity–independence

model, it can now be seen to be a special case of the conformity–independence–anticonformity model. In the total absence of anticonformity, variations in behavior are restricted to differences in position along line C I. It can be concluded that, while the formulation of Walker and Heyns (1962) is incorrect, that implied by Asch and Jahoda is merely too constricted.

In a previous study by Willis (1963), perceived task competence of partner and liking for partner were manipulated in a 2×2 factorial design in order to determine their effects on levels of independence and net conformity. If the Asch–Jahoda unidimensional framework suffices, then conformity and independence are representable as opposite ends of the same continuum. This in turn would imply that an analysis of results in terms of the independence scores would be tantamount to one in terms of the net conformity scores. If, on the other hand, the model of Figure 1 is appropriate, the two analyses *could* yield distinctly different patternings of results – and, in fact, this latter result was obtained. The mean independence scores for the four experimental groups did not differ significantly from one another. This was not the case for the mean net conformity scores; there was significantly ($p < 0.01$) less net conformity in the low liking, low perceived task competency condition than in the high liking, high perceived task competency condition. That these two differing patterns of means were obtained constitutes evidence in support of the two-dimensional model.

Despite the support for this model in the initial experiment, responses of conformity, independence, and anticonformity were not brought under experimental control to any appreciable degree. In none of the experimental groups did the mean location approach the limits set by the vertices of triangle C I A. All four means fell relatively close to line C I. Means were clustered approximately equidistant from each end of this line, but were a little nearer on the average to point I than to point C.

Procedure
Design

The present demonstration was conducted in order to experimentally manipulate proximity to each vertex of the triangle in Figure 1. Four variables (to be indicated presently) were manipulated simultaneously in an attempt to maximize differences among the three experimental groups.

Subjects and experimental conditions

Subjects were thirty-six volunteers from lower division classes at Washington University. Of these, twelve were male and twenty-four were female. Four males and eight females were randomly assigned to each of the three groups. All subjects were run in pairs in a pseudointeraction situation; that is, each subject was under the impression that he and his partner were each learning of the responses of the other, whereas in fact each was given a programmed sequence of 'partner's response'.

Subjects in one group, the C group, performed under conditions designed to elicit a high degree of conformity behavior; subjects in the second group, the I group, performed under conditions designed to elicit a high degree of independence behavior; and those in the third group, the A group, performed under conditions intended to evoke a high degree of anticonformity behavior.

Stimuli and task

The stimuli for the main task were 100 lines, ranging in length from three to nine inches. These were drawn on cardboard with four lines per 8×10 card. Under each line appeared a numerically expressed comparison length. In actuality, each stimulus line was exactly equal to the comparison length, but subjects were told that the stimulus lines were longer half the time and shorter half the time, and that they would do well to make about an equal number of plus (longer) and minus (shorter) responses over all.

Each response booklet contained twenty-five pages, all alike, 1 for each of the stimulus cards. For each card, the subject made an initial binary judgement of the length of each of the four lines. These responses were recorded in the first column of the appropriate page of the booklet. A plus mark was used to indicate that the line was longer than the numerically expressed length, while a minus mark was used to indicate that the line was shorter.

After both subjects had completed the initial series of judgements for a stimulus card, the experimenter indicated in the second column of each subject's response sheet the judgements that were presumably made by the partner. These responses actually were predetermined according to a schedule which specified agreement and disagreement with the subject's initial judgements equally often. After these programed responses had been indicated by the experimenter, each subject had an opportunity either to change any of his initial responses or to reaffirm them. After each subject had recorded his second set of responses in the third column, the experimenter indicated in the fourth column the responses that were supposedly correct. The last column was reserved for the use of the subject to keep a record of the number of points earned on each judgement in accordance with rules which varied from group to group.

Computation of scores

With two binary responses to each stimulus, plus an additional binary response attributed to the partner, there are eight possible outcomes on any trial. Considerations of symmetry allow these eight outcomes to be paired, yielding four distinct patterns of responding.

The first step in the computation of a subject's score was to count the frequency with which each of the four distinct response patterns appeared over all trials. These pattern frequencies are designated C, I, A and U (conformity, independence, anti-conformity and uniformity). Using a plus sign to represent a judgement of longer and a minus sign to represent a judgement of shorter, the four response patterns can be defined in terms of the eight possible trial outcomes:

C: + − − or − + +
I: + − + or − + −
A: + + − or − − +
U: + + + or − − − .

The frequencies of the C and I patterns sum to 50, and the same is true for the A and U frequencies. This is so because the half of the 100 trials on which 'the partner's response' disagrees with the subject's initial response yields C and I patterns, while the half of the trials on which there is agreement yields A and U patterns. Using these relations, frequencies are first converted to proportions of the maximum possible frequency. For example, if the C pattern appears fifteen times and the I pattern appears thirty-five times, the corresponding proportions are 0·30 and 0·70.

Letting c, i, a and u stand for the response pattern proportions, x and y are defined in the following way:

$$x = ui,$$
$$y = c - a.$$

These scores can be interpreted as the horizontal and vertical coordinates of the subject's position in triangle C I A of Figure 1, as measured from Point O as origin. A high x-score indicates a high degree of *independence*, while a high y-score indicates a high degree of *net conformity*. A negative y-score indicates that the tendency to anticonform is greater than the tendency to conform.[1]

Experimental manipulations

Because the purpose of this experiment was to demonstrate the possibility of bringing the three response modes – conformity, independence and anticonformity – under experimental control, several variables were manipulated simultaneously to maximize differences among the three experimental groups. The simultaneously manipulated independent variables were:

1. The perceived competency of *either* the subject *or* his partner in making judgements of the kind involved, as indicated by the results of the pretest.
2. The perceived competency of *either* the subject *or* his partner, as indicated by experimenter feedback on each trial concerning 'correct' responses.

1. The question arises as to the independence of x and y. An appropriate answer must be phrased in terms of contingencies. If $a = 0$, that is, if all traces of anticonformity are absent, then x and y exhibit no independence whatsoever. Specifically, they will be perfectly and inversely correlated, for under this condition $x = i$, and $y = c = 1 - i$. The Asch–Jahoda conceptualization applies here. If a is free to assume any value within its limits of zero and unity, then x and y are independent in the sense that the values they assume can be interrelated in any of a large number of possible ways. The limits on these possible relationships are shown graphically by triangle C I A in Figure 1. One of the major virtues of the x and y scoring system, in fact, is that the limits imposed on possible score combinations are perfectly isomorphic with the limits imposed by the theoretical framework.

Richard H. Willis and Edwin P. Hollander 295

3. Strength of set towards reaffirming initial judgements on second responses.
4. Reward structure.

The specific differences among experimental groups are indicated in Table 1. The pretest consisted of twenty stimulus lines of the

Table 1 Summary of Experimental Manipulations

	C-group	I-group	A-group
Performance on pretest	Partner: 18 out of 20	Subject: 18 out of 20	Partner: 3 out of 20
Set	Flexibility	Consistency	Flexibility
Feedback	Partner correct 90%	Subject correct 90%	Partner correct 10%
Reward structure	Subject wrong: 0 Subject only right: 1 Both right: 2 each (team score)	Subject wrong: 0 Subject right: 1 (no comparison)	Subject wrong: 0 Both right: 1 each Subject only right: 2 (competition)

same kind as those judged subsequently. These were presented one to a card, and each subject judged the series essentially at his own rate. Judgements of longer and shorter were required in equal numbers. Answer sheets were then sham-scored by the experimenter and predetermined results were reported to the subjects. In the C-group, each subject was informed that his partner had judged eighteen out of the twenty stimuli correctly. In the I group, each subject was told that he himself had received a score of 18. In the A-group, each subject was led to believe that his partner had scored only three correct on the pretest. Subjects in the C- and A-groups were told nothing about their own performance, while subjects in the I-group were told nothing about performance of partner.

In both the C-group and the A-group, instructions included a statement to the effect that subjects would be able to do better by adopting a flexible attitude which allowed the recognition and correction of mistakes, while the instructions for the I-group

stressed that it would be better to trust one's initial reaction, when in doubt.

Experimenter feedback was programed in the C-group so as to make the partner appear to be correct in his judgements 90 per cent of the time, while in the I-group, it was the subject himself who was presented as being correct 90 per cent of the time. The partner was allowed to appear correct on only 10 per cent of the trials in the A-group.

The simplest reward structure was that for the I-group. The subject received one point for every correct *second* judgement, and nothing for every incorrect second judgement. The object was for the subject to get as many points as he could. In the C-group, the subject received *two* points for every correct second response *only in the event* that his partner's response was also correct, and *one* point for every correct second response if his partner's response was incorrect. Furthermore, *all* points won by the subject and his partner were to be pooled at the end of the experimental session into a single *team score*.

In the A-group, the subject was under the impression that both he and his partner each received *one* point in the event that they both judged a stimulus correctly, but that if one were correct and the other incorrect, the former would receive *two* points and the latter none. Instructions further emphasized that the object for the subject was to get more points than his partner.

Results

As will be seen in Table 2, the three experimental groups differ, both with respect to x scores (independence) and y scores (net conformity). Analysis of variance indicates that both sets of means differ significantly among themselves. For the x-scores the F-ratio

Table 2 Group Means for Independence (x-Scores) and Net Conformity (y-Scores)

	C	I	A
	0·438	0·905	0·631
	0·542	0·075	−0·141

is 16·79, while that for the y scores is 22·36, each with df = 2/33. Both of these values are significant considerably beyond the 0·001 level.

Duncan range tests (Duncan, 1955; Edwards, 1960, pp. 136–40) were employed to test the significance of differences between adjacent means. The x means for the C- and A-groups differ significantly at the 0·05 level, while the corresponding difference between the I- and A-groups is significant at the 0·005 level. The difference between the C- and I-groups is significant at the 0·001 level.

Application of the Duncan test to differences between over-all y means also revealed each to be significantly different from the others. The difference between the I- and A-group means is significant at the 0·05 level, that between the C- and I-groups at the 0·001 level, and that between the C- and A-groups at the 0·001 level.

Table 3 presents independence and net conformity means for

Table 3 Group Means by Blocks of Twenty Trials

	I	II	III	IV	V	Move-ment
C						
x	0·598	0·433	0·450	0·300	0·372	0·226
y	0·337	0·567	0·534	0·701	0·601	0·264
I						
x	0·830	0·924	0·910	0·926	0·959	0·129
y	0·121	0·076	0·075	0·058	0·028	0·093
A						
x	0·717	0·608	0·666	0·641	0·587	0·130
y	0·074	−0·072	−0·075	−0·317	−0·301	0·375

each experimental group by blocks of twenty trials. The trends are, by and large, rather consistent. The I-group is highly independent during the first block of trials, and becomes even more so on successive blocks of trials. Both of the other groups show a tendency to become more dependent over blocks of trials. As anticipated, the C-group shows a strong tendency towards increasing conformity

as trials progress. Also as anticipated, the A-group exhibits considerable movement along the *y*-axis in the direction of anticonformity. An incidental observation is that the I-group shows a little movement in the direction of less net conformity.

Mean movement scores are shown in the last column of Table 3 and are plotted on triangle CIA in Figure 2. The *x* movement score

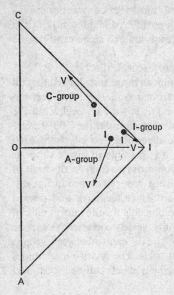

Figure 2 Location of first (I) and last (V) block of trials for each of the three experimental groups

for a group was computed by subtracting the *x* score on the first block of trials from that on the last block of trials. The *y* movement scores were computed in an analogous manner.

Movement scores were tested by means of *t*-tests. The C-group was the only one which showed a significant amount of movement along the *x*-axis; with $t = 2\cdot33$ and $df = 11$, this is significant at the 0·05 level. Both the C- and the A-groups showed a significant degree of movement along the *y* axis, and in opposite directions, with respective values for $t = 2\cdot55$ and $2\cdot59$ ($df = 11$), significant at the 0·05 level.

Perhaps the clearest statistical indication of the success of the experimental manipulations is that based on the differences among final positions, that is, the means on the last block of trials. Analysis of variance applied to the mean x-score differences yielded an F-ratio of 13·17, $df = 2/33$, which is significant beyond the 0·001 level. A Duncan range test indicated that the difference in x means between the C- and A-groups was not significant. However, the C- and I-groups differed significantly at the 0·001 level, while the I- and A-groups differed significantly at the 0·005 level.

As for final differences in mean y scores, the F-ratio is 22·35 ($df = 2/33$, $p < 0·001$), and a Duncan range test showed that all pairs of means differ significantly from one another. That between the I- and A-groups differs significantly at the 0·05 level, while the two remaining differences are both significant at the 0·001 level.

Although it is not possible to determine the effects of each independent variable separately, it is possible to divide the four independent variables into two groups of two each on the basis of producing initial differences between groups, or producing differential movement effects. Experimenter feedback and reward structure can be assumed to be responsible for movement effects, while the pretest and set (flexibility versus consistency) can be assumed to account for much of the difference between groups observed during the first block of trials. The relative magnitudes of the initial differences and movement effects can be ascertained from an inspection of Figure 2.

A short questionnaire was administered to each subject immediately after the experimental session. In general, the patterning of the differences between groups is in accordance with expectations. In particular, examination of the answers to the last question, an open-ended one inquiring as to the purpose of the experiment, disclosed that a majority of subjects were aware of the fact that the experiment dealt with the influence partners' responses might have on second judgements. Few subjects appeared to have achieved more specific insights into the nature of the experiment.

Responses given by subjects in the A-group to Question 4 ('How much help was your partner to you in making your judgements?'), merit particular attention. Mean y-scores for subjects in each response category on this question are given in Table 4, along with

Table 4 Mean Net Conformity Scores for the Subjects in the A-Group Checking Each Response Category on Question 4: 'How Much Help was Your Partner to You in Making Your Judgements?'

Response	f	y
Extremely helpful	4	−0·58
Fairly helpful	—	—
About average	1	0·12
No help at all	6	0·05
Worse than no help at all	1	0·20

category frequencies. There is a pronounced tendency for judgements that the partner was extremely helpful to be associated with a high level of anticonformity. Subjects who anticonform in the A-group earn large numbers of points, and such subjects acknowledge the fact that the systematically incorrect responses of their partners were helpful. This finding supports the interpretation that subjects failing to show appreciable anticonformity in the A-group were those who failed to solve the problem of utilizing the information made available to them through the responses attributed to partners.

Discussion

The findings warrant the conclusion that the experimental manipulations were in fact successful in producing the three basic reactions specified by the theoretical framework. This is important inasmuch as it demonstrates that these response modes can be brought under experimental control with the techniques which have been developed to date.

It should be noted, however, that in the cases of conformity and anticonformity reactions, the theoretical limits were not closely approached. On the other hand, the theoretical limit was almost attained in the case of the independence reaction, largely because this mode of behavior was quite pronounced during the first block of trials in the relevant experimental group.

The significance of this experiment resides in the fact that it demonstrates the possibility of evoking in considerable strength the three modes of reaction specified by the conceptual framework employed. While the earlier experiment by Willis (1963) demonstrated small, though statistically significant, differences relative to the theoretical limits, this experiment obtained differences between groups which were substantial relative to the theoretical limits. If not only conformity and independence behavior, but anticonformity behavior as well, can be produced in the laboratory, the path is cleared for a systematic exploration of the antecedent conditions associated with the various combinations of each.

These results support the two-dimensional model as a more adequate description of behavior than either of the two unidimensional conceptualizations cited earlier (see Hollander and Willis, 1964). Also, the findings of the present experiment shed light on the relationship between the perception of competence and the acceptance of influence, previously studied experimentally by, for example, Hollander (1960). A distinction is evident, however, between this process and the associated considerations of *how* conformity, independence, and anticonformity are perceived and responded to in interaction over time. An experiment on this last issue has recently been reported by the authors (Hollander and Willis, 1964).

References

ASCH, S. E. (1956), 'Studies of independence and conformity: I. A minority of one against a unanimous majority', *Psychol. Monogr.*, vol. 70, no. 9.

DUNCAN, D. B. (1955), 'Multiple range and multiple F tests', *Biometrics*, vol. 11, pp. 1–42.

EDWARDS, A. L. (1960), *Experimental Design in Psychological Research*, Holt, Rinehart & Winston, rev. edn.

HOLLANDER, E. P. (1958), 'Conformity, status, and idiosyncrasy credit', *Psychol. Rev.*, vol. 65, pp. 117–27.

HOLLANDER, E. P. (1960), 'Competence and conformity in the acceptance of influence', *J. abnorm soc. Psychol.*, vol. 61, pp. 365–9.

HOLLANDER, E. P. and WILLIS, R. H. (1964), 'The effects of conformity, independence, and anticonformity behavior', in E. P. Hollander (ed.), *Leaders, Groups, and Influence*, Oxford University Press, Inc., ch. 19.

JAHODA, M. (1959), 'Conformity and independence: a psychological analysis', *Hum. Rel.*, vol. 12, pp. 99–120.

KELMAN, H. C. (1961), 'Processes of opinion change', *Pub. Opin. Quart.*, vol. 25, pp. 57–78.

WALKER, E. L., and HEYNS, R. W. (1962), *An Anatomy for Conformity*, Prentice-Hall.

WILLIS, R. H. (1963), 'Two dimensions of conformity–nonconformity', *Sociometry*, vol. 26, pp. 499–513.

WILLIS, R. H. (1965), 'Conformity, independence, and anticonformity', *Hum. Rel.*, vol. 18, pp. 373–88.

Modes of Responding in Social Influence Situations[2]

In an experiment reported in a preceding study [Reading 15], evidence was obtained in support of a two-dimensional model of social response. This model can be diagrammed as a triangle, as shown in Figure 1 (p. 291).

Subsequently a refinement of the triangular model was developed, *the diamond model*, which incorporates a fourth mode of response (Willis, 1965). The diamond model can be visualized by imagining another triangle, the mirror image of the original, added to Figure 1 so that the response space assumes the shape of a diamond and becomes symmetrical about line CA. The vertex on the left would be labeled V for *variability*. Pure variability behavior would be exhibited by a subject who invariably changes his mind from his initial to his subsequent judgement on each trial.

Both models yield identical conclusions when applied to the data of the experiment in question. In the diamond model the scoring formula for independence becomes $x = i + u - 1$, while that for net conformity remains $y - c - a$. Applying this modification of scoring for independence to the data at hand reveals that the largest difference in the mean of x for a block of trials is 0·022, while the average difference in means for all fifteen blocks of trials is 0·005. The new configuration of movement from first to last block of trials is almost identical with that shown in Figure 2 (p. 299), and all levels of significance remain unchanged.

Although it makes little or no difference in this particular case, the diamond variant possesses distinct advantages under certain circumstances, and it is recommended as a distinct improvement over the earlier triangular model.

Space does not permit a discussion in detail, but an example can be given. Because the two dimensions of independence and

2. A supplementary note by Richard H. Willis and Edwin P. Hollander, appearing in *J. abnorm. soc. Psychol.*, vol. 69, 1964, p. 157.

Richard H. Willis and Edwin P. Hollander   303

net conformity can be employed as independent variables as well as dependent variables, the diamond model allows the experimental production, in a simulated dyadic interaction situation, of four varieties of *partner* behavior which are interrelated in a symmetrical fashion (Willis, 1964). As a result, a number of meaningful comparisons, obscured by the triangular version, are brought to light.

References

WILLIS, R. H. (1964), 'The phenomenology of agreement and disagreement in dyads', *Technical Report*, *Washington University, Office of Naval Research*.

WILLIS, R. H., (1965), 'Conformity, independence, and anticonformity', *Hum. Relat.*, vol. 18, pp. 373–88.

WILLIS, R. H., and HOLLANDER, E. P. (1964), 'An experimental study of three response modes in social influence situations', *J. abnorm. soc. Psychol.*, vol 69, pp. 150–56.

16 Gary I. Schulman

Asch Conformity Studies:
Conformity to the Experimenter and/or to the Group?

Gary I. Schulman, 'Asch conformity studies: conformity to the experimenter and/or to the group?', *Sociometry*, vol. 30, 1967, pp. 26–40.

A characteristic of the experimenter–subject relationship in almost all laboratory experiments is that the experimenter is an authority figure in position to observe and hence to evaluate the subject's behavior. The present study was designed to examine the effect of this characteristic in the Asch conformity situation (Asch, 1953). The Asch situation or modifications of it have been used in numerous studies to determine the relationship between independent variables (e.g. personality, status in the group, relative task competence) and the dependent variable, conformity (see, for example, Bartos, 1958; Cohen, Mayer, Schulman and Terry, 1961; Crutchfield, 1955; Dittes and Kelley, 1956; Kelley and Shapiro, 1954; Moeller and Applezweig, 1957). These studies have all been interpreted in terms of conformity to the group (see Homans, 1961, ch. 16) despite the fact that there are three possible types of influence that may be operating.

In the Asch situation, the subject knows the unanimous, incorrect judgements of the other members of the group before he makes his own response. Thus he may give the same answer as the others because he takes their answers as evidence about reality (informational conformity to the group). The subject gives his response publicly, hence his response may be a function of concern with the evaluation of his behavior by the group (normative conformity to the group) and/or by the experimenter (normative conformity to the experimenter).[1]

---

1. The conceptual distinction between informational and normative conformity as applied to the Asch situation is attributable to Deutsch and Gerard (1955). However, they were unsuccessful in operationalizing this distinction. The distinction between group and experimenter normative conformity in the Asch situation was made by the present author.

The study seeks to determine the extent to which behavior observed in the Asch situation is a function of each of these three possible types of influence. It was predicted that the rate of conformity responses would be raised by informational influence and by normative conformity to the group; while it would be decreased by normative conformity to the experimenter.

Method

Experimental conditions were varied in terms of whether the experimenter and/or the group were perceived by the subject to be in a position to observe (evaluate) him. In all experimental conditions the following basic features of the Asch situation were employed: (a) the subjects were instructed that they were participating in a study of perceptual judgement, in which they were to match accurately the length of a given line with one of three lines, (b) correct judgements were easy to make, (c) before responding, the subject knew the judgement of other persons and (d) on critical trials the judgements of the other persons were wrong and unanimous judgements.

The procedure differed from the classic Asch situation in the following ways: each group was made up of four subjects, two males and two females who were not previously acquainted. Each believed that he or she was subject number 4, the last to respond.[2] Live confederates were not used. The subjects indicated their answers by pressing a button on a panel, supposedly indicating the responses of persons 1, 2 and 3, but the responses were in fact controlled by an assistant located in an adjoining room. Subjects were seated in cubicles which prevented them from seeing that everyone pressed a button when person number 4 was asked to respond.

The stimuli were slides projected on a screen for seven seconds at a distance of approximately 8 feet. Subjects were asked to make their judgements after the slide was removed from the screen. The standard line was $11\frac{1}{2}$ inches high, while the three lines from which subjects were to select its match, were 9 inches, $11\frac{1}{2}$ inches and $9\frac{11}{16}$

---

2. Immediately upon coming into the experimental room, subjects were told to take any of the four seats. They were then asked to pick slips of paper to determine their number. All were number 4.

inches high. All slides were identical except for the identifying letters which appeared under each of the three lines.

On thirty critical trials, the subject received information immediately prior to his response that persons 1, 2 and 3 had chosen the $9\frac{11}{16}$ line. There were four neutral trials: on trials 1 and 2, subjects received the information that persons 1, 2 and 3 had chosen the $11\frac{1}{2}$ inch line, the correct answer; on trials 7 and 20, subjects received the information that persons 1, 2 and 3 had not been unanimous in their responses. Thus it was not possible to have, as Asch did, errors on critical trials in the direction of, but not identical to, that of the group. Subjects could choose the correct answer ($11\frac{1}{2}$ inches), the group's incorrect answer ($9\frac{11}{16}$ inches), or an even more incorrect answer (9 inches).

Each of these differences might affect the observed rate of conformity responses. However, the basic features of the experimental situation have been replicated, and concern is not with absolute rates but with the comparison across the experimental conditions.

The experimental conditions

The four conditions and the manipulations to achieve them were:

I: Neither the experimenter nor the group is in a position to observe the subject, thus only informational influence is possible.
IG: The group, but not the experimenter, is in a position to observe the subject; thus both informational and group normative influence are possible.
IE: The experimenter, but not the group, is in a position to observe the subject; thus both informational and experimenter normative influence are possible.
IEG: Both the experimenter and the group are in a position to observe the subject; thus informational, experimenter normative and group normative influence are possible.[3]

3. With male subjects and a three-man majority, Asch found, over twelve critical trials, an average of four responses identical to or in the direction of the confederates. In condition IEG we find an average of 11·3 identical errors for males and 17·3 for females, out of the thirty critical trials. We find that over all subjects the mean number of more extreme errors is only 0·42, and there are no significant differences by sex or condition. Thus, in presenting our data we will present the mean number of conformity responses (errors identical to the group).

In the control condition, the perceptual task was performed without any knowledge of others' responses. This provides an indication of the rate of incorrect responses given the character of the subject population and the stimuli. No influence process is possible in the control condition.

The informational effect is indicated by comparing the control condition with condition I. The group normative effect is indicated by comparing condition I with condition IG, and by comparing condition IE with condition IEG. The experimenter normative effect is indicated by comparing condition I with condition IE, and by comparing condition IG with condition IEG.

When the subject was to believe that the group was in a position to evaluate him, he was told that as each person responded, their responses would show on each of the other subjects' panels. When he was to believe that the group was not in a position to evaluate him, he was told that the responses of 1, 2 and 3 would show on all subjects' panels as they responded, but that the response of the last person to respond (4) would not show on any of the other subjects' panels, since the last response set off an automatic clearing mechanism.

When the experimenter was to be in a position to evaluate him, the subject was told that the experimenter had a panel from which he would record each person's response on each trial. When the experimenter was not to be in a position to evaluate him, the subject was told that the experimenter's panel would show nothing until all subjects had responded. Then, the responses would show on the experimenter's board but would be scrambled so that he could know only how many correct answers were given on each trial.

The remainder of the manipulation depended upon instructions about sheets on which the subjects in all conditions recorded their responses *after* having pushed their buttons.

When both the experimenter and the group were to be in a position to evaluate the subject, they were instructed to put both their name and their number on the sheet, which would be collected by the experimenter at the end of the trials. They were told the experimenter would announce to the group the name, number and individual score of each person at the end of the trials.

When the experimenter but not the group was to be in a position to observe, they were instructed to put their name and number on the sheet, which would be collected by the experimenter at the end of the trials. The experimenter would write the number correctly on these sheets, return them to each individual and then re-collect them. They were told they would not be allowed to show their score to any of the other subjects so that the experimenter would be the only person (besides the subject) who would know his name, number, and score.

When the group but not the experimenter was to be in a position to observe, they were instructed that at the end of the trials the experimenter would give each subject a key and the subject would be required to record his score next to his name and number. The subjects would then have to exchange their sheet with each of the other three subjects. After the exchange, each subject would take his sheet with him without the experimenter having seen them, so that only the group members would know the number, name and score of the subjects.

When neither the experimenter nor the group was to be in a position to evaluate him, subjects were told that at the end of the trials the experimenter would give each a key from which each could determine his own score. They would not be allowed to show their score to any of the others, and the experimenter would not see these sheets.

Success of the manipulation

At the end of the thirty-four slides, subjects were asked three questions in individual interviews: (a) Who knew when 4 gave the same or a different answer than the others? (b) Who would know at the end of the session that you were 4? (c) Who would know your individual score at the end of the session?

Giving one point for each correct response for the experimental condition intended and computing a mean score for each condition we find that the manipulation was reasonably successful. The lowest score was 2·00 for males in condition IG: the highest was 2·95 for females IE.[4]

4. In order to minimize distortion of results due to differential success in creating conditions the data were analysed for all subjects in a condition, and for only those subjects who gave the correct response on at least two of the three check questions. The latter are presented only where relevant differences appear.

Subjects

Undergraduate students in introductory sociology courses served as subjects. Most took part as a requirement of the course, others were volunteers. Each subject was randomly assigned to one of the conditions.

Table 1 Success in Creating Experimental Conditions: Mean Number of Check Questions Answered Correctly

	Males		Females	
Condition	Mean	N	Mean	N
IEG	2·26	23	2·52	21
IG	2·00	18	2·13	23
IE	2·82	24	2·95	21
I	2·52	23	2·38	21

Note: maximum score $= 3$.

Experimeter

The same twenty-eight-year-old male, first-year graduate student acted as experimenter for all conditions. He introduced himself as Dr James, and gave the instructions from a standard script for the appropriate condition.

Results

Table 2 presents the data bearing on the occurrence of the three types of conformity influences.

Informational influence

Comparing the control condition with condition I, there is, as predicted, an increase in the mean conformity rate for both males and females. Informational influence raises the mean conformity rate for male subjects 6·4 ($p = 0.02$), and 14·5 ($p < 0.001$) for female subjects.

Normative conformity to the experimenter

There is no significant experimenter effect for females. Comparing conditions IG and IEG there is a mean conformity response rate

Table 2 Mean Conformity Response Rate and Tests of Differences

Condition	Males Mean	N	Females Mean	N
IEG	11·3	23	17·3	21
IG	14·3	18	15·7	23
IE	6·6	24	16·1	21
I	10·5	23	14·5	21
Control	4·1	10	0·0	10

Experimenter				
IEG v. IG	$p = 0.24$	$p = 0.01$	$p = 0.48^*$	
IE v. I	$p = 0.03$		$p = 0.62^*$	
Group				
IEG v. IE	$p = 0.03$	$p = 0.04$	$p = 0.30$	$p = 0.30$
IG v. I	$p = 0.18$		$p = 0.30$	
Informational				
I v. Control	$p = 0.02$		$p < 0.001$	

Note: Probability figures are one-tailed using the Mann–Whitney Statistic U, except in the case of results in a direction other than predicted. For these the probabilities are two-tailed and indicated by an asterisk (*).

increase of 1.6 ($p = 0.48^*$), rather than the predicted decrease. Comparing females in conditions I and IE, there is an increase of 1.6 ($p = 0.62^*$). For male subjects, the same comparisons yield decreases of 3.0 ($p = 0.24$) and 3.9 ($p = 0.03$), respectively. Given that the latter results are in the predicted direction in both independent tests (IG v. IEG, and I v. IE) the χ^2 procedure described by Edwards for determining a composite probability for independent tests was followed (Edwards, 1954, pp. 391–3). The probability that both independent comparisons would be in the predicted direction due to chance is 0.01. Thus, for males there is, as predicted, an experimenter effect which decreases the conformity response rate.

Normative conformity to the group

There is no significant group normative effect for females. Comparing conditions I and IG there is an increase of 1.2 ($p = 0.30$) in the

Table 3 Subject's Report of Thinking about the Experimenter's and the Group's Reaction to Them (in appropriate conditions)

Question		Very frequently	A number of times	A few times	Never	No response or not asked	N
1. Had thoughts about 'Dr James's reactions (conditions IE and IEG)	Males	2	3	23	17	2	47
	Females	5	5	15	15	2	42
2. Had thoughts about the other three participants' reactions (conditions IG and IEG)	Males	3	4	22	12	0	41
	Females	6	13	15	10	0	44

mean conformity response rate, and comparing conditions IE and IEG there is an increase of 1·2 ($p = 0.30$). The composite probability was not significant ($p = 0.30$). For males, there is, as predicted, a group normative effect that increases the mean rate of conformity responses. Comparing conditions I and IG, there is an increase of 3·8 ($p = 0.18$); and comparing conditions IE and IEG there is an increase of 4·7 ($p = 0.03$). The composite probability for these two independent tests was 0·04.

Assumptions and controls

These data indicate that, for males, behavior in the Asch situation reflects informational, group normative, and experimenter normative effects; while for females, behavior in the Asch situation reflects only informational influence.

The absence of experimenter and group effects for females was unexpected and strange since the females say, in post session interviews, that (in the appropriate conditions) they thought about the experimenter's and the group's impression of them at least as much as did the males (see Table 3).

The prediction of a decrease in conformity responses due to the experimenter effect assumed that subjects would expect the experimenter's evaluation of them to be based primarily on whether they gave correct or incorrect answers. Thus, a decrease would be predicted only if subjects believed the nonconformity answer to be correct. An increase would be predicted if subjects believed the conformity answer to be correct, and no difference if subjects were uncertain as to which was correct.

Analysis of data from post-session interviews support the assumption as to the criteria the experimenter is expected to use (see Table 4). The assumption as to which response is believed to be correct is found to be valid only for males. Among males 61 per cent believed the nonconformity answer was correct, 15 per cent were uncertain, and 24 per cent believed that the conformity answer was correct. In contrast, among females the respective percentages were 35, 35 and 30.[5] Thus, for females, any experimenter effect

5. Subjects were asked to bet in the interview as to the number of trials on which they gave the same or a different answer from the group. They were also asked to bet how many of each type of answer would turn out to be correct answers. Those who bet that the nonconformity answer was correct

Table 4 Mean Evaluation Expected from Experimenter, and Tests of Differences between Situations

Situation (experimenter knows that you:)	Females (N = 41)	Males (N = 45)
A. agreed with others, but have no idea which is correct	+0·44	+0·34
D. disagreed with others, but have no idea which is correct	+0·23	+0·49
AC. agreed with others, and you are correct	+1·22	+1·09
AI. agreed with others, and you are incorrect	−1·07	−0·95
DC. disagreed with others, and you are correct	+2·05	+2·35
DI. disagreed with others, and you are incorrect	−0·54	−1·13
Tests for agreement		
A v. D	$p = 0·14$	$p = 0·18$
DC v. AC	$p < 0·001$	$p < 0·001$
DI v. AI	$p = 0·04$	$p = 0·18$
Tests for correctness		
A v. AC	$p = 0·002$	$p < 0·001$
A v. AI	$p < 0·001$	$p < 0·001$
D v. DC	$p < 0·001$	$p < 0·001$
D v. DI	$p < 0·001$	$p < 0·001$
DC v. DI	$p < 0·001$	$p < 0·001$
AC v. AI	$p < 0·001$	$p < 0·001$

Note: Responses tabled for subjects in conditions IEG and IE. The probabilities are one-tailed based on the Mann–Whitney Statistic U. Mean scores were based on ratings ranging from +3 (extremely favorable) to −3 (extremely unfavorable). Two males and one female were not asked these questions due to interviewer error.

on twenty or more of the thirty critical trials were classified as believing the nonconformity answer was correct. Those who bet that the conformity answer was correct on twenty or more of the critical trials were classified as believing the conformity answer was correct. Remaining subjects were classified as uncertain, as all trials used identical stimuli.

could not be seen with belief uncontrolled: a predicted decrease among the 35 per cent who believe the nonconformity answer is correct, would be balanced by a predicted increase among the 30 per cent who believe the conformity answer is correct.

Controlling for belief

For females who believe the nonconformity answer is correct, comparing conditions I and IE there is a predicted decrease of 5·18 ($p = 0·13$), and comparing conditions IG and IEG there is a decrease of 2·79 ($p = 0·38$). The composite probability for the two independent tests of experimenter effect is 0·19. When the data for only those who responded correctly on at least two of the three condition check questions are used, i.e. those for whom the experimental manipulations are most sure – there is a stronger experimenter effect (see Table 5).[6]

For females who believe that the conformity answer is correct, comparing conditions I and IE there is a predicted increase of 2·20 ($p = 0·11$); comparing conditions IG and IEG there is an increase of 3·25 ($p = 0·05$). The composite probability for the two independent tests of experimenter effect is 0·04. The data for only those who responded correctly on at least two of the three check questions shows a stronger experimenter effect in the I v. IE comparison and a weaker effect in the IG v. IEG comparison (see Table 5 and note 6).

For those females who are uncertain as to which answer is correct, no significant experimenter effect can be found in the I–IE, and IG–IEG comparisons.

For those males who believe the nonconformity answer is correct, comparing conditions I and IE, there is a predicted decrease of 2·13 ($p = 0·03$); comparing conditions IG and IEG

6. The data in Table 5 are for all subjects. However, in the following cases, relevant differences are found when the data are based only on subjects who gave the correct response for at least two of the three condition check questions:
1. *For females who believe the nonconformity answer is correct*, I v. IE shows a predicted decrease of 3·54, $p = 0·13$; IG v. IEG a decrease of 5·06, $p = 0·10$ (composite $p = 0·07$). I v. IG shows an increase of 3·72, $p = 0·10$; IE v. IEG an increase of 2·20, $p = 0·07$ (composite $p = 0·04$).
2. *For females who believe the conformity answer is correct*, I v. IE shows a predicted increase of 4·90, $p = 0·09$; IG v. IEG an increase of 1·33, $p = 0·30$ (composite $p = 0·13$).

Table 5 Mean Conformity Response Rate Controlling for Belief as to Which Answer is Correct, and Tests of Differences between Conditions

| | Males | | | | | | Females | | | | | |
| | Nonconformity correct | | Uncertain | | Conformity correct | | Nonconformity correct | | Uncertain | | Conformity correct | |
Condition	Mean	N	Mean	N	Mean	N	Mean	N	Mean	N	Mean	N
IEG	4·53	15	18·00	1	25·00	7	4·43	7	19·50	6	26·87	8
IG	5·44	9	24·00	2	22·86	7	7·72	9	18·00	6	23·62	8
IE	2·41	17	13·50	4	21·33	3	1·60	5	18·18	11	26·40	5
I	4·54	13	13·67	6	25·00	4	6·78	9	17·57	7	24·20	5

Experimenter effect

| | Males | | | | | | Females | | | | | |
	Nonconformity correct		Uncertain		Conformity correct		Nonconformity correct		Uncertain		Conformity correct	
IEG v. IG	$p=0.43$	0·07	$p=0.66$*	0·14	$p=0.19$		$p=0.38$	0·19	$p=0.94$*		$p=0.05$	0·04
IE v. I	$p=0.03$		$p=0.92$*		$p=0.22$*		$p=0.13$		$p=1.00$*		$p=0.11$	

Group effect

| | Males | | | | | | Females | | | | | |
	Nonconformity correct		Uncertain		Conformity correct		Nonconformity correct		Uncertain		Conformity correct	
IEG v. IE	$p=0.05$	0·10	$p=0.40$	0·14	$p=0.19$		$p=0.05$	0·11	$p=0.50$	0·55	$p=0.31$	
IG v. I	$p=0.41$		$p=0.07$		$p=0.64$*		$p=0.45$		$p=0.42$		$p=0.84$*	

Note: The probabilities are one-tailed using the Mann–Whitney Statistic U, except when the data are not in the predicted direction in which case they are two-tailed and indicated by an asterisk (*). See also footnote 6.

there is a decrease of 0·91 ($p = 0.43$). The composite probability for the two independent tests of experimenter effect is 0·07.

For those males who believe the conformity answer is correct, the data do not show a consistent effect due to the experimenter. Comparing conditions I and IE, there is, contrary to prediction, a decrease of 3·67 ($p = 0.22*$). Comparing conditions IG and IEG, there is an increase of 2·14 ($p = 0.19$).

For those males who are uncertain as to which answer is correct, there is, as predicted, no significant effect due to the experimenter to be seen in the I–IE and IG–IEG comparisons.

This analysis indicates that the conclusion that there is an experimenter effect for males, but not for females, must be reconsidered. For females, the absence of an experimenter influence when belief is not controlled is attributable to a balancing effect. For males, the significant decrease attributed to the experimenter when belief is not controlled, appears to be a function of (a) most males (61 per cent) believing that the nonconformity answer is correct, and this belief category producing a significant decrease, and (b) a decrease due to the experimenter in three of the four comparisons in the two remaining belief categories.

One possible explanation for the consistency among males in the direction of experimenter effect across the belief categories, might be that males are less willing than females to admit to the interviewer that they gave the conformity answer when they actually believed it was the wrong answer. If this is true, some proportion of those males otherwise classified should actually be in the 'nonconformity correct' category. Then, the predicted increase among those who believe the conformity answer to be correct would be covered up; and the predicted decrease among those who believe the nonconformity answer is correct would be underestimated.

Partial support for this interpretation is found. A ratio of the number of conformity responses given over the number of trials on which the subject is willing to bet that the conformity answer was correct, was computed for males and females who were classified as uncertain or believing that the conformity response was correct. A ratio greater than one, implying that the subject gave more conformity responses than he thought correct, can be taken as an indication of willingness to admit influence to the

interviewer. Among those classified as uncertain, there is a statistically significant difference ($p = 0.02$, one-tailed Mann–Whitney U)
between the mean ratios for males (0·90) and females (1·20),
suggesting that some proportion of males classified as uncertain
should be in the 'nonconformity is correct' category and that the
decrease observed in this category has been underestimated.
Among those classified as believing the conformity answer was
correct, there is no difference between males and females.

A similar analysis for group effect was made. This analysis shows
that while there is a general consistency, as predicted, in the direction of an increase in conformity response rate due to the group,
for both males and females, the only statistically significant increase
is found among those who believe the 'nonconformity answer
correct'.[7] It would seem that the findings of no significant group
effect for females and a significant group effect for males when
belief is not controlled, was again due to the considerably larger
proportion of the males, as compared to the females, in the
'nonconformity is correct' belief category.

The prediction of an increase in conformity response rate due to
the group was based on the assumptions that: (a) subjects would
expect the group to evaluate them on both agreement–disagreement, and on whether they gave the correct or incorrect answer;
and (b) at least during the task (before scores were reported or
answer keys distributed) subjects would think that the group
considers the answer the group gives unanimously to be the correct
answer.

Data from the post-session interview confirms the first assumption (see Table 6), while there are no data relevant to the second
assumption. The question thus arises as to why significant increases
due to the group are found only among those who believe the nonconformity answer to be correct. To the extent that subjects believe
that the group will evaluate them in terms of giving the correct or
incorrect answer, one would expect the least increase among those
who believe the nonconformity answer is correct.

A possible explanation exists. First, in the absence of the group's

7. Due to the probable misclassification of males in the 'nonconformity is
correct' category, as noted previously, and the large magnitude of increase
observed among males categorized as uncertain, the increase observed for
males in the nonconformity is correct category is probably underestimated.

Table 6 Mean Evaluation Expected from the Group, and Tests of Differences between Situations

Situation (the group knows that you:)	Females (N = 43)	Males (N = 40)
A. agreed with them, but have no idea which is correct	+0·80	+0·80
D. disagreed with them, but have no idea which is correct	−0·68	−0·35
AC. agreed with them, and you are correct	+1·23	+1·22
AI. agreed with them, and you are incorrect	+0·19	+0·32
DC. disagreed with them, and you are correct	0·00	+0·27
DI. disagreed with them, and you are incorrect	−0·56	−1·17
Tests for agreement		
A v. D	$p < 0.001$	$p < 0.001$
DC v. AC	$p < 0.001$	$p = 0.004$
DI v. AI	$p < 0.001$	$p < 0.001$
Tests for correctness		
A v. AC	$p < 0.001$	$p < 0.001$
A v. AI	$p < 0.001$	$p < 0.001$
D v. DC	$p < 0.001$	$p = 0.07$
D v. DI	$p < 0.001$	$p < 0.001$
DC v. DI	$p = 0.033$	$p < 0.001$
AC v. AI	$p < 0.001$	$p < 0.001$

Note: (See note to Table 4.) One male and one female were not asked these questions due to interviewer error.

observation, the more a person believes that the conformity response is correct the higher is the rate of conformity responses. Thus, when group observability is introduced, there is a ceiling effect among those who believe that the conformity response is the correct answer. There is considerably more room for an increase among those who believe the nonconformity answer is correct. Second, subjects may expect that the group's evaluation of them will be affected more by what the group believes is the correct answer *during the task*, than what the subject believes the group will find out is the correct answer when scores are computed.

Conclusions and implications

While behavior in the Asch situation has previously been interpreted as an indicator of conformity to the group, the data suggest that for both males and females the rate of conformity response in the Asch situation is a function of informational conformity, normative conformity to the experimenter and normative conformity to the group.

The implications of these findings are twofold. They add to the growing body of research and comment indicating that we must consider the experimental situation itself as a social system containing expectations and role relationships between the experimenter and his subjects, which may affect the results obtained (see Mills, 1962; Rosenthal, 1963).

Rosenthal has shown that an experimenter may unknowingly, and in some as yet unspecified way, bias results in the direction of the predictions. Mills has offered an explanation for some unexpected relationships observed between cohesiveness, task relevance, and rejection of a deviate; and he suggests that the results may be a function of systematic differences in the experimenter–subject relationship produced in the attempt to create the experimental variations in the independent variable.

To these experimenter effects, the present data add the indication that even when the experimenter–subject relationship is a constant, as it is in the classic Asch studies, that the nature of the experimenter–subject relationship is such that the dependent variable may be a function of this relationship.

Further, these results suggest that the interpretations placed upon results from studies which have used the Asch situation must be reconsidered. For instance, it has been found that persons of middle status in a group give a higher rate of conformity responses than high status persons. The interpretation has been that middle status persons conform more to the group. However, the present data suggest an alternative interpretation. Perhaps middle and high status persons are equally influenced by concern with the group's evaluation of them, but that high status persons are more influenced than middle status persons by concern with evaluations from authority figures (the experimenter). Given that the experimenter's effect is to reduce conformity responses among males (and the status-conformity findings cited were based on male subjects), it is possible that the high status person gives few conformity responses in the Asch situation not because the group exerts less normative influence over him, but because the experimenter exerts more (Bartos, 1958; Homans 1961).

References

ASCH, S. E. (1953), 'Effects of group pressure upon the modification and distortion of judgment', in D. Cartwright and A. Zander (eds.), *Group Dynamics*, Row, Peterson, pp. 151–62.

BARTOS, O. J. (1958), 'Leadership, conformity and originality', unpublished paper presented at meeting of American Sociological Society.

COHEN, B. P., MAYER, T. F., SCHULMAN, G. I., and TERRY, C. (1961), *Relative Competence and Conformity*, Department of Sociology, Stanford University.

CRUTCHFIELD, R. S. (1955), 'Conformity and character', *Amer. Psychol.*, vol. 10, pp. 191–8.

DEUTSCH, M., and GERARD, H. B. (1955), 'A study of normative and informational social influences upon individual judgment', *J. abnorm. soc. Psychol.*, vol. 51, pp. 629–36.

DITTES, J. E., and KELLEY, H. H. (1956), 'Effects of different conditions of acceptance on conformity to group norms', *J. abnorm. soc. Psychol.*, vol. 57, pp. 100–107.

EDWARDS, A. L. (1954), *Statistical Methods for the Behavioral Sciences*, Holt, Rinehart & Winston.

HOMANS, G. C. (1961), *Social Behavior, its Elementary Forms*, Harcourt, Brace & World.

KELLEY, H. H., and SHAPIRO, M. M. (1954), 'An experiment on conformity to group norms when conformity is detrimental to group achievement', *Amer. soc. Rev.*, vol. 19, pp. 667–77.

MILLS, T. M. (1962), 'A sleeper variable in small groups research: the experimenter', *Pacific soc. Rev.*, vol. 1, pp. 21–8.

MOELLER, G., and APPLEZWEIG, M. H. (1957), 'A motivational factor in conformity', *J. abnorm. soc. Psychol.*, vol. 55, pp. 114–20.

ROSENTHAL, R. (1963), 'On the social psychology of the psychological experiment', *Amer. Sci.*, vol. 51, pp. 268–83.

17 Bruce W. Tuckman

Developmental Sequence in Small Groups

Bruce W. Tuckman, 'Developmental sequence in small groups',
Psychological Bulletin, vol. 63, 1965, pp. 384–99.

The purpose of this article is to review the literature dealing with the developmental sequence in small groups, to evaluate this literature as a body, to extrapolate general concepts about group development and to suggest fruitful areas for further research.

While small-group processes have been given great attention in recent years by behavioral scientists, the question of change in process over time has been relatively neglected. Perhaps the major reason for this is the overwhelming tendency of the small-group researcher to run groups for short periods of time and thus avoid the 'problems' created by temporal change. Laboratory studies of developmental phenomena are quite rare. The majority of articles dealing with sequential group development come from the group-therapy setting and human relations training-group setting, neither of which features strict experimental control nor manipulation of independent variables. Moreover, the only major theoretical statements of group development which have appeared are those of Bach (1954), Bales (1953) and Schutz (1958).

In an attempt to bring the facts and the issues into sharper focus, existing research in the area of small-group development will be cited, and a framework within which this phenomenon can be better understood and further investigated will be presented. This framework will also serve to integrate the variety of studies cited in a meaningful way.

Classification model

The classification approach adopted for distinguishing between and within developmental studies is a threefold one. The delineations are based on (a) the setting in which the group is found, (b) the realm into which the group behavior falls at any point in time, that is, task or interpersonal, and (c) the position of the group in a hypothetical developmental sequence (referred to as the stage of development). It is this last delineation that allows not only for the separation and ordering of observations within each setting, but for the development of additional hypotheses as well.

Setting

Classification according to setting allows for the clustering of studies based on their similarity of features, for example, group size, group composition, duration of 'group life', etc. More similarity between observations made in the same setting than in different settings is expected.

In the *group-therapy setting* the task is to help individuals better deal with their personal problems. The goal is individual adjustment. Such groups contain from five to fifteen members, each of whom has some debilitating personal problem, and a therapist, and the group exists for three months or more. The developmental data for such groups consist of the observations of the therapist and those professional observers that are present, usually as trainees. Such data are highly anecdotal in nature and reflect the clinical biases of the observers. Furthermore, such accounts are usually formulated after the fact and based on the observation of a single group. Since the bulk of the literature reviewed comes from this setting, its generality must be limited by the limitations of the setting and the mode of data collection.

In the *human relations training-group (T-group) setting*, the task is to help individuals interact with one another in a more productive, less defensive manner, and to be aware of the dynamics underlying such interaction. The goal is interpersonal sensitivity. Such groups contain ordinarily from fifteen to thirty members, usually students or corporation executives, and one trainer or leader, and endure from about three weeks to six months.

The most striking differences between therapy- and training-group settings are in the areas of group composition, task, goal, and duration of group life. Such differences can account for different findings in the two settings. The most striking similarity is in the manner of data collection. Data in the training-group setting are highly anecdotal, subjective, collected by the trainer and his co-workers, and often based on the observations of a single group.

Again, this serves to limit the generality of these findings.

The *natural-group setting* is distinguished on the basis that the group exists to perform some social or professional function over which the researcher has no control. Members are not brought together for self-improvement; rather, they come together to do a job. Such groups may be characterized either by appointed or emergent leadership. Presidential advisory councils and industrial groups represent examples of natural groups. Similar limitations to generalization based on the manner of data collection and number of groups observed applies in this setting as in the previous settings.

The *laboratory-task setting* features groups brought together for the purpose of studying group phenomena. Such groups are small (generally under ten members), have a short life, and may or may not have leaders. In this setting, groups are given a task or tasks which they are to complete. Quantitative data are collected and analyzed based on multiple-group performances.

The last two settings have been combined due to the small number of studies in each (the dearth of group development studies in the industrial area is notable), and also because theoretical statements are reviewed which are generalized to cover both areas. All studies will be classified into one of the three setting categories according to best fit.

Realm: *interpersonal* v. *task*

Within the studies reviewed, an attempt will be made to distinguish between *interpersonal* stages of group development and *task* behaviors exhibited in the group. The contention is that any group, regardless of setting, must address itself to the successful completion of a task. At the same time, and often through the same behaviors, group members will be relating to one another interpersonally. The pattern of *interpersonal relationships* is referred to as *group structure* and is interpreted as the interpersonal configuration and interpersonal behaviors of the group at a point in time, that is, the way the members act and relate to one another as persons. The content of interaction as related to the task at hand is referred to as *task activity*. The proposed distinction between the group as a social entity and the group as a task entity is similar to the distinction between the task oriented functions of groups and the social-emotional-integrative functions of groups, both of which occur as simultaneous aspects of group functioning (Bales, 1953; Coffey, 1952; Deutsch, 1949; Jennings, 1947).

In therapy groups and T-groups, the task is a personal and interpersonal one in that the group exists to help the individuals deal with themselves and others. This makes the interpersonal-task distinction a fuzzy one. A further problem with this distinction occurs because the studies cited do not distinguish between the two realms and often talk about interpersonal development at one point in the sequence and task development at another point. The distinction will be maintained, however, because of the generic difference between the reaction to others as elements of the group task versus the reaction to others as social entities. Failing to separate stages by realm obscures the continuity of the developmental process. While the two realms differ in content, as will be seen their underlying dynamics are similar.

Proposed developmental sequence

The following model is offered as a conceptualization of changes in group behavior, in both social and task realms, across all group settings, over time. It represents a set of hypotheses reflecting the author's biases (rather than those of the researchers) and the perception of trends in the studies reviewed which become considerably more apparent when these studies are viewed in the light of the model. The model of development stages presented below is not suggested for primary use as an organizational vehicle, although it serves that function here. Rather, it is a conceptual statement suggested by the data presented and subject to further test.

In the realm of group structure the first hypothesized stage of the model is labeled as *testing and dependence*. The term 'testing' refers to an attempt by group members to discover what interpersonal behaviors are acceptable in the group, based on the reactions of the therapist or trainer (where one is present) and on the reactions of the other group members. Coincident to discovering the boundaries of the situation by testing, one relates to the therapist, trainer, some powerful group member, or existing norms and structures in a dependent way. One looks to this person, persons, or standards for guidance and support in this new and unstructured situation.

The first stage of task-activity development is labeled as *orienta-*

tion to the task, in which group members attempt to identify the task in terms of its relevant parameters and the manner in which the group experience will be used to accomplish the task. The group must decide upon the type of information they will need in dealing with the task and how this information is to be obtained. In orienting to the task, one is essentially defining it by discovering its 'ground rules'. Thus, orientation, in general, characterizes behavior in both interpersonal and task realms during this stage. It is to be emphasized that orientation is a general class of behavior which cuts across settings; the specifics of orientation, that is, what one must orient to and how, will be setting-specific.

The second phase in the development of group structure is labeled as *intragroup conflict*. Group members become hostile toward one another and toward a therapist or trainer as a means of expressing their individuality and resisting the formation of group structure. Interaction is uneven and 'infighting' is common. The lack of unity is an outstanding feature of this phase. There are characteristic key issues that polarize the group and boil down to the conflict over progression into the 'unknown' of interpersonal relations or regression to the security of earlier dependence.

Emotional response to task demands is identified as the second stage of task-activity development. Group members react emotionally to the task as a form of resistance to the demands of the task on the individual, that is, the discrepancy between the individual's personal orientation and that demanded by the task. This task stage will be most evident when the task has as its goal self-understanding and self-change, namely, the therapy- and training-group tasks, and will be considerably less visible in groups working on impersonal, intellectual tasks. In both task and interpersonal realms, emotionality in response to a discrepancy characterizes this stage. However, the source of the discrepancy is different in the different realms.

The third group structure phase is labeled as the *development of group cohesion*. Group members accept the group and accept the idiosyncrasies of fellow members. The group becomes an entity by virtue of its acceptance by the members, their desire to maintain and perpetuate it, and the establishment of new group-generated norms to insure the group's existence. Harmony is of maximum importance, and task conflicts are avoided to insure harmony.

The third stage of task activity development is labeled as the *open exchange of relevant interpretations*. In the therapy- and training-group context, this takes the form of *discussing oneself and other group members*, since self and other personal characteristics are the basic task inputs. In the laboratory-task context, exchanged interpretations take the form of opinions. In all cases one sees information being acted on so that alternative interpretations of the information can be arrived at. The openness to other group members is characteristic in both realms during this stage.

The fourth and final developmental phase of group structure is labeled as *functional role-relatedness*. The group, which was established as an entity during the preceding phase, can now become a problem-solving instrument. It does this by directing itself to members as objects, since the subjective relationship between members has already been established. Members can now adopt and play roles that will enhance the task activities of the group, since they have learned to relate to one another as social entities in the preceding stage. Role structure is not an issue but an instrument which can now be directed at the task. The group becomes a 'sounding board' off which the task is 'played'.

In task-activity development, the fourth and final stage is identified as the *emergence of solutions*. It is here that we observe constructive attempts at successful task completion. In the therapy- and training-group context, these solutions are more specifically *insight* into personal and interpersonal processes and constructive self-change, while in the laboratory-group context the solutions are more intellectual and impersonal. Here, as in the three preceding stages, there is an essential correspondence between group structural and task realms over time. In both realms the emphasis is on constructive action, and the realms come together so that energy previously invested in the structural realm can be devoted to the task.

The next section presents a review of relevant studies separated according to setting. The observations within each study are separated according to stage of development and realm.

Stages of development in therapy groups
Stage 1
Group structure: testing and dependence. Of the twenty-six studies

of development in therapy groups which were reviewed, eighteen identified a beginning stage as either testing or dependence or both. Bach (1954) speaks of *initial situation testing* to determine the nature of the therapy environment and discover the kinds of relationships the therapist will promote, followed closely by *leader dependence* where group members relate to the therapist dependently. Barton (1953), Beukenkamp (1952) and Mann and Semrad (1948) identify an initial stage in which the group tests to determine the limits of tolerance of the therapist and the group.

Researchers emphasizing the more dependent aspects of this initial stage are Bion (1961) who describes groups operating with the basic assumption of *dependency*, Cholden (1953) who has observed dependency in therapy groups of blind individuals, and Stoute (1950) who observed dependency in larger classroom therapy groups.

Others have observed this stage and have used a variety of names to label it. Corsini (1957), in an integration of other studies, identifies *hesitant participation* as an initial stage, in which members test the group and therapist to discover how they will respond to various statements. Grotjahn (1950) refers to an initial period of orientation and information, while King (1959) labels initial testing and orienting behavior in activity-group therapy as *acclimatization*. Abrahams (1949) and Powdermaker and Frank (1948) describe the initial period as one of orientation and testing where group members attempt to relate to the therapist and to discover the structure and limits of the therapy group. Schindler (1958), using bifocal-group therapy, labels the initial stage as *attachment to the group*, in which individuals discharge old ties and establish new ones. Taylor (1950) talks about qualifying for acceptance by the group at the start of therapy which implies both testing and conforming.

Four of the studies reviewed describe a stage preceding the testing-dependence stage which will be referred to as pre-stage 1. Thorpe and Smith (1953) and Osberg and Berliner (1956), in therapy with hospitalized narcotic addicts, describe an initial stage of resistance, silence and hostility followed by a testing period where patients attempt to discover what behaviors the therapist deems acceptable. Shellow, Ward and Rubenfeld (1958), who worked with institutionalized delinquents, described two such stages of resistance and hostility preceding the testing stage, while Martin and Hill (1957) theorized about a stage of isolation and 'unshared behavior' preceding one of stereotypic responding to fellow group members and a dependent orientation toward the therapist.

Three of the four studies identifying a pre-stage 1 were specifically based on observations of groups of antisocial individuals (drug addicts and delinquents) who probably must be won over to the situation and their initial extreme resistance overcome before the normal sequence of therapy-group development can begin. This would account for pre-stage 1.

The remaining studies did not identify an initial stage of testing-dependence but dealt either with task development (to be discussed below), or offered as an initial stage 1 which is postulated here as a second stage. Finally, a study by Parker (1958) described an initial stage of *cohesive organization* in which sub-groups are formed, rules followed, and harmony maintained – a description which is difficult to fit into the testing-dependence category.

Task activity: orientation and testing. During the initial stage, task development is characterized by indirect attempts to discover the nature and boundaries of the task, i.e. what is to be accomplished and how much cooperation is demanded, expressed specifically through (a) the discussion of irrelevant and partially relevant issues (Bion, 1961; Coffey *et al.*, 1950; Martin and Hill, 1957; Osberg and Berliner, 1956), (b) the discussion of peripheral problems (Stoute, 1950), (c) the discussion of immediate behavior problems (Abrahams, 1949), (d) the discussion of symptoms (Bach, 1954; Taylor, 1950), (e) griping about the institutional environment (Mann and Semrad, 1948; Shellow, Ward and Rubenfeld, 1958; Thorpe and Smith, 1953), and (f) intellectualization (Clapham and Sclare, 1958; Wender, 1946).

This stage is also characterized by more direct attempts at orientation toward the task as illustrated in (a) a search for the meaning of therapy (Cholden, 1953), (b) attempts to define the situation (Powdermaker and Frank, 1948), (c) attempts to establish a proper therapeutic relationship with the therapist through the development of rapport and confidence (Dreikurs, 1957; King, 1959; Wolf, 1949), (d) mutual exchange of information (Grotjahn,

1950), and (e) suspiciousness of and fearfulness toward the new situation which must be overcome (Corsini, 1957).

Stage 2

Group structure: intragroup conflict. Thirteen of the twenty-six studies of group therapy reviewed identified a stage of intragroup conflict (in eleven cases as a second stage and in two as a first stage). Abrahams (1949) identifies an interaction stage typified by defensiveness, competition and jealousy. Bion (1961) discusses a *fight–flight* period in which members conflict with the therapist or attempt to psychologically withdraw from the situation. Grotjahn (1950) identifies a stage of increasing tension, while Parker (1958) talks about a *crisis period* where friction is increased, anxiety mounts, rules are broken, arguments ensue, and a general structural collapse occurs. Powdermaker and Frank (1948) discuss a second stage featuring sharp fluctuation of relationships, sharp reversals of feelings, and 'intense but brief and brittle linkages'. Schindler (1958) talks about a stage of psychodramatic acting-out and localization of conflicts in the group, while Shellow, Ward and Rubenfeld (1958) describe a stage characterized by ambivalence toward the therapist which is expressed through the formation of conflicting factions in the group. Stoute (1950) describes a second stage beginning with derogation and negativity, while Thorpe and Smith (1953) describe a stage beginning with disintegration, distance, defenses out of awareness and disrupted communication. King (1959), in activity-group therapy, describes a second stage of *benign regression* characterized by extreme acting-out and unacceptable behavior. Martin and Hill (1957) theorize about a stage of polarization featuring the emergence of sub-groups following a stage of interpersonal exploration.

Coffey *et al.* (1950) identify an initial stage of defensiveness and resistance where members clash with one another. However, these authors also see 'pecking orders' being established during this period; perhaps their initial stage includes stages 1 and 2 as postulated in this review. Mann (1953) describes an initial phase of 'working through of hostility' followed by a stage of 'working through of anxieties'. The hostility phase is characterized by disruption and fragmentation which are reduced gradually in the anxiety phase.

The remaining studies fail to identify this stage. Some of them jump from stage 1 directly to stage 3, while others deal with task development as concerns the first two stages of therapy-group development.

Task activity: emotional response to task demands. The outstanding feature of this second task stage appears to be the expression of emotionality by the group members as a form of resisting the techniques of therapy which require that they 'expose' themselves and of challenging the validity and usefulness of therapy (Bach, 1954; Barton, 1953; Cholden, 1953; Clapham and Sclare, 1958; Mann, 1953; Mann and Semrad, 1948; Martin and Hill, 1957; Stoute, 1950; Wender 1964). Furthermore, mention is made of the fact that this is a period of extreme resistance to examination and disclosure (Abrahams, 1949; Barton, 1953), and an attempt at analysis of this resistance is made (Wolf, 1949). Others emphasize ambivalence toward the therapist (Shellow, Ward and Rubenfeld, 1958), the discussion of sensitive areas (Powdermaker and Frank, 1948), psychodrama (Schindler, 1958) and resistance via 'putting one on' (Thorpe and Smith, 1953).

Stage 3

Group structure: development of group cohesion. Twenty-two of the twenty-six studies reviewed identified a stage in which the group became a cohesive unit and developed a sense of being as a group. Bach (1954), Barton (1953) and Clapham and Sclare (1958) identify a stage during which ingroup consciousness is developed and establishment and maintenance of group boundaries is emphasized. Bion (1961) discusses the basic assumption of *pairing* in which the emphasis is on cohesion, but the unit is the pair as opposed to the whole group. Coffey *et al.* (1950), and Taylor (1950) describe a stage following the stage of intragroup hostility in which the group becomes unified and is characterized by the existence of a common goal and group spirit. Parker (1958) and Shellow, Ward and Rubenfeld (1958) see the stage of crisis and factions being followed by one featuring consensual group action, cooperation, and mutual support. Grotjahn (1950), Mann and Semrad (1948), and Powdermaker and Frank (1948) describe a third stage characterized by group integration and mutuality.

Noyes (1953) describes a middle stage of group integration, while Stoute (1950) and Thorpe and Smith (1953) see the stage of intragroup hostility grading into a period of unity, support, and freedom of communication. Martin and Hill (1957) theorize about a stage featuring awareness that the group is an organism preceding the final stage of development. Abrahams (1949) describes the development of 'we-consciousness' in the third stage, while Mann (1953) sees the third stage as one of personal mutual exploration and analysis during which the group attains unity.

The notion that the group becomes a simulation of the family constellation (that is, through transference members react to one another as members of their family), with the unity and cohesion generally accepted in that structure, fits as a close parallel to the stage of development of group cohesion being postulated. Beukenkamp (1952) describes the middle stage of *reliving the process of the family constellation* where the group becomes a familylike structure, while King (1959) utilizes a similar description (that is, family unity in the group) for the final stage in activity-group therapy. Wender (1946) and Wolf (1949) both describe a stage preceding the final stage in which the group becomes the new family through the displacement of parent love.

Studies that fail to identify this stage are those that deal primarily with task development or those that integrate it as part of the final stage.

Task activity: discussing oneself and other group members. Many researchers observed probing and revealing by group members at a highly intimate level during this period and labeled it as (a) confiding (Clapham and Sclare, 1958; Coffey *et al.*, 1950; Thorpe and Smith, 1953), (b) discussing personal problems in depth (Corsini, 1957; Mann and Semrad, 1948; Osberg and Berliner, 1956; Taylor, 1950), (c) exploring the dynamics at work within the individual (Dreikurs, 1957; Noyes, 1953), and (d) exploring the dynamics at work within the group (Bach, 1954; Martin and Hill, 1957; Powdermaker and Frank, 1948).

Beukenkamp (1952) observed that recalled material was related to the family; Abrahams (1949) observed the process of common ideation; and Shellow, Ward and Rubenfeld (1958) and Wolf (1949) emphasized patients' discussion of topics related to transference to the therapist and to other group members which took place during this period.

Stage 4

Group structure: functional role-relatedness. Only twelve of the therapy studies are at all explicit in their identification of this stage. Almost all of the therapists discuss the final stage of development of the therapy group in task terms as the therapeutic stage of under-standing, analysis and insight. The group is seen as serving a therapeutic function, but the nature of this therapeutic function is not spelled out. This is a stage of mutual task interaction with a minimum of emotional interference made possible by the fact that the group as a social entity has developed to the point where it can support rather than hinder task processes through the use of function-oriented roles.

Bach (1954) and Bion (1961) both refer to the group in its final stage as the *work group*. As such it serves a function supportive of therapy. Abrahams (1949) and Wender (1946) see the group as creating a therapeutic atmosphere in the final stage, while Corsini (1951), Stoute (1950) and Wolf (1949) describe this stage as one of *freedom and friendliness* supportive of insightful behavior and change. Both Coffey *et al.* (1950) and Dreikurs (1957) see the group as a therapeutic force producing encouragement and integrating problems with roles. Martin and Hill (1957) identify the group as an *integrative-creative-social instrument* in its final stage which facilitates problem solving, diagnosis and decision making. Osberg and Berliner (1956) describe the self-starting stage where the group environment supports analysis, while Mann (1953) discusses a final stage of *personal mutual synthesis*.

Other therapy researchers failing to specifically delineate this final stage in social development have tended to lump the third and fourth stages together and not make the distinction between the development of cohesion and the 'use' of cohesion (via functional roles) as a therapeutic force. Such descriptions were included in the section on the third stage. The small number of investigators identifying this final stage is most likely due to the high visibility of task functions occurring during this time period which obscure and minimize social processes occurring simultaneously.

Task activity: emergence of insight. There seems to be overwhelming agreement among the observers of therapy-group development that the final stage of task development is characterized by attainment of the desired goal, insight into one's own problems, an understanding of the cause of one's abnormal behavior and, in many cases, modification of oneself in the desired direction (Beukenkamp, 1952; Bion, 1961; Clapham and Sclare, 1958; Coffey *et al.*, 1950; Corsini, 1957; Dreikurs, 1957; King, 1959; Noyes, 1953; Schindler, 1958; Stoute, 1950; Thorpe and Smith, 1953; Wender, 1946; Wolf, 1949). Others (Abrahams, 1949; Bach, 1954; Barton, 1953; Cholden, 1953; Grotjahn, 1950; Shellow, Ward and Rubenfeld, 1958; Taylor, 1950) place more emphasis on the processes of attempting to develop insight and change during this last period as opposed to the development of such insight and change itself.

Two additional therapy-group studies are worthy of inclusion, both of which utilized a technique for collecting and analyzing data which was highly dissimilar to the approach used in the other therapy-group studies, namely, interaction-process analysis (Bales, 1950). Psathas (1960) found that groups phase from *orientation* to *evaluation* to *control*, based on an analysis of early, middle and late sessions. Talland (1955) failed to observe this phase movement based on an analysis of the first eight sessions.

Stages of development in training groups
Stage 1

Group structure: testing and dependence. Nine of the eleven training-group studies reviewed that deal with the development of group structure identify an initial stage characterized at least in part by testing and dependence, with the emphasis on the dependent aspect of this stage.

Herbert and Trist (1953), Bennis and Shepard (1956), Bradford, (1964a), and Bradford and Mallinson (1958) describe the initial group phase as one characterized by the strong expression of dependency needs by the members toward the trainer, and attempts at group structuring to work out authority problems by the quick acceptance of and dependence on such structure and arbitrary norms. Thelen and Dickerman (1949) discuss initial stage establishment of a leadership hierarchy catering to the dependency needs of the members. Hearn (1957) sees group members making an attempt to structure the unknown and to find their position in the group in the earliest group stage. Here again, structure reflects the expression of dependency needs.

Miles (1953) describes a first stage characterized by *establishment of the situation* through interpersonal exploration and testing, while Semrad and Arsenian (1961) identify an initial phase during which group members 'test' the central figure and 'test' the situation.

Whitman (1964) describes a beginning stage in which the chief 'vectors' are dependency and hostility. It would appear that Whitman has identified a first stage which combines the first two stages proposed in this article.

The two studies that do not yield an exact fit to the proposed scheme are those of Barron and Krulee (1948) and the Tulane Studies in Social Welfare (1957) which identify an initial period characterized by the emergence of leadership and orientation, respectively. In so far as these authors see the authority area as being of central concern and emphasize the orientation aspects of the first stage, there is overlap with the scheme proposed herein. Moreover, orientation as a first stage fits the hypothesized initial stage for task activities; perhaps the observation in the Tulane studies (1957) of a member orientation as an initial stage is better classified in the task-activity area.

Task activity: orientation. Bradford (1964b) identifies an initial stage of *learning how to learn* which is characterized by acceptance of the group's goal and orientation to the techniques to be used. Herbert and Trist (1953) label their initial stage as *discovery*, in which the members orient themselves to the consultant or trainer who serves an interpretive and educational role. Stock and Thelen (1958) discuss an initial stage characterized by little 'work' and a variable amount of 'emotionality', during which time the members are concerned with defining the directions the group will pursue.

As can be seen, initially interpersonal problems are dealt with via dependence, while task problems are met with task-orienting behavior (i.e. what is to be accomplished and how).

Stage 2

Group structure: intragroup conflict. Ten of the eleven studies identify intragroup conflict as a second stage, while the remaining study (Whitman, 1964) describes an initial stage encompassing both dependence and hostility, in that order.

Barron and Krulee (1948) and Bradford (1964a) discuss a second stage characterized by group cleavage and conflict. Both studies identify the emergence of polarities during this stage – members favoring a more active, less defensive approach versus those who are more passive and defensive and seek 'safety' via structure. Thelen and Dickerman (1949), Hearn (1957), the Tulane studies (1957) and Bradford and Mallinson (1958), as well, identify a similar polarization and resultant conflict, frustration and disruption during the second stage.

Herbert and Trist (1953) describe a second stage characterized in part by resistance, while Miles (1953) identifies anarchic rebellion during this stage of *anxiety, threat and resistance.* Semrad and Arsenian (1961) identify rivalry for the position of central figure and emotional struggles in this period, while Bennis and Shepard (1956) see a similar power struggle in which counterdependents seek to usurp the leader, resulting in a conflict between counterdependents and dependents.

There appears to be general agreement that the dependency stage is followed by a stage of conflict between warring factions representing each side of the polarized issue: dependence versus independence, safe retreat into the familiar versus risky advance into the unfamiliar, defensiveness versus experimenting.

Task activity: emotional response to task demands. Bradford (1964b) identifies a second stage in which individuals *learn how to give help* which requires that they remove blocks to learning about themselves, reduce anxiety, and express real reactions. Stock and Thelen (1958) see emotionality occurring in considerable excess of work during this period. The Tulane studies (1957) describe the second stage as one of experimental aggressiveness and hostility where individuals express themselves freely.

Thus, self-change and self-denial necessitated by the learning task is reacted to emotionally, as is the imposition of the group on the individual. Often the two (representative of the two realms) are difficult to separate.

Stage 3

Group structure: development of group cohesion. All of the relevant T-group development studies see the stage of conflict and polarization as being followed by a stage characterized by the reduction of the conflict, resolution of the polarized issues, and establishment of group harmony in the place of disruption. It is a 'patching-up' phase in which group norms and values emerge.

Hearn (1957), Miles (1953) and Thelen and Dickerman (1949) identify a third stage characterized by attempts to resolve conflict and the consequent development of group cohesion and mutual support. Semrad and Arsenian (1961) and the Tulane studies (1957) each describe two phases in their temporal sequences which would be included in stage 3. In the case of the former, their first cohesion phase is characterized by group cohesion processes and their second by the development of affection bonds; in the latter, the first cohesion stage features the emergence of structure, roles and 'we-feelings', while the second features increased group identification on a conscious level and vacillation in role acceptance. Whitman (1964) talks about a middle phase, following conflict, described as the development of a new group culture via the generation of norms and values peculiar to the group as an entity. Bradford and Mallinson (1958) describe stage 3 as one of reorganization, in which reforming and repair take place and a flexible organization emerges.

Bradford (1964a) describes a third stage in which the group norm of 'openness' emerges, and a fourth stage in which the group generates additional norms to deal with self-revelation and feedback. Furthermore, Bradford (1964b) identifies a third stage as one of developing a group climate of permissiveness, emotional support and cohesiveness in which learning can take place. This description would appear to subserve both interpersonal and task realms.

Bennis and Shepard (1956) describe a third stage in which resolution of authority problems occurs, and a fourth stage characterized by smooth relations and enchantment as regards the interpersonal sphere of group functioning. Finally, Barron and Krulee (1948) identify the third stage as increasing member responsibility and changing faculty role in which a definite sense of structure and goal orientation emerge in the group.

Task activity: discussing oneself and others. Herbert and Trist (1953) identify a second stage labeled as execution, in which the group settles down to the description of a single basic problem and learns to accept 'the examination of what was going on inside of itself as a regular part of the task . . . .' Stock and Thelen (1958) describe a third task phase in which the group shows a new ability to express feelings constructively and creatively. While emotionality is still high, it now contributes to work.

While the social function of the third stage is to cause a unique and cohesive group structure to emerge, the task function is to attempt to use this new structure as a vehicle for discovering personal relations and emotions by communicating heretofore private feelings.

Stage 4

Group structure: functional role-relatedness. There is some tendency for T-groupers, as there was for the therapy groupers, to emphasize the task aspects of the final stage, namely, the emergence of insight into the interpersonal process. In doing this, it is made implicit that the group as a social entity characterized by task-oriented role-relatedness makes the emergence of such insight possible by providing support and an opportunity for experimentation and discovery.

Bradford (1964a) sees the group becoming a work organization which provides member support, mutual acceptance, and has strong but flexible norms. Hearn (1957) discusses mutual acceptance and use of differences in the collaborative process during the fourth and fifth group stages, while Miles (1953) sees group structure as tending 'to be functional and not loved for itself alone' as it was in the preceding stage. The support function is further emphasized by Miles when he says (p. 94),

in groups where the interpersonal bonds are genuine and strong . . . members give one another a great deal of mutual evaluative support, which seems to be a prime requisite for successful behavior change.

Semrad and Arsenian (1961) describe a final phase of productive collaboration, while Thelen and Dickerman (1949) identify the group as an effective social instrument during this period. Barron and Krulee (1948) see, as one group function occurring during the final two meetings, the sharing and refining of feelings through the group process.

Bennis and Shepard (1956) see the stage of group cohesion being followed by another period of conflict, in which the issue is intimate social relations versus aloofness. The final stage is then one of consensual validation in which group interpersonal problems are solved and the group is freed to function as a problem-solving instrument.

The Tulane studies (1957) describe the stage following the emergence of cohesion as one in which behavior roles become dynamic, that is, behavior is changed as a function of the acceptance of group structure. An additional stage is also identified in this study in which structure is institutionalized by the group and thus becomes rigid. Perhaps this stage, not identified by other researchers, would most apply to groups with a long or indefinite group life.

The remaining T-group studies describe task development exclusively during the final group phase.

Task activity: insight. Bradford's (1964b) fourth phase is one in which members discover and utilize various methods of inquiry as ways of group development and individual growth, while, in his fifth and final stage, members learn how to internalize, generalize and apply learnings to other situations. Herbert and Trist (1953) label their final stage as *evaluation*. Stock and Thelen (1958) describe the fourth and final stage as one characterized by a high degree of work in the absence of affect. The issues are dealt with in a less excited way.

The over-all fit between stages of development postulated in this paper for application in all settings and those delineated by T-groupers is highlighted in the fourfold scheme presented by Golembiewski (1962), based on his examination of some T-group development studies already reviewed in this paper. Golembiewski describes his stages as: (a) establishing the hierarchy; (b) conflict and frustration; (c) growth of group security and autonomy; (d) structuring in terms of problems facing the group rather than in terms of stereotypic role prescriptions.

Stages of development in natural and laboratory groups

Few studies or theoretical statements have concerned themselves with the developmental sequence in natural groups or laboratory groups.

Stage 1

Group structure: testing and dependence. Modlin and Faris (1956), studying an interdisciplinary professional group, identify an initial stage of *structuralization*, in which members are dependent upon roles developed outside of the group, well-established traditions, and a fixed hierarchy of responsibility.

Schroder and Harvey (1963) describe an initial stage of *absolutistic dependency*, featuring the emergence of a status hierarchy and rigid norms which reduce ambiguity and foster dependence and submission.

Theodorson (1953) observed a tendency initially for only one leader to emerge and for group members to categorize one another so that they could define the situation and reduce ambiguity.

Schutz (1958)[1] sees the group dealing initially with problems of *inclusion* – to join or not to join; to commit oneself or not. The group concern, thus, is boundary problems, and the behavior of members is individually centered. This description is somewhat suggestive of testing.

Task activity: orientation. Bales (1953) and Bales and Strodtbeck (1951) using Bales's (1950) interaction-process categories, discovered that leaderless laboratory groups begin by placing major emphasis on problems of *orientation* (as reflected in Bales's categories: 'asks for orientation' and 'gives orientation'). This orientation serves to define the boundaries of the task (i.e. what is to be done) and the approach that is to be used in dealing with the task (i.e. how it is to be accomplished).

Stage 2

Group structure: intragroup hostility. Modlin and Faris (1956) describe *unrest* characterized by friction and disharmony as the second stage, while Schroder and Harvey (1963) identify a second

1. The classification of Schutz's theory as one primarily descriptive of natural and laboratory groups is arbitrary. Some would argue that Schutz is working the T-group tradition.

stage of *negative independence* featuring rebellion, opposition and conflict. In this stage the greater emphasis is on autonomy and individual rights. Theodorson (1953) observed more friction, disharmony and animosity early in the group life than during later periods.

Schutz (1958) postulates a second stage in which the group deals with problems of *control*. This entails a leadership struggle in which individual members compete to establish their place in the hierarchy culminating in resolution.

In the task area, the stage of *emotional response to task demands* is not delineated, presumably due to the impersonal and non-threatening nature of the task in these settings. When the task does not deal with the self at a penetrating level, extreme emotionality in the task area is not expected.

Stage 3

Group structure: development of Group Cohesion. Modlin and Faris (1956) identify *change* as the third stage, characterized by the formation of the concept of the group as a functioning unit and the emergence of a team 'dialect'. Schroder and Harvey (1963) refer to stage 3 as *conditional dependence*, featuring a group concern with integration and an emphasis on mutuality and the maintenance of interpersonal relationships.

Theodorson (1953) observed the following group tendencies over time (i.e. tending to occur later as opposed to earlier in group development): (a) discovering what is common to the members and developing a within-group 'parochialism'; (b) the growth of an interlocking network of friendship; (c) role interdependence; (d) mutual involvement and identification between members with a concomitant increase in harmony and solidarity; and (e) the establishment of group norms for dealing with such areas as discipline.

Schutz (1958) postulated a third stage wherein problems of *affectation* are dealt with. Characteristic of this stage are emotional integration, pairing, and the resolution of intimacy problems.

Task activity: expression of opinions. Bales (1953) and Bales and Strodtbeck (1951) observed that the orientation phase was followed by a period in which major emphasis was placed on problems of *evaluation* (as reflected by categories: 'asks for opinion' and 'gives opinion'). 'Evaluation' as a descriptor of the exchange of opinions appears to be comparable to the third task stage in therapy- and training-group development which was heretofore labeled as 'discussing oneself and others'. Because the therapy and training tasks are personal ones, task opinions must involve self and others. When the task is an impersonal one, the content of task opinions varies accordingly.

Stage 4

Group structure: functional role-relatedness. Modlin and Faris (1956) identify integration as the fourth and final stage in which structure is internalized and the group philosophy becomes pragmatic, that is, the unified-group approach is applied to the task.

Schroder and Harvey (1963) postulate a final stage of *positive interdependence*, characterized by simultaneous autonomy and mutuality (i.e. the members can operate in any combination, or as a unit), and an emphasis on task achievement which is superordinate to social structure.

Theodorson (1953) sees the group as developing into a subculture over time, along with the development of member responsibility to the group.

Schutz (1958) does not identify a fourth stage; rather, he sees his three postulated stages continually cycling over time.

Task activity: emergence of solution. The third and final phase observed by Bales (1953) and Bales and Strodtbeck (1951) is one in which major emphasis is placed on problems of *control* (as reflected by categories: 'asks for suggestion' and 'gives suggestion'). The purpose of suggestions is to offer solutions to the task based on information gathered and evaluated in previous developmental periods. This then represents an analogue of final stages in therapy- and training-group task development where the emergence of insight yields solutions to personal problems.

These authors do not identify a period of task development in laboratory groups comparable to the second task stage in therapy- and training-group development which features the expression of emotional material. Again, because therapy and training tasks are personal ones, this will be reflected in the content of discussion, specifically by the manifestation of resistance prior to dealing with the personal task at a level of confidence and honesty. This task stage does not appear to be quite relevant in laboratory discussion groups, and its existence has not been reported by Bales (1953) and Bales and Strodtbeck (1951).

Philp and Dunphy (1959) have further substantiated the findings of Bales (1953) and Bales and Strodtbeck (1951) by observing the same phase-movement pattern in groups working on a different type of discussion problem.[2] Furthermore, Philp and Dunphy (1959) present evidence which indicates that sex of the participants does not affect the pattern of phase movements.

Finally, Smith (1960) has observed that experimental groups show early concentration on matters not related to the task, and, only later in the development sequence, concentrate on task-relevant activities. Again, this finding suggests a strong similarity between task development in laboratory groups and in therapy and training groups, since, in the latter settings, constructive task-relevant activity appears only late in the developmental sequence.

Discussion

The literature that has been reviewed can be criticized on a number of grounds. First, it may be pointed out that this literature cannot be considered truly representative of small-group developmental processes, since certain settings have been over-represented, primarily the therapy-group setting, and others under-represented, primarily the natural group and laboratory-group settings. This shortcoming cannot be rectified within the existing literature; rather, it must serve as a stimulus for further research in the latter group settings. Furthermore, the inequality of setting representation necessitates caution in generalizing from this literature. Generalization must, perforce, be limited to the fact that what has been presented is mainly research dealing with sequential development in therapy groups.

A second source of criticism concerns the extent of experimental

2. As mentioned earlier, Psathas (1960), working with therapy groups, observed the same phase movement, namely, orientation to evaluation to control. However, Talland (1955) failed to get this phase movement in therapy groups.

rigor characteristic of the majority of studies cited in this review. Most of the studies carried out in the therapy-group, training-group and natural-group settings are based on the observation of single groups. Furthermore, these observations are qualitative rather than quantitative, and as such are subject to the biases of the observer, ordinarily the therapist or trainer. This is not to suggest that the therapy-group setting is not appropriate for studying group processes, but that the study of such processes should be more subject to methodological considerations. A good instance of the application of such considerations is the study of Psathas (1960) conducted in the therapy-group setting. Psathas coded group protocols using Bales's (1950) scheme of interaction-process analysis. After satisfactory reliabilities were obtained, the data could be considered as highly quantitative and objective, and could then be subjected to statistical analysis. Approaches of equal rigor are recommended for other studies conducted in the therapy-group setting and other settings as well.

A final criticism concerns the description and control of independent variables. Since most of the studies in the therapy-, training- and natural-group settings used a single group, the control and systematic manipulation of independent variables was impossible. In the absence of the manipulation of independent variables and the consequent discovery of their differential effects within studies, these effects can only be approximately discerned by comparing studies. However, many independent variables are likely to vary from study to study, for example, group composition, duration, etc., and little light will be shed on the effects of these variables on the developmental process. Therefore, no conclusions about the specific effects of independent variables on developmental phenomena will be drawn, and further work along these lines is encouraged.

In order to isolate those concepts common to the various studies reviewed (across settings), a developmental model was proposed. This model was aimed at serving a conceptual function as well as an integrative and organizational one. The model will be summarized here.

Groups initially concern themselves with orientation accomplished primarily through testing. Such testing serves to identify the boundaries of both interpersonal and task behaviors. Coincident with testing in the interpersonal realm is the establishment of dependency relationships with leaders, other group members or pre-existing standards. It may be said that orientation, testing and dependence constitute the group process of *forming*.

The second point in the sequence is characterized by conflict and polarization around interpersonal issues, with concomitant emotional responding in the task sphere. These behaviors serve as resistance to group influence and task requirements and may be labeled as *storming*.

Resistance is overcome in the third stage in which ingroup feeling and cohesiveness develop, new standards evolve and new roles are adopted. In the task realm, intimate, personal opinions are expressed. Thus, we have the stage of *norming*.

Finally, the group attains the fourth and final stage in which interpersonal structure becomes the tool of task activities. Roles become flexible and functional, and group energy is channeled into the task. Structural issues have been resolved, and structure can now become supportive of task performance. This stage can be labeled as *performing*.

Although the model was largely induced from the literature, it would seem to withstand the test of common sense as well as being consistent with developmental theory and findings in other areas. It is not unreasonable to expect 'newness' of the group to be greeted by orienting behavior and resultant unsureness and insecurity overcome through dependence on an authority figure, as proposed in the model. Such orienting responses and dependence on authority are characteristic of the infant during the first year (Ilg and Ames, 1955), the young child when first apprehending rules (Piaget, 1932), and the patient when first entering psychotherapy (Rotter, 1954).

After the 'newness' of the group has 'worn off', the members react to both the imposition of the group and the task emotionally and negatively, and pose a threat to further development. This proposal is mirrored by the rebelliousness of the young child following his 'obedient' stages (Ilg and Ames, 1955; Levy, 1955).

Such emotionality, if overcome, is followed by a sense of 'pulling together' in the group and being more sensitive to one another. This sensitivity to others is mirrored in the development of the child (Ilg and Ames, 1955; Piaget, 1932) and represents an essential aspect of the socialization process (Mead, 1934).

Finally, the group becomes a functional instrument for dealing with the task. Interpersonal problems lie in the group's 'past', and its present can be devoted to realistic appraisal of and attempt at solutions to the task at hand. This interdependence and 'marriage to reality' is characteristic of the 'mature' human being (Erikson, 1950; Fromm, 1941) and the 'mature' nine-year-old child (Ilg and Ames, 1955).[3]

The suggested stages of group development are highly visible in the literature reviewed. The fit is not perfect, however. Some of the studies identify some but not all of the suggested stages. In some of these cases, two of the suggested stages have been welded into one by the observer. For instance, Barton (1953) describes three stages; the first and second fit the first two conceptual stages closely, while Barton's third stage is descriptive of the third and fourth conceptual stages in so far as it is characterized by both the emergence of cohesiveness and the working through of problems. In other cases, one or more of the hypothesized stages have been clearly missing, and thus not recognized in the group or groups being observed. For instance, Powdermaker and Frank (1948) identify three stages that fit the first three conceptual stages fairly closely, but they do not identify any fourth stage. Perhaps cases like this can be accounted for on the basis of independent variables such as duration of group life.

A few studies identify more than four stages. Some of these additional stages represent a greater degree of differentiation than that of the model and are of less generality (i.e. highly specific to the independent conditions of the study). For instance, therapy-group studies with delinquents and dope addicts identify a stage prior to conceptual stage 1 in which the antisocial group member must be won over to the point where they will take the therapy seriously.

Some of the studies identify a stage that is clearly not in the model. Parker (1958) describes a first stage of cohesive organization. This divergence from the model may reflect a different way of

3. A more detailed model of individual development (similar to the group model proposed here), along with many citations of supporting literature, may be found in Harvey, Hunt and Schroder (1961).

describing much the same thing or may reflect an unusual set of independent conditions. Parker was observing a ward population of about 25, rather than a small weekly therapy group. It may be that the hypothesized first stage is somewhat inappropriate for larger, living-together groups.

While the suggested sequence appeared to hold up under widely varied conditions of group composition, duration of group life and specific group task (i.e. the sequence held up across settings), it must be assumed that there is a finite range of conditions beyond which the sequence of development is altered, and that the studies reviewed did not exceed this assumed range to any great extent. Setting-specific differences and within-setting differences may affect temporal change as regards the specific content of the stages in the developmental sequence, the rate of progression through the sequence, or the order of the sequence itself. In the therapy-group setting, for instance, task information in the third stage is considerably more intimate than it is in the laboratory-group setting, and this stage may be attained at a later chronological time in therapy groups than in laboratory groups.

Certainly duration of group life would be expected to influence amount and rate of development. The laboratory groups, such as those run for a few hours by Bales and Strodtbeck (1951), followed essentially the same course of development as did therapy groups run for a period of a year. The relatively short life of the laboratory group imposes the requirement that the problem-solving stage be reached quickly, while no such imposition exists for the long-lived therapy group. Consequently, the former groups are forced to develop at a rapid rate. The possibility of such rapid development is aided by the impersonal and concrete nature of the laboratory task. Orientation is still required due to the newness of the task but is minimized by task rules, players' manuals and the like, that help to orient the group members. Emotionality and resistance are major features of therapy-group development and represent personal and interpersonal impediments to group development and solution attainment as a function of the highly emotionally charged nature of the therapy-group task. The impersonal laboratory task features no such impediments and consequently the stage of emotionality is absent. The exchange of relevant information is as necessary to the laboratory task as it is to the therapy task, but the information to be exchanged is limited in the laboratory task by the nature of the task and time considerations. The behavior of 'norming' is common to both settings but not so salient in the laboratory where the situation is so task-oriented. Finally, the problem-solving or 'performing' stage is an essential stage in both settings.

One would expect the laboratory group to spend relatively more time in the fourth stage relative to the first three stages because of the task orientation in the laboratory setting. In the therapy task, with its unavoidable deep interpersonal penetration, we would expect relatively equal time to be spent in each stage. This, however, can undoubtedly be further modified by group composition as well as by the duration of group life and specific nature of the laboratory task. Undoubtedly there is an interaction between setting and development such that the sequence proposed here will be altered.

Unfortunately the above hypotheses cannot be substantiated with available data, though certain of the studies are suggestive of the explanations offered. The articles reviewed do not deal with rate of temporal change nor do they give sufficiently complete and detailed time data associated with each stage to make calculations of rate possible. Furthermore, they do not systematically describe their independent variables nor relate them to the developmental phenomena through systematic variation and the observation of cause and effect. The major task of systematically studying the effects of a variety of appropriate independent variables on development still remains. The value of the proposed model is that it represents a framework of generic temporal change within which the above explorations can be tested and which should lead to the derivation of many specific hypotheses relating independent variables to the sequence of temporal change. Such quantitative explorations will undoubtedly lead to refinements and perhaps major modifications of such a model.

References

ABRAHAMS, J. (1949), 'Group psychotherapy: implications for direction and supervision of mentally ill patients', in Theresa Muller (ed.), *Mental Health in Nursing*, Catholic University Press, pp. 77–83.

BACH, G. R. (1954), *Intensive Group Psychotherapy*, Ronald Press, pp. 268–93.

BALES, R. F. (1950), *Interaction Process Analysis: A Method for the Study of Small Groups*, Addison-Wesley.

BALES, R. F. (1953), 'The equilibrium problem in small groups', in T. Parsons, R. F. Bales and E. A. Shils (eds.), *Working Papers in the Theory of Action*, Free Press, pp. 111–61.

BALES, R. F., and STRODTBECK, F. L. (1951), 'Phases in group problem-solving', *J. abnorm. soc. Psychol.*, vol. 46, pp. 485–95.

BARRON, M. E., and KRULEE, G. K. (1948), 'Case study of a basic skill training group', *J. soc. Iss.*, vol. 4, pp. 10–30.

BARTON, W. E. (1953), 'Group psychotherapy of the psychoses', *Dig. Neurol. Psychiat.*, vol. 21, pp. 148–9.

BENNIS, W. G., and SHEPARD, H. A. (1956), 'A theory of group development', *Hum. Rel.*, vol. 9, pp. 415–37.

BEUKENKAMP, C. (1952), 'Some observations made during group therapy', *Psychiat. Quart. Suppl.*, vol. 26, pp. 22–26.

BION, W. R. (1961), *Experience in Groups*, Basic Books.

BRADFORD, L. P. (1964a), 'Trainer-intervention: case episodes', in L. P. Bradford, J. R. Gibb and K. D. Benne (eds.), *T-Group Theory and Laboratory Method*, Wiley, pp. 136–67.

BRADFORD, L. P. (1964b), 'Membership and the learning processes', in L. P. Bradford, J. R. Gibb and K. D. Benne (eds.), *T-Group Theory and Laboratory Method*, Wiley, pp. 190–215.

BRADFORD, L. P., and MALLINSON, T. (1958), 'Group formation and development', in *Dynamics of Group Life*, National Education Association, National Training Laboratories, Washington.

CHOLDEN, L. (1953), 'Group therapy with the blind', *Group Psychother.*, vol. 6, pp. 21–9.

CLAPHAM, H. I., and SCLARE, A. B., (1958), 'Group psychotherapy with asthmatic patients', *Int. J. group Psychother.*, vol. 8, pp. 44–54.

COFFEY, H. S. (1952), 'Socio and psyche group process: integrative concepts', *J. soc. Iss.*, vol. 8, pp. 65–74.

COFFEY, H., FREEDMAN, M., LEARY, T., and OSSORIO, A. (1950), 'Community service and social research – group psychotherapy in a church program', *J. soc. Iss.*, vol. 6(1), pp. 14–61.

CORSINI, R. J. (1951), 'On the theory of changes resulting from group therapy', *Group Psychother.* vol. 4, pp. 179–80.

CORSINI, R. J. (1957), *Methods of Group Psychotherapy*, McGraw-Hill, pp. 119–20.

DEUTSCH, M. A. (1949), 'A theory of cooperation and competition', *Hum. Rel.*, vol 2, pp. 129–52.

DREIKURS, R. (1957), 'Group psychotherapy from the point of view of Adlerian psychology', *Int. J. group Psychother.*, vol. 7, pp. 363–75.

ERIKSON, E. H. (1950), *Childhood and Society*, Norton, pp. 213–20.

FROMM, E. (1941), *Escape from Freedom*, Holt, Rinehart & Winston.

GOLEMBIEWSKI, R. T. (1962), *The Small Group*, University of Chicago Press, pp. 193–200.

GROTJAHN, M. (1950), 'The process of maturation in group psychotherapy and in the group therapist', *Psychiatry*, vol. 13, pp. 63–7.

HARVEY, O. J., HUNT, D. E., and SCHRODER, H. M. (1961), *Conceptual Systems and Personality Organization*, Wiley.

HEARN, G. (1957), 'The process of group development', *Autonom. Groups Bull.*, vol. 13, pp. 1–7.

HERBERT, E. L., and TRIST, E. L. (1953), 'The institution of an absent leader by a student's discussion group', *Hum. Rel.*, vol. 6, pp. 215–48.

ILG, F. L., and AMES, L. B. (1955), *Child Behavior*, Harper & Row.

JENNINGS, H. H. (1947), 'Sociometric differentiation of the psychegroup and sociogroup', *Sociometry*, vol. 10, pp. 71–9.

KING, C. H. (1959), 'Activity group therapy with a schizophrenic boy – follow-up two years later', *Int. J. group Psychother.*, vol. 9, pp. 184–94.

LEVY, D. M. (1955), 'Oppositional syndromes and oppositional behavior', in P. H. Hoch and J. Zubin (eds.), *Psychopathology of Childhood*, Grune & Stratton, pp. 204–26.

MANN, J. (1953), 'Group therapy with adults', *Amer. J. Orthopsychiat.*, vol. 23, pp. 332–7.

MANN, J., and SEMRAD, E. V. (1948), 'The use of group therapy in psychoses', *J. soc. Casework*, vol. 29, pp. 176–81.

MARTIN, E. A., and HILL, W. F. (1957), 'Toward a theory of group development. Six phases of therapy group development', *Int. J. group Psychother.*, vol. 7, pp. 20–30.

MEAD, G. H. (1934), *Self, Mind and Society*, University of Chicago Press.

MILES, M. B. (1953), 'Human relations training: how a group grows', *Teachers College Record*, vol. 55, pp. 90–96.

MODLIN, H. C., and FARIS, M. (1956), 'Group adaptation and integration in psychiatric team practice', *Psychiatry*, vol. 19, pp. 97–103.

NOYES, A. P. (1953), *Modern Clinical Psychiatry*, Saunders, 4th edn, pp. 589–91.

OSBERG, J. W., and BERLINER, A. K. (1956), 'The developmental stages in group psychotherapy with hospitalized narcotic addicts', *Int. J. group Psychother.*, vol. 6, pp. 436–47.

PARKER, S. (1958), 'Leadership patterns in a psychiatric ward', *Hum. Rel.*, vol. 11, pp. 287–301.

PHILP, H., and DUNPHY, D. (1959), 'Developmental trends in small groups', *Sociometry*, vol. 22, pp. 162–74.

PIAGET, J. (1932), *The Moral Judgment of the Child*, Harcourt, Brace & World.

POWDERMAKER, F., and FRANK, J. D., (1948), 'Group psychotherapy with neurotics', *Amer. J. Psychiat.*, vol. 105, pp. 449–55.

PSATHAS, G. (1960), 'Phase movement and equilibrium tendencies in interaction process in psychotherapy groups', *Sociometry*, vol. 23, pp. 177–94.

ROTTER, J. B. (1954), *Social Learning and Clinical Psychology*, Prentice-Hall.

SCHINDLER R. (1958), 'Bifocal group therapy', in J. Masserman and J. E. Moreno (eds.), *Progress in Psychotherapy*, vol. 3, Grune & Stratton, pp. 176–86.

SCHRODER, H. M., and HARVEY, O. J. (1963), 'Conceptual

organization and group structure', in O. J. Harvey (ed.), *Motivation and Social Interaction*, Ronald Press, pp. 134–66.

SCHUTZ, W. C. (1958), *FIRO: A Three-Dimensional Theory of Interpersonal Behavior*, Holt, Rinehart & Winston, pp. 168–88.

SEMRAD, E. V., and ARSENIAN, J. (1961), 'The use of group processes in teaching group dynamics', in W. G. Bennis, K. D. Benne and R. Chin (eds.), *The Planning of Change*, Holt, Rinehart & Winston, pp. 737–43.

SHELLOW, R. S., WARD, J. L., and RUBENFELD, S. (1958), 'Group therapy and the institutionalized delinquent', *Int. J. group Psychother.*, vol. 8, pp. 265–75.

SMITH, A. J. (1960), 'A developmental study of group processes', *J. genet. Psychol.*, vol. 97, pp. 29–39.

STOCK, D., and THELEN, H. A. (1958), *Emotional Dynamics and Group Culture*, National Education Association, National Training Laboratories, Washington.

STOUTE, A. (1950), 'Implementation of group interpersonal relationships through psychotherapy', *J. Psychol.*, vol. 30, pp. 145–56.

TALLAND, G. A. (1955), 'Task and interaction process: some characteristics of therapeutic group discussion', *J. abnorm. soc. Psychol.*, vol. 50, pp. 105–9.

TAYLOR, F. K. (1950), 'The therapeutic factors of group-analytic treatment', *J. ment. Sci.*, vol. 96, pp. 976–97.

THELEN, H., and DICKERMAN, W., (1949), 'Stereotypes and the growth of groups', *Educ. Leadership*, vol. 6, pp. 309–16.

THEODORSON, G. A. (1953), 'Elements in the progressive development of small groups', *Social Forces*, vol. 31, pp. 311–320.

THORPE, J. J., and SMITH, B. (1953), 'Phases in group development in treatment of drug addicts', *Int. J. group Psychother.*, vol. 3, pp. 66–78.

TULANE UNIVERSITY, (1957), *The Use of Group Methods in Social Welfare Settings*, Tulane University School of Social Work.

WENDER, L. (1946), 'The dynamics of group psychotherapy and its application', *J. nerv. ment. Dis.*, vol. 84, pp. 54–60.

WHITMAN, R. M. (1964), 'Psychodynamic principles underlying T-group processes', in L. P. Bradford, J. R. Gibb and K. Benne (eds.), *T-Group Theory and Laboratory Methods*, Wiley, pp. 310–35.

WOLF, A. (1949), 'The psychoanalysis of groups', *Amer. J. Psychother.*, vol. 3, pp. 16–50.

18 Daryl J. Bem, Michael A. Wallach and Nathan Kogan

Group Decision Making under Risk of Aversive Consequences

Daryl J. Bem, Michael A. Wallach and Nathan Kogan, 'Group decision making under risk of aversive consequences', *Journal of Personality and Social Psychology*, vol. 1, 1965, pp. 453–60.

In two previous studies of individual and group decision making, Wallach, Kogan and Bem (1962, 1964) found that group decisions reached through discussion and consensus tended to be more risky than decisions made by the group members as individuals. In our first investigation, the decisions involved a number of hypothetical life situations in which a protagonist was faced with the choice between a more risky and a less risky course of action. The second experiment inquired whether these risk-taking tendencies in groups would be found in a decision situation in which the group members were actually exposed to the consequences of their decisions. Using risks and payoffs based on monetary gain and loss for problem-solving performance, we observed that groups were considerably more likely than individuals to select the more difficult, higher payoff (for correct solution) problems, even though problem solving itself was carried out by a single group member. In both of the above experiments, the 'risky shift' phenomenon was interpreted as the outcome of a process of responsibility diffusion.

The present experiment seeks to extend the generality of our previous findings to a type of group decision making in which negative consequences are emphasized. In order to accomplish this end, we selected physical pain and discomfort, coupled with monetary loss, as the potential negative outcomes of risk taking. A second purpose of the present investigation was to examine in more detail whether processes other than a diffusion of responsibility might account for, or contribute to, a risk-taking shift in group decision making. We consider two possible alternative processes in turn below.

First, there is the possibility that risk taking, by connoting boldness, may be more socially desirable than conservatism. Such an association might be quite strong in the present experiment where physical pain and discomfort are being risked, since conservatism under such circumstances could imply cowardice. Further, the association may be especially likely to appear in a group setting where one's 'image' is on public display. Accordingly, an experimental condition involving anticipated disclosure of one's decisions to others has been incorporated in the study design.

Second, an expectation that the consequences of one's decisions will not be experienced alone, but in the company of group members who are undergoing the same experience, may enhance the level of risk selected. This possibility might well be derived from Schachter's (1959) observations concerning subjects' strong preference for awaiting impending painful stimulation in the company of others in the same predicament. In the present case, subjects may be inclined toward greater risk taking if they know that others will be present to serve as a potential source of comfort during the course of any negative consequences ensuing from their risk-taking behavior. Accordingly, we have included an experimental condition in which subjects were informed that like-minded peers would be present during any experimental session involving possible aversive stimulation.

The two conditions outlined above might or might not be sufficient, when considered separately, to elicit the 'risky shift' effect. Suppose, however, that the processes at work in the preceding two conditions were allowed to operate simultaneously. Would such a state of affairs yield a shift in the direction of greater risk taking? To explore this third possibility, we added an experimental condition in which subjects would make their decisions on the basis of an anticipated discussion to consensus. The possible social desirability of high risk taking would be expected to emerge even more dramatically under these circumstances, for beyond having one's decisions disclosed to others, one anticipates defending the selected risk level in the discussion to follow. In addition, the presence of others while consequences of the decisions are being experienced is also anticipated in this condition, Thus, only the discussion to consensus itself is omitted in the present case.

If we can show that the conditions stated above are unable or insufficient to account for the observed shift of group decisions in the risky direction, then we will possess a strong basis for proposing that the group discussion to consensus is an active causal factor. Such a finding would, of course, reinforce the 'diffusion of responsibility' interpretation discussed earlier. On the other hand, if the conditions described produce a risky shift as large as that obtained under group discussion to consensus, then we shall know that diffusion of responsibility cannot be the sole explanatory principle.

Method

Subjects and general procedure

One hundred and twenty-six male subjects, students at the summer session of the University of Colorado, were recruited to serve in an experiment disguised as a study of various 'physiological effects on problem solving'. The mean age of the subjects was 22·6 years, and they were randomly assigned to five treatment conditions. The written description of the experiment used for recruiting subjects was designed to minimize self-selection; in particular, neither the risk-taking nature nor the possible aversive features of the experiment were mentioned. Potential subjects were told that there would be two sessions, a preliminary session of half an hour during which they would fill out nonpersonal information forms, and a one-hour experimental session to be arranged at their convenience sometime later. Payment of $2.00 was offered for the preliminary session in addition to payment (of unspecified amount) for the experiment itself. The 'preliminary session', in actual fact, constituted the complete experiment. Subjects were paid $2.50 after all participants had completed the experiment, at which time the deception was fully explained.

The experimental procedures were administered to groups of three previously unacquainted subjects at a time by a male experimenter. The subjects were seated along one side of a long table in a small experimental room which contained assorted pieces of mechanical and electrical apparatus. Movable wooden partitions separated the subjects' work spaces at the table. As soon as the subjects were seated, they were given a paper-and-pencil questionnaire with the request that they read the initial instructions and the first item and then wait for further instructions. The six-item questionnaire was entitled, 'Preliminary session for psychophysiological experiment', and its instructions read as follows:

With the recent interest in manned space exploration, scientists have become increasingly concerned with the effects of various physiological stimulations on the ability to perform various tasks. For example, it is well known that background noise interferes with the ability to solve simple arithmetic problems. In our research we are interested in having people undergo various physiological stimulations for a period of fifteen minutes before engaging in a forty-five-minute session of solving simple verbal and mathematical problems. An experimental session, then, lasts a total period of one hour.

Each of the following sheets describes one of the six experiments we are conducting. Through a random drawing procedure, you may be selected to participate in one of these; no person will serve in more than one. If you are so selected, the information you provide on these sheets will then be consulted for selecting the exact procedure to be employed. Within the next few weeks, you will be informed by mail whether or not you have been selected to participate in one of these experiments. Whether you are selected or not, you will be paid $2.00 for the present preliminary session at that time.

We are employing this rather unusual preliminary session and selection procedure in order to partially overcome a difficulty which has impeded the research. This is the occurrence of unwanted disruptive side effects which sometimes result from the physiological stimulations under investigation. When such side effects do occur, it is impossible for the individual to provide meaningful results on the problem solving and his participation in the experiment must then necessarily be terminated. Although we do know that all of the side effects subside within an hour and never leave any permanent effect, it is still not possible to prevent such side effects nor to predict in advance who is likely to suffer them. For these reasons, then, we are offering more money to those willing to undergo stimulation which is more likely to produce a side effect, with the understanding that those suffering the side effect cannot be used in the problem solving and, hence, will be excused from the experiment and paid a flat fee of $1.00 for their time and inconvenience. That is, the greater compensation is paid only to those who complete the experiment after undergoing stimulation which was more likely to have produced the side effect, but did not do so.

The forms of stimulation, side effects and schedule of payments are described on the following sheets. For each experiment you are asked to indicate your preference on the stimulation to be employed; you are also given the option in each experiment of not undergoing the stimulation at all, but participating only in the problem solving portion of the experiment.

The first 'experiment' was entitled, 'Olfactory stimulation', and follows in its entirety:

In the olfactory experiment, we are interested in assessing the effects on subsequent problem solving of a fifteen-minute exposure to an odor. Some of the odors we are testing are known to produce side effects of nausea and intense sinus pain in a portion of the population. The side-effects subside within an hour and leave no permanent effect. The table below indicates the approximate percentage of the population likely to suffer these side effects. You will note that the payment is larger if you are willing to choose an odor for which the likelihood of the side effects is greater. That is, greater compensation is offered to those who complete the experiment after experiencing a stimulation which had a greater likelihood of producing the side effects. If you happen to suffer the side effects, you will be excused from the experiment and paid a flat fee of $1.00 for your time and inconvenience.

Please select one of the odors by circling its identification code letter. If you are selected for an olfactory experiment, this will be the odor which you will experience. If you prefer not to expose yourself to any odor but only to participate in the problem solving part of the experiment, circle 'none'.

Odor	Percentage of population experiencing side effects	Pay in addition to 75 cents for the hour of the experimental session
None	–	$0.00
a	10%	$2.80
b	20%	$3.15
c	30%	$3.60
d	40%	$4.20
e	50%	$5.00
f	60%	$6.25
g	70%	$8.35
h	80%	$12.50
i	90%	$25.00

The six experiments described in the questionnaire were identical in format to the one just presented, differing only in the stimulation employed and the possible side effects which might occur. The five other experiments were: (b) 'Chromatic stimulation', in which bright color patterns would be presented for fifteen minutes by means of special goggles containing prisms. Possible side effects were severe headache and intense burning sensation in the eyes. (c) 'Movement stimulation', in which a motor-driven apparatus used for flight simulation would provide bodily and vibratory movement. Possible side effects were dizziness and loss of muscular control in the limbs. (d) 'Taste stimulation', in which various tastes would be presented by means of flavored sticks held in the mouth. The possible side effect was an intense burning sensation in the mouth. (e) 'Auditory stimulation', in which complex sound patterns would be presented through high-fidelity earphones. Possible side effects were intense, throbbing headache and ringing in the ears. (f) 'Odorless gases', in which nontoxic odorless gases would be presented for the fifteen minutes preceding the problem solving. The possible side effect was stomach cramps.

After subjects had read the instructions and examined the first experiment, further verbal clarification of the procedures was given. The following points were covered:

1. Subjects for the various experiments will be selected by a random procedure; in other words, responses on the questionnaire will not enter into the selection. Each individual will serve either in one or none of the experiments.
2. Responses on the questionnaire will be held confidential and the experimental sessions themselves will be private; you will undergo the stimulation and problem-solving alone.
3. We are equally interested in all of the stimulations; therefore, you should be guided only by your own preferences in making your decisions.
4. The side effects are all-or-none affairs; it is easy to tell when one is suffering from them, they appear almost immediately, and they cannot be hidden.
5. The scales of stimulation do not represent intensity scales; that is, the side effect from odor 'a', for example, would be just as severe as the side effect from odor 'i'. The only feature which varies as one goes down the scale is the probability that the given side effects will occur. Similarly, the stimulations themselves are not

unpleasant – including the movement stimulation – nor do they differ very much from one another within a particular experiment. It is only the side effects which would be unpleasant.

6. The salary scale has been arranged to suit the percentages. Thus, for example, if you select the 90 per cent level, you have a 10 per cent chance of being paid – of not suffering the side effect; if you select the 80 per cent level, you then have a 20 per cent chance of being paid. Since the chances have doubled, the salary has been halved. All of the salaries have been arranged in this way so that we can calculate our budget ahead of time.

These points were all emphasized so that they could not arise as new information in a group discussion and lead, thereby, to an artifactual shift in risk taking under the group-discussion condition. As the last point made clear to the subjects, the probability of being paid multiplied by the size of the payoff is a constant. Therefore, since the side effects have negative utilities, the expected values of the various alternatives decrease as one becomes more risky. Hence, a 'rational' decision-making strategy of maximizing expected values would lead to conservatism in the present situation.

This first administration of the questionnaire provided the individual base lines against which all subsequent shifts in risk taking were evaluated. After all subjects had completed the initial questionnaire, they either were told to return the following week or were given a second questionnaire (as noted below in the appropriate treatment conditions).

Test–retest control (N = eighteen subjects)

Subjects in this control condition were asked to return the following week in order to receive their salary and, possibly, to provide additional information. At that time they were told that selection of subjects had not yet been made and that a number of people had expressed a desire to change their responses either up or down after thinking about their participation. Since it is very important that nobody be asked to undergo stimulation which they do not really want, the experimenter explained further, they were being encouraged to make any changes they desired before experimental subjects were actually selected. Thus, change was encouraged rather than discouraged. Separating partitions remained in place as in the first administration. This condition provides data on the test–retest reliability of the questionnaire as well as a practice or familiarity control for any shifts in risk levels observed in the other conditions.

Discussion to consensus (N = eighteen groups)

Group decisions. This condition was designed to answer the basic question: will discussion to consensus lead to increased risk taking in the present decision-making context? Subjects were told:

This questionnaire I have just handed you is identical to the one you have just completed. It is to be used for a second phase of our research. In this second phase, we are interested in examining an even more important problem than individual problem solving, that of the effects of various stimulations on the ability of a crew or group of men who must perform joint tasks, tasks which require them to coordinate their efforts. It is for this reason that three of you were asked to be here at the same time. If you are selected for an individual experiment, then the information you gave on your first questionnaire will still be consulted; but we are also selecting groups of three, at random, to participate in a group problem solving session after undergoing the same stimulation. In these sessions, if one person suffers a side effect, he will be paid his dollar and dismissed and a stand-in will replace him; if two suffer the side effects, then two replacements will be used. In any case, if you do not suffer the side effect, you will be solving problems with two other individuals who have experienced the same physiological stimulation. If you are selected for a group experiment, you will not also serve in an individual experiment. Since this group may be selected for one of the six experiments, we would like you to go through the questionnaire and decide among yourselves which stimulation you would like to experience in each case. That is, you should discuss each experiment and come to a unanimous decision regarding the stimulation to be employed; be sure the decision is unanimous and that a majority is not just bulldozing the third member into something.

At this point, the partitions which had separated the subjects' working space on the table were removed. As in our previous experiments, the subjects were encouraged to take ample time for their deliberations.

Private decisions. In order to assess the possible effects on individual risk-taking levels of the discussion to consensus, the above subjects went over the questionnaire again following the group decisions and indicated their private opinions. They did this, the subjects were told, since

it is important to us that nobody in this research be required to undergo an experience he has not chosen for himself, if possible. . . . If it is at all possible, then, we will put you in a group of two others who have selected the same level of stimulation rather than placing you in this group.

Partitions were again placed between the subjects.

Anticipated public disclosure (N = eighteen subjects)

As one check on the possibility that the social desirability of increased risk taking might enhance the risk levels selected, this condition was identical to the test-retest control except that the subjects were further told at the retest session that each person's decisions would be made public and discussed after they filled out the questionnaire, since 'a number of people have expressed an interest in knowing what the other people have been deciding'. In addition, the wooden partitions which had previously separated the work spaces were not present this time. Again, change was encouraged rather than discouraged. Note that subjects still anticipated that the experimental session itself would be private.

Anticipated presence of others (N = eighteen subjects)

This condition examined the effect on risk-taking levels of expecting to undergo the consequences of one's decisions in the company of others who have selected the same levels of risk. Subjects received the second questionnaire immediately after the first one. The first paragraph of instructions was identical to the first paragraph for the condition of discussion to consensus – group decisions. The subjects then were requested to go through the questionnaire and

mark the stimulation in each experiment you would prefer to undergo for this group problem solving. If you are selected for an experiment on group problem solving, then you will participate in the experiment with two other individuals who have selected the same stimulation.

Anticipated discussion to consensus (N = eighteen subjects)

This condition contained all the features of the discussion-to-consensus condition except for the discussion itself. Subjects were given the second questionnaire immediately following the first one. Again, the first paragraph of instructions was identical to the first paragraph for the condition of discussion to consensus – group decisions. The instructions then continued:

If this group is selected for an experiment, then it will be necessary for the three of you to reach an agreement as to which stimulation you will all undergo. For this reason, we would like each of you to go through the questionnaire, marking the stimulation in each experiment which you would prefer to undergo in the group experience. When and if you are selected for an experiment, then your decisions on that experiment will be made available to the three of you so you can discuss them and make a unanimous selection on just which stimulation is to be employed. In other words, you should now mark the stimulation in each experiment which you would want to suggest to the group for the stimulation to be used.

Results

In the presentation of results, risk scores on the questionnaire represent the percentage level (probability of side effect) selected by a subject or group for the average of the six 'experiments'. Thus, scores can range from 0 per cent (for the 'none' alternative) to 90 per cent, with higher scores reflecting greater risk taking. A shift score for an individual is computed by subtracting his score on the first administration of the questionnaire from his score on the second administration ($N =$ number of subjects). When group decisions are under consideration, a shift score represents the group questionnaire score minus the mean of the questionnaire scores obtained by the same three individuals in the first administration ($N =$ number of groups). When private decisions after group consensus are under study, a shift score represents the mean of the postconsensus private decisions by a group's members minus the mean of their scores on the first administration ($N =$ number of groups). All subjects thus serve as their own controls. Positive shift scores represent shifts in the risky direction. One sample t-tests of the difference scores (Walker and Lev, 1953, pp. 151–3) are used to evaluate the null hypothesis that the mean shift for a condition is zero.

The mean initial risk score for the 126 subjects was 65·5 per cent, with a standard deviation of 16·8 per cent. Table 1 displays the

Table 1 Percentage of Degree of Shift in Risk Taking for Each of the Experimental Conditions

Condition	Mean degree of shift in percentage	SD	t
1. Test-retest control (N = 18 subjects)	+1·11	12·78	0·36
2a. Discussion to consensus – group decisions (N = 18 groups)	+5·43	7·82	2·86***
2b. Discussion to consensus – private decisions (N = 18 groups)ª	+3·97	6·02	2·71***
3. Anticipated public disclosure (N = 18 subjects)	+1·85	11·86	0·64
4. Anticipated presence of others (N = 18 subjects)	−1·30	2·52	2·12*
5. Anticipated discussion to consensus (N = 18 subjects)	−4·91	8·14	2·48**

a Test based on subjects pooled within groups in order to preserve independence. Hence $df = 17$.

* $p < 0.05$, two-tailed test.
** $p < 0.25$, two-tailed test.
*** $p < 0.02$, two-tailed test.

mean shift score obtained in each of the conditions, and its statistical test.

With regard to the test–retest control (Table 1, row 1), permitting subjects to reconsider their decisions after a period of one week and under circumstances that encourage change, does not lead to any systematic shift in either direction. The r between the first and second administrations of the questionnaire is 0·79, thus indicating that the test-retest reliability of the instrument is quite satisfactory.

Concerning discussion to consensus, group decisions are significantly more risky than the mean of the decisions made by the group members as individuals (Table 1, row 2a). The groups selected levels of risk which averaged over one-half a scale step more risky than individual decisions. Sixteen of the eighteen groups in this condition display a shift in the risky direction, which argues for the consistency of the effect. Row 2b of Table 1 indicates, in turn, that the private decisions of these same subjects, obtained after completion of the group discussions, also shifted significantly in the risky direction. Thus, subjects did not revert to their original prediscussion decisions, but rather showed a high degree of personal acceptance of the greater risk taking ensuing from discussion to consensus.

Regarding anticipated public disclosure, there is no evidence for either a risky or conservative shift due to knowing that one's decisions are to be disclosed to others rather than being held confidential (Table 1, row 3). The results are quite comparable to those for the test–retest control condition.

The data for anticipated presence of others (Table 1, row 4) indicate that individuals actually tend to be more conservative when they anticipate undergoing the consequences of the decisions in the company of others who have selected the same levels of risk. Although the magnitude of the shift is small, it is statistically significant, given the consistency of the effect. Note the very small standard deviation relative to that of the other conditions.

Finally, concerning anticipated discussion to consensus, decisions made under this expectation are considerably more *conservative* than decisions made by those same individuals under conditions of confidentiality (Table 1, row 5). The shift in the conservative direction under anticipated discussion to consensus is about as large as the shift in the risky direction which appears when the discussion is actually held.

Discussion

The present investigation has demonstrated in a context of aversive consequences that unanimous group decisions concerning matters of risk show a shift toward greater risk taking when compared with individual decisions, and postdiscussion individual decisions that follow group consensus reflect the risky shift of the group rather than the original prediscussion decisions. Hence, the general conclusions drawn from our two previous experiments (Wallach, Kogan and Bem, 1962, 1964) can now be extended to include decision-making contexts emphasizing negative consequences.[1]

The proposal that a diffusion of responsibility is the process underlying such group - induced risky shifts received further support in the present experiment. Each of the alternative explanations that has been suggested in order to account for the group-induced risky shift phenomenon has been found inapplicable.

Consider first the proposal that higher risk taking has greater social desirability than conservatism. If this were the causal factor at work in the group discussion, one would also expect higher risk taking to appear when a person knows that his decisions, rather than remaining private, will be made available to others for inspection. Yet, in the anticipated-public-disclosure condition, such enhanced risk taking failed to appear. Furthermore, a dramatic conservative shift appeared in the anticipated-discussion-to-consensus condition where each subject not only knew that his decisions would be disclosed to others, but also knew that he would be expected to defend his decisions before the other members of the group.

Second, the proposal that increased risk taking might be caused simply by knowing that one would be experiencing the consequences of one's decisions in the company of others who had made similar decisions, also was clearly disconfirmed. Such a proposal followed from the consideration that a person might accept greater risk of aversive consequences if he knew that others would be present as a source of potential sympathy and comfort during the period when those aversive consequences might be experienced. We find, however, a significant conservative shift in the anticipated-presence-of-others condition. Perhaps, male subjects faced with the uncertainty of how they will 'take' the side effects of physiological stimulation are concerned about the possibility of conveying an impression of weakness in the presence of peers. Such a process would enhance conservatism.

In a previous experiment (Wallach, Kogan and Bem, 1964), a conservative shift was displayed by individual decision makers

1. The content of the discussions revealed that the present experiment was indeed successful in shifting the focus of the decision making to the negative or aversive consequences of risk taking. In fact, the monetary payoffs were rarely mentioned in achieving consensus; rather, discussion centered around the relative aversiveness of the various side effects for the group members.

when responsibility for others was introduced in the absence of group interaction. The conservative shift which appeared in the present experiment's condition of anticipated discussion to consensus seems to be an example of the same phenomenon, even though here the individual's decisions are not yet binding on the other members of the group. In the present condition, the individual is proposing a decision which he presumably intends to urge upon the group, a decision whose consequences, therefore, will be experienced by all. It seems likely that a feeling of responsibility for others would be generated under such circumstances. When no discussion to consensus has yet occurred but is only expected, the effect of these forces is to make the individual favor conservative decisions. When the discussion to consensus actually takes place, on the other hand, increased risk taking is the result. These findings offer direct support for explaining the group induced risky shift phenomenon in terms of a diffusion of responsibility.[2]

In our previous paper (Wallach, Kogan and Bem, 1964), we touched upon some of the implications of our work for committee decision making concerning national and military policy. While recognizing that these latter concerns introduced risks and deterrents likely to be qualitatively different from those capable of study in a laboratory context, we nevertheless felt that our research might be of some relevance to the decision making characterizing affairs of state. Indeed, the present experiment may be viewed as a closer approximation to the real-life cases cited above, for the reason that the risk of aversive consequences is here an important ingredient of the decision-making process. It is precisely such risks that under-

2. Wallach, Kogan and Bem (1962) reported low but significant positive correlations between initial risk-taking levels and perceived influence exerted in the group discussion. While this finding could well represent an outcome of a responsibility diffusion process, the possibility remains that high risk takers may dominate the group discussion and hence exert a disproportionate influence in the risky direction on the other members of the group. Although quantitative data on this point were not obtained in the discussion-to-consensus condition of the present study, the experimenter observed that group members appeared eager to defer to and sympathize with any member who found a given side effect particularly aversive. There appeared to be little indication of particular group members urging an across-the-board strategy of high risk taking.

lie the deterrence policies of the major powers. Of course, the decisions reached in this experiment affect only the group members participating in the study; the decisions have no impact on the larger populations from which the subjects are drawn. Despite this important qualification, it would be most surprising if the shifts toward risk taking observed here and in our previous experiments did not have some counterpart in the actions of government decision-making bodies. Such matters would clearly be worthy of careful study.

References

SCHACHTER, S. (1959), *The Psychology of Affiliation*, Stanford University Press.

WALKER, H. M., and LEV, J. (1953), *Statistical Inference*, Holt, Rinehart & Winston.

WALLACH, M. A., KOGAN, N., and BEM, D. J. (1962), 'Group influence on individual risk taking', *J. abnorm. soc. Psychol.*, vol. 65, pp. 75–86.

WALLACH, M. A., KOGAN, N., and BEM, D. J. (1964), 'Diffusion of responsibility and level of risk taking in groups', *J. abnorm. soc. Psychol.*, vol. 68, pp. 263–74.

19 James P. Flanders and
Donald L. Thistlethwaite

Effects of Familiarization and Group Discussion upon
Risk Taking

James P. Flanders and Donald L. Thistlethwaite, 'Effects of familiarization
and group discussion upon risk taking', *Journal of Personality and
Social Psychology*, vol. 5, 1967, pp. 91–7.

Several experiments using pre-test/post-test control-group designs
have demonstrated a 'risky shift' effect, in which subjects advocated riskier solutions to risk-taking problems after discussing the
problems than they did before discussion. In the initial experiments
(Bem, Wallach and Kogan, 1965; Stoner, 1961; Wallach, Kogan
and Bem, 1962, 1964) the discussion treatments which produced
sizeable risky shifts were invariably accompanied by unanimous
group decisions. Recently, Wallach and Kogan (1965) found that
groups exposed to discussion without the requirement of consensus
exhibited risky shifts fully as great as those in a condition requiring
discussion to consensus. They interpreted these results as indicating that group discussion is both a necessary and sufficient condition for generating the risky shift effect. Wallach and Kogan
proposed a responsibility diffusion interpretation, which states
that direct verbal confrontation provided by group discussion leads
to the development of affective interdependencies, which in turn
mediates a process of responsibility diffusion. According to this
interpretation the increased willingness to take risks which follows
group discussion is produced by a decreased feeling of personal
responsibility.

A rival explanation, which may be called a comprehension interpretation, is suggested by Bateson's (1966) experiment. In this
experiment similar risky shifts were obtained in a condition providing interpolated individual study of the risk-taking problems
instead of group discussion. Moreover, the risky shift effect obtained in such a familiarization condition was fully as great as
that obtained in a condition requiring discussion to consensus.
According to Bateson, the effective ingredient in both discussion

and familiarization treatments may be the more thorough consideration and comprehension of the risk-taking problems which additional study provides. Presumably better comprehension of the relevant information in each test item, or of the alternative probabilities from which choices are to be made, leads to reduced cautiousness (increased willingness to advocate risky solutions).

Since Bateson's experiment did not include a condition in which subjects were exposed to both familiarization and group discussion, it is impossible to say whether the responsibility diffusion and comprehension explanations should be considered mutually exclusive. One of the main purposes of this experiment was to explore the compatibility of the responsibility diffusion and comprehension interpretations by examining the interaction of the independent variables of familiarization and group discussion. Depending upon the theoretical processes assumed, varying predictions concerning this interaction may be made.

Let us suppose first that (a) group discussion produces responsibility diffusion, (b) familiarization produces improved comprehension and (c) both theoretical processes (responsibility diffusion and improved comprehension) contribute to the production of the risky shift effect. To predict the presence or absence of an interaction we must of course make more specific assumptions about the joint operation of these processes. If we assume that the operation of one of these processes does not affect the operation of the other, then it follows that the joint effect of the two independent variables should reflect a simple additivity of the main effects. On the other hand, if it is assumed that the two processes are complementary and mutually facilitative, then it follows that the joint effect of the two independent variables should be an enhanced risky shift significantly greater than would be produced from a simple addition of the main effects.

An alternative set of assumptions, postulating only a single theoretical process, might include the following: (a) Group discussion produces improved comprehension; (b) familiarization produces improved comprehension; and (c) improved comprehension is the sole process contributing to the risky shift effect. As before, in order to make specific predictions about the interaction effect, we must be more specific about the hypothesized process when both independent variables are operative. If we assume that the level of comprehension reaches an asymptote with only moderate levels of familiarization or of group discussion, then it follows that the joint effect of both independent variables should be no greater than the effect of one variable acting alone. But if we assume that the level of comprehension reaches an asymptote only after extensive levels of familiarization or of group discussion, then it follows that the joint effects of both variables should consist of a simple additivity of main effects.

A second purpose of the present investigation was to provide data for evaluating a third hypothetical process which may be involved in the risky shift effect: namely, high risk takers may more readily take the initiative in social situations and exert more influence in group discussions, so that the greater interpersonal influence of high risk takers is the cause of the groups' movement toward greater risk taking. First, it may be noted that if we substitute such a process of differential interpersonal influence for responsibility diffusion in the first set of assumptions outlined above, then the initial expectations concerning interaction effects follow. Second, this study sought to provide a test of the related hypothesis that perceived influence in group discussions is positively correlated with initial risk-taking dispositions. In fact, Wallach, Kogan and Bem (1962) found these two variables to be significantly correlated even when judgements of popularity were held constant. The present experiment also tested the related hypotheses that extraversion would be positively correlated with both initial risk level and perceived influence.

It was hoped that with knowledge of the interaction effect between the independent variables and of the related correlations between risk taking and other variables it would be possible to determine which set of assumptions offers the best over-all predictions of risky shift effects under a variety of conditions.

Method
Pre-test procedures

Three subjects were scheduled to appear in the experimental room at a given time. Subjects were seated about a round table, on which partitions were placed to separate each subject from the view of the others, and given the same instructions employed by Wallach and Kogan (1965) for completing the risk-taking dilemmas. These risk-taking measures consisted of a set of twelve real-life dilemmas first devised by Wallach and Kogan (1959, 1961) and reproduced in full by Kogan and Wallach (1964, appendix E). Each of the dilemmas describes a situation in which a protagonist is faced with a choice between two actions, X and Y, whose outcomes differ in attractiveness and probability of occurrence. The successful outcome associated with Alternative X is always more attractive than the successful outcome associated with Alternative Y, but the probability of attaining the former is less than that of attaining the latter. Subjects are asked to consider themselves as advisors to the protagonist in each story, and to indicate the minimum probability of success they would consider acceptable in order to recommend the action X which potentially leads to the more attractive outcome. The probabilities listed for each of the twelve dilemmas include 1, 3, 5, 7 and 9 chances out of 10; in addition each item includes a category (scored 10) in which the respondent may indicate his belief that the protagonist should not take action X 'no matter what the probabilities'. Risk-taking scores were computed for a given measurement occasion by adding the chosen probabilities for each item and multiplying by 10. Thus, a subject who chose 5/10 on each of the twelve dilemmas would have a risk-taking score of $(12) \times (5/10) \times (10) = 60$. Low scores reflected a greater willingness to advocate risky solutions.

Eysenck's (1956) twenty-four-item extraversion scale was administered to all subjects as the last part of the pre-test. Following administration of the personality measure, the procedures for the different experimental conditions varied as indicated below.

Experimental manipulations

A 2×2 factorial design was used in which the independent variables of familiarization and discussion with consensus were manipulated. Instructions used in each of the four cells of the design follow.

Familiarization without discussion. After collecting the pre-test materials, the experimenter handed out new blank copies of the dilemma booklets and said:

You will now *prepare* for a group discussion which will involve all three of you. You will discuss each of the twelve situations. Your task now is to restudy each choice, with the view of making certain that you have not overlooked some relevant information. Try to clarify for yourself the nature of each choice open to the central person and the character of the odds attached to each alternative. We want each of you to be prepared to discuss the choices to be made so that you will not have to spend group discussion time restudying the problem. Also, the discussion should then concentrate only on the important issues relevant to each choice. It is strongly recommended that in the twenty-five minutes you now have to restudy that you note in the questionnaire booklet what you consider to be the important issues. Use whatever method you use every day, such as underlining, starring, jotting in the margin, or making lists of pros and cons. You will be allowed to refer to your markings in this booklet during the discussion. Feel free to read between the lines. You have twenty-five minutes.

During the period of individual study of the dilemmas, the partitions remained in place on the table, and none of the subjects communicated with each other. The experimenter next gave the following instructions for the post-test measure of risk taking:

Before proceeding to the group discussion, we will have a short bit of further individual work. I want you to go back over each of these situations and indicate your own present personal decision with a 'P'. It is quite natural that some further thoughts have occurred to you since you indicated your reactions to the situations the first time. You need not consider yourself bound by *any* of the past decisions, because your task now is simply to indicate the recommendation you would give to the central figure *at the present time*. Remember, you are to indicate your own personal decision at the present time with a P.

Since subjects in this condition anticipated a discussion but did not actually participate in one, the experimenter provided at the conclusion of the session a debriefing which explained the need for deception and requested subjects not to discuss the experiment with others.

Discussion without familiarization. Having collected the pre-test materials, the experimenter removed the partitions separating subjects and distributed new blank copies of the booklets. He proceeded by saying:

We are now ready to begin the group discussion. What we are really interested in *now* is having the group discuss every situation in turn and arrive at a unanimous decision on each. You will recognize that your unanimous decision is different from a majority vote, by the way. You all must agree. This time you may not return to a question; discuss each one until the group decision is reached and then go on to the next. When the group reaches its decision, you are to mark it on the questionnaire you have so that you have a record of the group's decisions. I am not going to participate in the discussion, although I will be here to answer any procedural questions which may arise. Remember that it is only the group's final decision in which we are interested.

After each group had discussed – and reached a unanimous consensus with respect to – each of the dilemmas the experimenter gave the instructions for the post-test measure of risk taking. These instructions were virtually identical for all conditions. The only variation was that in the two experimental conditions involving group discussion, the experimenter omitted the phrase 'before proceeding to the group discussion' from the second paragraph of instructions for the immediately preceding condition.

Familiarization and discussion. Specific instructions for this condition duplicated the first paragraph of instructions for the familiarization without discussion conditions, and the complete set of instructions for the immediately preceding discussion without familiarization condition.

Neither familiarization nor discussion. Following administration of the personality measure, the experimenter proceeded immediately to the instructions for the post-test measure of risk taking described above for the familiarization without discussion condition.

Influence measures

Participants in the group discussions described above were asked, as part of an exercise following the post-test, to rank order the group members (including themselves) with respect to over-all 'degree of influence' in the discussion. A subjects' perceived influence score was the sum of the three ranks assigned to him; a low sum indicated greater perceived influence.

Subjects

Subjects were 180 male undergraduates at Vanderbilt University enrolled in the introductory psychology course. All subjects volunteered for this experiment, and each group of three subjects volunteering for a given experimental session was randomly assigned to one of the four experimental conditions. Fifteen groups of three persons each were assigned to each condition.

Results

In the analysis of results, a group's risk-taking score, whether based on the pre-test or post-test measure, was the arithmetic sum of the risk-taking score of its three members. Shift scores for each group were obtained by subtracting pre-test from post-test scores.

An F-test comparing the mean pre-test scores of groups in the four experimental conditions was insignificant ($F < 1$); thus the random assignment of groups to the conditions was effective in ruling out initial differences in risk-taking dispositions.

An analysis of variance was performed on the group shift scores and is presented in Table 1. It reveals that there was a highly

Table 1 Analysis of Variance of Shift Scores of Groups in Experimental Conditions

Source	df	MS	F
Familiarization (A)	1	1025·07	8·56****
Discussion (B)	1	232·07	1·94
A × B	1	777·60	6·49**
Error	56	119·74	
Total	59	148·14	

** $p < 0.02$.
**** $p < 0.005$.

significant main effect attributable to the familiarization manipulation. Also there was a significant interaction between the familiarization and group-discussion variables. The group-discussion manipulation did not have a significant main effect.

Table 2 contains average group risk-taking and shift scores for each experimental condition and presents t-tests for evaluating whether each of the mean shifts was significantly different from zero. The mean shift in riskiness was significantly greater than

Table 2 Shifts in Risk Taking under Each Condition

Condition	Mean pre-test score	Mean post-test score	Mean shift[a]	t
F – Familiarization without discussion	216·3	202·4	−13·9	5·38***
FD – Familiarization and discussion	220·3	209·6	−10·7	3·36***
D – Discussion without familiarization	209·7	200·1	− 9·6	3·40***
N – Neither familiarization nor discussion	218·1	219·6	+ 1·5	0·57

Note: N=fifteen groups within each condition.
[a] Negative sign indicates increase in riskiness.
*** $p < 0.001$ (two-tailed).

zero in conditions F (familiarization without discussion), FD (familiarization and discussion), and D (discussion without familiarization). The slight increase in conservatism shown by condition N (neither familiarization nor discussion) was not significantly different from zero.

Risk-taking shifts among the four experimental conditions are compared in Table 3. Conditions, F, FD and D each exhibited

Table 3 Comparison of Risk-Taking Shifts between Pairs of Conditions

Comparison	
F *v*. N	4·15***
FD *v*. N	2·94**
D *v*. N	2·86**
F *v*. D	1·13
F *v*. FD	0·80
FD *v*. D	0·25

** $p < 0.02$ (two-tailed).
*** $p < 0.001$ (two-tailed).

greater risky shifts than condition N, but they did not differ significantly from each other.

Correlations between initial risk-taking scores and other variables were based on the scores of the ninety subjects participating in group discussions. As expected, initial risk-taking scores had a significant correlation with perceived influence scores ($r = 0.30$), but – contrary to the hypothesis – had only an insignificant correlation with extraversion scores. Also the correlation between extraversion and perceived influence scores was insignificant.

Finally, an analysis of the items making up the dilemma test was performed to investigate the internal homgeneity of this risk-taking measure. Using the risk-taking data for all 180 subjects an alpha coefficient of 0.61 was found for the pre-test scores, while a coefficient of 0.59 was obtained for the post-test scores. Correlations between each item response and the individual risk-taking scores based upon all twelve dilemmas were computed from the pre-test data; these correlations ranged from 0.52 to 0.33. Using the numbering of the dilemmas described by Kogan and Wallach (1964, appendix E), the eighth and twelfth had the lowest item total-score correlations and were the only two on which the 180 subjects exhibited an average shift score which was positive (i.e. in the conservative direction).

Discussion

The present experimental results indicate that discussion to consensus has the effect of producing a risky shift among subjects who have *not* had interpolated familiarization with the risk-taking problems. However, among subjects who have been given the opportunity of further individual study of the risk-taking problems, discussion to consensus has no effect upon risk-taking scores.

The responsibility-diffusion interpretation can account for the former, but not for the latter finding. These findings concerning the interaction of the two variables of familiarization and group discussion provide a more persuasive disconfirmation of the responsibility-diffusion hypothesis than Bateson's (1966) finding – which was confirmed by the present comparisons – that a familiarization without discussion condition was as effective in producing risky shift as a discussion without familiarization condition. One might maintain, in attempting to account for the latter result, that responsibility diffusion may be one of many sufficient causes of the risky shift and that improved comprehension of the risk-taking tasks may be another. However, the present findings pose a particularly difficult explanatory problem for the responsibility-diffusion explanation. It cannot explain why group discussion to a consensus, which should increase affective interdependencies and responsibility diffusion in 'familiarized' as well as 'unfamiliarized' subjects, failed to have any effect upon the risk-taking scores of subjects who first had the opportunity of additional study of the risk-taking problems. The possibility that the particular discussion procedures used were ineffectual seems to be ruled out since discussion did produce a significant risky shift effect among subjects not exposed to a familiarization procedure.

Bateson (1966) acknowledged, in attempting to reconcile his findings with those of Wallach and Kogan (1965), that since he had employed only five of the twelve dilemmas his groups remained in existence a shorter period of time, and therefore may not have developed the same degree of affective interdependency as groups which consider the entire set of dilemmas. The present experiment seems to rule out this possibility, however, since it employed the entire set of twelve dilemmas and included instructions which were virtually identical to those used in the discussion and consensus condition of Wallach and Kogan (1965). Moreover, the present item analysis of the twelve dilemmas revealed a pattern of risky shifts on individual items quite similar to that found previously: Wallach, Kogan and Bem (1962) found that the average shift scores for both men and women were negative (in a risky direction) for ten of the twelve dilemmas; furthermore, both studies found that the average shift score was positive (in a conservative direction) for the twelfth item in the set. The chief difference was that the latter investigators found an over-all conservative shift on the fifth item rather than the eighth item. It is of interest to note that the fifth, eighth and twelfth items were not included among the five employed by Bateson (1966), so that his results cannot be attributed to an unrepresentative selection of test items.

In order to determine whether there was any evidence in the present experiment suggesting that influence attempts operate to bring opinion deviates into closer conformity with a group norm, an additional analysis was made of the changes in within-group variability of risk-taking scores among group members under each of the experimental conditions. Wallach and Kogan (1965) found that the two discussion conditions which produced the greatest shifts in risk taking also produced marked reductions in within-group variability. For this analysis, we used a measure of within-group variability similar to that employed by Wallach and Kogan; within each group the range of the three individual post-test risk-taking scores was subtracted from the range of the three individual pre-test risk-taking scores, yielding a single difference score (d) for each group of three subjects. A positive difference between these two ranges, of course, indicates a reduction in within-group variability. An analysis of variance of the d-scores reveals a significant main effect associated with the discussion manipulation ($F = 31.20$, $p < 0.001$), but there is neither a significant main effect for the familiarization manipulation ($F < 1$) nor a significant interaction between the two independent variables ($F < 1$). Table 4 contains t-tests for evaluation whether the shift in within-group

Table 4 Shifts in Within-Group Range of Risk-Taking Levels under Each Condition

Condition	Average shift (d)	SE_d	t
D	11·00	3·20	3·44***
FD	6·87	2·02	3·40***
N	−4·33	1·84	2·35*
F	−4·33	2·21	1·96

Note: N=fifteen groups within each condition.
* $p < 0.05$ (two-tailed).
*** $p < 0.001$ (two-tailed).

variability was significantly different from zero in each condition.

These results essentially duplicate the findings of Wallach and Kogan (1965) and indicate that there was a significant reduction in within-group variability for conditions D and FD – the two conditions providing group discussion – but no significant reduction in variability for conditions F and N – the two conditions in which group discussion was not present. In fact, condition N showed a marginally significant *increase* in within-group variability. Separate comparisons indicate that conditions D and FD did not differ significantly from each other in the degree of narrowing of intragroup heterogeneity, but that each differed significantly from the average shifts in variability in conditions F and N. It seems clear that group-influence processes were at work in the groups which discussed the dilemmas.

However, these influence processes are generally unrelated to the risky shifts shown by the groups. For example, condition F which produced the largest risky shift, showed an average increase, rather than a decrease, in within-group variability. As a further check on the possible role of group-influence processes in the production of the risky shift, a correlation was computed between the group risk-taking shift scores and the shifts in within-group variability (d-scores) of the sixty groups; this correlation was low and insignificant ($r = -0.11$). These comparisons indicate that the observed reductions in within-group variability played little or no role in the risky shift effects in the present experiment. Presumably, in the discussion groups influence processes are directed with more or less equal intensity toward deviates on both the risky and the conservative sides of the average initial risk-taking levels.

The foregoing results provide no support for the view that group processes mediate the risky shift effect. Consequently the significant correlation between initial risk taking and perceived influence scores probably should not be interpreted as indicating that high risk takers exercise greater interpersonal influence in the group discussions. This correlation may be explained equally well by supposing that influence ranks were assigned on the basis of noting that the group's consensus usually most closely matched the initial position of the high risk taker in the group. In other words, the group's movement toward riskier solutions may have resulted in group members ascribing more influence to the initially high risk taker.

On the other hand, the interpretation suggested by Bateson (1966) can readily explain both the main and interaction effects observed in this experiment. Improved comprehension may be the outcome of a discussion without familiarization condition, just as it may be the outcome of a familiarization without discussion condition. When subjects are given the opportunity to more adequately grasp the relevant facts or choices posed by a hypothetical dilemma, they become less cautious and more willing to advocate risky solutions to the dilemmas. According to this interpretation, discussion produces risky shifts among unfamiliarized subjects because the discussion provides time for further study and understanding of the tasks. Moreover, discussion has no effect upon the risk-taking dispositions of familiarized subjects (who have already achieved an adequate comprehension of the task) simply because further study has little to add.

References

BATESON, N. (1966), 'Familiarization, group discussion, and risk-taking', *J. exper. soc. Psychol.*, vol. 2, pp. 119–29.

BEM, D. J., WALLACH, M. A., and KOGAN, N. (1965), 'Group decision making under risk of aversive consequences', *J. Personal. soc. Psychol.*, vol. 1, pp. 453–60.

EYSENCK, H. J. (1956), 'The inheritance of extraversion–introversion', *Acta Psychol.*, vol. 12, pp. 95–110.

KOGAN, N., and WALLACH, M. A. (1964), *Risk Taking: A Study in Cognition and Personality*, Holt, Rinehart & Winston.

STONER, J. A. F. (1961), 'A comparison of individual and group decisions involving risk', unpublished master's thesis, Massachusetts Institute of Technology, School of Industrial Management.

WALLACH, M. A., and KOGAN, N. (1959), 'Sex differences and judgmental processes', *J. Personal.*, vol. 27, pp. 555–64.

WALLACH, M. A., and KOGAN, N. (1961), 'Aspects of judgment and decision making: interrelation shifts and changes with age', *Behav. Sci.*, vol. 6, pp. 23–36.

WALLACH, M. A., and KOGAN, N. (1965), 'The roles of information, discussion, and consensus in group risk taking', *J. exper. soc. Psychol.*, vol. 1, pp. 1–19.

WALLACH, M. A., KOGAN, N., and BEM, D. J. (1962), 'Group influence on individual risk taking', *J. abnorm. and soc. Psychol.*, vol. 65, pp. 75–86.

WALLACH, M. A., KOGAN, N., and BEM, D. J. (1964), 'Diffusion of responsibility and level of risk taking in groups', *J. abnorm. soc. Psychol.*, vol. 68, pp. 263–74.

20 Edwin P. Hollander

Competence and Conformity in the Acceptance of Influence

Edwin P. Hollander, 'Competence and conformity in the acceptance of influence', *Journal of Abnormal and Social Psychology*, vol. 61, 1960, pp. 365–9.

When one member influences others in his group it is often because he is competent in a focal group activity. A member may show such competence by individual actions that further the attainment of group goals (cf. Carter, 1954); more specific situational demands may variously favor the ascent of the expediter, advocate or what Bales and Slater (1955) have termed the task specialist. An additional condition for the acceptance of influence involves the member's perceived adherence to the normative behaviors and attitudes of his group. His record of conformity to these expectancies serves to sustain eligibility of the sort Brown (1936) calls 'membership character'.

A person who exhibits both competence and conformity should eventually reach a threshold at which it becomes appropriate in the eyes of others for him to assert influence; and in so far as these assertions are accepted he emerges as a leader. But it is still necessary to account for the 'nonconformity' that leaders display as they innovate and alter group norms. Certain shifts must therefore occur in the expectancies applicable to an individual as he proceeds from gaining status to maintaining it.

This process has been considered recently in a theoretical model of status emergence (Hollander, 1958). It features the prospect that behavior perceived to be nonconformity for one member may not be so perceived for another. Such differentiations are seen to be made as a function of status, conceived as an accumulation of positively disposed impressions termed 'idiosyncrasy credits'. A person gains credits, i.e. rises in status, by showing competence and by conforming to the expectancies applicable to him at the time. Eventually his credits allow him to nonconform with greater impunity.[1] Moreover, he is then subject to a new set of expectancies which direct the assertion of influence. Thus, whether for lack of motivation or misperception, his failure to take innovative action may cause him to lose status.[2]

It is readily predictable that in task oriented groups a member giving evidence of competence on the group task should with time gain in influence. If he simply nonconforms to the procedures agreed upon, the opposite effect should be observed, but the sequential relationship of nonconformity to competence is especially critical.

From the model, it should follow that, with a relatively constant level of manifest competence, the influence of a person who nonconforms *early* in the course of group interaction should be more drastically curtailed than in the case of a person who nonconforms *later*. Indeed, a reversal of effect would be predicted in the latter instance. Once a member has accumulated credits, his nonconformity to general procedure should serve as a confirming or signalizing feature of his status, thereby enhancing his influence. Accordingly, it may be hypothesized that given equivalent degrees of task competence, a member should achieve greater acceptance of his influence when he has conformed in the past and is now nonconforming than he should when nonconformity precedes conformity.

Method
Design

Twelve groups, each composed of four male subjects, were engaged in a task involving a sequence of fifteen trials. A group choice was required for each trial from among the row alternatives in a 7×7 payoff matrix (see Table 1). In every group, a fifth member was a confederate whose prearranged response was contrived to be correct on all but four trials, i.e. 2, 3, 6 and 12, thus reflecting considerable competence on the task. All interactions among participants took place through a system of microphones and

1. This is a newer formulation of an observation long since made regarding the latitude provided leaders (e.g. Homans, 1950, p. 416). It is further elaborated in Hollander (1959).

2. This proposition is consistent with various findings suggestive of the greater social perceptiveness of leaders (e.g. Chowdhry and Newcomb, 1952).

Table 1 Matrix Used in Group Task

	Green	Red	Blue	Yellow	Brown	Orange	Black
Able	−1	−12	+5	−1	−2	+15	−4
Baker	+10	−1	−2	−7	+4	−3	−1
Charlie	−5	+5	−3	+3	−11	−1	+12
Dog	+5	−7	+10	−2	−5	+1	−2
Easy	−4	−1	−1	+1	+13	−10	+2
Fox	−6	+15	−5	−1	−3	−1	+1
George	−1	−1	−2	+10	+4	−2	−8

headsets from partitioned booths. Subjects were assigned numbers from 1 to 5 for communicating with one another. The central manipulation was the confederate's non-conformity to procedures agreed upon by each group in a pretrial discussion. In terms of a division of the fifteen trials into three zones – early, middle and late – of five trials each, six treatments were applied: nonconformity throughout, nonconformity for the first two zones, for the first zone alone, for the last two zones, for the last zone alone, and a control with no nonconformity. In one set of treatments the confederate was designated number 5, and in the other number 4, to test possible position effects. Acceptance of the confederate's influence was measured by the number of trials by zone in which his recommended response was accepted as the group's. This was supplemented by post-interaction assessments.

Subjects

The forty-eight subjects were all juniors in the College of Engineering and Science at the Carnegie Institute of Technology. All had volunteered from introductory psychology sections after being told only that they would be taking part in a study of problem solving in groups. Care was taken in composing the twelve groups so as to avoid either placing acquaintances together or having membership known in advance. Thus, no two subjects from the same class section were used in the same group, and subjects reported at staggered times to different rooms. By the time a subject reached the laboratory room where the experiment was actually conducted, he had been kept apart from the others and was not aware of their identity. The subjects never saw one another during the entire procedure, nor were their names ever used among them.

Instructions and set

Once seated and assigned a number, every subject was given a sheet of instructions and the matrix used for the task. These instructions fell into two parts, both of which were reviewed aloud with each subject individually, and then with the entire group over the communication network. The first part cautioned the subjects to always identify themselves by number (e.g. 'This is station 3 . . .') before speaking and not to use names or other self-identifying references. The second part acquainted them with the procedures to be used, emphasized the aspect of competition against a 'system', and established the basis for evident procedural norms. It read as follows:

1. You will be working with others on a problem involving a matrix of plus and minus values. Everyone has the same matrix before him. The goal is to amass as many plus units as possible, and to avoid minus units. Units are worth one cent each to the group; the group begins with a credit of 200 units. You cannot lose your own money, therefore. There will be fifteen trials in all.
2. In any one trial, the task involved is for the group to agree on just *one* row – identified by Able, Baker, Charlie, etc. – which seems to have strategic value. Once the group has determined a row, the experimenter will announce the column color which comes up on that trial. The intersecting cells indicate the payoff. Following this announcement, there will be thirty seconds of silence during which group members can think individually about the best strategy for the next trial, in terms of their notion about the system; note please that there are several approximations to the system, although the equation underlying it is quite complex. But work at it.
3. At the beginning of each trial the group members must report, one at a time, in some order, as to what they think would be the best row choice on the upcoming trial. Members may 'pass' until the third time around, but must announce a choice then. Following this, groups will have three minutes on each trial to discuss choices and reach some agreement; this can be a simple majority, or unanimous decision; it is up to the group to decide. If a decision is not reached in three minutes, the group loses five units.

4. Before beginning the trials, the group will have five minutes to discuss these points: (a) The order of reporting; (b) How to determine the group choice for a given trial; (c) How to divide up the money at the end. These decisions are always subject to change, if the group has time and can agree. After the fifteenth trial, group members may have as much as five minutes to settle any outstanding decisions. Then headsets are to be removed, but group members remain seated for further instructions, and the individual payment of funds.

Instruments and procedure

The matrix was specially constructed for this study to present an ambiguous but plausible task in which alternatives were only marginally discrete from one another.[3] The number of columns and rows was selected to enlarge the range of possibilities beyond the number of group members, while still retaining comprehensibility. The fact that the rows are unequal in algebraic sum appears to be less important as a feature in choice than the number and magnitude of positive and negative values in each; there is moreover the complicating feature of processing the outcome of the last trials in evaluating the choice for the next. All considered, the matrix was admirably suited to the requirements for ambiguity, challenge, conflict, immediate reinforcement and ready manipulation by the experimenter.

The confederate, operating as either 4 or 5 in the groups, suggested a choice that differed trial by trial from those offered by other members; this was pre-arranged but subject to modification as required. Since subjects rather typically perceived alternatives differently, his behavior was not unusual, especially during the early trials. For the eleven trials in which the confederate's row choice was 'correct', the color that 'came up' was contrived to yield a high plus value without at the same time providing a similar value for intersection with another person's row choice. Had his recommendations been followed by the group on these trials, high payoffs would have accrued.

The device of a five-minute pretrial discussion had special utility for establishing common group expectancies, in the form of procedures, from which the confederate could deviate when called for in the design. Predictable decisions on these matters were

3. The matrix is an adaptation, at least in spirit, of a smaller one used with success by Moore and Berkowitz (1956).

reached unfailingly, but their importance lay in having a *public affirmation* of member intent. Thus, on order of reporting, it was quickly agreed to follow the order of the numbers assigned members. Each group, despite minor variants suggested, decided on simple majority rule. Regarding division of funds equal sharing prevailed, sometimes with the proviso that the issue be taken up again at the end.

In the zones calling for nonconformity, the confederate violated these procedures by speaking out of prescribed turn, by questioning the utility of majority rule, and by unsupported – but not harsh – challenges to the recommendations made by others. He manifested such behaviors on an approximate frequency of at least one of these per trial with a mean of two per trial considered optimum. Thus, he would break in with his choice immediately after an earlier respondent had spoken and before the next in sequence could do so; when there were periods of silence during a trial he would observe aloud that maybe majority rule did not work so well; and he would show a lack of enthusiasm for the choice offered by various others on the matter of basis. Lest he lose credibility and become a caricature, in all instances he chose his moments with care and retained an evident spontaneity of expression.

Results and discussion

The task gave quite satisfactory signs of engrossing the subjects. There was much talk about the 'system' and a good deal of delving into its basis, possibly made the more so by the subjects' academic background; the returned matrices were littered with diagrams, notations and calculations. Though quite meaningless in fact, the confederate's tentative accounts of his 'reasoning' were evidently treated with seriousness, perhaps as much because of the contrived time constraint, which prevented probing, as of his jargon regarding 'rotations' and 'block shifts'. In any case, the confederate at no time claimed to have the system completely in hand. He delayed his response from the sixth trial onward to suggest calculation of an optimum choice in the face of conflicting alternatives; and the four trials on which he was 'wrong' were spaced to signify progressive improvement, but not total perfection.

Most pertinent, however, is the fact that there were no manifestations of suspicion concerning the confederate's authenticity. The others seemed to believe that he was one of them and that he was 'cracking' the system; the post-interaction data were in full agreement.

Since all of the interactions were available on tape, it was possible to derive a number of indices of acceptance of influence. The most broadly revealing of these appeared to be the frequency of trials on which the confederate's recommended solution was followed.

In Table 2 this index is employed to discern the effects of three major variables. The analysis is arranged by zones (Z) of trials, and in terms of the confederate's nonconformity (NC) in the *current* zone and immediate *past* zone.[4] The means given in each cell indicate the number of trials, out of five per zone, on which the confederate's choice was also the group's. In a chi-square test, the effect of position upon this measure was found to be nonsignificant, and is therefore omitted as a distinction in the analysis of variance.

The significant F secured from zones is in accord with prediction. It reveals the ongoing effect of task competence in increasing the acceptance of the confederate's choice, to be seen in the rising means across zones. While current nonconformity does not yield a significant effect, past nonconformity does. Viewing the table horizontally, one finds that the means for 'without' *past* NC exceed the means for 'with' *past* NC in all instances but one. Regarding the significant interaction of *current* and *past* NC, the combination 'without–without' has a sequence (2·00, 3·75, 4·75) of persistently higher value than has 'with–with' (1·67, 3·25, 4·00); this, too, is in line with prediction. Finally, the maximum value of 5·00 in zone II for the combination 'without' *past* NC but 'with' *current* NC confirms the key prediction from the model, at least within the context of the relative magnitudes there; the same value is also seen in zone III for the identical combination; still another reading of 5·00 holds there, however, for the inverse combination, but in a tight range of values quite beyond separation of effects for interpretation.

4. For Zone I, the 'past zone' refers to the discussion period. If he was to nonconform there, the confederate would question majority rule and suggest that the division of funds be left until the end rather than agree then on equal shares.

Table 2 Mean Number of Trials on Which a Group Accepts Confederate's Recommended Solution

	Zone I (trials 1–5)		Zone II (trials 6–10)		Zone III (trials 11–15)	
Confederate's Previous Conformity	Nonconforming[a]	Conforming	Nonconforming	Conforming	Nonconforming	Conforming
With Procedural nonconformity in immediate *past* zone	1·67	—	3·25	3·00	4·00	5·00
	6[b]		4	2	4	2
Without Procedural nonconformity in immediate *past* zone	—	2·00	5·00	3·75	5·00	4·75
		6	2	4	2	4

Analysis of Variance

Source	SS	df	MS	F
Current nonconformity	0·20	1	0·200	—
Zones	47·05	2	23·525	35·01**
Past nonconformity	3·36	1	3·360	5·00*
Int: current NC × Z	1·22	2	0·610	—
Int: current NC × past NC	13·52	1	13·520	20·12**
Int: Z × past NC	0·72	2	0·360	—
Int: current NC × Z × past NC	4·11	2	2·055	3·06
Residual	16·12	24	0·672	
Total	86·30	35		

[a] Confederate showed procedural nonconformity on the trials in this zone.
[b] Indicates number of groups upon which cell is based.

* $p < 0.05$.
** $p < 0.001$.

Considerable consistency was found too in the post-interaction data. On the item 'over-all contribution to the group activity,' forty-four of the forty-eight subjects ranked the confederate first; on the item 'influence over the group's decisions,' forty-five of the forty-eight ranked him first. Two things bear emphasis in this regard: subjects had to individually write in the numbers of group members next to rank, hence demanding recall; and their polarity of response cut across all six treatments, despite significant differences among these in the actual *acceptance of influence*. That the confederate therefore made an impact is clear; but that it had selective consequences depending upon the timing of his nonconformity is equally clear.

In detail, then, the findings are in keeping with the predictions made from the model. The operational variable for measuring acceptance of influence was confined to the task itself, but non-task elements are touched as well. In that respect, the findings corroborate the subtle development of differential impressions as a function of even limited interpersonal behavior.

Some unquantified but clearly suggestive data are worth mentioning in this regard. Where, for example, the confederate began nonconforming *after* the first zone, his behavior was accepted with minimal challenge; by the third zone, his suggestion that majority rule was faulty yielded a rubber stamping of his choice. Again, if he had already accrued credit, his pattern of interrupting people out of turn not only went unhindered but was taken up by some others. Quite different effects were elicited if the confederate exhibited nonconformity from *the outset*, notably such comments of censure as 'That's not the way we agreed to do it, five.'

The findings are especially indicative of the stochastic element of social interaction and its consequence for changing perception. Especially interesting is the fact that these effects are produced even in a relatively brief span of time.

Summary

A study was conducted to test the relationship between competence on a group task and conformity or nonconformity to procedural norms in determining a person's ability to influence other group members. Data were gathered from twelve groups engaged in a problem solving task under controlled conditions. Each was made up of five members one of whom was a confederate who evidenced a high degree of competence during the fifteen trials. His nonconformity to the procedural norms agreed upon by the group was introduced at various times, early, middle or late, in the sequence of trials. Influence was measured by the number of trials (per segment of the entire sequence) in which the confederate's recommended solution was accepted as the group's choice. As a broad effect, it was found that a significant increase in his influence occurred as the trials progressed, presumably as a function of the successive evidences of competence. Past conformity by the confederate was also found to be positively and significantly related to the acceptance of his influence; finally, there was a statistically significant interaction between past and current nonconformity reflected in high influence in the groups in which the confederate had conformed earlier in the sequence of trials but was presently nonconforming. These results were all thoroughly consistent with predictions made from the 'idiosyncrasy credit' model of conformity and status.

References

BALES, R. F., and SLATER, P. E. (1955), 'Role differentiation in small decision-making groups', in T. Parsons and R. F. Bales (eds.), *Family, Socialization, and Interaction Process*, Free Press.

BROWN, J. F. (1936), *Psychology and the Social Order*, McGraw-Hill.

CARTER, L. F. (1954), 'Recording and evaluating the performance of individuals as members of small groups', *Personnel Psychol.*, vol. 7, pp. 477–84.

CHOWDHRY, K., and NEWCOMB, T. M. (1952), 'The relative abilities of leaders and non-leaders to estimate opinions of their own groups', *J. abnorm. soc. Psychol.*, vol. 47, pp. 51–7.

HOLLANDER, E. P. (1958), 'Conformity, status, and idiosyncrasy credit', *Psychol. Rev.*, vol. 65, pp. 117–27.

HOLLANDER, E. P. (1959), 'Some points of reinterpretation regarding social conformity', *Soc. Rev.*, vol. 7, pp. 159–68.

HOMANS, G. V. (1950), *The Human Group*, Harcourt, Brace & World.

MOORE, O. K., and BERKOWITZ, M. I. (1956), 'Problem solving and social interaction', *ONR Technical Report*, no.1, Yale University Department of Sociology.

Part Six Intergroup Relations

The primary focus of this volume has been on the small group, with some reference also to the constraints which the environment imposes on its development. This focus reflects the way research in the field has so far developed. Very little attention has been paid to the study of intergroup relations. And yet, if one accepts the value of an open-system analysis of group behaviour (as exemplified in this volume by Reading 3), it must be clear that almost every small group is a component of an intergroup system. This often means for example that a group is able to resolve or stave off conflict within the group by uniting against the perceived threat of some relevant other group.

The work of Sherif has long stood alone (see Reading 21). More recently other researchers have begun to see the potentialities of the area. Likert (1961) has developed a theory of organization whose central tenet is that an organization is a multigroup system held together by 'linkpins' who have membership roles in several different groups.

Findings from partially naturalistic studies as those of Sherif do not permit one to differentiate some of the numerous variables which may operate concurrently in intergroup relationships. One possible more analytic approach is that of simulation, which as Druckman shows (Reading 22) may enable us to establish more precisely just what it is that determines the development of intergroup conflict.

The central dilemma of intergroup relations – partially incompatible goals, plus mutual misperceptions – may well turn out not to require any explanatory concepts additional to those developed by Thibaut and Kelley in their analysis of the dyad. In analysing interpersonal behaviour, one is faced not so much with different areas, but with a choice as to which level is the most fruitful one at which to attempt to explain the behaviour. For those concerned with the analysis of small group behaviour within larger organizations, the intergroup level promises much. For those more concerned with the development of general explanations of social behaviour, the dyadic level may increasingly hold the stage.

Reference

LIKERT, R. (1961), *New Patterns of Management*, McGraw-Hill.

21 M. Sherif

Group Conflict and Co-operation

Excerpt from M. Sherif, *Group Conflict and Cooperation*, Houghton Mifflin, 1966, pp. 71–93.

The hypotheses to be tested experimentally were derived from the orientation stated in chapter 4 [not included in this excerpt]. The orientation required a study design with a definite sequence of stages, each designed to establish experimental conditions for hypotheses whose testing also depended upon the outcome of the previous stage. The sequence can be described briefly.

For experimental purposes it was important to start from scratch with individuals who had no previous relationships with one another. The individuals were chosen very carefully, as we shall see, to rule out explanations of the results other than those being tested.

In order to test our formulation of the essential characteristics of intergroup relations, the next step was to produce distinct groups, each with a definite organization (leader and followers) and a set of norms for behavior. To insure control over conditions in which groups formed and came into contact, the experiments were conducted in isolated camp sites completely at the disposal of the research program.

Groups were formed. The natural history of their formation was traced step by step. Then for the first time the groups were brought into functional contact. They were brought into contact initially under conditions designed to produce competition, hostility and social distances between them. Later, they met under conditions designed to test hypotheses about the reduction of hostility and derogatory stereotypes.

Three separate experiments were conducted, each lasting approximately three weeks, in different locations and with different subjects (cf. Sherif, 1951; Sherif and Sherif, 1953; Sherif, White, and Harvey, 1955; Sherif *et al.*, 1961). A composite picture of the conduct and findings of the three studies will be presented here, with specification of the source when this is feasible without confusing the account. The first experiment, conducted in 1949 in Connecticut, was carried through the stage of intergroup conflict. All the hypotheses presented here were formulated before the second study, but the systematic sequence of stages in that study had to be terminated after the rise of intergroup hostility. The third experiment, conducted at Robbers Cave, Oklahoma, was carried through the sequence of group formation, intergroup conflict and reduction of intergroup conflict which was contingent upon cooperative activities between erstwhile hostile groups.

Choice of subjects

Because the experiments were performed at camp sites, subjects were selected who would find camping a natural and fascinating activity: boys between eleven and twelve years old. In order to eliminate, as much as possible, alternative explanations for events that transpired in the experiments, the selection procedures were long and careful. Interviews were held with each boy's teachers, school officials, and family. School and medical records were studied, and scores were obtained on psychological tests. Each boy was observed in natural give-and-take with agemates in the classroom and during athletic and informal interpersonal activities.

As a result of the methods of selecting subjects, the results could not be explained in any of the following alternative ways:

1. Previous acquaintance or personal ties among the boys. Boys were chosen from different schools and neighborhoods to eliminate this possibility.
2. Neurotic tendencies, undue instability or excessively frustrating situations in past history. The boys were healthy, well adjusted in school and neighborhood, members of stable families with both parents living at home (no broken homes) and with no record of past disturbances in behavior. Members of minority groups who might have suffered from social discrimination were not included.
3. Pronounced differences in background or physical appearance. All subjects were selected from stable, white Protestant families from the middle socio-economic level. While they displayed the normal range of individual differences, these were equalized during

the stage of group formation by matching boys in the different groups as much as possible according to size and skills.

Research procedures and the validity problem

As in any experiment, the chief claim to validity must lie in the correspondence between the research conditions and the actualities the experiment purports to study. Our concern with validity led to the particular sequence of the study just described. It also dictated the major features of the research procedures and methods for data collection.

The experimental conditions for each successive stage were defined in terms of the *properties* of problem situations the subjects faced. All problem situations were introduced in a naturalistic setting, in keeping with activities usually carried out in such settings. All problem situations were selected to be highly appealing, on the basis of prior study of the subjects' interests. Through manipulation of objects, facilities and timing, it was possible to introduce the procedures with a minimum of verbal instruction and without the individuals being aware that each step was planned to study inter-group relations experimentally. The experimental nature of the study required that the problem situations at each stage meet the criteria specified for conditions of that stage. Beyond this, every effort was made so that the activities and the flow of interpersonal interaction as they occurred were as natural as possible.

Since the knowledge that one is a 'research subject' and is being observed constantly has definite effects on behavior, the subjects were not aware that data were being collected or that the sequence of events was experimentally planned. All research staff appeared in the roles of personnel in a usual camp situation: senior counselors (observers), camp director, handyman, and so on. In these capacities, they observed the boys throughout their waking hours, recording symbols and other notes only when out of the subjects' sight and expanding them into a report later each day.

The validity of the findings was cross-checked by using a *combination of data-gathering methods* at every step. In addition to reports of observation on interaction and ratings made by 'senior counselors', independent ratings were made by observers not familiar with the groups in situations in which the group was engaged in lively interaction. Sociometric choices were obtained from the subjects themselves in interviews that appeared to them as casual conversations. At choice points, laboratory-like techniques were introduced to assess their attitudes through judgement tasks presented to them as games.

In summarizing the research, we rely on recurrent observations that were checked by one or more of these techniques.

Stage of spontaneous interpersonal friendship choices

Hypotheses: A. When unacquainted individuals with similar backgrounds meet in interaction situations of common appeal to them, interpersonal friendship clusters will develop on the basis of personal attractions, common interests, and affinities.

B. These spontaneous friendship ties will be reversed in favor of fellow group members when friends participate separately in the formation of different groups.

The primary purpose of this stage was to reduce the possibility that groups formed in the experiment proper would be based initially on sheer personal attraction. When the boys arrived at the site, they were all housed in one large bunkhouse. All activities were camp-wide, with free choice of buddies, eating companions, and the like.

After the boys had begun to be consistent in associating with one or two others in various activities, each was asked informally who his best friends were (sociometric choices). Then the boys were divided into two different cabins, so that about two-thirds of their best friends were in the other cabin. (The pain of separation was eased by allowing each cabin to go at once on an overnight hike and camp-out, something all had wanted to do.) Following the stage of group formation, they were again asked who their best friends were, specifying that they could choose from the entire camp.

Table 1 gives the data from the 1949 study showing how friendship choices based on personal attraction were reversed after groups had actually formed. These procedures were replicated in 1953 with almost identical results.

Conclusions and implications

From the results in this stage, we conclude that interaction in pleasant activities among similar individuals is conducive to

Table 1 Reversal of Friendship Choices Before and After Group Formation

| Persons chosen in: | Persons choosing from: Group A | | | Group B | | |
	Before	After	Difference	Before	After	Difference
	%	%	%	%	%	%
Group A	35·1	95·0	59·9	65·0	12·3	−52·7
Group B	64·9	5·0	−59·9	35·0	87·7	52·7

formation of small friendship clusters based on personal attraction and common interests. By separating the friendship clusters before the stage of group formation, the possibility of explaining group formation primarily on that basis is eliminated. Further, the findings show that choice of friends is affected by the formation of groups, more than half of the choices shifting away from strictly personal preferences toward friendship within their own group.

These findings may tell us something about the choice of friends and personal associates in daily life. The popular notions that, 'I choose friends because of my own personal preferences' or that 'We all should be free to choose our friends' are misleading, particularly when used to justify exclusionist practices by organized groups (cf. Lee, 1955). As the results show, friendship choices shift readily from strictly interpersonal attractions toward ingroup exclusiveness, as a part of group formation and functioning. Freedom to choose friends on the basis of personal preferences within an organization turns out to be freedom to choose among persons selected according to the rules of membership established by the organization.

Stage of group formation

Hypotheses: 1. When a number of individuals without previously established relationships interact in conditions that embody goals with common appeal value to the individuals and that require interdependent activities for their attainment, a definite group structure consisting of differentiated status positions and roles will be produced.

1a. Appraisals of performance by group members will vary with the status of the member being judged, status being defined as effective initiative in group interaction. The higher an individual's status the greater will be the tendency to overestimate his performance.

2. When individuals interact under the conditions stated in Hypothesis 1, norms regulating their behavior in relations with one another and in activities commonly engaged in will become standardized, concomitant with the rise of group structure.

This stage of the experiment started by dividing the subjects into two bunches, matched as closely as possible in terms of size and skills of the individuals composing them. In the 1954 experiment at Robbers Cave, this stage was the first, since the previous experiments had eliminated explanation of friendship choices on the basis of strictly personal preference. The boys arrived on two separate buses and settled in cabins at a considerable distance. Thus, belonging to their cabin seemed entirely natural. Contact between the two groups was prevented until the next stage.

In this stage, the boys engaged in many activities, but all were in harmony with specifications for group formation. All required interdependent activities among the boys in a cabin to reach a common goal as specified in the hypotheses. They included camping out, cooking, improving swimming places, transporting canoes over rough terrain to the water and various games.

As they faced problem situations, played and worked together, the boys in each unit pooled their efforts, organized duties and divided up tasks of work and play. Different individuals assumed different responsibilities. One excelled in cooking. Another led in athletics. Others, though not outstanding in any particular skill, could be counted on to pitch in and do their level best in anything the group attempted. One or two boys seemed to disrupt activities, to start teasing at the wrong moment or offer useless suggestions. A few boys consistently had good suggestions and showed ability to coordinate the efforts of others in carrying them through. Within a few days, one person had proved himself more resourceful in the latter respect than the others. Thus, rather quickly, a leader and lieutenants emerged. Some boys sifted toward the bottom of the heap, while others jockeyed for higher positions of respect.

This process of group formation may be illustrated during a cookout in the woods. The staff supplied the boys with unprepared food. When they got hungry, one boy started to build a fire, asking for help in getting wood. Another attacked the raw hamburger to make patties. Others prepared a place to put buns, relishes, and the like. Two mixed soft drinks from flavoring and sugar. One boy who stood around without helping was told by others to 'get to it'. Shortly the fire was blazing and the cook had hamburgers sizzling. Two boys distributed them as rapidly as they became browned. Soon it was time for the watermelon. A low-ranking member took a knife and started toward the melon. Some of the others protested. The most highly regarded boy in the group took the knife, saying, 'You guys who yell the loudest get yours last.'

The relative positions in the group were rated by observers and independent raters primarily on the basis of their *effective initiative* in the group. These ratings were also checked by informal sounding of the boys' opinions as to who got things started, who got things done, and who could be counted on to support group activities (see Figure 1). When these measurements by observers and sociometric choice checked, we could conclude that a group organization had formed, as predicted in the hypotheses.

In the 1953 experiment, we obtained data for Hypothesis 1a on the status relations in each group through a game requiring each boy to evaluate the performance of his fellow members. Before an important baseball game, a target board was set up, with the pretense of making practice in pitching more interesting. There were no marks on the front of the board for the boys to judge objectively how close the ball came to a bull's-eye, but, unknown to them, the board was wired to flashing lights behind so that an observer could see exactly where the ball hit. The result was that the boys consistently overestimated the performance of the most highly regarded members of their group and tended to underestimate the scores of low-ranking members. In other words, estimation of performance and status in the group, as determined from observation, were significantly correlated (Sherif, White and Harvey, 1955).

As the group became an organization, the boys coined nicknames. In 1949, the big, blond, hardy leader of one group was dubbed 'Baby Face' by his admiring followers. A boy with a rather long head became 'Lemon Head' to his group. Each group

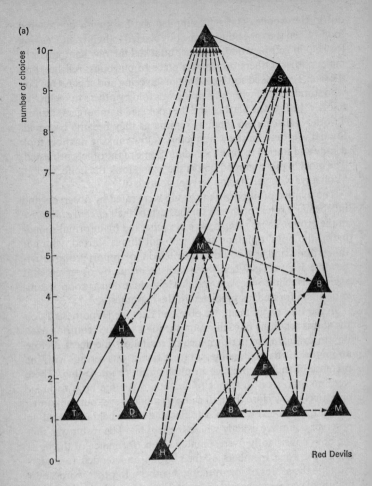

(a)

number of choices

Red Devils

——————— reciprocated choices

— — — — — one-way choices

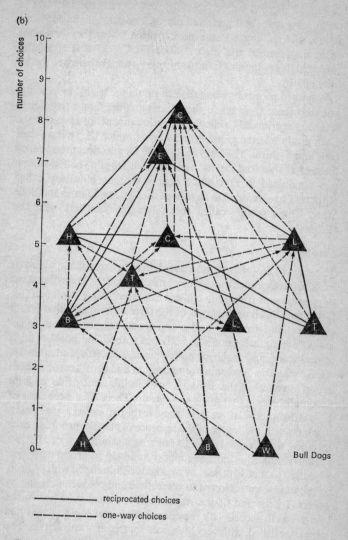

Figure 1 Status structures of (a) the Red Devils and (b) the Bull Dogs

developed its own jargon, special jokes, secrets, special ways of performing tasks and preferred places. For example, in 1954 one group, after killing a snake near a place where they had gone swimming, named the place 'Moccasin Creek' and thereafter preferred this swimming hole to any other, though there were better ones nearby.

Wayward members who failed to do things 'right' or who did not contribute their bit to the common effort found themselves receiving reprimands, ridicule, 'silent treatment' or even threats. Each group selected symbols and a name, which they put on their caps and T-shirts. The boys in the 1949 Connecticut study called themselves the 'Red Devils' and the 'Bull Dogs'. The 1954 camp was conducted in Oklahoma near a famous hideaway called Robbers Cave, reputed to have been used by Jesse James and Belle Starr. These groups called themselves the 'Rattlers' and the 'Eagles'.

Conclusions

The stage of group formation lasted, in each experiment, approximately a week. Since the choice of subjects and the preceding stage of spontaneous friendship choices minimized other explanations, it was concluded on the basis of the three experiments that group organization (structure) and group norms are products of inter-action among individuals in activities embodying goals of high appeal value, and requiring performance of interdependent tasks. Along with the developing organization and local customs, each group manifested the signs of 'we' feeling and pride in joint accomplishments that mark an ingroup. There even were signs of comparison between 'we' and 'they' in the two earlier experiments, in which each was aware of the presence of another group. In each instance, the edge was given to one's own group.

Individuals who did not support and help in group activities, who tried to 'bully' others, or who actively interfered with projects in progress were subjected to correctives and cold-shouldering by others. By the end of the stage, however, most behavior in the group was in accord with the customary *modus operandi* that had been established, with very little need for frequent correctives. The Bull Dogs, at the initiative of their leader, instituted a standard penalty for getting 'out of line' (removing a given number of stones from their swimming hole), which was administered by the leader with the consent of the entire membership.

Though isolated from currents of ordinary life, the groups that formed inevitably reflected the general culture and the surrounds of which they were parts. The names chosen for the groups are one example; nicknames, preferences in activities, the development of democratic procedures, and the interest in competitive games are others. Even these little experimental groups reflected a cultural framework and, as the next stage showed, no group structure had a wall impenetrable from the outside.

Stage of intergroup conflict

Hypotheses: 1. When members of two groups come into contact with one another in a series of activities that embody goals which each urgently desires, but which can be attained by one group only at the expense of the other, competitive activity toward the goal changes, over time, into hostility between the groups and their members.
2. In the course of such competitive interaction toward a goal available only to one group, unfavorable attitudes and images (stereotypes) of the outgroup come into use and are standardized, placing the outgroup at a definite social distance from the ingroup.
3. Conflict between two groups tends to produce an increase in solidarity within the groups.
4. The heightened solidarity and pride in the group will be reflected in overestimation of the achievements by fellow group members and lower estimates of the achievements by members of the outgroup.
5. Relations between groups that are of consequence to the groups in question, including conflict, tend to produce changes in the organization and practices within the groups.

The rise of persistent conflict between groups and hostile attitudes toward each other were predicted even though each group was composed of normal, well-adjusted individuals, and even though there were no differences between the groups in terms of socio-cultural background or marked physical characteristics.

In order that contact between the groups could be specified, the groups had no encounters as groups prior to this stage. (Indeed, in 1954 the two groups were not even aware of each other's presence until just before this stage.)

Because these were American boys, who are keenly interested in competitive sports, the necessary experimental conditions were easily created. As though acceding to the boys' requests, the staff arranged a tournament of games: baseball, touch football, tug of war, a treasure hunt, and so on, with prizes for the winning group.

The tournament started in a spirit of good sportsmanship, but as it progressed good feeling began to evaporate. The 'good sportsmanship' cheer customarily given after a game, '2, 4, 6, 8 – who do we appreciate,' followed by the name of the other group, turned into '2, 4, 6, 8 – who do we appreci-*hate*.' Soon members of each group began to call their rivals 'stinkers', 'sneaks' and 'cheats'. The boys in the 1949 camp turned against buddies whom they had chosen as 'best friends' when they first arrived. The rival groups made threatening posters and planned raids, collecting secret hoards of green apples as ammunition.

In the Robbers Cave study, the Eagles, after defeat in a game, burned a banner left behind by the Rattlers. The next morning the Rattlers seized the Eagles' flag when they arrived on the athletic field. From that time on, name-calling, scuffling and raids were the rule of the day. A large proportion of the boys in each group gave negative ratings to the character of *all* boys in the other. When the tournament was over, they refused to have anything more to do with members of the other group.

However, another effect of intergroup conflict was to increase solidarity, cooperativeness and morale *within* each group. It is noteworthy that the heightening of cooperativeness and democratic interaction *within* each group did *not* carry over to a group's treatment of the other group.

Near the end of this stage, the members of each group found the other group and its members so distasteful that they expressed strong preferences to have no further contact with them at all. In fact, they were subsequently reluctant even to be in pleasant situations (eating, movies, entertainments), if they knew the other group would also be in the vicinity.

At this point in 1954, a game of bean toss was introduced, with a cash prize, the aim being to see which group could collect the largest number of beans scattered on the ground within a limited time. Each person collected beans in a sack with a restricted opening, so that he could not check the number of beans in it. Through an opaque projector, the beans purportedly collected by each individual were shown briefly, and everyone wrote down his estimate of the number. Actually, thirty-five beans were exposed each time, a number sufficiently large that it could not be counted in the time available. The findings showed that members of each group, on the average, *over*estimated the number of beans collected by fellow members and made much lower estimates of the detested outgroup's performance. The tendency to *over*estimate was much greater for the group that had won the tournament of games just concluded. The losers *over*estimated their own performance and *under*estimated that of their rivals on this task.

The course of conflict between the groups did produce changes in the status and role relationships *within* groups as predicted. In one group, leadership actually changed hands when the leader who had emerged during group formation proved reluctant to take front-line action in the conflict. In another, a 'bully' who had been castigated during the peaceful days of group formation, and had been rather low in status, emerged as a hero during encounters with the outgroup. Practices established within the group, including techniques for team play and for executing the tug of war, were altered during the intergroup encounters. During a tug of war, one group adopted the strategy of its opponents. A great deal of time and energy within each group went into making plans and strategies to outwit and defeat the outgroup, which now appeared as an 'enemy'.

Perhaps the net effect of intergroup conflict upon the ingroups can be illustrated best by a test situation near the end of this stage. In the 1954 study, the groups were taken to the beach at a nearby lake for an outing on a day when the beach was crowded with visitors and afforded many distractions. Despite the sheer effort needed not to get 'lost in the crowd', each group stuck together, entirely absorbed in its own activities. Watching carefully for diversions of attention, the observers could find only such incidents as a boy bumping into a stranger and murmuring 'Pardon me', as he rushed to join his fellows. Psychologically, other people did not 'count' as far as the boys were concerned. Such intensive concentration of interests and activities within the group would have been impossible in this situation had not the groups attained a high degree of solidarity.

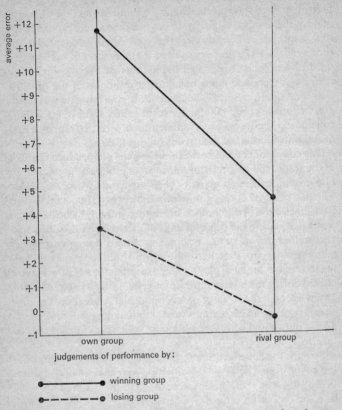

Figure 2 Errors in estimating a performance by victors and defeated group in intergroup tournament

This instance of ingroup solidarity and cooperativeness was observed at the very time when intergroup conflict was at its peak, during the period when the groups asserted emphatically that they would have nothing more to do with one another.

Conclusions

There can be no doubt that cultural and observable physical differences between groups facilitate discriminatory reactions toward members of an outgroup. There can be no doubt that such differences play a part in intergroup hostility and prejudice. Yet this stage of intergroup conflict has shown that neither cultural, physical, nor economic differences are *necessary* for the rise of intergroup conflict, hostile attitudes, and stereotyped images of outgroups. Nor are maladjusted, neurotic or unstable tendencies necessary conditions for the appearance of intergroup prejudice and stereotypes.

The *sufficient condition* for the rise of hostile and aggressive deeds (including raids on each other's cabins with destruction of property) and for the standardization of social distance justified by derogatory images of the outgroup was the existence of two groups competing for goals that only one group could attain, to the dismay and frustration of the other group.

During the course of rising intergroup hostility, solidarity and cooperativeness within each group did increase. There was no indication of any transfer of these modes of behavior to the out-group. The intergroup conflict did produce changes in the patterns of relationships within each group and in the issues and practices of concern to the members of each. The sequence of events did affect the judgement of the members in their appraisals of their own and the outgroup's performance.

If an outside observer had entered the situation at this point, with no information about preceding events, he could only have concluded on the basis of their behavior that these boys (who were the 'cream of the crop' in their communities) were wicked, disturbed and vicious bunches of youngsters.

Stage of intergroup cooperation: reduction of intergroup conflict

How can two groups in conflict, each with hostile attitudes and negative images of the other and each desiring to keep the members of the detested outgroup at a safe distance, be brought into co-operative interaction and friendly intercourse? When the 1954 study was done, we were not aware that this had ever been accomplished through controlled conditions that were specified in advance.

We were aware, however, of various proposals that for one reason or another were insufficient or inadequate to reduce conflict once it had heightened, to bring conflicting groups into cooperative interaction, or to reduce hostile attitudes and images.

Perhaps the most persistent concept about reducing intergroup hostility is that groups should have 'accurate' (hence favorable) *information* about each other. There can be no quarrel with this proposal. Indeed, groups must know something about each other before there is any possibility of changing hostile relationships. However, all the available evidence shows that 'information' is subordinate to the existing state of relationships between groups, and actually succeeds in changing this state only when it contains definite evidence of a shift in their relative power (as with the advent of Sputnik). Otherwise, the available research indicates that favorable information about the adversary is ignored, is reinterpreted to fit one's own designs, or is otherwise ineffective as the sole means of reducing intergroup conflict.

As for the related notion that information couched in appeals to moral values is sufficient in itself, the experiments contain numerous examples to the contrary. Religious services, held on Sunday (as is customary in camps of Protestant boys) with their enthusiastic support, were conducted by the same minister for each group. At our request, the topics were brotherly love, forgiveness of enemies and cooperation. The boys arranged the services except for the sermon, to which the response was uniformly enthusiastic. Upon solemnly departing from the beautiful outdoor setting of Sunday ceremony, they returned within minutes to their concerns in defeating the detested outgroup, or avoiding it, as the case might be at the time.

In the 1949 experiment, we found that the introduction of a *common enemy* in the form of another competing group was at least temporarily effective. But for two reasons, this expedient measure was not attempted again. First, the uniting of hostile groups to defeat another group is, after all, a widening of intergroup conflict on a large scale. If pursued to its logical limits, the end result is simply a repetition of the stage of intergroup conflict with larger, hence potentially more deadly flare-ups. Second, history is replete with examples of conflicting groups who close ranks to face an enemy and then resume the same old conflicts when the enemy is vanquished.

Both on a community, regional and international scale, *conferences of leaders* are frequently held and proposed as the means to settle intergroup conflicts. There can be no doubt of the value of such conferences, either for learning more about the other group and its leadership or for taking steps, backed by the power of each group, to build mutual trust in dealing with problems that concern them. But our survey of literature led us to suspect that this procedure, unaided by other considerations, would be insufficient to initiate cooperative interaction across group lines.

The reasons may be stated briefly: in order to be a 'leader', in any sense other than an autocratic monarch or a dictator with total power over every segment of one's group, an individual must be responsible to pursue the goals of his group within the prevailing bounds for acceptable means. If he transgresses these limits, someone – sooner or later – will expose him as a traitor or as being soft on the adversary. For groups gripped in severe conflict, these bounds of propriety surely include behavior with the outgroup, even extending to the point of proscribing personal encounters with the leader of the outgroup. (As of this writing, the reader can understand this stricture by imagining the reactions within their countries if either the President of the United States or the Premier of China should propose a joint 'summit meeting'.) Therefore, we concluded that realistic appraisals of the role of meetings between leaders had to assume that *some* cooperative interaction or some common interests already existed between the groups. This was not the case in our experiments.

Individual competition according to the abilities of persons also has been proposed as a means of furthering intergroup cooperation. In classroom and recreation situations, this measure appears to be used pragmatically to break up groups that adults detect. On a larger scale, we find no evidence that track meets between Negroes and whites, or Olympic games between nations, have materially advanced cooperation between the groups represented by the respective winners and losers.

The hypotheses in regard to these questions were formulated in the light of these considerations.

Hypotheses: 1. Contact between groups on an equal status in activities that, in themselves, are pleasant for members of both groups, but that involve no interdependence among them, will not decrease an existing state of intergroup conflict.
2. When conflicting groups come into contact under conditions

embodying goals that are compelling for the groups involved, but cannot be achieved by a single group through its own efforts and resources, the groups will tend to cooperate toward this superordinate goal. Our definition of superordinate goal emphasizes that it is unattainable by one group, singly; hence, it is not identical with a 'common goal'. Another implication of the definition is that a superordinate goal supersedes other goals each group may have, singly or in common with others; hence its attainment may require subordination of either singular or common goals.

3. Cooperation between groups arising from a series of superordinate goals will have a cumulative effect toward reducing the social distance between them, changing hostile attitudes and stereotypes, and hence reducing the possibility of future conflicts between them.

It may be seen that the measures actually tested in our experiment were introduced with the objective of clarifying the necessary conditions for *contact as equals* to be effective in reducing existing conflicts between groups and changing attitudes of their members.

Phase one

In order to test the first hypothesis, a series of situations was introduced involving *contact* between groups in activities highly pleasant to each group but not involving interdependence between them. Examples were going to the movies, eating in the same dining room, shooting off fireworks on the fourth of July, and the like. Far from reducing conflict, these situations served as occasions for the rival groups to berate and attack each other. In the dining-hall line, they shoved each other, and the group that lost the contest for the head of the line shouted 'Ladies first!' at the winner. They threw paper, food, and vile names at each other. An Eagle bumped by a Rattler was admonished by his fellow Eagles to brush 'the dirt' off his clothes. The mealtime encounters were dubbed 'garbage wars' by the participants.

Phase two: superordinate goals

The measure that was effective was suggested by a corollary to our assumptions about intergroup conflict: *if conflict develops from mutually incompatible goals, common goals should promote cooperation. But what kind of common goals?*

In considering group relations in the everyday world, it seemed that the most effective and enduring cooperation between groups occurs when *superordinate goals* prevail, superordinate goals being those that have a compelling appeal for members of each group, but that neither group can achieve without participation of the other. To test this hypothesis experimentally, we created a series of urgent and natural situations that challenged individuals in both groups.

One was a breakdown in the water supply system. Water came to the camp in pipes from a tank about a mile away. The flow of water was interrupted and the boys in both groups were called together to hear of the crisis. Both groups promptly volunteered, in their own distinctive ways, to search the water line for trouble. They explored separately, then came together and jointly located the source of the difficulty. But despite the good spirits aroused, the groups fell back on their old recriminations once the immediate crisis was over.

A similar opportunity was offered when the boys requested a movie that both groups had high on their list of preference. They were told that the camp could not afford to pay for it. The two groups got together, figured out how much each group would have to contribute, chose the film by a common vote and enjoyed the show together. It should be kept in mind that this followed the episode of their cooperation in the water crisis.

One day the two groups went on an outing at a lake some distance away. A large truck was to go for food. But when everyone was hungry and ready to eat, it developed that the truck would not start (the staff had taken care of that). The boys got a rope – the same rope they had used in their acrimonious tug of war – and all pulled together to start the truck.

Joint efforts in situations such as these did not *immediately* dispel hostility. But gradually, the series of activities requiring interdependent action reduced conflict and hostility between the groups. As a consequence, the members of the two groups began to feel friendlier. For example, a Rattler whom the Eagles had disliked for his sharp tongue and skill in defeating them became a 'good egg'. The boys stopped shoving each other in the meal line. They no longer called each other names and began to sit together at the table. New friendships developed, cutting across group lines.

In the end, the groups were actively seeking opportunities to intermingle, to entertain and 'treat' each other. Procedures that 'worked' in one activity were *transferred* to others. For example, the notion of 'taking turns' developed in the dining hall and was transferred to a joint campfire, which the boys themselves decided to hold. The groups took turns presenting skits and songs.

Given the alternative of returning in separate buses or on the same bus, members of both groups requested that they go home together on the same bus. As a whole neither group paid attention to a few *die-hards* who muttered 'Let's not'.

On the way home, a stop was made for refreshments. One group still had five dollars won as a prize. They decided to spend this sum on refreshments for both groups, rather than using it solely for themselves and thereby having more to eat. On their own initiative they invited their former rivals to be their guests for malted milks.

Interviews with the boys confirmed the change in their attitudes. From choosing their best friends almost exclusively in their own group, many of them shifted to listing some boys in the other group. They were glad to have a second chance to rate the boys in the other group as to personal qualities. Some remarked that they were inclined to change their minds since the first rating made after the tournament. Indeed they had. The new ratings were largely favorable. It is probably not accidental that the group that had been declared victorious in the intergroup tournament was also more prone to continue attributing negative qualities to the outgroup and to remain more exclusive in ingroup choices.

Conclusions

1. Intergroup conflict and its by-products of hostility and negative stereotypes are not *primarily* a result of neurotic tendencies on the part of individuals, but occur under conditions specified here even when the individuals involved are normal, healthy, and socially well adjusted.

2. Cooperative and democratic procedures *within* groups are not directly transferable to intergroup relations. On the contrary, cooperativeness and solidarity within groups were at their height when intergroup conflict was most severe.

3. Important intergroup relations affect the patterning of roles

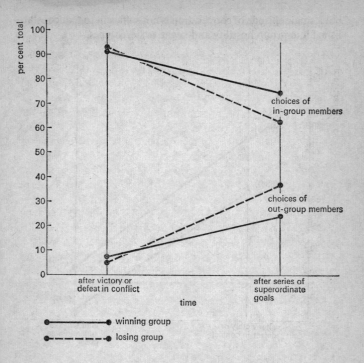

Figure 3 Changes in percentages of friendship choices of ingroup and outgroup members by winning and defeated groups

and the norms within each group. As noted earlier, one group deposed a leader who could not 'take it' in contests with the adversary. Another made a hero of a big boy who had previously been regarded as a bully. Similarly, the change to intergroup cooperation was accompanied by shifts in the status structure, particularly in one group in which some members looked back on the former days of rivalry with nostalgia.

4. Contact between hostile groups as equals in contiguous and pleasant situations does not in itself necessarily reduce conflict between them.

5. Contact between groups involving interdependent action toward superordinate goals is conducive to cooperation between groups,

but a single episode of cooperation is not sufficient to reduce established intergroup hostility and negative stereotypes.

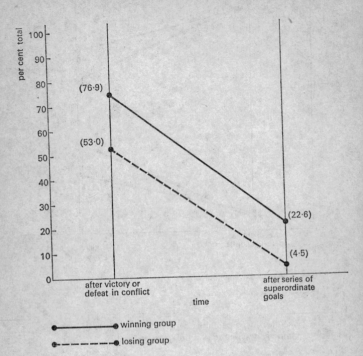

Figure 4 Percentages of categorically unfavorable ratings of outgroup after intergroup conflict and after series of superordinate goals

6. A series of cooperative activities toward superordinate goals has a cumulative effect in reducing intergroup hostility. This cumulative effect involves the successful development of procedures for cooperating in specific activities and their transfer to new situations, so that established modes of intergroup cooperation are recognized.

7. Tools and techniques found useful in problem solving within groups and in intergroup conflict may also serve in intergroup cooperation. (In the experiments, the tug-of-war rope was used to

pull the stalled truck.) But their use in intergroup cooperation requires recognition that the procedures involve not merely so many individuals within a group, but different groups of individuals contributing to the attainment of a common goal.

8. Cooperative endeavor between groups toward superordinate goals alters the significance of other measures designed to reduce existing hostility between them:

Intergroup *contacts* in the course of striving toward superordinate goals were used for developing plans, for making decisions, and for pleasant exchanges.

Information about the other group became interesting and sought after, rather than something to be ignored or interpreted to fit existing conceptions of the outgroup.

Exchange of persons for the performance of tasks was not seen as 'betrayal' of one's own group.

Leaders found that the trend toward intergroup cooperation widened the spheres in which they could take positive steps toward working out procedures for joint endeavor and future contact. In fact, a leader who tried to hold back from intergroup contact found that his group was ceasing to listen to him.

In short, the findings suggest that various methods used with limited success in reducing intergroup hostility may become effective when employed within a framework of cooperation among groups working toward goals that are genuinely appealing to all and that require equitable participation and contributions from all groups.

References

LEE, A. M. (1955), *Fraternities without Brotherhood*, Beacon Press.

SHERIF, M. (1951), 'A preliminary experimental study of inter-group relations', in J. J. Rohrer and M. Sherif (eds.), *Social Psychology at the Crossroads*, Harper & Row.

SHERIF, M., and SHERIF, C. W. (1953), *Groups in Harmony and Tension*, Harper & Row.

SHERIF, M., WHITE, B. J., and HARVEY, O. J. (1955), 'Status in experimentally produced groups', *Amer. J. Psychol.*, vol. 60, pp. 370–79.

SHERIF, M., HARVEY, O. J., WHITE, B. J., HOOD, W. R., and SHERIF, C. W. (1961), *Intergroup Conflict and Cooperation: The Robbers Cave Experiment*, University of Oklahoma Book Exchange.

22 Daniel Druckman

Dogmatism, Pre-Negotiation Experience and Simulated Group Representation as Determinants of Dyadic Behaviour in a Bargaining Situation

Daniel Druckman, 'Dogmatism, prenegotiation experience and simulated group representation as determinants of dyadic behavior in a bargaining situation', *Journal of Personality and Social Psychology*, vol. 6, 1967, pp. 279–90.

Several investigators in the area of conflict resolution have been concerned with the problem of how people approach one another as individuals or group representatives in a situation where they come together to resolve differences and where compromise is possible. Two orientations, characterized by Gladstone (1962), seem especially appropriate to this type of confrontation. An egoistic orientation is defined by a strong motive to win, evidenced in noncompromise behavior, a perception of the other in terms of stereotypical categories and the judgement of an outgroup product to be of inferior quality. Blake and Mouton (1962) spelled out a similar syndrome which they called 'win–lose' motivation. The experimental production of egoistic motivation was demonstrated by Sherif *et al.* (1961) with children in a camp setting, and Blake and Mouton (1962) with adults in an industrial setting. An integrative orientation is one in which the importance of collaboration for mutual benefit is realized. Compromise as a means of conflict resolution is predicted to result from this orientation.

Few investigators have attempted to specify the variables responsible for the predominance of one or the other orientation or have separated individual style from situational variables in accounting for the behavior observed. Instead, explanations have relied upon either group relatedness or personality viewed largely as mutually exclusive alternatives.

Group relatedness

Blake and Mouton (1962) and Sherif and Sherif (1965) observed that there has been a tendency among many investigators to attribute motivation to factors within the individual rather than to properties of the group in which he is a member. They called this the 'psychodynamic fallacy'. Committedness, according to these authors, should account for more variance in intergroup posture than should personality.

Studies on intergroup relations have demonstrated the production of competitive motivation after having teams independently develop a position or group product. Unilateral participation, rather than attachment to the group *per se*, may have been responsible for such behavior as the inability objectively to assess the value of competing positions and competitive nonyielding. The constraints placed upon a representative due to unilateral position formation have been illuminated by Blake (1959), Mack and Snyder (1957) and Rusk (1955). Pearson (1959) claimed that ambiguity serves as an aid to problem solving. Turk and Lefcowitz (1962), in a recent restatement of a major part of Sumner's (1906) ethnocentrism syndrome, considered acts of assertion on the part of representatives to be more likely under high ingroup solidarity (position consensus).

In the human relations training laboratories created by Blake and Mouton (1961, 1962) members interacted only with their own group on the development of an assigned problem, and representatives were elected to debate the merits of their group's product. Deadlock in agreeing on the best solution was the invariable result. A unilateral definition of the problem was apparent in so far as, after studying the competitor's position, most participants showed that they knew more about their own solution and saw little that the positions shared in common. Bass and Dunteman (1963), Blake and Mouton (1961), and Ferguson and Kelley (1964) produced evaluative bias under conditions in which laboratory groups worked independently on the creation of one or more products. From the subject's point of view it is probable that group problem-solving effectiveness was at stake.

However, in most of the experimental studies of intergroup relations, unilateral participation in the development of a product was not separated from group membership or group representation (e.g. Bass and Dunteman, 1963; Blake and Mouton, 1962; Sherif *et al.*, 1961). Another example of a possible confounding factor was seen in a study by Campbell (1960). He found that two-person union and management teams had difficulty in finding a compromise acceptable to both teams after having formed independent strategies. Is this rigid behavior a function of prenegotiation experience or group loyalty, or is it due to an interaction between these two variables?

A few investigators were able to examine the effects of one of these variables while holding the other constant. Bass (1963) had individuals negotiate as representatives of abstract organizations rather than laboratory groups. Agreement was reached quickly if negotiators did not form strategies or spell out positions before bargaining. That is, when future negotiators defined the problem from a bilateral perspective, compromise resulted without deadlock. However, when they spelled out their own position before bargaining, a significantly longer time period was necessary before agreement could be reached, and negotiations often ended in deadlock. Vegas, Frye and Cassens (1964) and Ferguson and Kelley (1964) found group membership to be the important variable. The former study demonstrated no perceptual distortion and early agreement among two individuals on which one produced the best essay when neither represented a group product. The latter investigators found that subjects who were members of laboratory groups but who did not participate in the formation of the group product overvalued both the ingroup and its products as much as members who took part in product formation. The extent of bias was correlated with attraction to the group irrespective of taking part in product formation. However, without an orthogonal design it is not possible to determine the relative amount of variance accounted for by each of these variables. The Bass study yielded no information on the effect of group membership, while the Ferguson and Kelley study was inconclusive with respect to unilateral product formation.

Personality

Whether a representative behaves competitively or in a conciliatory fashion may depend partially on attributes that he brings to the situation, other than those determined by his role. While several investigators argue against psychodynamic explanations, some experimental work points toward personality correlates of bargaining behavior.

Some personality variables which have been shown to be related to cooperative or competitive choices in a Prisoner's Dilemma game include internationalism–isolationism (Lutzker, 1960), cooperative, individualistic or competitive motivational orientations (Deutsch, 1962), family orientation (Crowne, 1966) and F-scale authoritarianism (Deutsch, 1960). However, Robinson and Wilson (1965) failed to replicate the latter finding when two-man teams competed. While they found a significant ingroup–outgroup bias in both competitive choices and personality-trait ratings, this was not related to authoritarian attitudes.

A correspondence between behavior at the interpersonal and intergroup levels was provided in the research of Blake and Mouton (1961). The elected representatives shared certain rated behavioral characteristics that distinguished them from non-representatives. These subjects were rated by all participants as significantly more nonyielding, independent, and resistant to external influences during the ingroup caucus. This is also an accurate description of how they behaved in the intergroup session. Thus the variables of personality type, unilateral planning and group commitment could not be separated in accounting for the nonyielding behavior of representatives during the intergroup debate.

Among the characteristics of the dogmatic personality delimited by Rokeach (1960) is blind loyalty to a system. He presented experimental evidence on the tendency of closed-minded subjects not to defect from instructions coming from an external authority. There were significant differences between closed-minded and open-minded subjects on defection from the experimenter's instructions even when they made no sense. Jamias (1964) demonstrated that closed-minded respondents were significantly affected by the values of the social systems within which they lived, while open-minded participants were not. Thus another individual difference variable may have relevance for the behavior of a group representative.

The intention of the present study was to investigate the relative contribution of personality and situational variables as determinants of orientation in a non-zero-sum, simulated, labor–management bargaining game. The investigator sought to determine whether an egoistic orientation or nonyielding behavior is a function of commitment to a planned bargaining posture. The behavior of groups that had formulated a strategy was contrasted with the behavior of groups which had not previously decided upon a strategy. Lack of significant differences in behavior between the conditions indicates that the manipulation made no difference, but does not exclude the possibility that nonyielding behavior is a function of group loyalty. In order to determine if this is the case it was necessary to examine bargaining behavior on the part of representatives not coming from laboratory groups. The personality variable is discussed in the design section.

Method
Design

The manipulations were arranged into a $2 \times 2 \times 2$ design with fifteen replications (nine male dyads and six female dyads) in each cell. The first variable represented an attempt to produce a unilateral versus a bilateral definition of the problem by manipulation of prebargaining environments. The second variable attempted to separate the effects of group commitment *per se* from the constraints imposed by position taking. Finally, to see whether personality made a difference, representatives were chosen on the basis of extreme scores on a modification of the Dogmatism Scale devised by Rokeach (1960). Each session was homogeneous in attitudinal disposition and sex. Across all eight conditions 120 dyads or 240 subjects were run through the simulation. A brief discussion of the basis for role assignments will be followed by specific details on each manipulation.[1]

Union versus company. Participants were assigned to either a union (employee role) or company (employer role) team on the basis of their scores on a twenty-four-item attitude scale. The scale is balanced with an equal number of items worded in the directions of prounion, anticompany, antiunion and procompany. The split-half reliability, corrected by the Spearman–Brown formula, is 0·72. This selection criterion was used with the intention of increasing the identification of subjects with the position that they were given. Subjects indicated, on a post-negotiation question, that their assigned role coincided highly with their own general

1. The instructions for each condition, questionnaires, attitude scales and additional information concerning the procedure are contained in Druckman (1966).

beliefs. The mean across all subjects was 2·16 on a five-point scale ranging from 'completely coincided' to 'did not coincide at all'. The differences in role identification between males and females, company or employer and union or employee representatives, and high and low dogmatics were nonsignificant.

Typical of the scale are the following items, worded in each of the four directions:

Anticompany
Most violence found at picket lines is instigated by management itself.

Procompany
Management should have the sole right to determine fringe benefits.

Prounion
Unions struggle to keep existing work rules in order to ensure the health and safety of the worker, not to make unnecessary work or featherbed.

Antiunion
The motives governing the actions of top union officials are prestige and financial gain, and not the welfare of the workers.

Approximately the upper and lower quartiles of the labor–management scale distribution were eligible for participation. However, only those also scoring in the upper or lower quartiles of a modified Dogmatism Scale were used. The scores ranged from 33 to 118, with a mean of 76·09. The mean score of the union and employee representatives was 62·73 ($V = 0·112$),[2] while the mean for the company and employer representatives was 89·47 ($V = 0·097$).

Unilateral position formation versus bilateral discussion. In the strategy condition the two teams (or individuals) were separated into different rooms for approximately forty minutes. The instructions for the group condition were as follows:

The next forty minutes will be spent with your own team. You are to use this time to plan your bargaining strategy. First gain an understanding of the issues. Then you may formulate a list of points defining the rationale or arguments for your team's position on each issue. You should decide on items that you think each man representing you should remain firm on. This strategy may be prepared so as to guide the negotiators

2. The coefficient of variability $\{V - (s/\bar{x})\}$ rather than the standard deviation was used as a measure of dispersion for both scales. Blalock (1960, p. 73) claimed that when the means are large and spread out it might be somewhat misleading to compare the absolute magnitudes of the standard deviations.

through the bargaining session. It may also include potential concessions, anticipations for trading, setting goals, and the like.

In general, it is felt that these strategy instructions set the stage for more typical pre-bargaining environment under which collective bargaining takes place.

Joint study conditions were created with the intent of releasing bargainers from commitment to a rigid position. The instructions for the group condition were as follows:

The next forty minutes will be spent in bilateral study. You are to use this time for learning as much as possible about company and union perspectives. Study the issues in order to gain understanding of both points of view as well as areas of greater or lesser agreement between proponents of either. Do not formulate or plan any strategies for bargaining from either position. Do not take a position and argue its merits against someone who might profess to the opposite position. Finally, do not form coalitions with other team members to bargain or debate from a position.

If at any point the discussion seems to break down into an interteam competition, the experimenter will stop it and remind participants of the goal. You should act bipartisan with respect to the issues during this session. There is no need to use any form of propaganda in order to obtain later gains. Feel free to enter the discussion at any point and openly discuss the issues. The emphasis is on informality and there is no one observing you or recording data. Understanding is the goal![3]

Blake and Mouton (1962) used a similar procedure where members from opposing teams questioned each other to gain understanding of both positions. However, this came after each team formulated a strategy, and biases were found in comprehension of the two positions, even when members admitted to understanding both solutions.

Group versus no group. Some subjects debated their position as employers or employees in a simulated nonunionized company, while others were members of laboratory teams and representatives of abstract labor or management organizations. Since three bargaining pairs were run in one group session, there were twenty group runs and sixty individual runs. Each participant in the

3. Apart from the creation of unilateral and bilateral groups the nature of the instructions concerning appropriate behavior during these sessions may have influenced negotiating behavior. Experiments are in progress in an attempt to clarify the effect of varying the instructions for the prebargaining session both for unilateral and bilateral arrangements.

individual conditions was explicitly told that he was only bargaining for himself, and any decision on a settlement applied only to that particular employee and had no direct relevance for the contracts of other employees. The instructions, including the nature of the hypothetical company and the task, were essentially the same for both conditions except for modifications in wording which took into account the change in structure when individuals rather than teams competed. In fact, just two changes in format were necessitated in order that the task be made more appropriate to employer–employee interaction. Details on these procedures are discussed in the section on the task description.

Personality. Since two subject variables were used in selection, care had to be taken to avoid confounding them. Due to an apparent ideological bias in the F-scale it might have been rather difficult to find high-F prolaborites or low-F antilaborites. Rokeach (1960) successfully developed a scale which is somewhat impervious to ideological content. Correlations between his Dogmatism Scale and scales of political-economic conservation are low and non-significant. The D-Scale was further modified by the investigator in order to remove vestiges of apparent ideological content which might have been associated with prolabor or promanagement attitudes. An attempt was also made to choose or construct items which sampled certain conceptual components of the dogmatism variable such as resisting pressures to change one's opinion, rejection of disbelievers, etc. There are forty-eight items fairly evenly divided over these various categories. Sixteen were borrowed from Rokeach (1960). In order to obviate an acquiescent response set from influencing the results, items are worded in two directions, reflecting both a high- and a low-dogmatic ideology. The split-half reliability, corrected by the Spearman–Brown formula, is 0·72.

Typical of the scale are the following original items, worded in both directions:

High dogmatic
I feel quite justified in sticking to a position that I feel strongly about even in the face of strong opposition.

One must be as critical as possible of the ideas of one's opponents.

Low dogmatic
If progress is ever to be made in this world, we must encourage cooperation between conflicting political and religious groups.

A leader should look to his opponents for good ideas as well as to his supporters.

Approximately the upper and lower quartiles of the modified D-scale distribution were eligible for participation. However, only those also scoring in the upper and lower quartiles of the labor–management scale were used. That correlated subject variables were avoided is attested to by the interscale correlation of 0·011. There was no problem in recruiting procompany and prounion subjects at both extremes of the modified D-scale. The scores ranged from 87 to 177, with a mean of 128·30. The mean score for high dogmatics was 143·70 ($V = 0·062$), while the mean for low dogmatics was 112·92 ($V = 0·067$).

Recruitment of subjects

Items from the labor–management scale and the modified Dogmatism Scale were administered together. The position of a given item was randomly determined. Respondents were to indicate the extent of their agreement on a five-point scale ranging from strongly agree to strongly disagree. In order to attain enough subjects at the extremes of both scale distributions, the questionnaire was administered to 850 students from five undergraduate psychology classes at Northwestern University. Respondents were informed that we were interested in recruiting people who had similar attitudes for participation in an interesting experiment.

As soon as both scales were scored, eligible respondents were placed in one of eight categories arranged by sex, dogmatism and prounion or procompany. Conditions were assigned to sessions each week before subjects were contacted. Both levels of the three variables were interspersed in a random-like manner in sessions during a given week.

Procedure

The situation facing the subjects was constructed in such a way so as to incorporate a number of parameters of a particular real world conflict. A complex simulation model was chosen over simpler, more popular situations on the presumption that subject behavior might come closer to their behavior in other conflict of interest situations, and the results might have more predictive validity for the situation being simulated. The simulation technique used also lends itself to the study of the effects of group commitment. A non-zero-sum collective bargaining game devised by

Campbell (1960) was considerably modified for this experiment.

The following task description is for those subjects who were assigned to be representatives of laboratory teams which simulated an organization. Slight modifications, discussed below, were introduced when individuals bargained for themselves. Upon entering the laboratory the participants were told that they were being given the opportunity to learn about the bargaining process through participation and informed of research evidence indicating that simulations of processes were a more effective learning device than attending lectures or reading case studies.

Participants were then assigned to a three-member union or company team. They were told that assignment was made specifically on the basis of attitudes toward labor unions and management, but similarity on other more general attitudes was also used as a criterion. The hypothetical company was called the Acme Steel Corporation. They were told that negotiations had been going on for a while, but no contract had been signed. They were the newly chosen representatives. Both teams received four issues, each arranged on a seventeen-step scale with the position of the union and company, when negotiations broke off, at either extreme. Between these extremes some possible compromises were listed for the convenience of the bargainers. Below each position on the scale the estimated cost to the company in thousands of dollars for the duration of the contract, if the issue were settled at that position, was listed. In the individual sessions the cost was in dollars, but the scale was identical (e.g., $320 rather than $32,000). An example of an issue scale is as follows:

Percentage of company payment[4]

Company	0	10	20	30	40	50	60	70	80	Union
	(0)	(4)	(8)	(12)	(16)	(20)	(24)	(28)	(32)	

An issue was chosen on the basis of relevance to broader problems or a widely publicized grievance and whether it could be quantitatively defined. The scale range for each issue was as follows:

4. This is a seventeen-step scale in so far as bargainers were able to use intervals of 5 per cent.

Issue	Company position	Union position
Wages	No raise	$0.16 raise per hour
Off-job training	No vocational school payment	80% tuition fees paid by company
Hospital plan	20% premium payment	100% premium payment by company
Paid vacation	2 weeks for 1 year of service (no increase for more years)	3 weeks for 10 years of service (scale started at 3 weeks for 25 years)

In terms of cost to the company and union demands, the wage issue was the most expensive, while paid vacation was the least expensive. The other two were equally expensive and fell in between.

In order to give the bargainers some perspective and to provide a common starting point for position formation, a page of background information was provided. A brief statement of company and union rationale for their demands and 'going rates' at four other similar hypothetical companies in the industry were included. The average going rate on each issue was between the starting union and company positions at Acme. Such information as profit and loss statements, company budgets, union funds and a detailed history of company operations was not provided in an attempt to insure that the results would not be a function of built-in parameters and so that the teams would be given sufficient latitude to be flexible or rigid.

The experiment was divided into two phases. The first phase consisted of either studying the issues on a bilateral basis or planning strategies unilaterally. Participants in both conditions were not told of the exact procedure to be used in the bargaining session. Before the next phase all participants were asked to privately rank the importance of the four issues. The second phase consisted of randomly dividing the six bargainers into three union-company pairs for contract negotiations. In order to reduce the potential influence on any dyad coming from another pair or to insure independence, the pairs were separated into three corners of the room, and screens were placed around each bargaining table. To make sure that team identification was maintained, the representatives were told that the results of their negotiations would be included with the results of the bargaining efforts of their partners, and net gains in terms of a total score for the team would be computed. Thus each subject was bargaining for his team and, perhaps, expected to be measured against how well his two colleagues fared. This competitive set was pitted against the advantages of a quick settlement. The latter pressure was created by informing the bargainers that each eight minutes of debate time would cost $5000 (or $50 in the no-group condition) to each side in lost wages or profits.

The intergroup phase lasted for thirty minutes and was divided into five-minute intervals, each five minutes representing a simulated day. Announcement of each five minutes of debate time was made by the experimenter. The latter's role was that of 'referee', but he did not specifically observe each bargaining pair. In order for a contract to be settled, agreement must have been reached on each of the four issues. Bargainers were provided with contracts. If an issue was settled, they were asked to circle the position of settlement or write it in if it fell between two listed positions and initial their contract opposite the scale. If an issue was not settled at the deadline, the bargainers were asked to indicate, independently, the amount of movement that they were willing to concede in order to obtain an agreement.

Bargaining pairs were instructed to provide some indication of the approximate amount of time needed to discuss each issue. Each bargainer was given a time sheet arranged such that he would only have to record the time on his watch at the start of discussion of an issue and then again when ready to move on to another issue. If two or more issues were being discussed simultaneously, they were to record the same time for each of the issues. Many dyads did discuss issues simultaneously, and 'package agreements' were occasionally negotiated. Bargainers did not have to settle an issue to move on to another one. They could go back to unsettled issues.

At the end of the second phase all representatives were brought together to fill out postnegotiation-reaction questionnaires. Some of the questions included the defensibility of one's starting position on each issue, the degree to which one wanted to see his team (or himself) come out favorably, and the extent to which compromise was perceived as defeat. None of the subjects was sophisticated enough about the manipulations to have his data invalidated.

While the participants were filling out the post-negotiation questionnaire, the experimenter combined the results for all dyads in order to give each team an idea of how it fared relative to the other. The resulting figures indicated how far the company and union teams were willing to move from their starting positions. The computational procedure is discussed in Druckman (1966).

Results

It was assumed that the firmness of the two negotiators' commitment to their respective positions would be reflected in four measures of conflict resolution: the speed of resolution, average distance apart, average amount of yielding and number of unresolved issues. Since the behavior of one representative in a bargaining dyad was not independent of the behavior of his opponent, the unit of analysis was the bargaining dyad rather than the individual bargainer. A special attempt was made to insure the independence of the three dyads in a group session during bargaining. Any given dyad was kept virtually unaware of the progress, situation, or completion of any other pair of bargainers. Since the independence of issues during debate is questionable, the effect of the manipulated conditions was assessed across the four issues.

Due to the imposition of a deadline on bargaining, there were both settled and unsettled contracts. Since it is hypothesized that the outcome of bargaining is a function of the manipulated conditions, both settled and unsettled contracts must be given equal consideration in any statistical analysis. The technique for inclusion of all contracts is specific to the measure used and is discussed below.

Speed of resolution

A reciprocal transformation was performed on the time measure in order to insure stability in the variances (Edwards, 1960) and so that deadlocks could be taken into consideration. Deadlocks were assumed to be settled in an infinite amount of time. The reciprocal of infinity is zero so that deadlocks could be treated as zero values and included in the distribution with the reciprocals of all the other obtained values. Thus all unsettled contracts received the same score.

The harmonic mean times (the reciprocal of the mean of the reciprocals of the original values) are presented in Table 1. Bass

Table 1 Means for Three Measures of Conflict Resolution

	Unilateral Strategy		Bilateral study		High dogmatic	Low dogmatic
	Group representation	Self-representation	Group representation	Self-representation		
Speed of resolution (in min.)						
High dogmatic	67·35	58·24	28·91	23·76	44·57[a]	
Low dogmatic	32·51	37·42	23·92	23·33		29·30[a]
Unilateral strategy	48·90[b]		Bilat. study 24·98[b]			
Group representation	38·17[c]			Self-rep. 35·69[c]		
Average distance apart						
High dogmatic	2·450	1·683	1·500	0·667	1·575[a]	
Low dogmatic	0·733	1·350	0·300	0·250		0·658[a]
Unilateral strategy	1·554[b]		Bilat. study 0·679[b]			
Group representation	1·246[c]			Self-rep. 0·988[c]		
Average yielding						
High dogmatic	6·942	7·208	7·250	7·667	7·267[a]	
Low dogmatic	7·642	7·325	7·850	7·875		7·673[a]
Unilateral strategy	7·279[b]		Bilat. study 7·660[b]			
Group representation	7·421[c]			Self-rep. 7·519[c]		

a Means for dogmatism main effect.
b Means for unilateral strategy/bilateral study main effect.
c Means for group-representation/self-representation main effect.

(1963) claimed that the harmonic mean time can be interpreted as the speed with which the conflict is resolved, while the mean time is the length of time required to resolve the conflict. The harmonic means are somewhat inflated due to deadlocks. Table 2 reports the results of an analysis of variance performed on the reciprocals of the time measure. The strategy-study effect is highly significant. While the mean difference between high and low dogmatics is large and in the predicted direction, the effect does not quite reach significance. The group/no group main effect and the interactions account for a negligible portion of the total variance.

Average distance apart and average yielding

The indication of how far a bargainer was willing to go in order to obtain agreement on unsettled issues made it feasible to include all contracts, resolved and unresolved, in determining the average distance apart across all issues as well as the average yielding per contract.[5] Since each scale had the same number of steps, it was possible to equate yielding from one scale to another.

Since the results for these two measures were highly similar, they are reported together. The results of analyses of variance for both measures, as reported in Table 2, show two main effects to be significant. High dogmatics were significantly further apart in their positions at the end of the bargaining session and yielded significantly less than low dogmatics. Strategy experience kept bargainers significantly further apart and resulted in significantly less yielding than study experience. While bargainers who represented groups were further apart and yielded less than bargainers who represented themselves, the mean difference was not large enough to be significant. The means are reported in Table 1. None of the interactions for either measure approached significance. When issues were included as a classification category, for both measures, neither the issue main effect nor any issue × condition interaction was significant. Thus high scores on the modified Dogmatism Scale and strategy prenegotiation experience kept bargainers further apart and produced less yielding irrespective of the issue being bargained for.

5. Yielding to compromise and the amount of movement that one is willing to concede in order to obtain an agreement were equated in obtaining the measure of average yielding. Both are indicative of a 'desire to compromise' rather than 'the most desirable position for settlement'.

Table 2 Analyses of Variance of Three Measures of Conflict Resolution

Source	Reciprocal of time to complete contracts		Average distance apart		Average yielding	
	MS	F	MS	F	MS	F
Dogmatism (A)	0·00211	2·30	25·208	5·34*	4·951	4·46*
Strategy–Study (B)	0·00965	10·54**	22·969	4·86**	4·361	3·93*
Group–No group (C)	0·00009	<1·00	2·002	<1·00	0·288	<1·00
A×B	0·00058	<1·00	0·352	<1·00	0·000	<1·00
A×C	0·00030	<1·00	8·802	1·86	1·782	1·60
B×C	0·00019	<1·00	1·008	<1·00	0·453	<1·00
A×B×C	0·00000	<1·00	0·675	<1·00	0·069	<1·00
Within replicates	0·00092		4·722		1·111	

* $p < 0.05$, $df = 1/112$.
** $p < 0.01$, $df = 1/112$.

Number of unresolved issues

Each contract was represented by a score ranging from 0 to 4, depending upon how many issues were not settled. The Mann–Whitney U-Test, with a correction for ties, was used to analyse this data for each variable. A feature of this test is that the effect of tied ranks on p is practically negligible.

Table 3 shows the number of bargaining dyads or contracts

Table 3 Number of Bargaining Dyads with 0, 1, 2, 3 or 4 Unresolved Issues

	No. unresolved issues				
	0	1	2	3	4
Strategy	31	6	9	4	10
Study	43	7	4	3	3
High dogmatic	31	7	8	5	9
Low dogmatic	43	6	5	2	4
Group	38	8	5	4	5
No group	36	5	8	3	8

with 0, 1, 2, 3 or 4 issues unresolved for each condition. Strategy experience before bargaining led to a higher rate of unresolved issues per contract than bilateral study experience. A Mann–Whitney U-Test yielded a z of 2·53 which is highly significant ($p < 0·005$). High dogmatics resolved fewer issues, on the average, per contract than low dogmatics. A z of 2·40 is highly significant ($p < 0·008$). Whether an individual represented himself or a group did not seem to have an effect on how many issues were resolved. A z of 0·608 is not significant.

Role differences in yielding behavior

Dyadic analyses could not take into account differential bargaining behavior as a function of assigned role or the defensibility of the built-in positions. Thus, a five-way analysis of variance was performed with the intention of examining differential yielding as a function of assigned role and issue rather than in the effect of the manipulated conditions *per se*. Role and the role $\times$ issues interaction were highly significant and together accounted for 78 per cent of the controlled variance. The dogmatism × role interaction was not significant indicating that high or low dogmatics behaved the same irrespective of their assigned role.

The mean amount of yielding for each role by issue across the three manipulated conditions is presented in Table 4. Observation of the means reveals that the role main effect seems to be a function of differential yielding on one issue – hospital plan. The difference between the average yielding by company or employer representatives across the four issues is 2·329. When the hospital plan issue is excluded, the mean difference drops to 0·197.

Reference to data on perceived defensibility of the built-in starting positions by company or employer and union or employee representatives may provide an explanation for the role × issue interaction. Participants were to place each issue on a five-point scale ranging from 'more defensible than other side' to 'not as defensible as other side'. The position endorsed by the union representative or employee was subtracted from the position endorsed by the company representative or employer in each dyad. The higher the mean across the 120 contracts in a positive direction, the more defensible was the union's position perceived to be; the higher the mean in a negative direction, the more defensible was the company's position perceived to be. The mean for each issue is as follows:

Wages	Off-job training	Paid vacation	Hospital plan
+0·4298	+0·1974	−0·2818	−0·6360

The difference between the means is highly significant ($p < 0·001$). Application of Duncan's multiple-range test indicated that only the mean difference between wages and off-the-job training is not significant or near significant ($p < 0·1$). The hospital plan issue was thus significantly less defensible to union and employee representatives than the other three issues. It was shown that differential yielding on hospital plan was considerably greater than on any of the other issues.

Table 4 also shows that company or employer representatives yielded less on paid vacation, while union or employee bargainers yielded less on wages and off-the-job training. The union position was considered to be more defensible on wages and off-the-job

Table 4 Mean Yielding by Company or Employer and Union or Employee Representatives by Issue

	Wages	Off-job training	Paid vacation	Hospital plan	Mean by role
Company or employer	7·750	7·742	6·675	3·058	6·306
Union or employee	7·475	6·850	8·433	11·738	8·635
Mean by issue	7·613	7·296	7·554	7·421	

training, while less defensible on paid vacation and hospital plan. Thus, in a general way, differential yielding by role corresponds to the perceived defensibility of the built-in positions.

Data were not collected concerning reasons for defensibility ratings. However, a general correspondence between the average going rates and the defensibility ratings may be noted. The average going rate for wages and off-the-job training was half the distance between the company and union starting positions. The average going rate for the paid-vacation issue was four steps on the scale from the company starting position, while for hospital plan it was only three steps from the company position. The presumed relation between defensibility, going rates and differential yielding is more suggestive than conclusive. As such these data suggest hypotheses which may be tested in another setting by, perhaps, manipulating defensibility and determining amount of yielding.

Agreement on the ranked importance of the issues

If the study session was effective in facilitating communication between bargainers, this should be reflected in agreement on the ranked importance of the four issues. The method for determining the extent of agreement between two members of a bargaining dyad was to take the absolute difference between the ranks assigned to each issue by each member and sum the differences. The 'agreement scores' were ranked and a Mann–Whitney U-Test was performed. The hypothesis was confirmed. Bargainers who studied the issues before negotiation agreed more on their relative importance than bargainers who planned strategies apart from one another. A z of 2·23 is highly significant ($p < 0.01$). The difference in amount of agreement between high dogmatics and low dogmatics or between group and individual representatives was slight and nonsignificant.

The amount of time spent discussing each issue corresponded to its average rank in importance. The wage issue was considered to be the most important ($\bar{x} = 1.26$) and was discussed longest in debate (8·15 minutes), off-the-job training was second in both importance (2·19) and time to discuss (7·18 minutes), followed by hospital plan (3·03 and 4·13 minutes) and paid vacation (3·52 and 3·65 minutes). The order of ranked importance was not affected by condition or role.

Involvement and the perception of compromise as defeat

In general, representatives wanted themselves or their teams to come out favorably in the negotiations. The over-all mean was 1·45 on a four-point scale. Group representatives wanted their team to come out favorably significantly more than individuals wanted themselves to come out favorably. The means were 1·37 in the case of group representatives and 1·54 for bargainers representing themselves ($t = 2.51$, $p < 0.01$). The differences between the other conditions were small and nonsignificant.

High dogmatics viewed compromise as defeat significantly more than did low dogmatics. The question was asked on a three-point scale. The means were 2·11 for high dogmatics and 2·37 for low dogmatics ($t = 3.36$, $p < 0.001$). The differences between the other conditions were small and nonsignificant.

Discussion

The results appear to be quite consistent across the measures of conflict resolution used. Strategy experience before bargaining led to a hardening of positions as reflected in measures of agreement and amount of yielding. Bilateral study experience, on the other hand, resulted in faster agreement and more yielding on the part of bargainers. These results were a function of pre-negotiation experience apart from the effects of group commitment *per se*. Whether bargainers represented groups or themselves did not have a significant effect on compromise behavior. That study experience was more effective in facilitating communication may have been revealed in the greater agreement on the ranking of the importance of the issues by bargainers after bilateral study.

The modified Dogmatism Scale was also predictive of conflict resolution. Irrespective of strategy or study pre-negotiation experience, high dogmatics were more resistant to compromise than low dogmatics. A post-negotiation question revealed that high dogmatics viewed compromise as defeat more than low dogmatics. The dogmatic subjects behaved in keeping with the theory and evidence presented by Rokeach (1960) and the evidence of Jamias (1964). They were less willing to defect from given positions. Blake and Mouton (1962) and Sherif and Sherif (1965) dismissed the relevance of psychodynamic explanations of behavior in an intergroup situation. The results of this study suggest that these explanations cannot be dismissed so lightly. The low correlation between the modified Dogmatism Scale and the labor-management attitude scale suggests that the former may be tapping a general disposition not related to political or specific content attitudes. Also there were no differences between high- or low-dogmatic union representatives and high- or low-dogmatic company representatives on yielding behavior. It might be interesting to examine the relationship between this scale and extant measures of misanthropy.

Bargainers who represented groups behaved no differently than those who bargained for themselves. A careful attempt was made to maintain group identification during the bargaining session. Bargainers were told, before negotiations, that a team score would be determined and a 'winner' and 'loser' announced. The results of a postnegotiation question indicated that this manipulation might have been effective. Group representatives wanted their team to come out favorably more than individuals wanted themselves to come out favorably. It is conceivable that such alternative procedures as having all three representatives bargain together as a team or choosing one to represent the team during bargaining might have intensified the salience of representing a laboratory team. However, both alternatives would require a greatly increased number of group sessions and the possibility of unwanted constraints on the bargainers from the bargaining session itself due to the 'public' nature of the situation. Only further investigations can clarify this issue.

Experimental studies of intergroup relations have been characterized by the use of short-lived *ad hoc* groups. The Sherif *et al.*

(1961) boys' camp study is perhaps the only exception. While certain steps were taken in this study to increase group cohesion, group identification or the intensity of competition might have been increased if the groups interacted over a longer period of time. At the current stage of empirical development it is difficult to assess the relevance of findings from simulated groups for groups with their own developmental history.

The implications of this study are clear. While the negotiation situation facing professional diplomats and bargainers is more complicated and more is at stake, these results may be suggestive to those social engineers responsible for creating situations more conducive to agreement. The unilateral attachments of representatives may not lie in their group identifications, but may be the result of a disciplined reticence toward their opponents. When representatives are given positions to defend but compromise is the desired goal, a problem-solving atmosphere, with no sanctions against open discussion from either side, is recommended. However, this should take place before representatives have a chance to develop a rationale or a cognitive context for their own position. This may be similar to the situation in labor–management contract negotiations where arbitrators assign starting positions to the contending parties and have them discuss their relative merits in the context of both vantage points. It also appears that efforts aimed at reducing conflict have a better chance of succeeding if carried out by people who are more collaborative in interpersonal relations and who do not view compromise as defeat.

References

BASS, B. M. (1963), 'Effects on negotiators of their prior experience in strategy or study groups', *Technical Report No. 1, Office of Naval Research*.

BASS, B. M., and DUNTEMAN, G. (1963), 'Biases in the evaluation of one's own group, its allies and opponents', *J. conflict Resol.*, vol. 7, pp. 16–20.

BLAKE, R. R. (1959), 'Psychology and the crisis of statesmanship', *Amer., Psychol.*, vol. 14, pp. 87–94.

BLAKE, R. R., and MOUTON, J. S. (1961), 'Competition, communication, and conformity', in I. A. Berg and B. M. Bass (eds.), *Conformity and Deviation*, Harper & Row, pp. 199–229.

BLAKE, R. R., and MOUTON, J. S. (1962), 'The intergroup dynamics of win–lose conflict and problem solving collaboration in union–management relations', in M. Sherif (ed.), *Intergroup Relations and Leadership*, Wiley, pp. 94–140.

BLALOCK, H. M. (1960), *Social Statistics*, McGraw-Hill.

CAMPBELL, R. J. (1960), *Originality in Group Productivity: III. Partisan Commitment and Productive Independence in a Collective Bargaining Situation*, Ohio State University Research Foundation.

CROWNE, D. P. (1966), 'Family orientation, level of aspiration, and interpersonal bargaining', *J. Personal. and soc. Psychol.*, vol. 3, pp. 641–5.

DEUTSCH, M. (1960), 'Trust, trustworthiness, and the F scale', *J. abnorm. soc. Psychol.*, vol. 61, pp. 138–40.

DEUTSCH, M. (1962), 'Cooperation and trust: some theoretical notes', in M. R. Jones (ed.), *Nebraska Symposium on Motivation: 1962*, University of Nebraska Press, pp. 275–320.

DRUCKMAN, D. (1966), 'Dogmatism, prenegotiation experience and simulated group representation as determinants of dyadic behavior in a bargaining situation', unpublished doctoral dissertation, Northwestern University.

EDWARDS, A. L. (1960), *Experimental Design in Psychological Research*, Holt, Rinehart & Winston.

FERGUSON, C. K., and KELLEY, H. H. (1964), 'Significant factors in over-evaluation of own-group's product', *J. abnorm. soc. Psychol.*, vol. 69, pp. 223–8.

GLADSTONE, A. I. (1962), 'Relationship orientation and processes leading toward war', *Background*, vol. 6, pp. 13–25.

JAMIAS, J. F. (1964), 'The effects of belief system styles on the communication and adoption of farm practices', Unpublished doctoral dissertation, Michigan State University.

LUTZKER, D. R. (1960), 'Internationalism as a predictor of cooperative behavior', *J. conflict Resol.*, vol. 4, pp. 426–30.

MACK, R. W., and SNYDER, R. C. (1957), 'The analysis of social conflict – toward an overview and synthesis', *J. conflict Resol.*, vol. 1, pp. 212–48.

PEARSON, L. B. (1959), *Diplomacy in the Nuclear Age*, Harvard University Press.

ROBINSON, C., and WILSON, W. (1965), 'Intergroup attitudes and strategies in non zero sum dilemma games: II. Selective bias in both authoritarians and nonauthoritarians', unpublished manuscript, University of Hawaii.

ROKEACH, M. (1960), *The Open and Closed Mind*, Basic Books.

RUSK, D. (1955), 'Parliamentary diplomacy – debate versus negotiation', *World Affairs Interpreter*, vol. 26, pp. 121–38.

SHERIF, M., HARVEY, O. J., WHITE, B. J., HOOD, W. R., and SHERIF, C. W. (1961), *Intergroup Conflict and Cooperation: The Robbers Cave Experiment*, University of Oklahoma Book Exchange.

SHERIF, M., and SHERIF, C. W. (1965), 'Research on intergroup relations', in O. Klineberg and R. Christie (eds.), *Perspectives in Social Psychology*, Holt, Rinehart & Winston, pp. 153–77.

SUMNER, W. G. (1906), *Folkways*, Ginn.

TURK, H., and LEFCOWITZ, M. J. (1962), 'Towards a theory of

representation between groups', *Social Forces*, vol. 40, pp. 337–41.

VEGAS, O. V., FRYE, R. L. and CASSENS, F. P. (1964), 'Learning set as a determinant of perceived cooperation and competition', *Amer. Psychol.*, vol. 19, p. 482 (abstract).

Further Reading

A number of the Readings are drawn from whole volumes on group processes, some of which are included in the following list.

General

D. Cartwright and A. Zander (eds.), *Group Dynamics*, Tavistock, 3rd edn, 1969.

R. T. Golembiewski, *The Small Group*, University of Chicago Press, 1962.

A. P. Hare, *Handbook of Small Group Research*, Free Press, 1962.

G. C. Homans, *Social Behavior: Its Elementary Forms*, Harcourt, Brace & World, 1961.

E. E. Jones and H. B. Gerard, *Foundations of Social Psychology*, Wiley, 1968.

G. Lindzey and E. Aronson (eds.), *Handbook of Social Psychology*, vol. 4, Addison-Wesley, 1969.

J. W. Thibaut and H. H. Kelley, *The Social Psychology of Groups*, Wiley, 1959.

Structural models

R. G. Barker and P. V. Gump, *Big School, Small School*, Stanford University Press, 1964.

T. Caplow, *Two Against One*, Prentice-Hall, 1968.

F. Emery and E. L. Trist, 'The causal texture of the organisational environment', *Hum. Rel.*, vol. 18, 1964, pp. 21–32.

L. Festinger, S. Schachter and K. W. Back, *Social Pressures of Informal Groups*, Harper & Row, 1950. (1963 edn, Stanford University Press and Tavistock.)

R. Sommer, 'Small group ecology', *Psychol. Bull.*, vol. 67, 1967, pp. 145–52.

Interpersonal models

M. Deutsch and R. M. Krauss, 'The effects of threat upon interpersonal bargaining', *J. conflict. Resol.*, vol. 6, 1962, pp. 52–76.

B. Eisman, 'Some determinants of group cohesiveness', *Hum. Rel.*, vol. 12, 1959, pp. 183–9.

P. S. Gallo and C. G. McClintock, 'Cooperative and competitive behavior in mixed-motive games', *J. conflict Resol.*, vol. 9, 1965, pp. 68–78.

H. H. Kelley, 'Experimental studies of threats in negotiations', *J. conflict Resol.*, vol. 9, 1965, pp. 79–105.

A. J. Lott and B. E. Lott, 'Group cohesiveness as interpersonal attraction', *Psychol. Bull.*, vol. 64, 1965, pp. 259–309.

T. M. Newcomb, *The Acquaintance Process*, Holt, Rinehart & Winston, 1961.

R. L. Swinth, 'The development of trust', *J. conflict Resol.*, vol. 11, 1967, pp. 335–44.

R. F. Winch, *Mate Selection: A Study of Complementary Needs*, Harper & Row, 1958.

Social roles

B. J. Biddle and E. J. Thomas (eds.), *Role Theory: Concepts and Research*, Wiley, 1966.

F. E. Fiedler, *A Theory of Leadership Effectiveness*, McGraw-Hill, 1967.

C. A. Gibb (ed.), *Leadership*, Penguin Books, 1969.

N. E. Gross, W. S. Mason and A. W. McEachern, *Explorations in the School Superintendency Role*, Wiley, 1958.

R. L. Kahn, D. Wolfe, R. P. Quinn, J. D. Snoek and R. A. Rosenthal, *Organizational Stress: Studies in Role Conflict and Ambiguity*, Wiley, 1964.

H. H. Kelley, 'Attribution theory in social psychology', in *Nebraska Symposium on Motivation*, vol. 17, pp. 192–240, University of Nebraska Press, 1967.

R. K. White and R. Lippitt, *Studies in Autocracy and Democracy: An Experimental Inquiry*, Harper & Row, 1960.

Norms and behaviour change

V. L. Allen, 'Conformity', in L. Berkowitz (ed.), *Advances in Experimental Social Psychology*, vol. 2, Academic Press, 1965.

E. P. Hollander, *Leaders, Groups and Influence*, Oxford University Press, 1964.

H. Hyman and E. Singer (eds.), *Readings in Reference Group Theory and Research*, Free Press, 1968.

C. A. Kiesler and S. B. Kiesler, *Conformity*, Addison-Wesley, 1969.

N. Kogan and M. A. Wallach, 'Risk-taking as a function of solution, person and group', in G. Mandler *et al.* (eds.), *New Directions in Psychology*, vol. 3, Holt, Rinehart & Winston, 1967, pp. 224–80.

T. M. Mills, *Group Transformation: An Analysis of a Learning Group*, Prentice-Hall, 1964.

E. H. Schein and W. G. Bennis, *Personal and Organisational Change through Group Methods: The Laboratory Approach*, Wiley, 1965.

D. S. Whitaker and M. A. Lieberman, *Psychotherapy through the Group Process*, Prentice-Hall, 1965.

Intergroup relations

M. Sherif, *Group Conflict and Cooperation*, Routledge & Kegan Paul, 1967.

M. Sherif (ed.), *Intergroup Relations and Leadership*, Wiley, 1962.

Acknowledgements

Permission to reproduce the Readings in this volume is acknowledged to the following sources:

1 University of Chicago Press and R. T. Golembiewski.
2 Harper & Row, Publishers, Inc.
3 Tavistock Publications Ltd
4 John Wiley & Sons, Inc., Publishers
5 Academic Press, Inc., and Marvin E. Shaw
6 *Journal of Conflict Resolution* and John Thibaut
7 American Psychological Association and Theodore M. Newcomb
8 American Psychological Association and Walter R. Borg
9 Duke University Press and R. V. Exline
10 John Wiley & Sons, Inc., Publishers
11 John Wiley & Sons, Inc., Publishers
12 American Sociological Association and Philip E. Slater
13 Holt, Rinehart & Winston, Inc.
14 American Sociological Association and Richard de Charms
15 American Psychological Association, Richard H. Willis and Edwin P. Hollander
16 American Sociological Association and Gary I. Schulman
17 American Psychological Association and Bruce W. Tuckman
18 American Psychological Association and Daryl J. Bem
19 American Pyschological Association, James P. Flanders and Donald L. Thistlethwaite
20 American Psychological Association and Edwin P. Hollander
21 Routledge & Kegan Paul Ltd, Houghton Mifflin Company and Muzafer Sherif
22 American Psychological Association and Daniel Druckman

Author Index

Subject Index